Non-Conventional Energy Resources

Second Edition

ASHISH CHANDRA
TARU CHANDRA

KHANNA BOOK PUBLISHING CO. (P) LTD.

Publisher, of Science, Technology and Engineering Books

4C/4344, Ansari Road, Darya Ganj, New Delhi-110002
Phone: 011-23244447-48 **Mobile:** +91-99109 09320
E-mail: contact@khannabooks.com,
sales@khannapublishers.com
Website: www.khannabooks.com

Price: ₹ 475.00

Non Conventional Energy Resources

Ashish Chandra

ISBN: 978-93-82609-82-7

Second Edition: 2019
Reprint: 2022, 2023, **2026**

Published by:

KHANNA BOOK PUBLISHING CO. (P) LTD.
4C/4344, Ansari Road, Darya Ganj, New Delhi-110 002
Phone: 011-23244447-48 **Mobile:** +91-9910909320
E-mail: contact@khannabooks.com

Printed in India.

Preface to the Second Edition

We are extremely grateful and thankful to all the readers of our previous edition. In this new edition, we have incorporated the suggestions and also included new topics for better understanding.

We wish to say a special thanks to Mr. Puneet Seth & Mr. Mukul Seth, engineering publishers for publishing this revised edition. Their patience and perseverance have made this task most pleasant.

Finally, we welcome suggestions and feedbacks from the readers towards the further improvement of the book.

Ashish Chandra
Taru Chandra

Preface to the First Edition

India is one of the five fast developing countries.

Energy is the primary and most universal measure of all kinds of work by human beings and nature. Whatever happens in the world, is only the expression of flow of energy in either of its forms.

Energy is a crucial input in the process of economic, social and industrial development. Energy consumption in the developing countries is increasing at a faster rate. According to world energy report, we get around 80% of our energy from conventional fossil fuels like oil (36%), natural gas (21%) and coal (23%). It is well known that the time is not so far when all these sources will be completely exhausted. Nuclear energy is a comparatively clean source of energy. However, safe handling of nuclear energy reactor is a sophisticated task and only around 7% of the world's total energy requirement is being satisfied by it today. Thus, as conventional energy sources are depleting day by day, utilization of alternative energy sources is the only solution.

India has made rapid strides towards economic self-reliance over the last few years. On the energy demand and supply side, India is facing severe shortages. To overcome energy crisis, government has developed many projects related to alternative energy sources. The new agricultural technologies can be developed, based on non-conventional energy sources. Utilization of renewable energy, efficient conversions of fossil fuel are not only environmentally and climatically beneficial, but also they preserve the finite energy sources.

Various forms of alternative energy sources are solar, wind, biogas/ biomass, tidal, geothermal, fuel cell, hydrogen energy, small hydropower etc.

This book covers all the upcoming technologies and uses of alternative energy resources and helps the teaching fraternity to update themselves in this upcoming field so that the teachers, who are the pillars in our education system, can lay a strong foundation for generations to come. Lastly, we are thankful to all of them who have contributed in the development of this book.

Lastly, we are thankful to all of them who have contributed in the development of this book.

Ashish Chandra

Taru Chandra

Contents

1

INTRODUCTION TO NON-CONVENTIONAL SOURCES OF ENERGY

1.1 INTRODUCTION TO ENERGY

Energy gives personal comfort and mobility to people, and is essential for the generation of industrial, commercial and societal wealth. On the other hand, energy production and consumption place considerable pressures on the environment (including heat and electricity production, oil refining and its final use in households, services, industry and transport). These pressures include the emission of greenhouse gases and air pollutants, land-use, waste generation and oil spills. They contribute to climate change, damage natural ecosystems and the man-made environment, and cause adverse effects to human health.

Energy is the primary and most universal measure of all kind of work by human beings and nature. Everything that happens in the world is the expression of flow of energy one of its form.

Today every country draws its energy needs from a variety of sources. We can broadly categorize these sources as commercial and noncommercial. The commercial sources include the fossil fuels (coal, oil and natural gas), hydro-electric power and nuclear power, while the noncommercial sources include wood, animal waste and agricultural wastes. In an Industrialized country like U.S.A. most of the energy requirements are met from commercial sources, while in an industrially less developed country like India, the use of commercial andnon-commercial sources is about equal.

1.1.1 Common Forms of Energy

Energy is the ability to do work or cause change. We use many created objects that require or produce energy, and elements in nature, such as humans/plants/animals, rely on gaining and using energy to survive.

There are five common forms of energy that we encounter daily.

(i) **Mechanical Energy** is the sum of kinetic and potential energy in an object that is used to do work. It is the energy used based on motion or position of an object.

Kinetic energy is the energy of an object that is due to motion. All moving objects have kinetic energy. The amount of kinetic energy an object has depends on its mass and speed. Kinetic energy increases as mass increases and as speed increases.

$$\textit{Kinetic Energy} = \frac{1}{2}mv^2$$

Where m = mass of an object (kg) and v = velocity of an object (m/sec).

Potential energy is the energy that an object has due to its position, condition, or chemical composition. Potential energy that is the result of an object's position is called gravitational potential energy. Gravitational potential energy increases as the object's height or mass increases.

$$\textit{Potential Energy} = mgh$$

Where m = mass of an object (kg), g = acceleration due to gravity = 9.81 m/s^2, h = distance of fall of an object (m).

(ii) **Sound Energy** is the movement of energy through waves that travel through a medium, such as water or air, for humans to hear.

(iii) **Electrical Energy** is created when tiny charged particles called electrons move from one atom to another through magnetic forces, such as batteries, or wires.

(iv) **Light Energy** is the movement of visible light (a part of radiant energy) through space. It can be reflected, refracted, and absorbed.

(v) **Heat/Thermal Energy** is the vibration or movement of electrons that heats objects. Heat always moves from a warmer object to a cooler object to later stabilize in temperature.

There can be more than one form of energy applied to something or someone. For example, the sun heats up the Earth and shares its light. It therefore has both Light Energy and Heat/Thermal Energy.

1.1.2 Energy Chain

The energy chain (EC) concept is defined as energy paths from source to energy consumption to final end-use energy benefit. EC diagram can represent visually the flow of energy.

Below are some examples of how energy can change from one form to another. These are called energy chains.

(i) When a kettle is boiled, electrical energy is converted to heat energy.

electrical energy → heat energy

(ii) When a mass is dropped from a height gravitational potential energy is converted to kinetic energy as the mass falls and then to sound and heat as it hits the ground.

potential energy → kinetic energy + heat and sound

(iii) Energy changes occur in chemical processes, such as the burning of coal, as well as biological and physical ones. The energy changes involved in the burning of coal are:

chemical energy → heat + light

Energy changes also play a vital role in biological processes. When sunlight falls on green plants, it provides energy which causes a chemical reaction. Carbon dioxide and water combine to form biomass/carbohydrate and oxygen. This process is called photosynthesis. The energy (originally provided by the Sun) can later be released in living cells during the process called respiration. Alternatively it can be released when the biomass is burnt. In each of these cases the biomass and oxygen recombine to produce carbon dioxide and water again and release energy.

1.1.3 Energy Scenario in India

The energy scenario can be explained in detail as:

1. The Indian economy has experienced unprecedented economic growth over the last decade. Today, India is the ninth largest economy in the world, driven by a real GDP growth of 8.7% in the last 5 years (7.5% over the last 10 years).
2. A projection in the Twelfth Plan document of the Planning Commission indicates that total domestic energy production of 669.6 million tons of oil equivalent (MTOE) will be reached by 2016-17 and 844 MTOE by 2021-22.
3. . India's energy basket has a mix of all the resources available including renewables. At present India's coal dependence is borne out from the fact that 54 % of the total installed electricity generation capacity is coal based.Furthermore, over 70 % of the electricity generated is from coal based power plants. Other renewables such as wind, geothermal, solar, and hydroelectricity represent a 2 percent share of the Indian fuel mix. Nuclear holds a one percent share.
4. In 2011-12, India was the fourth largest consumer in the world of Crude Oil and Natural Gas, after the United States, China, and Russia.
5. Combustible renewables and waste constitute about one fourth of Indian energy use.
6. The power sector in India has an increase of 14% over that of March 2011. Thermal power plants constitute 66% of the installed capacity, hydroelectric about 19% and rest being a combination of wind, small hydro-plants, biomass, waste-to-electricity plants, and nuclear energy.
7. As of March 2012, the per capita total consumption in India was estimated to be 879 kWh. India's electricity sector is amongst the world's most active players in renewable energy utilization, especially wind energy.

8. Energy exploration and exploitation, capacity additions, clean energy alternatives, conservation, and energy sector reforms will, therefore, be critical for energy security. Conservation and efficient utilization of energy resources play a vital role in narrowing the gap between demand and supply of energy.

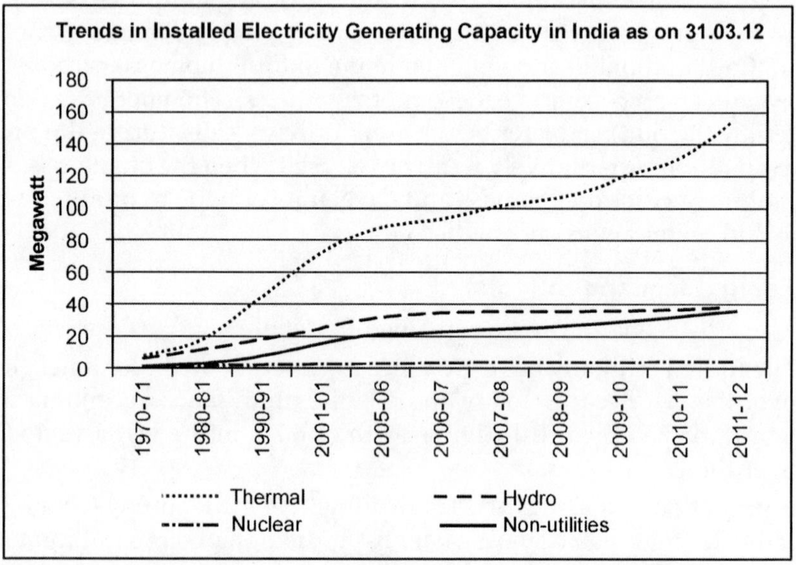

Fig. 1.1

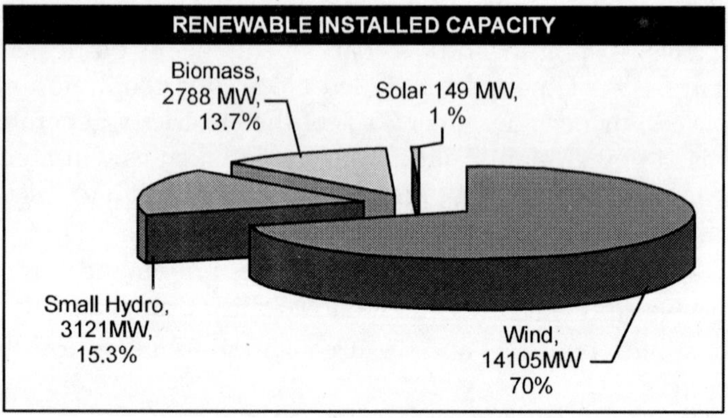

***Fig. 1.2** All India Installed Capacity (Renewable) As on 31st December, 2011*

1.1.4 World Energy Status

Figure 1.3 shows both the historical and projected growth in world energy consumption between 1990 and 2030. World energy consumption is expected to have grown by 44% by 2030. Much of this growth will happen in the developing economies, the biggest of which are China and India.

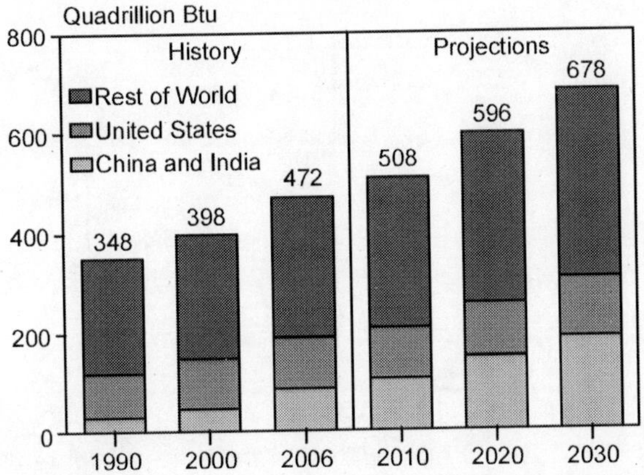

Figure 1.3: Historic and projected world energy consumption by region 1990 to 2030

The projected energy consumption is further categorised according to fuel type in Fig. 1.4, which shows the continuous dominance of oil in the future energy portfolio of the world. Renewable energy and coal are the fastest growing energy resources , with consumtion increasing by 2.1% and 2% respectively.

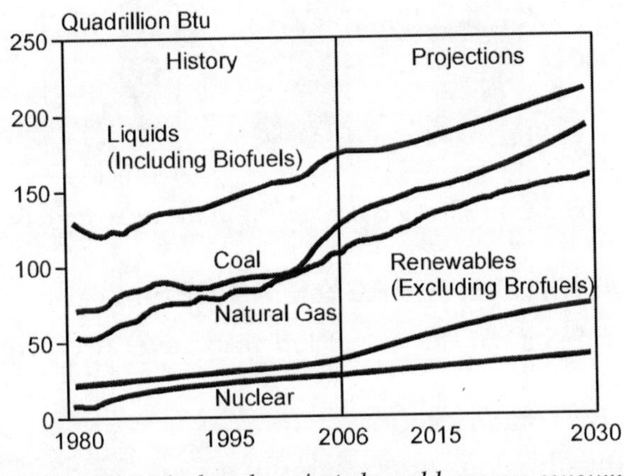

Figure 1.4: Historical and projected world energy consumption by fuel type 1980 to 2030

It is estimated that for electricity generation worldwide, the natural gas share increases from 20% to 25% , and the coal share increases from 41% to 46% by 2030.

The projected world energy consumption in the three growth cases (Fig. 1.5) and in the three price cases (Fig. 1.6) are estimated.

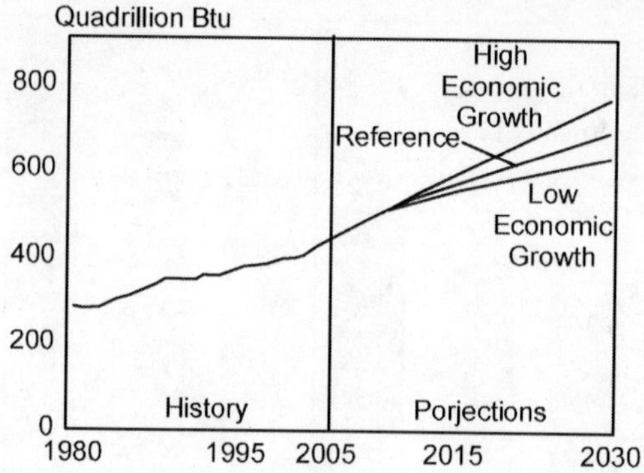

Fig. 1.5. Projectd World Energy consumption in the three growth cases (EIA, 2008)

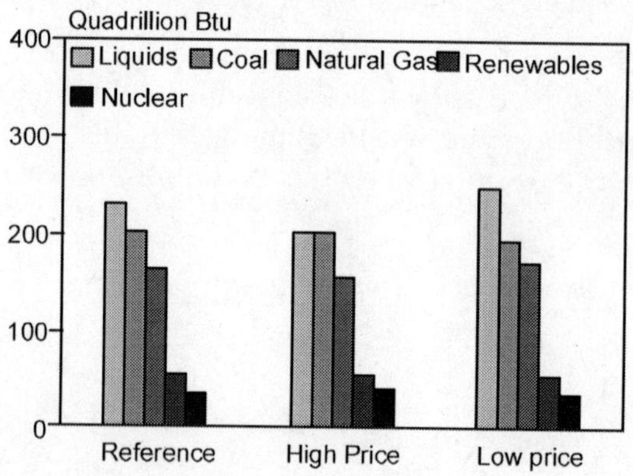

Fig. 1.6 Projectd (2030) world energy consumption in the three price cases (EIA, 2008)

1.2 CLASSIFICATION OF ENERGY SOURCES

The energy sources can be classified into several types based on the following criteria:

(*i*) Primary and Secondary sources

(*ii*) Commercial and Non-commercial sources

(*iii*) Renewable and Non-renewable sources

1.2.1 Primary and Secondary Sources

Primary forms of energy are those that are either found or stored in nature. Common primary energy sources are coal, oil, natural gas, and biomass (such as wood). Other primary energy sources available include nuclear energy from radioactive substances, thermal energy stored in the earth's interior (geothermal energy), and potential energy due to the earth's gravity.

Secondary forms of energy are those forms which are derived from the primary forms of energy; for example, coke, oil or gas converted into steam and electricity.

1.2.2 Commercial and Non-Commercial Sources

Commercial forms of energy are available in the market for a definite price. The most important forms of commercial energy are electricity, eoal and refined petroleum products. Commercial energy serves the basis of industrial, agricultural, transport and commercial development in the modern world.

Non-commercial forms of energy are not available in the commercial market for a definite price. Non-commercial energy sources include fuels such as firewood, cattle dung and agricultural wastes, which are traditionally gathered, and not bought at a price, and used especially in rural households. These are also called traditional fuels. Non-commercial energy is often ignored in energy accounting.

1.2.3 Renewable and Non-renewable Sources

Renewable energy sources are *not exhaustible.* These are freely available in nature and can be continuously used and re-generated. Examples of renewable resources include wind power, solar power, geothermal energy, tidal power, ocean therm al energy, fuel cells, energy from biomass and hydraulic energy. The most important feature of renewable energy source is that it can be harnessed without the released of harmful pollutants. These sources are also named as *non-conventional energy sources.*

Non-renewable energy sources are conventional fossil fuels such as coal, oil and gas, nuclear fuels, and heat traps which are accumulated in the earth crust. These have been in use for several decades. The sources of non-renewable energy are depleting at a fast rate and may not be sufficient to meet the increasing energy demand in future. Therefore, these sources are also called *exhaustible sources* of energy and they cannot be replenished immediately. These sources are also named as *conventional energy sources.*

1.3 CONVENTIONAL AND NON-CONVENTIONAL ENERGY SOURCES

1.3.1 Conventional Energy Sources

Conventional Energy Sources are non-renewable energy sources which exist in the form of fossil fuels (such as oil, petroleum, natural gas and coal) and radioactive fuel (uranium). Conventional energy sources are available on the earth in limited quantity. Non-renewable energy is not sustainable. The energy reserves will inevitably be empty if we continue to use them. Non-renewable sources are not environmental friendly and can have serious affect on our health. They are called non-renewable because they cannot be re-generated within a short span of time.

Advantages

- Non-renewable sources are cheap and easy to store and use.
- Non-renewable sources are more convenient than renewable resources.

- Natural gas and oil are easily transferred through- pipelines -to many areas at a lesser cost. Thus they can be located easily.
- Non-renewable sources are integrated into the global infrastructure, since they provide the majority of the world's power. Making transition to renewable sources will need wholesale changes not only in production but also in the technology to dispense these resources.
- The technology for using non-renewable energy sources is already highly developed, and widely deployed in the World.

Disadvantages

- Non-renewable sources are finite and in limited quantity.
- Burning fossil fuels produces carbon dioxide (CO_2), which is the primary cause of global warming.
- Burning fossil fuels also produces other kinds of air pollution, including sulfur dioxide, which causes acid rain, and also nitrous oxides, mercury pollution, and uranium pollution.
- Processing and using nuclear fuel (uranium) creates many radioactive by-products, which are very dangerous to living things. Disposing of these by-products and the spent (used) nuclear fuel is therefore difficult to do.
- Coal mining, uranium mining, and drilling for oil and gas can have very strong impacts on the landscape and on water supplies.
- Dependence of foreign energy resources can make a nation vulnerable to energy supply disruption, corrupt a nation's good intentions towards its neighbours, and also make a nation more susceptible to foreign exploitation.

Some of the main conventional energy sources are:

(*a*) Fossil fuel energy

Coal, petroleum, and natural gas are called Fossil fuel as these are formed by the decomposition of the remains of dead plants and animals buried under the earth for a long time. These are non-renewable sources of energy, which, if exhausted, cannot be replenished in a short time.

(i) Coal

Coal is a complex mixture of compounds of carbon, hydrogen and oxygen. Small amounts of nitrogen and Sulphur compounds are also present in coal. It is mainly available in Bihar, West Bengal, Orissa and Madhya Pradesh. The big coal mines in our country are at Jharia and Bokaro in Bihar and at Raniganj in West Bengal. It is considered as the backbone of the energy sector for its use in industry, transportation and electric power generation.

Depending upon the carbon contents of coal, it is classified as follows:

Type of coal Carbon content (%)

1. Peat – 60%
2. Lignite (soft coal) – 70%
3. Bituminous (house hold coal) – 80%
4. Anthracite (hard coal) – 90%

It is clear that peat is the most inferior quality of coal whereas anthracite is the most superior quality of coal. Bituminous is most commonly used in households and industry. On strong heating, coal breaks up to produce coal gas, ammonia, coal tar and coke. Coke is 98% carbon, obtained after losing all its volatile constituents during destructive distillation of coal. It can be used as smoke free fuel.

Availability of Coal and Lignite

(*i*) The total availability of raw coal in India during 2011-12 stood at 638.84 MTs and that of lignite at 41.89 MTs.

(*ii*) The availability of coal in the year 2011-12 increased by 8.30% compared to 2010-11, the availability of lignite also increased by 11.15% during the same period.

(*iii*) The availability of coal has increased at a CAGR of about 5.36% during the period from 1970-71 to 2011-12 and that of lignite has increased at a CAGR of about 1.41% during the period from 1998-99 to 2011-12.

Table 1.1 : Statewise Estimated Reserves of Coal in India as on 31.03.2011 and 31.03.2012

(in billion tonnes)

States/UTs	Proved		Indicated		Inferred		Total		Distribution (%)	
	31.03.2011	31.03.2012	31.03.2011	31.03.2012	31.03.2011	31.03.2012	31.03.2011	31.03.2012	31.03.2011	31.03.2012
Andhra Prasedh	9.30	9.57	9.73	9.55	3.03	3.03	22.05	22.16	**7.71**	**7.55**
Arunachal Pradesh	0.03	0.03	0.04	0.04	0.02	0.02	0.09	0.09	**0.03**	**0.03**
Assam	0.47	0.47	0.05	0.05	0.00	0.00	0.51	0.51	**0.18**	**0.17**
Bihar	0.00	0.00	0.00	0.00	0.16	0.16	0.16	0.16	**0.06**	**0.05**
Chhattisgarh	12.88	13.99	32.39	33.45	4.01	3.41	49.28	50.85	**17.24**	**17.32**
Jharkhand	39.76	40.16	32.59	33.61	6.58	6.58	78.94	80.36	**27.61**	**27.38**
Madhya Pradesh	8.87	9.31	12.19	12.29	2.06	2.78	23.13	24.38	**8.09**	**8.31**
Maharashtra	5.49	5.67	3.09	3.11	1.95	2.11	10.53	10.88	**3.68**	**3.71**
Meghalaya	0.09	0.09	0.02	0.02	0.47	0.47	0.58	0.58	**0.20**	**0.20**
Nagaland	0.01	0.01	0.00	0.00	0.31	0.31	0.32	0.32	**0.11**	**0.11**
Odisha	24.49	25.55	33.99	36.47	10.68	9.43	69.16	71.45	**24.19**	**24.34**
Sikkim	0.00	0.00	0.06	0.06	0.04	0.04	0.10	0.10	**0.04**	**0.03**
Uttar Pradesh	0.87	0.88	0.20	0.18	0.00	0.00	1.06	1.06	**0.37**	**0.36**
West Bengal	11.75	12.43	13.13	13.56	5.07	4.83	29.96	30.62	**10.48**	**10.43**
All India Total	**114.00**	**118.15**	**137.47**	**142.17**	**34.39**	**33.18**	**285.86**	**293.50**	**100.00**	**100.00**
Distribution (%)	**39.88**	**40.25**	**48.09**	**48.44**	**12.03**	**11.31**	**100.00**	**100.00**		

Table 1.1(A) : Statewise Estimated Reserves of Lignite in India as on 31.03.2011 and 31.03.2012

(in billion tonnes)

States/UTs	Proved		Indicated		Inferred		Total		Distribution (%)	
	31.03.2011	31.03.2012	31.03.2011	31.03.2012	31.03.2011	31.03.2012	31.03.2011	31.03.2012	31.03.2011	31.03.2012
Gujarat	1.24	1.28	0.32	0.28	1.16	1.16	2.72	2.72	**6.65**	**6.49**
Jammu & Kashmir	0.00	0.00	0.02	0.02	0.01	0.01	0.03	0.03	**0.07**	**0.06**
Kerala	0.00	0.00	0.00	0.00	0.01	0.01	0.01	0.01	**0.02**	**0.02**
Pondicheny	0.00	0.00	0.41	0.41	0.01	0.01	0.42	0.42	**1.02**	**0.99**
Rajasthan	1.17	1.17	2.15	2.15	1.52	1.59	4.84	4.91	**11.82**	**11.69**
TamilNadu	3.74	3.74	22.90	22.90	6.26	7.24	32.89	33.88	**80.41**	**80.73**
West Bengal	0.00	0.00	0.00	0.00	0.00	0.00	0.00	0.00	**0.00**	**0.00**
India	**6.15**	**6.18**	**25.80**	**25.768.97**	**10.02**	**40.91**	**41.96**	**41.96**	**100.00**	**100.00**
Distribution (%)	**15.02**	**14.73**	**61.67**	**61.40**	**21.92**	**23.88**	**100.00**	**100.00**		

(ii) Oil

India has total reserves (proved and indicated) of 1201 million metric tonnes of crude oil. The consumption of petroleum products increased by 3.6% from 2008-09 to 2009-10. India has a total installed capacity of 1199.75 MW of oil based power plants which is not substantial.

India is not particularly rich in petroleum reserves. The potential oil bearing areas are located in Assam, Tripura, Manipur, West Bengal, Ganga valley, Punjab, Himachal Pradesh, Kutch, eastern and western coastal area (in Tamil Nadu, Andhra Pradesh and Kerala), Andaman and Nicobar Islands, Lakshadweep, and in the continental shelves adjoining these areas.

Availability of Crude Oil and Petroleum Products

(*i*) The availability of crude oil in the country increased from 106.52 MTs during 2000-01 to 209.82 MTs during 2011-12.

(*ii*) During this period crude oil production increased from 6.82 MTs to 38.09 MTs and the net import increased from 11.68 MTs to 171.73 MTs. There was 4.24% increase in availability of crude oil during 2011-12 over 2010-11.

(iii) Natural Gas

India has total reserves (proved and indicated) of 437 billion cubic meters of natural gas as of 1st April 2010. Gross Production of Natural Gas in the country during 2009-10 was 44.63% higher than the production during 2008-09. The total installed capacity of gas fired plants as of February 2011 stood at 17706 MW. Natural gas can replace existing fuels in various sectors both for feedstock as well as for energy purposes.

Availability of Natural Gas

The availability of natural gas has steadily increased from a mere 17.86 BCMs during 1970-71 to 150.87 BCMs during 2011-12, registering a CAGR of 5.21%. Most of this increase in the indigenous production is due to discovery of new reserves.

Table 1.2(A) : Statewise Estimated Reserves @ of Crude Oil and Natural Gas in India as on in 31.03.2011 and 31.03.2012

States/UTs	Crude Petroleum (milion tonnes) 31.03.2011		31.03.2012		Natural Gas (billion cubic metres) 31.03.2011		31.03.2012	
	Estimated Reverse	Distribution (%)	Estimated Reverse	Distribution (%)	Estimated Reverse	Distribution (%)	Estimated Reverse	Distribution (%)
Andhra Pradesh	5.22	0.69	5.59	0.74	40.58	3.18	42.30	3.18
Arunachal Pradesh	3.39	0.45	3.41	0.45	2.21	0.17	2.15	0.16
Assam	170.33	22.49	172.54	22.71	139.64	10.93	139.82	10.51
CBM	0.00	0.00	0.00	0.00	87.63	6.86	97.54	7.33
Eastern Offshore[1]	36.18	3.46	24.12	3.18	438.03	34.27	462.08	34.73
Gujarat	137.43	18.14	135.72	17.87	78.96	6.18	78.19	5.88
Nagaland	2.69	0.36	2.69	0.35	0.12	0.01	0.12	0.01
Rajasthan	75.33	9.95	68.87	9.07	12.04	0.94	12.13	0.91
Tamil Nadu	8.87	1.12	8.86	1.17	36.88	2.89	39.30	2.95
Tripura	0.88	0.01	0.07	0.01	33.09	2.59	36.05	2.71
Western Offshore[2]	328.27	43.34	337.72	44.46	408.88	31.99	420.63	31.62
Total	**757.40**	**100.00**	**759.59**	**100.00**	**1278.06**	**100.00**	**1330.26**	**100.00**

CBM : Cold Bed Methane

(*b*) Nuclear energy

According to modern theories of atomic structure, matter consists of minute particles known as atoms. Heavier unstable atoms such as U_{235}, Th_{239}, liberate large amount of heat energy. The energy released by the complete fission of one Kg of Uranium (U_{235}), is equal to the heat energy obtained by burning 4500 tonnes of coal (or) 220 tons of oil. The heat produced by nuclear fission of the atoms of fissionable material is utilized in special heat exchangers for the production of steam which is then used to drive turbogenerators as in the conventional power plants.

However there are some limitations in the use of nuclear energy namely high capital cost of nuclear power plants, limited availability of raw materials, difficulties associated with disposal of radioactive waste and shortage of well trained personnel to handle the nuclear power plants.

The Uranium reserves in the world at present are small. These reserves are recoverable but are expensive. The presently working power plants are:

1. Tarapur atomic power station in Maharashtra
2. Ranapratap sagar atomic power station near Tota, Rajasthan

3. Kalpakkam atomic power station near Madras, Tamilnadu.
4. Narora atomic power station in U.P.

About 3% of the energy produced in India is obtained from nuclear

Availability of Electricity

(*i*) Since thermal electricity is not a primary source of energy, being produced either from coal or natural gas in India, electricity availability is considered only for that electricity which is generated from Hydro and Nuclear sources.

(*ii*) Without taking into account the transmission and distribution losses, the total availability is equal to the total generation, and this figure increased from 53,031 GWh during 1970-71 to 8,11,506 GWh during 2011-12, registering a CAGR of 6.71% over the period.

1.3.2 Non-conventional energy sources

The sources of energy which are being produced continuously in nature and are not exhaustible are called renewable sources of energy or non-conventional energy sources. For example, solar energy, wind energy, bio-energy - bio-fuels grown sustain ably), hydropower etc., are some of the examples of non-conventional energy sources.

A renewable energy system converts the energy found in sunlight, wind, falling-water, sea-waves, geothermal heat, or biomass into a form, we can use such as heat or electricity. Most of the renewable energy comes either directly or indirectly from sun and wind and can never be exhausted, and therefore they are called renewable.

Advantage

- The sun, wind, geothermal, ocean energy are available in the abundant quantity and free to use.
- The non-renewable sources of energy that we are using are limited.
- Renewable sources have low carbon emissions, therefore they are considered as green and environment friendly.
- Renewable helps in stimulating the economy and creating job opportunities.
- Renewable sources can cost less than consuming the local electrical supply.

Disadvantage

- It is not easy to set up a plant as the initial costs are quite steep.
- Solar energy can be used during the day time and not during night or rainy season.

- Geothermal energy which can be used to generate electricity has side effects too. It can bring toxic chemicals beneath the earth surface onto the top and can create environmental changes.
- Hydroelectric provide pure form of energy but building dams across the river which is quite expensive can affect natural flow and affect wildlife.
- To use wind energy, you have to rely on strong winds therefore you have to choose suitable site to operate them. Also, they can affect bird population as they are quite high.

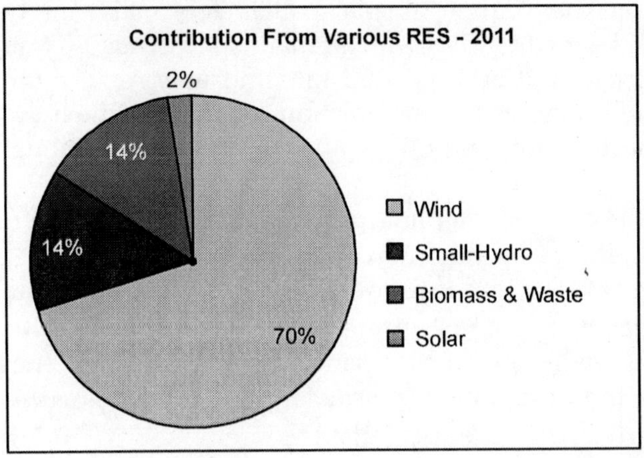

***Fig. 1.7** Contribution from various Renewable Energy Sources*

1.3.2.1 Various forms of renewable energy

(*a*) Solar Energy

Solar energy is the most readily available and free source of energy since prehistoric times.

Solar energy can be utilized through two different routes, as solar thermal route and solar electric (solar photovoltaic) routes. Solar thermal route uses the sun's heat to produce hot water or air, cook food, drying materials etc. Solar photovoltaic uses sun's heat to produce electricity for lighting home and building, running motors, pumps, electric appliances, and lighting.

Advantages of Solar Energy

1. No Pollution: Solar energy is non-polluting, clean, reliable and renewable source of electricity. It does not pollute the air by releasing harmful gases like carbon dioxide, nitrogen oxide and sulphur oxide.

2. Long lasting solar cells: Solar cells make no noise at all and there are no moving parts in solar cells which make them long lasting and require very little maintenance.

3. Renewable Source: Solar energy is a renewable source of energy and will continue to produce electricity as long as sun exists.

4. Low maintenance: Solar cells generally don't require any maintenance and run for long time.

5. Easy Installation: Solar panels are easy to install and does not require any wires, cords or power sources.

Disadvantages of Solar Energy

1. Initial Cost: The initial cost of purchasing and installing solar panels always become the first disadvantage when the subject of comes up.

2. Location: The location of solar panels is of major importance in the generation of electricity. Areas which remains mostly cloudy and foggy will produce electricity but at a reduced rate and may require more panels to generate enough electricity for your home. Houses which are covered by trees, landscapes or other buildings may not be suitable enough to produce solar power.

3. Pollution: Most of the photovoltaic panels are made up of silicon and other toxic metals like mercury, lead and cadmium. Pollution in the environment can also degrade the quality and efficiency of photovoltaic cells.

4. Inefficiency: Since not all the light from the sun is absorbed by the solar panels therefore most solar panels have a 40% efficiency rate which means 60% of the sunlight gets wasted and is not harnessed.

5. Reliability: They are less reliable.

6. Installation area: For home users, a solar energy installation may not require huge space but for big companies, a large area is required for the system to be efficient in providing a source of electricity.

Applications of Solar Energy

1. Growing our food: *Farming:* The most basic and ancient use of solar energy!

2. Cooking our food: This can be done with "solar ovens" or "solar cookers" which use mirrors to concentrate solar energy to make heat.

3. Drying our clothes: It takes a lot of energy to dry clothes with clothes dryers. A *clothesline* works just as well, and uses only solar energy!

4. Generating Electricity to power appliances, and for many other things: Solar energy can be used to generate electricity with "photovoltaic solar collectors". This can also been done by using very large mirrors to concentrate solar energy to first make heat to make steam or hot air to drive a turbine (generator). This is called "concentrating solar power".

5. Heating our homes and other buildings (directly): This can be done using "solar heating panels", which use solar energy to heat air or water.

6. Heating hot water for showers and dishwashing (directly): This can be done using solar heating panels, which use solar energy to heat water (the same type which can be used to heat a house).

7. Distilling/Purifying water: This can be done by using solar heat to evaporate water, leaving impurities behind.

8. Generating hydrogen for transportation fuel and for generating electricity with fuel cells: This can be done with solar generated electricity via the process of "electrolysis", or directly with "photocatalytic" processes.

9. Solar Energy, is also the ultimate source of wind power and biomass power.

(*b*) Wind energy

Wind energy is basically harnessing of wind power to produce electricity. The kinetic energy of the wind is converted to electrical energy. When solar radiation enters the earth's atmosphere, different regions of the atmosphere are heated to different degrees because of earth curvature. This heating is higher at the equator and lowest at the poles. Since air tends to flow from warmer to cooler regions, this causes what we call winds, and it is these airflows that are harnessed in windmills and wind turbines to produce power.

Wind Energy Technology: The basic wind energy conversion device is the wind turbine. Although various designs and configurations exist, these turbines are generally grouped into two types:

1. Vertical-axis wind turbines, in which the axis of rotation is vertical with respect to the ground (and roughly perpendicular to the wind stream),

2. Horizontal-axis turbines, in which the axis of rotation is horizontal with respect to the ground (and roughly parallel to the wind stream.)

Wind Potential: The following table represents a guideline of different wind speeds and their potential in producing electricity.

Table 1.3

Average Wind Speed km/h (mph)	Suitability
UP to 15 (9.5)	No good
18 (11.25)	Poor
22 (13.75)	Moderate
25 (15.5)	Good
29 (18)	Excellent

A wind generator will produce lesser power in summer than in winter at the same wind speed as air has lower density in summer than in winter.

Similarly, a wind generator will produce lesser power in higher altitudes - as air pressure as well as density is lower -than at lower altitudes.

The wind speed is the most important factor influencing the amount of energy a wind turbine can produce. Increasing wind velocity increases the amount of air passing the rotor, which increases the output of the wind system.

Applications

(*i*) Utility interconnected wind turbines generate power which is synchronous with the grid and are used to reduce utility bills by displacing the utility power used in the household and by selling the excess power back to the electric company.

(*ii*) Wind turbines for remote homes (off the grid) generate DC current for battery charging.

(*iii*) Wind turbines for remote water pumping generate 3 phase AC current suitable for driving an electrical submersible pump directly. Wind turbines suitable for residential or village scale wind power range from 500 Watts to 50 kilowatts.

Advantages of Wind Energy

1. Renewable Energy:

2. Reduces Fossil Fuels Consumption: Dependence on the fossil fuels could be reduced to much extent. Apart from this, it can also help to curb harmful gas emissions which are the major source of global warming.

3. Less Air and Water Pollution: Wind energy doesn't pollute at all. It does not destroy the environment or release toxic gases.

4. Initial Cost: The cost of producing wind energy has come down steadily over the last few years. Also, when combine with solar power, it provides cheap, reliable, steady and great source of energy for the developed and developing countries.

5. Create Many Jobs: Wind energy on the other hand has created many jobs for the local people. From installation of wind turbines to maintenance of the area where turbines are located, it has created wide range of opportunities for the people.

Disadvantages of Wind Energy

1. Noise Disturbances: Though wind energy is non pollution, the turbines may create a lot of noise. This alone is the reason that wind farms are not built near residential areas.

2. Threat to Wildlife: Due to large scale construction of wind turbines on remote location, it could be a threat to wild life nearby.

3. Wind Can Never Be Predicted: The main disadvantage of wind energy is that wind can never be predicted. In areas where large amount of wind is needed or winds strength is too low to support wind turbine, there solar or geothermal energy could prove to be great alternatives.

4. Suited To Particular Region: Wind turbines are suited to the coastal regions which receive wind throughout the year to generate power.

(*c*) Bio Energy

Bio-gas, a mixture containing 55-65% methane, 30-40% carbon dioxide and the rest being the impurities hydrogen (hydrogen sulphide and some nitrogen), can be produced from the decomposition of animal, plant and human waste. It is clean but slow burning gas and usually has a calorific value 5000 to 5500 kcal/kg. It can be used directly in cooking, reducing the demand for firewood. Moreover, the material from which the bio-gas is produced retains its value as a fertilizer and can be returned to soil.

Bio-gas is produced by digestion, pyrolysis or hydrogasification. Digestion is a biological process that occurs in the absence of oxygen and in the presence of anaerobic organisms at ambient pressures and temperatures of 35-70°C. The container in which this digestion takes place is known as the digester.

Advantages

1. Less dependence on fossil fuels
2. Reduction in landfill disposal
3. Easily available and inexhaustible fuel source
4. Has the potential to reduce greenhouse gases. Though it also emits carbon-dioxide, but carbon-dioxide released by it is largely balanced by the carbon dioxide captured in its own growth. Where as carbon-dioxide released by fossil fuels was captured by photosynthesis millions of years ago.

Disadvantages

1. Could contribute a great deal to global warming and particulate pollution if directly burned.
2. An expensive source and research is needed to reduce the cost of production of bio-energy based fuels.
3. Bio energy conversion projects are limited and therefore on a smaller scale there is more likely a net loss of energy.
4. Land needed to produce bio energy may be in demand for other purposes such as conservation or housing or agriculture use.

(*d*) Tidal Energy

The periodic rise and fall of the water level of sea which are carried by the action of the sun and moon on water of the earth is called the 'tide'.

The main feature of the tidal cycle is difference in water surface elevations at the high tide and at the low tide. If this differential head could be utilized in operating a hydraulic turbine, the tidal energy could be converted into electrical energy by means of an attached generator.

(*e*) Geothermal Energy

Our earth's interior - like the sun - provides heat energy from nature. This heat - geothermal energy - yields warmth and power that we can use without polluting the environment.

Advantages of Geothermal Energy

1. Significant Cost Saving: Geothermal energy generally involves low running costs since it saves 80% costs over fossil fuels and no fuel is used to generate the power.

2. Reduce Reliance on Fossil Fuels: Dependence on fossil fuels decreases with the increase in the use of geothermal energy.

3. No Pollution: Being the renewable source of energy, geothermal energy has helped in reducing global warming and pollution.

4. Direct Use: Since ancient times, people having been using this source of energy for taking bath, heating homes, preparing food and today this is also used for direct heating of homes and offices. This makes geothermal energy cheaper and affordable.

5. Job Creation and Economic Benefits: Government of various countries is investing hugely in creation of geothermal energy which on other hand has created more jobs for the local people.

Disadvantages of Geothermal Energy

1. Not Widespread Source of Energy: Since this type of energy is not widely used therefore the unavailability of equipment, staff, infrastructure, and training pose hindrance to the installation of geothermal plants across the globe.

2. High Installation Costs: To get geothermal energy, requires installation of power plants, to get steam from deep within the earth and this require huge one time investment and require hiring a certified installer and skilled staff needs to be recruited and relocated to plant location.

3. Can Run Out Of Steam : Geothermal sites can run out of steam over a period of time due to drop in temperature or if too much water is injected to cool the rocks and this may result huge loss for the companies which have invested heavily in these plants.

4. Suited To Particular Region: It is only suitable for regions where temperature below the earth is quite low and can produce steam over a long period of time. Some of these regions are near hilly areas or high up in mountains.

5. May Release Harmful Gases: Geothermal sites may contain some poisonous gases and they can escape deep within the earth, through the holes drilled by the constructors. The geothermal plant must therefore be capable enough to contain these harmful and toxic gases.

The estimated potential of various Renewable Energy technologies in India by IREDA are given below.

Table 1.2

Energy source estimated potential

Solar Energy	20 MW / sq. km
Wind Energy	20,000 MW
Small Hydro	10,000 MW
Ocean Thermal Power	50,000 MW
Sea Wave Power	20,000 MW
Tidal Power	10,000 MW
Bio energy	17,000 MW
Draught Animal Power	30,000 MW
Energy from MSW	1,000 MW
Biogas Plants	12 Million Plants
Improved Wood Burning Stoves	120 Million Stoves
Bagasse-based cogeneration	3500 MW

Table 1.3

Cumulative achievements in renewable energy sector (As on 31.03.2000)

Sources/Technologies	Unit Upto31.03.2000
Wind Power	MW1167
Small Hydro	MW217
Biomass Power & Co-generation	MW 222
Solar PV Power	MW / Sq. km 42
Urban & MSW	MW 15.21
Solar Heater	m^2.Area 480000
Solar Cookers	No. 481112
Biogas Plants	Nos. in Million 2.95
Biomas Gasifier	MW 34
Improved Chulhas	Nos. in Million 31.9

1.4 ENVIRONMENTAL AND ECOLOGICAL ASPECTS OF ENERGY USE

The environment is everything that surrounds the humans and where all the economic activity occurs. The lithosphere, the atmosphere and the hydrosphere are the three distinct components of the environment. Processes and events interact in different ways with the environment.

Ecology is the study of the relationships of organisms with one another and the relationship of organisms to their environment.

The exponential increase of energy consumption, since the beginning of the industrial revolution, has produced significant changes in the global environment, chief among which is the increase of the average concentration of carbon dioxide in the atmosphere from 280 ppm in 1750 to more than 390 ppm in 2011.

Climatologists predict that this change will cause an increase of the average temperature of the planet as well as regional and global and climatic changes. Other significant environmental effects of energy consumption are: the several ecological problems caused by acid rain, which has threatened in the past the ecosystems of several lakes and rivers; lead contamination of the atmosphere; nuclear waste, which is produced by the more than 430 nuclear power plants in continuous operation worldwide; and, the waste heat rejection by all thermal power plants, which is accompanied by fresh-water consumption.

1.4.1 Global Warming

The most pressing environmental issue of the early twenty-first century is the accumulation of carbon dioxide (CO_2) and the expected global warming.

Global warming is a phenomenon caused by increase in the atmospheric temperature of the earth's surface, due to increase in concentration of greenhouse gases such as carbon dioxide, methane, nitrous oxide, chlorofluorocarbons (CFC), etc. These greenhouse gases trap the solar rays and cause temperature rise in the earth's atmosphere. This process of trapping solar energy is called greenhouse effect. Increase in population causes demand in energy sources by burning of fossil fuels and cutting down trees (deforestation) which is major cause for global warming. It is clear that, burning of fossil fuels directly contributes to global warming by releasing greenhouse gases, but how does deforestation contribute to global warming? Trees and plants take in carbon dioxide and give out oxygen. If these plants and trees are cut down, the carbon dioxide will remain unused in the atmosphere, and increase the temperature of the earth's surface, which is called global warming!

All fossil fuels-coal, petroleum and natural gas-are composed of carbon and other atoms, typically hydrogen. The carbon atoms form CO_2 upon combustion, as for example in the following complete combustions of coal and methane:

$$C + O_2 \rightarrow CO_2 \quad ; \quad CH_4 + 2O_2 \rightarrow CO_2 + 2H_2O$$

Figure 1.8 shows the average concentration by volume of the CO_2 in the Earth's atmosphere since the beginning of the industrial revolution.

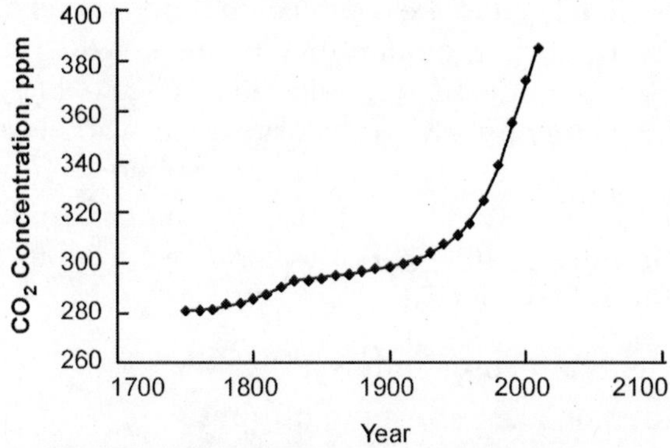

Fig. 1.8 Average atmospheric concentration of CO_2, since the beginning of the industrial revolution

Some of the global warming impacts are:

(*i*) Melting of the polar icecaps, the Greenland Ice sheet, glaciers, and the permafrosts.

(*ii*) Hotter average temperatures almost everywhere.

(*iii*) Increased drought in many places.

(*iv*) Increased flooding in many places.

(*v*) Increased numbers and strengths of tornados and hurricanes.

(*vi*) Migration and/or extinction of many species, many of which are already under pressure from human encroachment or other invasive species.

(*vii*) Large sea level rise, causing coastlines, islands, and coastal wetlands (like the Everglades) to disappear.

(*viii*) The increase in the atmosphere's carbon dioxide level also causes the oceans to become more acidic (through the formation of carbonic acid), which is thought to harm the growth of coral.

The following list includes some of the actions individual nations and the global community may take to, first, reduce the growth of CO_2 emissions and, secondly, to reduce the actual concentration of the gas in the atmosphere.

1. Reduction of energy consumption per capita
2. Sequestration of CO_2 at the production sites, that is at the power plants, and subsequent storage:
3. Substitution of coal with nuclear fuel for the production of electricity
4. Reforestation:
5. Seeding large ocean regions with iron and nitrogen-rich fertilizer
6. Higher use of renewable energy sources

1.4.2 Acid Rain

Acid rain is a rain or any other form of precipitation that is unusually acidic, meaning that it possesses elevated levels of hydrogen ions (low pH).

Acid rain is closely related to the combustion of fossil fuels. Fossil fuels, and especially coal, contain large quantities of sulfur which forms SO_2 upon combustion. In addition CO_2 and a series of nitrogen oxides with the general formula NOx (or, commonly, NOX) are formed during coal combustion. These oxides combine with water vapor in the atmosphere to form mild acids.

As a consequence of acid precipitation, the concentration of the H+ increases significantly and the pH of water drops from its natural range of 6.8-7.4 to significantly lower values.

The effects of acid rain are as follows:

- o Acidification of lakes, streams, and soils
- o Direct and indirect effects (release of metals, For example: Aluminum which washes away plant nutrients)
- o Killing of wildlife (trees, crops, aquatic plants, and animals)
- o Decay of building materials and paints, statues, and sculptures
- o Health problems (respiratory, burning- skin and eyes)

Some of the major procedures that must be followed to control acid rain are as follows:

1. Reduce amount of sulphur dioxide and oxides of nitrogen released into the atmosphere using methods like Flue gas desulphurization and Catalytic Converters.
2. Use cleaner fuels such as coal that contains less sulphur. Natural Gas can be used.
3. Use other sources of electricity (such as wind energy, geothermal energy, solar energy etc.)
4. Reduce the effects of acid rain by Liming. Powdered limestone/ limewater can be added to water and soil to neutralize acid.

1.5 SUSTAINABLE DEVELOPMENT

Sustainable development or 'sustainability' is development that meets the needs of the present without compromising the ability of future generations to meet their own needs.

The aim of sustainable development is to define viable schemes combining the economic, social, and environmental aspects of human activity. The ultimate goal of sustainable development is to find a coherent and long-lasting balance between these three aspects.

Benefits of Sustainable Development

1. It protects technological resources.
2. It provides basic human needs such as food, water and shelter for the long run.

3. Sustainable agriculture practices like crop rotation and effective seeding practices can help to promote high yields while protecting the integrity of the soil as it produces food for larger amounts of people.
4. It accommodates city development for rising population by reducing the use of fossil fuels.
5. It controls climatic changes with lower use of fossil fuels, which are not sustainable and which produce greenhouse gases.
6. Sustainable development can also produce more financially sustainable economies throughout the world. Resource-poor economies will gain access to free and accessible energy through renewables while also having the opportunity to train workers for jobs.
7. It sustains biodiversity.

REVIEW QUESTIONS

1. What is energy? Comment on classification of energy resources.
2. What are conventional sources of energy? Give detailed explanation along with examples.
3. What are non-conventional sources of energy? What are the various forms of renewable energy? Discuss them in detail.
4. Differentiate between conventional and non-conventional sources of energy.
5. Discuss the merits and demerits of non-conventional energy resources.
6. List various non-conventional energy resources. Give their availability, relative merits and their classification.
7. Discuss the main features of various types of renewable and non-renewable energy sources and explain the importance of non-conventional energy sources in the context of global warming.
8. Discuss the main feature of non-conventional energy sources.
9. Discuss different renewable sources of energy with special reference to the Indian context.
10. Discuss about Indian and global energy resources. Also describe the future of non-conventional energy resources in India.
11. Explain Energy Scenario in India.
12. Write a short note on Trends in Installed Electricity Generating Capacity in India.
13. Write a short note on 'Global Warming'.
14. Write a short note on Sustainable Development.

❑

2

PHOTOVOLTAIC SOLAR SYSTEMS

2.1 INTRODUCTION

The term "photo" means light and "voltaic," electricity. Photovoltaic (PV) comprises the technology which converts the sunlight energy directly into electric energy.

The solar PV cells (vital component of Solar PV System) are the devices which are used to convert the incident sunlight energy into electric energy in DC form and made up of semi-conducing materials (see Fig. 2.1).

A single converter cell is called a solar cell or, more generally, a photovoltaic cell, and combination of such cells; designed to increase the electric power output is called a solar module or solar array. These devices have theoretical efficiencies of the order of 25%. Actual operating efficiencies are less than half of this value, and decrease fairly rapidly with increasing temperature.

Mostly often silicon based solar PV cells are used today. The simplest PV cells power are used in watches and calculators, while more complex systems can light houses and provide power to the electrical grid.

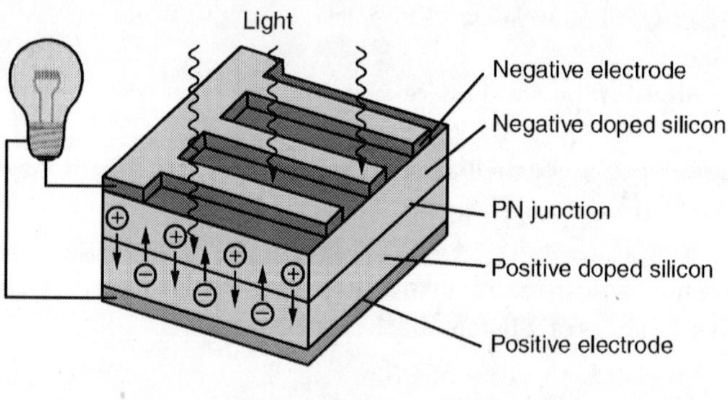

Fig. 2.1 Solar cell

2.2 SOLAR CELL FUNDAMENTALS

Typically, solar cells are made of silicon. A pure silicon crystal is an intrinsic semiconductor which has a two dimensional structure consists of covalent bonding. The silicon crystal forms the so-called diamond lattice (Fig. 2.2) where each atom has four nearest neighbours at the vertices of a tetrahedron. The four-fold tetrahedral co-ordination is the result of the bonding arrangement which uses the four outer (valence) electrons of each silicon atom. Each bond contains two electrons, and you can easily see that all the valence electrons are taken up by the bonds.

This crystal structure has a profound effect on the electronic and optical properties of the semiconductor. According to the quantum theory, the energy of an electron in the crystal must fall within well-defined bands. The energies of valence orbital which form bonds between the atoms represent just such a band of states, the valence band. The next higher band is the conduction band which is separated from the valence band by the energy gap, or band gap. The width of the band gap $E_c - E_v$ is a very important characteristic of the semiconductor and is usually denoted by E_g. (as depicted in Fig. 2.3)

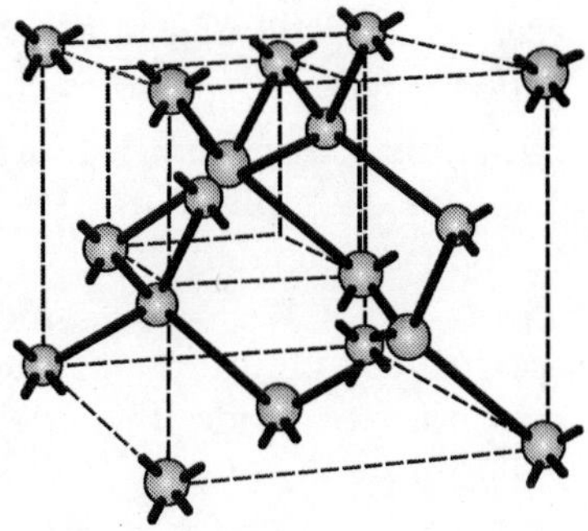

***Fig. 2.2** Silicon Lattice*

A pure semiconductor (which is called intrinsic) contains just the right number of electrons to fill the valence band, and the conduction band is therefore empty. Electrons in the full valence band cannot move - just as, for example, marbles in a full box with a lid on top. For practical purposes, a pure semiconductor is therefore an insulator.

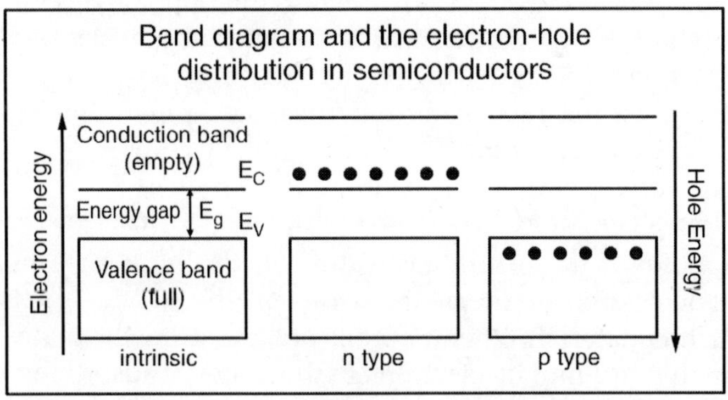

Fig. 2.3

Semiconductors can only conduct electricity if carriers are introduced into the conduction band or removed from the valence band. One way of doing this is by alloying the semiconductor with an impurity. This process is called doping. As we shall see, doping makes it possible to exert a great deal of control over the electronic properties of a semiconductor, and lies in the heart of the manufacturing process of all semiconductor devices.

Suppose that some group 5 impurity atoms (for example, phosphorus) are added to the silicon melt from which the crystal is grown. Four of the five outer electrons are used to fill the valence band and the one extra electron from each impurity atom is therefore promoted to the conduction band. For this reason, these impurity atoms are called *donors*. The electrons in the conduction band are mobile, and the crystal becomes a conductor. Since the current is carried by negatively charged electrons, this type of semiconductor is called *n type*.

A similar situation occurs when silicon is doped with group 3 impurity atoms (for example, boron) which are called *acceptors*. Since four electrons per atoms are needed to fill the valence band completely, this doping creates electron deficiency in this band. The missing electrons - called *holes* - behave as positively charged particles which are mobile, and carry current. A semiconductor where the electric current is carried predominantly by holes is called *p-type*.

2.3 WORKING PRINCIPLE OF SOLAR CELL

Solar Cell works on the principle of Photovoltaic Effect. By definition, the photovoltaic effect is the generation of a potential when radiation (photons) ionizes the region in or near the built-in potential barrier of a semiconductor.

When the two types of material (n-type and p-type) are brought together, say, with the n-material on the top, a very interesting thing happens. Some of the extra, mobile electrons in the n-material migrate over into the p-material and fill some of the holes there. This makes the upper layer of the p-material negatively charged, while the nearby n-material now lacks electrons and becomes positively charged. In the Fig. 2.1, these charges are symbolized with minus signs (for the negative charges), and plus signs (for the positive charges). These charges create an electric field, or voltage, across the junction of the two wafers, called a p-n junction, balances (stops) further (net) migration. This electric field remains permanently "built-in".

When there is no sunlight shining on the material, there is no net movement of electrons in the material, despite the fact that there is an electric field inside the material. When photons of light strike the material, however, some normally non-mobile electrons in the material absorb the photons, and become mobile by virtue of their increased energy. This creates new holes too - which are just the vacancies created by the newly created mobile electrons. Because of the "built in" electric field, the new mobile electrons in the n-material cannot cross over into the p-material.

In fact, if they are created near or in the junction where the electric field exists, they are pushed by the field towards the upper surface of the n-material (such an event is shown in the diagram below). If a wire is connected from the n-material to the p-material, however, they can flow through the wire, and deliver their energy to a load.

On the other hand, the holes created in the n-material, which are positively charged, are pushed over into the p-material. Thus an electron from the p-material, which was also made mobile by the absorption of a photon, is pushed by the electric field across the junction and into the n-material to fill the newly created hole. This completes the circuit and we see that there are electrons flowing all the way around the circuit, dropping the energy they acquired from photons at a load.

The crucial step in the whole process is that just described - the pushing of mobile electrons across the p-n junction. This suggests a nice way to think of the PV process - like a tennis player making an overhead serve: First, an electron absorbs a photon and become mobile. This is like the first step in a tennis player's serve, when they throw the ball upwards into the air. Secondly, the built-in electric field pushes the electron into the n-material. This is like the tennis racket crashing into the ball, and accelerating across the net.

2.4 SILICON SOLAR CELL CHARACTERISTICS

The silicon Solar cell used in this experiment can essentially be represented by the simplified equivalent circuit shown in Fig. 2.4, which consists of a constant current generator in parallel with nonlinear junction impedance (Z_J) and a resistive load (R_L). When light strikes the cell, a current I_S (short-circuit current) is generated which is equal to the sum of the current through the load, I_L, and the current flowing in the nonlinear junction, I_j.

Therefore, I_{SC} or $I_S = I_L + I_J$ ...(2.1)

Where $I_J = I_O (e^{qV/kT} - 1)$ ...(2.2)

where q is the electron charge, V is the applied junction voltage, k is the Boltzmann constant, T is the absolute temperature, and Io is the dark (reverse) saturation current. Hence, the current through the load is given

$$I_L = I_S - I_O (e^{qV/kT} - 1) \quad ...(2.3)$$

and the maximum voltage obtained from the cell, V_{max}; occurring when $I_L = 0$, is :

$$V_{max} = 1/(q/kT) \ln (I_S/I_O + 1)$$
$$= 1/\lambda \ln (I_S/ I_O + 1) \quad ...(2.4)$$

Where $\lambda = q/kT$.

I_o is obtained when the negative voltage is applied across the diode.

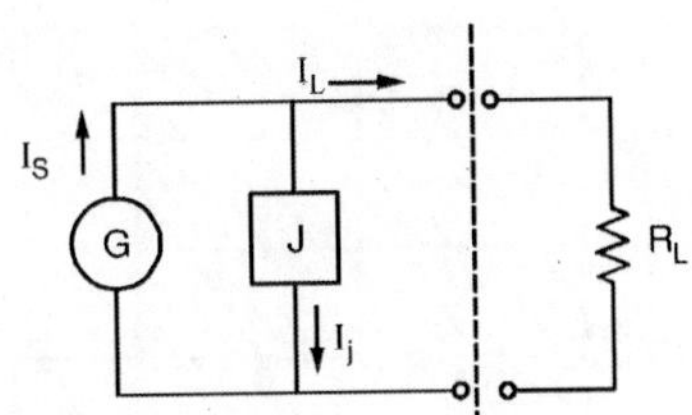

Fig. **2.4** *Equivalent Circuit*

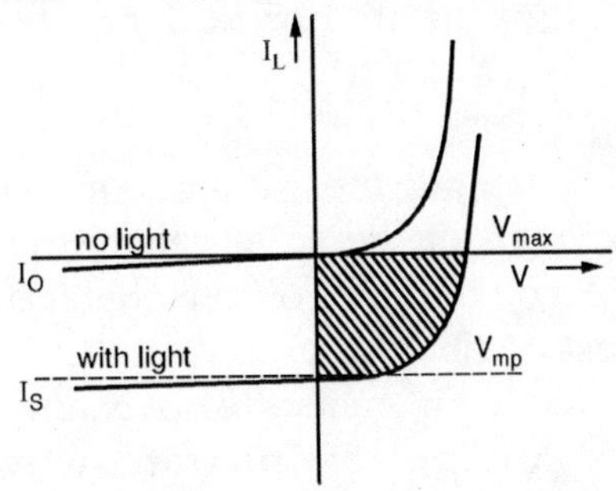

Fig. **2.5** *Solar Cell V-I Characteristics*

Shown in Fig. 2.5 is a general solar cell V-I characteristic with both I_O and I_S Plotted. Note that the curves appear in the fourth quadrant, therefore power can be extracted from the device according to Theory. The short circuit current I_{SC}, and the open-circuit voltage V_{OC}, are determined far a given light level by the cell properties, whereas the maximum current and voltage deliverable to the load is determined by the largest area rectangle that can be fit under the V-I curve as shown in Fig. 2.6. The point where this rectangle is tangent to the V-I curve is therefore defined as the Maximum power delivered to the load :

$$P_m = V_m \times I_m \qquad ...(2.5)$$

and is a very important value in calculating the efficiency of the unit.

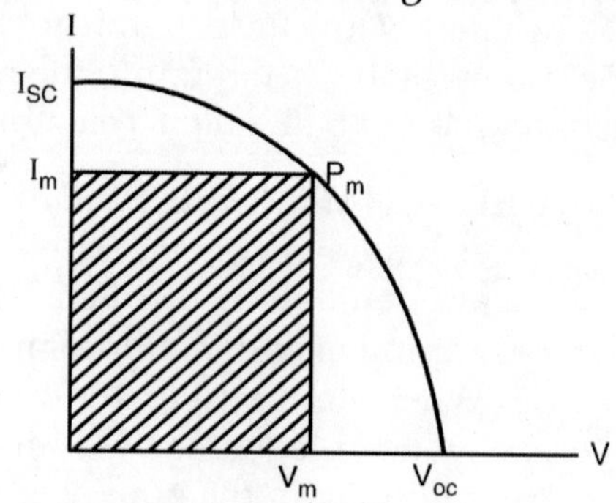

Fig. 2.6 *V-I Curve*

Another important value very useful in evaluating the overall efficiency of a solar cell is the "fill factor", defined as the ratio :

$$F.F = V_M I_M / I_{SC} V_{OC} = P_M / I_{SC} V_{OC} \qquad ...(2.6)$$

The fill factor, which is always less than unity, is typically used to describe quantitatively the "squareness" or "sharpness" of the V-I curve. The squarer such a curve is, the greater the maximum power output, P_m. Typical fill factors of contemporary silicon solar cells range from 0.75 to 0.80.

Plotted in Fig. 2.7 are the V-I characteristics for four different silicon solar cells.

Changing the illumination intensity incident on the solar cell has a great effect on the cell's output characteristic, most notably I_{SC} and V_{OC}, shifting the V-I curve but generally not changing its shape. Fig. 2.8 illustrates how the

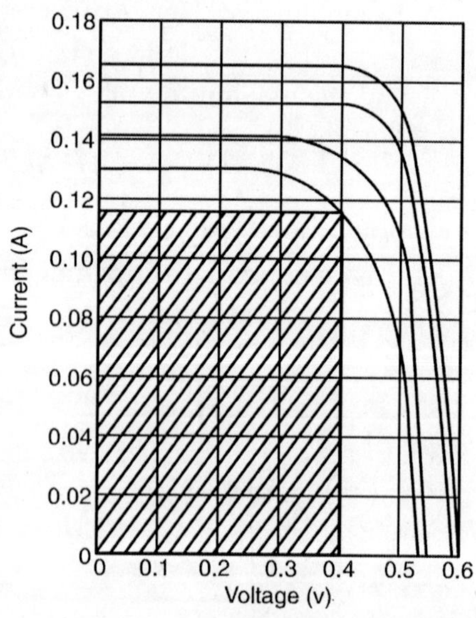

Fig. 2.7

voltage and current vary as functions of the sunlight intensity, technically known as the radiant solar energy flux density. As is obvious from the figure, the short-circuit current is directly proportional to the flux while the open-circuit voltage varies as the log of the flux. Note that at high flux densities, the voltage exhibits a saturation level. Therefore, even with fluctuations in the intensity in this saturation range, the voltage will essentially be insensitive to the changes. This is quite an advantage in that the cell can be employed for the charging of storage batteries without the need of a constant light source.

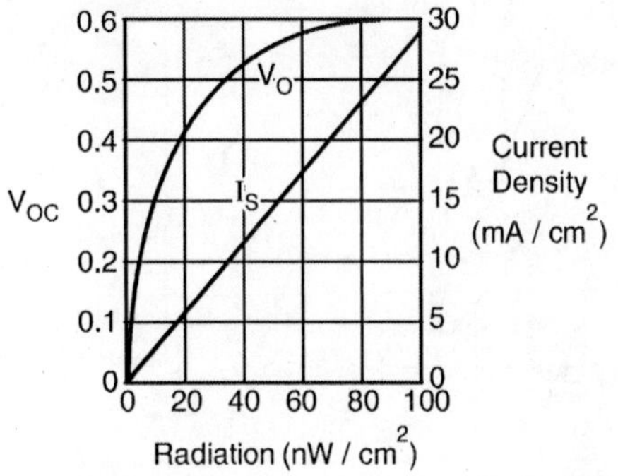

Fig. 2.8 Voltage and Current variation as a function of the sunlight intensity

2.4.1 EFFECTS OF TEMPERATURE AND INTERNAL RESISTANCES

An Increase in the operating temperature of a solar cell typically has the effect of slightly increasing the cell's short-circuit current and significantly decreasing the cell voltage. Therefore, as the temperature of the solar cell rises, the result is that the maximum efficiency decreases. (The area of the power rectangle under the V-I curve decreases).

A solar cell contains internal resistances (series and shunt) that reduce the cell's maximum efficiency. The simplified circuit of Fig. 2.4 can be modified as illustrated in Fig. 2.9 to show these internal resistances.

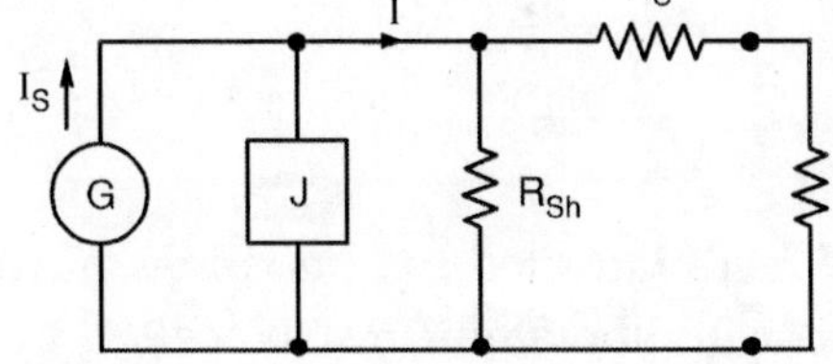

Fig. 2.9 Modified Equivalent Circuit

In the above Fig. 2.9, R_S is the cell's series resistance and R_{sh} is the shunt resistance. The solar cell's series resistance represents in lumped fashion all distributed resistance elements in the device, its ohmic contacts, and the semiconductor/contact interfaces.

The solar cell's shunt resistance, on the other hand, represents the portion of the generated electrical energy lost through the cell's internal leakage paths such as that through the *p-n* junction (recombination current), and along the outer cell edges (surface leakage).

The effect of both R_S and R_{sh} on the V-I characteristic curve for a 2 × 2 cm solar cell is shown in Fig. 2.10.

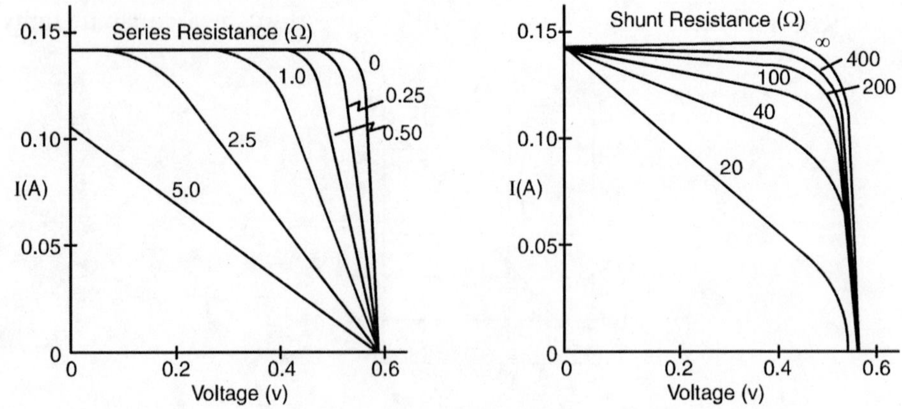

Fig. 2.10 *V-I Characteristics showing effect of both* R_S *and* R_{sh}

2.5 THEORETICAL AND PRACTICAL EFFICIENCIES OF A SOLAR CELL

The efficiency of a typical solar cell is defined by the following eqn. (2.6) :

$$\eta = P_{out}/P_{in} = P_{out}/A_c \rho_{in} \quad ...(2.6)$$

Where P_{out} is the electrical power output of the cell, P_{in} is the energy input to the cell, ρ_{in} is the solar illumination level per unit area, and A_c is the active solar cell area upon which the solar energy is incident.

The Fill Factor is the available power at the maximum power point (POUT) divided by the open circuit voltage (VOC) and the short circuit current (ISC). Thus,

$$FF = \frac{P_{OUT}}{V_{OC} \times I_{SC}} \quad ....(2.7)$$

The fill factor is directly affected by the values of the cell's series and shunt resistances. Increasing the shunt resistance (R_{sh}) and decreasing the series resistance (R_s) lead to a higher fill factor, thus resulting in greater efficiency, and bringing the cell's output power closer to its theoretical maximum.

According to theory, the maximum theoretical efficiency obtainable from silicon solar cell is approximately 22%. This value results from an analysis of the eqn. (2.8) for the maximum solar conversion efficiency;

$$\eta_{max} = k\left(\frac{\lambda V_{mp}}{1+\lambda V_{mp}}\right)\frac{n_{ph}(E_g)\,V_{mp}}{N_{ph}\,E_{av}} \quad ...(2.8)$$

Where k is a constant depending on the reflection and transmission coefficients and the collection efficiency,

V_{mp} is the voltage delivered at maximum power,

$n_{ph}(E_g)$ is the number of photons that generate EHP's in a semiconductor of energy gap E_g, and $N_{ph}E_{av}$ is the input power where N_{ph} is the number of incident photons and

E_{av} is their average energy in electron volts.

Assuming $\lambda V_{mp} \gg 1$ and $k \cong 1$, this equation reduces to :

$$\eta_{max} \cong \frac{n_{ph}(E_g)V_{mp}}{N_{ph}E_{av}} \quad ...(2.9)$$

By further assuming that for silicon, $n_{ph} \cong (2/3)N_{ph}$ and $V_{mp} \cong (1/3)E_{av}$, the equation yields :

$$\eta_{max} \cong \frac{\frac{2}{3}N_{ph}\frac{1}{3}E_{av}}{N_{ph}E_{av}} = \frac{2}{9} = 22\% \quad ...(2.10)$$

This is considered the ultimate maximum theoretical efficiency obtainable for a silicon solar energy converter. An interesting note here is that if monochromatic light is used with an energy equal to the band gap, n_{ph} will be equal to N_{ph} and $V_{mp} = .75\,E_{av}$, therefore, the maximum theoretical efficiency could be approximately 75%. As is evident from the equation for η_{max}, the theoretical maximum efficiency is a function of the semiconductor energy gap. Although for increasing values of the energy gap, the number of photons absorbed decreases, because I_O is also reduced, the cell voltage is thus increased.

Shown in Fig. 2.11 is a graph illustrating the relation between η_{max} and E_g for several solar cell materials.

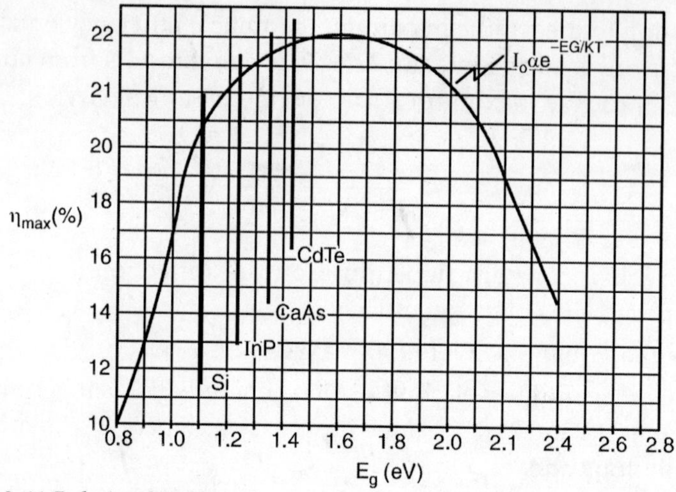

Fig. 2.11 Relationship between η_{max} and E_g for several solar cell materials.

2.6 TYPES OF SOLAR CELLS

According to the type of crystal, the solar cells are of three types:

(i) Monocrystalline silicon solar cell

This solar cell is produced from pure silicon (single crystal). The main technique for producing single-crystal silicon is the Czochralski (CZ) method. High-purity polycrystalline is melted in a quartz crucible. A single crystal silicon seed is dipped into this molten mass of polycrystalline. As the seed is pulled slowly from the melt, a single crystal ingot is formed. The ingots are then sawed into thin wafers about 200-400 micrometers thick (1 micrometer = 1/1,000,000 meter). The thin wafers are then polished, doped, coated, interconnected and assembled into modules and arrays.

They are more expensive but cost effective in the long run. The efficiency ranges between 15-20%.

(ii) Polycrystalline silicon solar cell

A common approach to produce polycrystalline silicon PV cells is to slice thin wafers from blocks of cast polycrystalline silicon. Another more advanced approach is the "ribbon growth" method in which silicon is grown directly as thin ribbons or sheets with the approach thickness for making PV cells.

Compared to single-crystalline silicon, polycrystalline silicon material is stronger and can be cut into one-third the thickness of single-crystal material. It also has slightly lower wafer cost and less strict growth requirements. The energy conversion efficiency for a polycrystalline silicon ranges between 10 to 14%.

(iii) Amorphous silicon solar cell

Amorphous silicon is obtained by depositing silicon film on the substrate like glass plate. The layer thickness is less than 1 μm. The energy conversion efficiency ranges between 5-9%.

2.7 PV CELL MATERIALS

PV cells are made of semiconductor materials. Solar Cells can be fabricated from a number of semiconductor materials, most commonly (Si)- crystalline, polycrystalline and amorphous. Solar cell materials are largely chosen on the basis of how well their absorption characteristics match with solar spectrum and upon their cost of fabrication.

2.7.1 Crystalline Materials

- ***Single-crystal silicon***

Single crystal silicon has a uniform molecular structure. Compared to noncrystalline materials, its high uniformity results in higher energy conversion efficiency -- the ratio of electric power produced by the cell to the amount of available sunlight power i.e. power-out divided by power-in. The higher a PV cell's conversion efficiency, the more electricity it generates for a given area of exposure to the sunlight. The conversion efficiency for single-silicon commercial modules ranges between 15-20%. Not only are they energy efficient, single-silicon modules are highly reliable for outdoor power applications.

- ***Polycrystalline silicon***

Consisting of small grains of single-crystal silicon, polycrystalline PV cells are less energy efficient than single-crystalline silicon PV cells. The grain boundaries in polycrystalline silicon hinder the flow of electrons and reduce the power output of the cell. The energy conversion efficiency for a commercial module made of polycrystalline silicon ranges between 10 to 14%.

Compared to single-crystalline silicon, polycrystalline silicon material is stronger and can be cut into one-third the thickness of single-crystal material. It also has slightly lower wafer cost and less strict growth requirements.

- ***Gallium Arsenide (GaAs)***

A compound semiconductor made of two elements: gallium (Ga) and arsenic (As), GaAs has a crystal structure similar to that of silicon. An advantage of GaAs is that it has high level of light absorptivity. To absorb the same amount of sunlight, GaAs requires only a layer of few micrometers thick while crystalline silicon requires a wafer of about 200-300 micrometers thick. Also, GaAs has much higher energy conversion efficiency than crystal silicon, reaching about 25 to 30%. Its high resistance to heat makes it an ideal choice for concentrator systems in which cell temperatures are high. GaAs is also popular in space applications where strong resistance radiation damage and high cell efficiency are required.

The biggest drawback of GaAs PV cells is the high cost of the single-crystal substrate that GaAs is grown on. Therefore it is most often used in concentrator systems where only a small area of GaAs cells is needed.

2.7.2 Thin Film Materials

In a thin-film PV cell, a thin semiconductor layer of PV materials is deposited on low-cost supporting layer such as glass, metal or plastic foil. Thin-film materials have higher light absorptivity than crystalline materials. Also, the deposition techniques in which PV materials are sprayed directly onto glass or metal substrate are cheaper. So the manufacturing process is faster, using up less energy and mass production is made easier.

However, thin film PV cells suffer from poor cell conversion efficiency due to non-single crystal structure, requiring larger array areas and increasing area-related costs such as mountings.

Materials used for thin film PV modules are as follows :

- ***Amorphous Silicon (a-Si)***

Amorphous silicon is a non-crystalline form of silicon i.e. its silicon atoms are disordered in structure. A significant advantage of a-Si is its high light absorptivity, about 40 times higher than that of single-crystal silicon. Also, a-Si can be deposited on various low-cost substrates, including steel, glass and plastic, and the manufacturing process requires lower temperatures and thus less energy. So the total material costs and manufacturing costs are lower per unit area as compared to those of crystalline silicon cells.

Disadvantages are low cell energy conversion efficiency, ranging between 5-9%, and efficiency degrades within a few months of exposure to sunlight, losing about 10 to 15%.

- ***Cadmium Telluride (CdTe)***

As a polycrystalline semiconductor compound made of cadmium and tellurium, CdTe has a high light absorptivity level -- only about a micrometer thick can absorb 90% of the solar spectrum. Another advantage is that it is relatively easy and cheap to manufacture by processes such as high-rate evaporation, spraying or screen printing.

The instability of cell and module performance is one of the major drawbacks of using CdTe for PV cells. Another disadvantage is that cadmium is a toxic substance.

- ***Copper Indium Diselenide ($CuInSe_2$, or CIS)***

A polycrystalline semiconductor compound of copper, indium and selenium. CIS has been one of the major research areas in the thin film industry.

CIS is also one of the most light-absorbent semiconductors -- 0.5 micrometers can absorb 90% of the solar spectrum.

CIS is an efficient but complex material. Its complexity makes it difficult to manufacture. Also, safety issues might be another concern in the manufacturing process as it involves hydrogen selenide, an extremely toxic gas.

2.8 SOLAR PV MODULE AND PV ARRAYS

Solar cells are devices that convert photons into electric potential in a PN silicon junction (or other material). A PV cell is a basic unit that generates voltage in the range of 0.5 to 0.8 volts depending on cell technology being used. This small generation is not of much commercial use if these cells are not integrated and connected together in the module to give the handsome voltage at least to charge a standard battery of 12 volts.

To increase their utility, dozens of individual PV cells are interconnected together in a sealed, weatherproof package called a module.

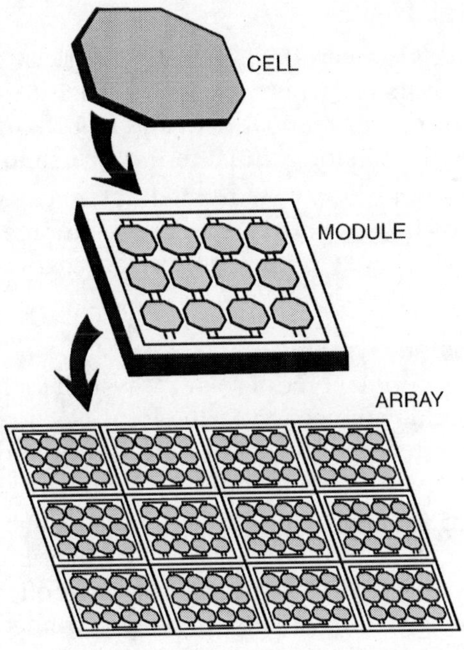

Fig. 2.12 Photovoltaic cells, modules and arrays

When two modules are wired together in series, their voltage is doubled while the current stays constant. When two modules are wired in parallel, their current is doubled while the voltage stays constant. To achieve the desired voltage and current, modules are wired in series and parallel into what is called a PV array. (see figure 2.12)

2.9 POWER OF A SOLAR PANEL, ARRAY AND MODULE

Let

n = Number of solar cells in a module

m = Number of modules in an array or a panel

Pc = Power per solar cell, watts

Power per module = n Pc

Power per array or panel = $m \times n \times$ Pc in Watts

For full light, solar panel will deliver power Pc. With power Pc and external resistance R, the voltage and current can be calculated DC voltage of the PV panel Vp, current delivered by the PV panel Ip, and the external DC load R are correlated by the basic equations of the ohms law.

$$Pp = Vp^2/R = Ip^2R = VpIp \quad ...(2.11)$$

$$\text{Power of a Solar Panel} = Pp = m \quad n\, Pc \quad ...(2.12)$$

$$\text{Voltage across panel } Vp = Pp/Ip \quad ...(2.13)$$

$$\text{Current delivered by panel } Ip = \sqrt{}Pp/R \quad ...(2.14)$$

2.10 SOLAR PV SYSTEMS

Solar Photovoltaic's convert daylight into electricity and can be used in Grid-Tied Solar PV Systems, where excess electricity is exported (sold) to energy companies using the National Grid and in Off-Grid situations where electricity is generated and stored in batteries for use locally.

Solar PV systems can broadly be divided in two categories; one is stand alone PV system which uses battery for energy storage and other is grid-connected systems which may or may not use any battery and interact with the grid.

2.10.1 Grid Connected Systems

These are the most popular type of solar PV system for homes and business in the developed world. Connection to the local electricity network allows any excess power produced to be sold to the utility, and electricity is then imported from the network outside daylight hours.

Inverters are used to convert the DC power generated by a PV array into AC, which is compatible with the local electricity distribution netowrk—this is essential for grid-connected PV systems. The inverter often includes elements to protect the system against instability in the grid connection as well.

A Grid-Tied PV system offers the potential to make a profit on the energy you generate, whilst significantly reducing your energy bills and making a contribution to lowering CO_2 emissions.

Normally, the efficiency of grid-connected inverters is quite good. The inverters are available with as high efficiency as 98%. Though the efficiencies are high, still some power loss occurs in the DC power to AC power conversion. Based on the above discussion, the following can be written:

Power output = Power input × Inverter efficiency

Power loss in inverter = Output power – Input power

Below is an overview of what equipment is needed in a typical Grid-Tied Solar PV installation.

(*i*) **Solar PV Panels / PV Modules:** The head end of a PV system that converts daylight into electrical current. As well as traditional Solar Panels, Solar PV panels can also be integrated into building materials where you may have traditionally used glass such as into canopies, skylights and balconies.

(*ii*) **A Grid-Tie Inverter:** Is used to convert DC power into AC power ready for use and export to the grid.

(*iii*) **Cables and Accessories:** Used to safely connect the various components, cables should be specified in relation to the maximum load current and the potential operating temperatures.

(*iv*) **Isolators:** Used to disconnect parts or all of the system for maintenance and/or in an emergency.

(*v*) **Mounting System:** There is a wide choice of mounting systems. Solar PV panels and modules can be mounted onto roofs (bolted on top or integrated within) Free Standing Frames and Building Integrated PV solutions are also available.

(*vi*) **Monitor:** Used for measuring how much energy is being generated.

(*vii*) **Export Meter:** An export meter monitors how much electricity is generated in kW hrs. Most meters will also show you at a glance how much electricity is being generated at the time.

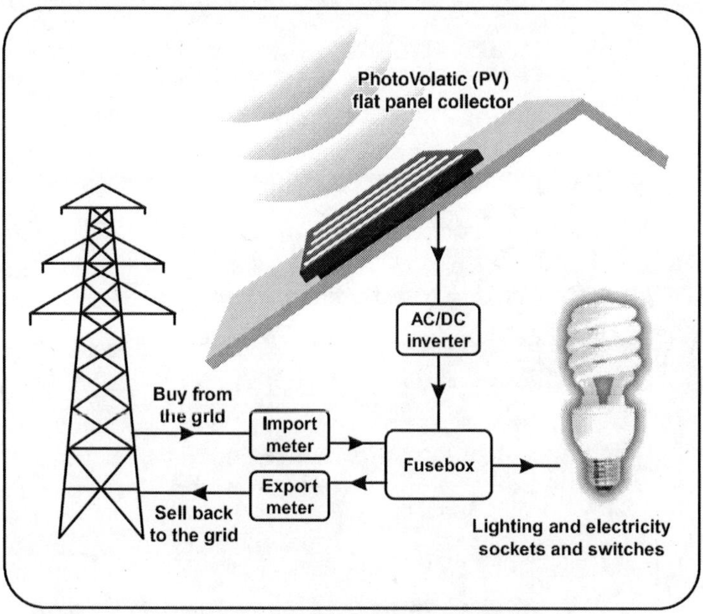

Fig. 2.13 *Grid Connected System*

Grid-connected system can also be broadly divided in two categories:

(*i*) Grid-connected PV system for small power applications e.g. in households.

(*ii*) Grid-connected PV system for large power applications e.g. in solar power plants

The main purpose of the grid-connected systems that are used for small power household applications is to generate energy and consume it within the household itself. Typically, the power rating of this type of PV system can be in the range of 1 kW to several 10s of kWs. The role of grid connectivity in case of small power household system is to supply excess generated energy to the grid (if more energy is generated by PV system then required by the load) or take energy from the grid if there is any shortage. However, in many cases, some batteries are added to ensure that loads always get the energy, even if grid power is not available.

The grid-connected PV systems for large power applications are mainly designed to act as power plants and the main purpose of these power plants is to generate power and supply it to the grid. In this way, they are equivalent to coal power plant or hydro power plants. Since the main purpose of this type of grid-connected PV system is to supply the power to the grid, their power ratings are normally in the range of 1 MW to several 10s of MW. No battery storage is planned in such plants.

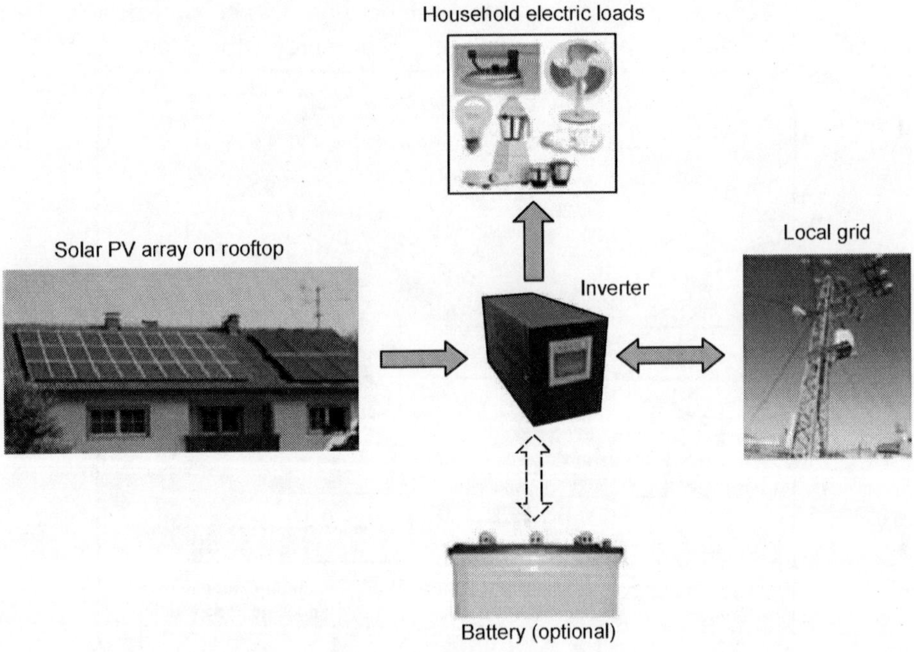

Fig. 2.14 Grid-connected PV system with small power applications

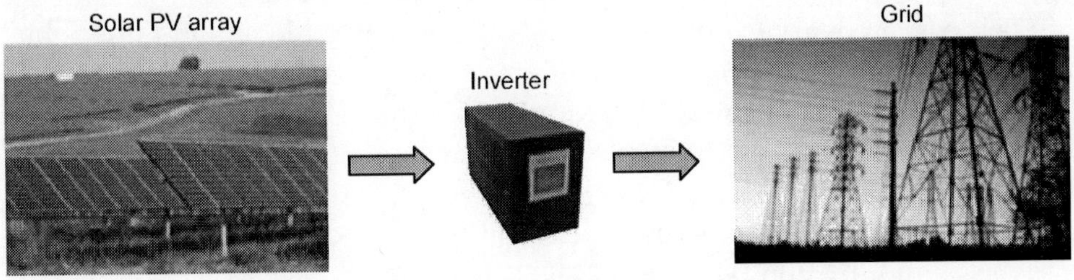

Fig. 2.15 Grid-connected PV system for large power applications

Advantages of Grid Connected PV System

Power from grid-connected PV systems directly replaces power generation at a power plant. Also, batteries take a lot of energy to make, and use dangerous chemicals and metals like lead, so not having batteries is good environmentally. Finally, compared to an off-grid PV system, all the solar power gets used by someone because the excess electricity is fed directly back into the power grid. In an off-grid system, electricity generated after the batteries are charged is often wasted. Some people still use an off-grid PV system because they live in a place far away from the electrical power grid, and an off-grid PV system is a lot cheaper than extending a power line (and more environmentally friendly than either the power line or the power from the power plant).

2.10.2 Off-Grid Solar Photovoltaic (PV) Systems

An Off-Grid Solar PV System is self contained and uses batteries to store and release electricity when the Solar PV Panels aren't active such as at night. An Off-Grid PV solution is ideal for remote buildings application specific functions such as for powering machinery, temporary solutions, pumps, boats pretty much anywhere where mams electricity isn't available and or isn't needed.

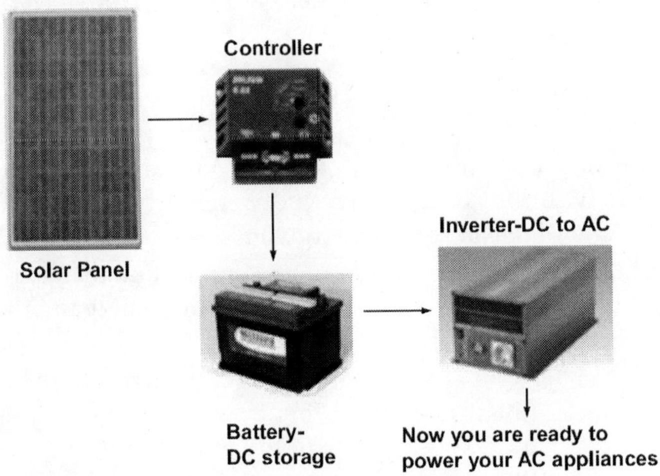

Fig. 2.16 Off-Grid Solar Photovoltaic (PV) Systems

Below is an overview of what equipment is needed in an Off-Grid Solar Photovoltaic (PV) System:

(*i*) **Solar PV Panels / PV Modules:** The head end of the system that converts daylight into electrical current.

(*ii*) **Power Inverters:** Used to convert DC power provided by Solar panels and stored in batteries into AC Electricity to be integrated into the buildings electrical system.

(*iii*) **Charge Controller:** Used to prevent damage to batteries through overcharging and reverse current.

(*iv*) **Cables & Accessories:** Used to safely connect the various components.

(*v*) **Isolators:** Used to disconnect parts or all of the system for maintenance and/or in in an emergency.

(*vi*) **Monitor:** Used for measuring how much energy is being generated.

(*vii*) **Batteries:** Used to store and release power.

(*viii*) **Mounting System:** Used to install Solar panels on a roof or other suitable structure.

First, the Sun shines on the panels to produce electrical power. That power is routed through the "charge controller" to the batteries. The charge controller regulates the charging of the batteries - the voltage on the batteries needs to be increased slowly, because charging them too fast or routinely overcharging the batteries quickly degrades them. Next, the "inverter" converts the DC (direct current) electrical power from the batteries into AC (alternating current) electrical power at 110 volts. This can then be fed to household appliances via a wall socket. For certain loads such as positive-displacement water pumps, a type of electronic DC-DC converter, called a maximum power point tracker (MPPT), and is used between the array and load to help better utilize the available array maximum power output. These are also known as Stand-alone PV systems.

2.10.3. Hybrid Solar Photovoltaic (PV) Systems

A Hybrid system gives all the benefits of both systems with the added benefits from protection from power cuts and outages (from either solar or mains), coupled with the ability to live independently of fossil fuels whilst supplying others with clean, green energy.

A Hybrid Solar PV System would utilize a connection to the grid enabling power to be exported and also use batteries to protect against power cuts and store power for use locally.

Please note that as with all grid connected PV systems, in hybrid systems we need to protect against islanding, this is where the PV system would continue to generate and export power to the grid even if the mains power was unavailable. For safety the PV system will disconnect itself from the grid if the mains power is unavailable.

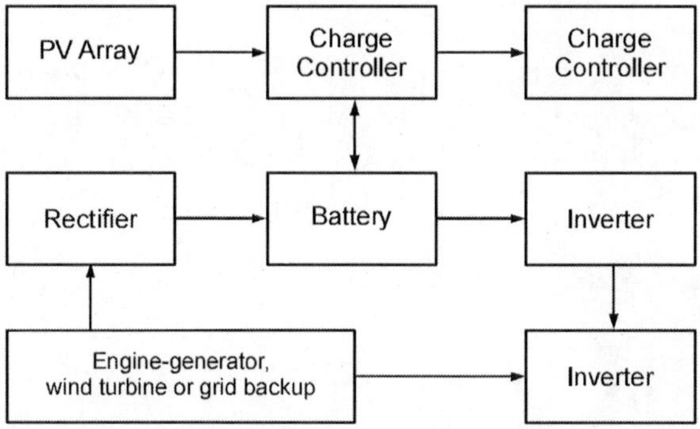

Fig. 2.17 *Photovoltaic Hybrid System*

2.11 MPPT

MPPT or **Maximum Power Point Tracking** is algorithm that included in charge controllers used for extracting maximum available power from PV module under certain conditions. The voltage at which PV module can produce maximum power is called 'maximum power point' (or peak power voltage). Maximum power varies with solar radiation, ambient temperature and solar cell temperature.

Typical PV module produces power with maximum power voltage of around 17 V when measured at a cell temperature of 25°C, it can drop to around 15 V on a very hot day and it can also rise to 18 V on a very cold day.

2.11.1 MPPT Working

The major principle of MPPT is to extract the maximum available power from PV module by making them operate at the most efficient voltage (maximum power point). That is to say:

MPPT checks output of PV module, compares it to battery voltage then fixes what is the best power that PV module can produce to charge the battery and converts it to the best voltage to get maximum current into battery. It can also supply power to a DC load, which is connected directly to the battery.

MPPT is most effective under these conditions:

- **Cold weather, cloudy or hazy days:** Normally, PV module works better at cold temperatures and MPPT is utilized to extract maximum power available from them.
- **When battery is deeply discharged:** MPPT can extract more current and charge the battery if the state of charge in the battery is lowers.

2.11.2 MPPT Solar Charge Controller

A MPPT **solar charge controller** is the charge controller embedded with MPPT algorithm to maximize the amount of current going into the battery from PV module.

MPPT is DC to DC converter which operates by taking DC input from PV module, changing it to AC and converting it back to a different DC voltage and current to exactly match the PV module to the battery.

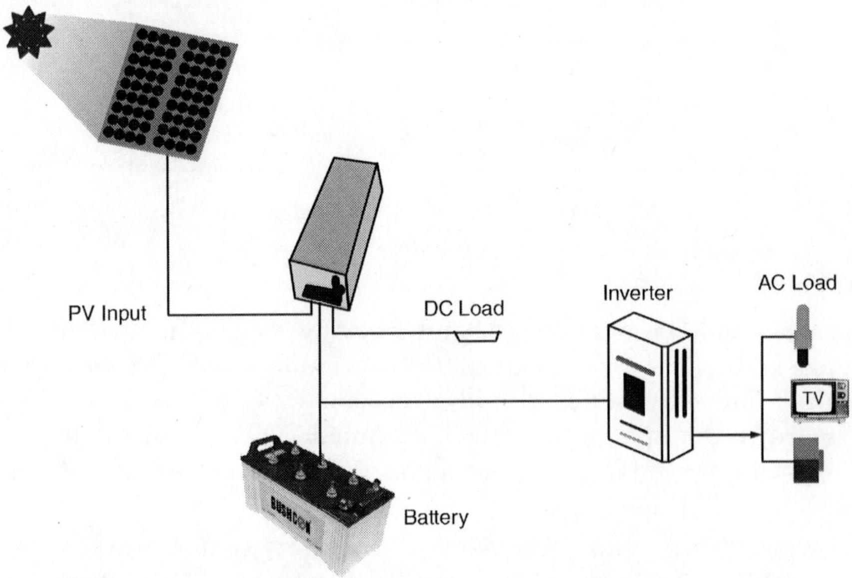

Fig. 2.18 *General configuration of the MPPT solar charge controller*

Examples of DC to DC converter are

(*i*) **Boost converter** is power converter which DC input voltage is less than DC output voltage. That means PV input voltage is less than the battery voltage in system.

(*ii*) **Buck converter** is power converter which DC input voltage is greater than DC output voltage. That means PV input voltage is greater than the battery voltage in system.

MPPT algorithm can be applied to both of them depending on system design. Normally, for battery system voltage is equal or less than 48 V, buck converter is useful. On the other hand, if battery system voltage is greater than 48 V, boost converter should be chosen.

MPPT **solar charge controllers** are useful for off-grid solar power systems such as stand-alone **solar power system, solar home system and solar water pump system, etc.**

Main features of MPPT solar charge controller

(*i*) In any applications in which PV module is energy source, MPPT solar charge controller is used to correct for detecting the variations in the current-voltage characteristics of solar cell and shown by I-V curve.

(*ii*) MPPT solar charge controller is necessary for any solar power systems need to extract maximum power from PV module; it forces PV module to operate at voltage close to maximum power point to draw maximum available power.

(*iii*) MPPT solar charge controller allows users to use PV module with a higher voltage output than operating voltage of battery system.

(*iv*) MPPT solar charge controller reduces complexity of system while output of system is high efficiency.

(*v*) MPPT solar charge controller can be applied to other renewable energy sources such as small water turbines, wind-power turbines, etc.

2.12 APPLICATIONS OF SOLAR CELL

Although the cost of solar energy is still too expensive, yielding power ten times more costly than that generated by oil, there are still applications for which solar power is economically feasible. It is particularly suited for remote applications where there is no direct tie-in to an electric utility feeder, or where the transportation of fuel to the generator site is impractical. In conjunction with an electrochemical storage battery and suitable charge control electronics, solar cell arrays can be designed to provide practically continuous power.

Some examples of this type of application include :

1. Electronic and optical beacons and warning devices such as channel buoys and shoreline barkers.
2. Remote television and radio receiver stations.
3. Radio transmitters and transponders, microwave repeater stations.
4. Weather and earthquake monitoring stations.
5. Electronic (galvanic) corrosion protection of metal structures such as bridges and towers.
6. Solar panels installed on the rooftops of homes can provide either heating and hot water or a percentage of the total electricity consumed.
7. Solar panels installed on the rooftops of commercial and public buildings can provide can provide a portion of the total electricity consumed; some examples where implementation has already occurred include a national park headquarters, some schools, and a daytime country music station in Ohio.
8. Irrigation projects.
9. Use of solar cells for hydrolysis and other electrochemical processes.
10. Emergency, surveillance, and security systems.

2.13 ADVANTAGES OF SOLAR PV SYSTEMS

1. Absence of moving parts.
2. Modular in nature in which desired currents, voltage and power levels can be achieved by mere integration.
3. They consume no fuel to operate on solar energy.
4. Maintenance cost is low as they are easy to operate.
5. They do not create pollution.
6. They have long effective life.
7. They have high power to weight ratio.
8. They have wide power handling capabilities from microwatts to kilowatts or megawatts when modules are combined into large area arrays. Solar cells can be used in combination with power conducting circuits to feed power into utility grid.

2.14 LIMITATIONS OF SOLAR PV SYSTEMS

1. Irregular, intermittent supply of solar energy
2. Need for storage batteries
3. High capital cost (Rs./kW) due to large number of PV cells, low output power, low efficiency and high technology involved.
4. Not economical for central power plants of MW rating due to very large area of PV panels and very large storage battery system.
5. Require storage batteries and or additional diesel generator sets for supplying power during night and during cloudy periods.
6. Do not generate power during cloudy season. Not suitable during rainy season.
7. Space for installing large PV-panels is not available in large cities, industrial cities etc. except on roofs of buildings.
8. Advanced PV technology required for producing PV cells.
9. Very low efficiency of PV cells (10 to 14%)

2.15 COST OF PV SYSTEMS

Some of the factors which affect the PV system costs and feasibility are

1. **Grid Connection:** Grid-connected systems do not need batteries which reduces considerably initial capital costs and energy costs.
2. **Location of Solar Resource:** Location affects the cost of producing energy hence affects the payback period investment.
3. **Types of Installation, Mounting, Size and Space:** Retrofit installations are more expensive than for new buildings. Maximization of flat roof lowers mounting expenses. Large scale systems are tending to be less expensive on a per watt basis.

4. **Module Technology :** Modules account for 40-50% of total system costs. PV modules that require less material, energy and time to develop, have lower costs.
5. **Indirect Benefits such as GHG reduction :** Customers would pay 10% more for a solar equipped residence.

SOLVED EXAMPLE

Example 1 : A solar cell (0.9 cm^2) receives solar radiation with photons of 1.8 eV energy having an intensity of 0.9 mW/cm^2. Measurements show open-circuit voltage of 0.6 V/cm^2, short-circuit current of 10 mA/cm^2, and the maximum current is 50% of the short-circuit current. The efficiency of cell is 25%. Calculate the maximum voltage that the cell can give and find the 'fill factor'.

Solution:

$$\eta = \frac{V_{max} I_{max}}{P_{in}}$$

$$V_{max} = \frac{P_{in} \times \eta}{I_{max}} = \frac{0.9 \times 10^{-3} \times 0.25}{5 \times 10^{-3}}$$

$$= 0.045 \text{ V/cm}^2$$

$$P_{max} = V_{oc} \times I_{sc} \times FF$$

$$FF = \frac{I_{max} \times V_{max}}{V_{oc} \times I_{sc}} = \frac{5 \times 10^{-3} \times 0.045}{0.6 \times 10 \times 10^{-3}}$$

$$= 0.0375$$

Example 2 : A solar PV array is rated at 100 V/50 A DC. System power losses are 20%. What is the AC power fed into the grid? If the grid voltage is 240 V AC, what is the AC current fed into the grid?

Here,

DC power = 100 V × 50 A = 5000 W = 5 kW

$$\text{Power lost} = 5000 \times \frac{20}{100} = 1000 \text{ W} = 1 \text{ kW}$$

AC power fed into grid = DC Power – Power loss = 5 kW – 1 kW = 4 kW = 4000 W

$$\text{AC current fed into grid} = \frac{\text{AC power}}{\text{AC voltage}} = \frac{4000}{240} = 16.67 \text{ A}$$

REVIEW QUESTIONS

1. What is a solar cell? Describe the fundamentals of solar cell.
2. Describe the principle of solar photovoltaic energy conversion.
3. Explain the V-I characteristics of a solar cell. Also explain the equivalent circuit of solar cell.
4. What are the different types of materials used to fabricate the solar cell? Explain them.
5. Derive the relation of maximum efficiency of a solar cell and prove that the ultimate theoretical efficiency obtained for a silicon solar cell is 22%.
6. What is a solar PV module and PV array? Explain.
7. Discuss the effects of temperature and internal resistance on solar cell efficiency.
8. How the power of a solar panel, array and module is are calculated? Explain.
9. Explain and discuss the grid-connected PV system.
10. What are the different applications of solar cell?
11. What are the advantages and disadvantages of a solar PV system?
12. Explain with suitable diagrams, the working of various types of solar photovoltaic power plants.

❑

3

SOLAR RADIATION AND ITS MEASUREMENT

3.1 INTRODUCTION

3.1.1 Nature of Sun

Sun is a medium sized yellow star that may be considered as a sphere of intensely hot gaseous matter with an average diameter of 1.39×10^9 m at an average distance of 1.495×10^{11} m (or 1 Astronomical unit) from the earth. The sun coalesced from a cloud of gas and dust formed 4.5 billion years ago. Earth goes round the sun in an elliptic orbit as shown in Fig. 3.1(a) not to scale. The earth is closest to the sun at 1.471×10^{11} m, the perihelion around January 2 each year; it is farthest at 1.526×10^{11} m around July 2 each year.

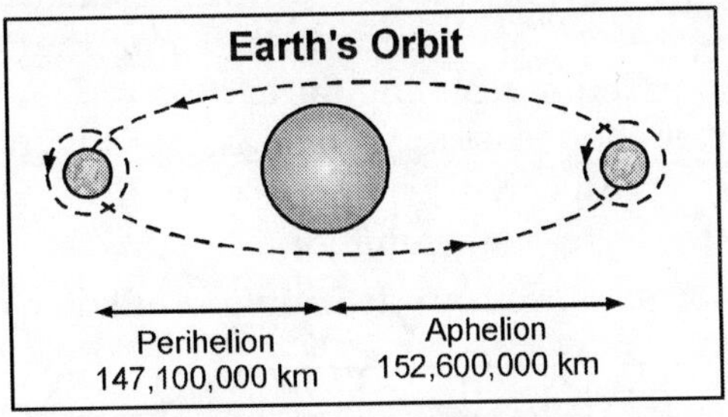

Fig. 3.1(a) The Perihelion and the Aphelion

Sun, in effect is a continuous fusion reactor and the constituent gases are a containing vessel retained by gravitational forces. Most important fusion reaction is hydrogen combining to form helium. Energy is produced in the sun (and other stars also) by continuous fusion in which four nuclei of hydrogen fuse in a series of reactions involving other particles that continually appear and disappear in the course of the reactions, such as He3, nitrogen, carbon and other nuclei, but culminating in one nucleus of helium and two positrons resulting in a mass decrease.

$$4\,{}_1H^1 \rightarrow {}_2He^4 + 2\,({}_{+1}e^0)$$

This reaction results in a mass decrease of about 0.0276 amu, corresponding to 25.7 MeV. The heat produced in these reactions maintains temperatures of the order of several million degrees in the core region of the sun and serves to trigger and sustain succeeding reactions.

The Sun is made up of about 2×10^{30} kilograms of gas. It is composed of about 75% hydrogen and 25% helium. About 0.1% is metals made from hydrogen via nuclear fusion. It has been estimated that the sun has used up about half of its initial hydrogen available4.5 billion years ago, i.e., the time of formation.

3.1.2. Solar Radiation

Solar Radiation is the electromagnetic radiation energy emitted from the sun. This energy is distributed over a wide range of continuous spectrum ranging from ultraviolet to infrared rays. In this spectrum, solar radiation in short wavelengths (0.29 to 3.0 μm) accounts for about 97% of the total energy. We can capture and convert this solar radiation energy into useful forms of energy such as heat and electricity using a variety of technologies.

Extraterrestrial radiation is the amount of solar radiation received if the earth's atmosphere had not been there, or, the atmospheric transmittance is unity.

Terrestrial Radiation is the solar radiation as received on earth's surface. This radiation can be once again expressed as intensity or an integrated energy quantity over a time period of interval. Further, the solar radiation while passing through the atmosphere is attenuated, partly due to absorption by O_3, CO_2 and H_2O. Other attenuation is due to scattering in the atmosphere by air molecules, water vapor and dust. Thus, the terrestrial radiation comprises of solar radiation reaching the earth's surface without a change in the direction and radiation reaching in all possible directions due to scattering in the atmosphere. Thus the terrestrial radiation will be less than the corresponding extra-terrestrial radiation.

Fig. 3.1 (b) shows a spectrum distribution of solar radiation.

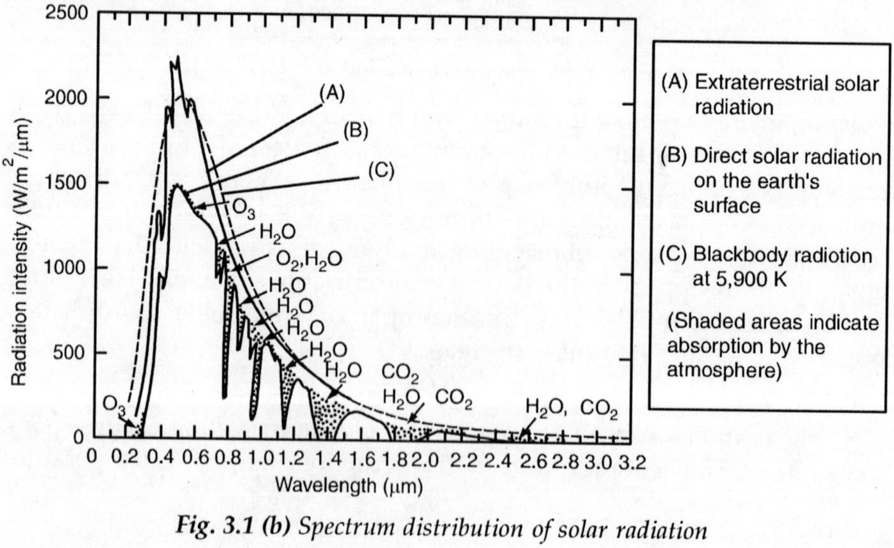

Fig. 3.1 (b) Spectrum distribution of solar radiation

3.2 SOLAR CONSTANT

The sun produces a constant amount of energy. The intensity of the solar radiation at the surface of the Sun is about 6.33×10^7 W/m^2. As the Sun's rays spread out into space the radiation becomes less intense and by the time the rays reach the edge of the Earth's atmosphere they are considered to be parallel.

The ***solar constant*** (**I_{SC}**) is the average radiation intensity falling on an imaginary surface, perpendicular to the Sun's rays and at the edge of the Earth's atmosphere Fig. 3.2.

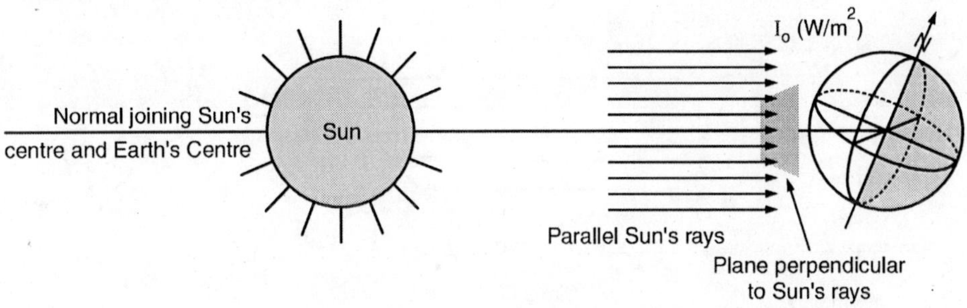

Fig. 3.2 *The Sun's rays incident on the Earth where I_0 is the irradiance on a plane perpendicular to the Sun's rays*

The term 'constant' is misleading as the solar constant varies by ± 3% because of the Earth's slightly elliptical orbit around the sun. The sun – earth distance is smaller when the Earth is at perihelion (first week in January) and larger when the Earth is at aphelion (first week in July). A yearly average value is thus taken and the solar constant equals 1367 W/m^2.

Thus, ***solar constant*** can be defined correctly as ***the power per unit area received at the average Earth-solar distance of one "Astronomical Unit" or AU which is 149.59787066 million kilometers.***

The solar radiation intensity falling on a surface is called ***irradiance*** (**I_0**) and is measured in **W/m^2**. The solar constant can be used to calculate the irradiance incident on a surface perpendicular to the Sun's rays outside and the Earth's atmosphere on any day of the year, as the distance between the sun and the earth changes throughout the year, with the help of following relation:

$$I_0 = I_{SC}\left[1 + 0.034\cos\left(\frac{2\pi n}{365}\right)\right] \quad ...(3.1)$$

Where

- I_0 is the extraterrestrial (outside the atmosphere) irradiance on a plane perpendicular to the Sun's rays (W/m^2)
- I_{SC} is the solar constant (1367 W/m^2)
- n is the day of the year such that for January 1st , n = 1.

As not all points on the Earth's surface are perpendicular to the Sun's rays, so it is become necessary to calculate the solar irradiance incident on an imaginary surface that is parallel to a horizontal plane on the Earth's surface. Using cosine effect Fig. 3, the irradiance intensity on the horizontal plane can be calculated from the following equation:

$$I_{oh} = I_o \cos \theta_z = I_o (\cos \delta \cos \phi \cos \omega + \sin \delta \sin \phi) \quad ...(3.2)$$

Where θ_z is the solar zenith angle which is the angle of the sun relative to a line perpendicular to the earth's surface.

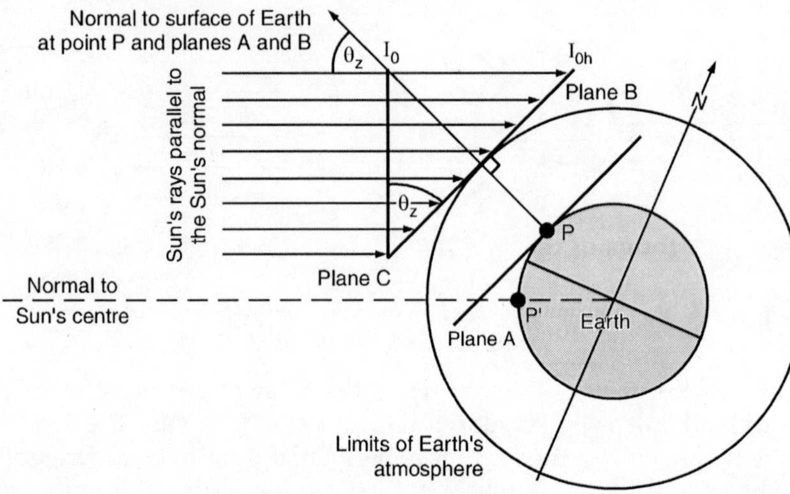

Fig. 3.3 The cosine effect

Fig. 3.3 shows three plane surfaces:

- *plane A*, a horizontal plane at the point P on the Earth's surface;
- *plane B*, a surface parallel to plane A but on the edge of the Earth's atmosphere, often referred to as the horizontal plane;
- *plane C*, a surface perpendicular to the Sun's rays, often referred to as *the normal plane.*

Note that since cosine values fall between 1 and –1, **I_{oh} will never be greater than I_o**, and $I_{oh} = I_o$ at point P' where $\cos \theta_z = 1$ ($\theta_z = 0°$).

However, the total amount of solar radiation energy is called ***irradiation* (H)** and is measured in the units of energy per unit area **(J/m²)**.

3.3 SOLAR RADIATION AT THE EARTH'S SURFACE

As the sun's rays pass through the atmosphere certain wavelengths are absorbed, scattered and reflected by molecules, aerosols, water vapor and clouds and reaches the Earth's surface from all directions as ***diffuse radiation.*** The radiation which has not been absorbed or scattered and reaches the ground directly by the sun is called ***"direct radiation" or "beam radiation"***. Solar irradiance on a horizontal surface due to both direct sun rays and diffuse sky radiation is called ***global solar irradiance***.

Fig. 3.4(*a*) shows that a plane on the Earth's surface receives

- *Beam (or direct) radiation* – coming straight through the atmosphere to hit the plane (very directional);
- *Diffused radiation* – scattered in all direction in the atmosphere and then some arrives at the plane on the Earth's surface (not directional);
- *Reflected radiation* – beam and diffused radiation that hits the Earth's surface and is reflected onto the plane.

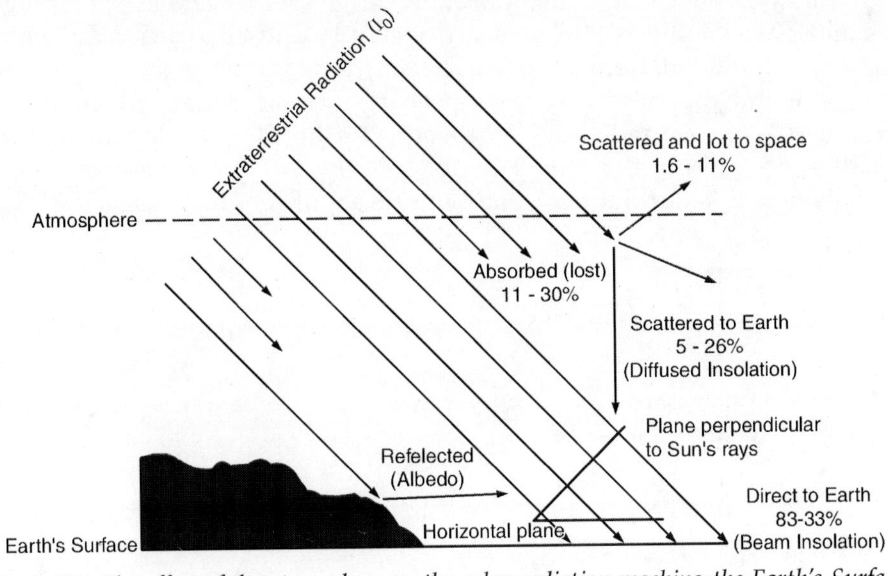

Fig. 3.4(a) *The effect of the atmosphere on the solar radiation reaching the Earth's Surface*

Atmospheric attenuation of solar radiation

There are some atmospheric processes which modify the solar radiation passing through our atmosphere destined to the Earth's surface. These processes act on the radiation when it interacts with gases and suspended particles found in the atmosphere. This results in the alteration of the amount, spectrum and directionality of solar radiation at the ground, which occur in two main ways, by scattering and dry absorption.

Some of the radiation is scattered by the gas molecules that make up the air, and this is called *Rayleigh scattering*. Solar radiation is scattered preferentially at lower wavelengths by gas molecules and it is the resulting scattered blue radiation that we see the associate with clear sky above us. Additional scattering of solar radiation occurs due to the atmospheric aerosols such as dust and smoke in the air.

All scattering processes alter the direction of solar radiation and some radiant energy is scattered back and does not the surface. In addition, some radiant energy is absorbed from the solar beam as it passes through the atmosphere, giving rise to atmospheric warning. Absorption occurs preferentially in wavelength bands that correspond to excited states in important minority gases in the air, notably ozone in the stratosphere, which mainly absorbs ultraviolet radiation, but also water vapor, carbon dioxide and other so-called *radiatively active* gases. Figure 3.4(*b*) shows how the incoming spectrum of solar radiation is progressively eroded through the atmosphere by these several scattering and absorbing processes in clear sky conditions.

If the sky is not clear, substantial energy in the solar beam is lost through the atmosphere because of the presence of clouds. The ice particles and water droplet in clouds interfere strongly. The scatter radiation mainly backward into space and they also absorb solar energy. Thick clouds will reflect as much as 70% of solar radiation and absorb a further 20%, while transmitting just 10%. As a result, the proportion of solar radiation absorbed, which is typically just 25% in cloudless conditions, is about 75% for overcast skies.

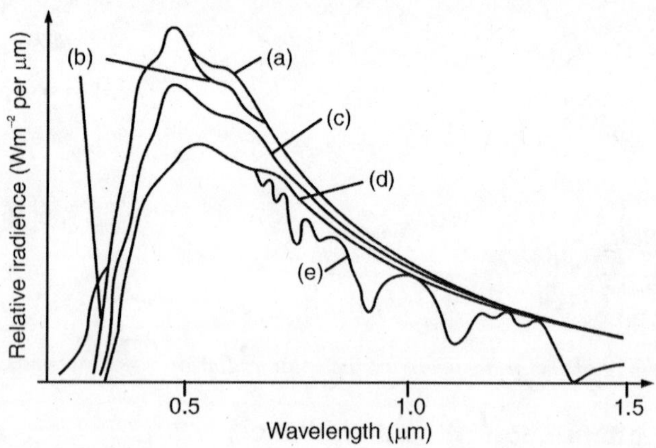

Fig. 3.4(b) *The progressive loss of energy in the solar beam by scattering in the solar beam by scattering and absorption as it passes through the atmosphere in typical clear sky conditions showing the representative spectra (a) of extraterrestrial radiation, (b) after absorption by ozone, (c) after Rayleigh scattering, (d) after aerosol interactions, and (e) after absorption by* H_2O, CO_2, *etc.*

Atmospheric conditions can reduce direct beam radiation by 10% on clear, dry days and by 100% during thick, cloudy days. Fig. 3.5 shows the normally incident solar spectrum at sea level on a clear day.

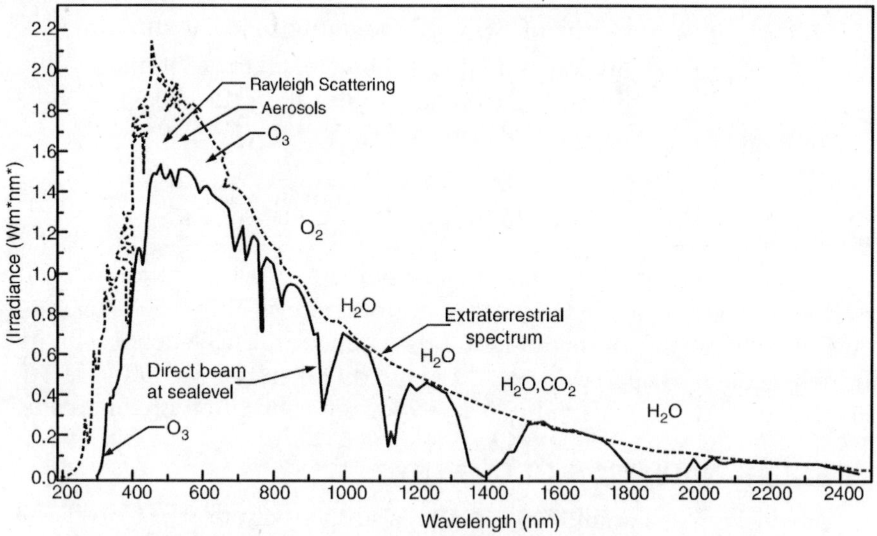

Fig. 3.5 Normally incident solar spectrum at sea level on a clear day. The dotted curve shows the extraterrestrial spectrum

3.4 AIR MASS

The amount of energy reflected, scattered and absorbed depends on the amount of atmosphere that the incident radiation travels through as well as the levels of dust particles and water vapour present in the atmosphere. The latter is difficult to judge but the distance travelled through the atmosphere by incident radiation depends on the angle of the Sun (Fig. 3.6).

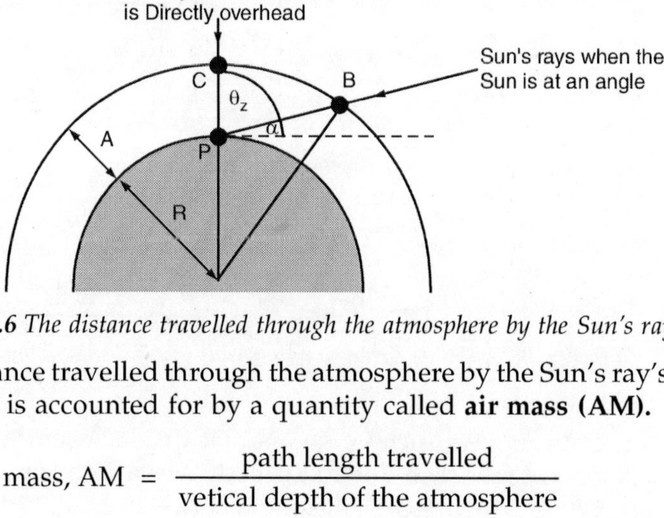

Fig. 3.6 The distance travelled through the atmosphere by the Sun's rays

The distance travelled through the atmosphere by the Sun's ray's incident on the Earth is accounted for by a quantity called **air mass (AM).**

$$\text{Air mass, AM} = \frac{\text{path length travelled}}{\text{vetical depth of the atmosphere}}$$

$$\text{AM} = \frac{\text{BP}}{\text{CP}} = \left[\left(\frac{\text{R}}{\text{H}}\cos\theta_z\right)^2 + 2\frac{\text{R}}{\text{H}} + 1\right]^{1/2} - \frac{\text{R}}{\text{H}}\cos\theta_z \quad ...(3.3)$$

Where R = radius of the earth, taken to be 6370 km.

H = thickness of atmosphere, taken to be 7991 km. (although it is thicker at the equator than the poles).

For angles, $\theta_z < 70°$;

$$AM \cong \frac{1}{\cos \theta_z} = \sec \theta_z \qquad ...(3.4)$$

Therefore, outside the earth's atmosphere AM = 0, when the sun is directly overhead. The entry point into the atmosphere is called "Air Mass-0" or "AM-0", where "0" points out that there is no air mass. When $\theta_z = 0$, AM = 1 and when the $\theta_z = 60°$, AM = 2. AM is nearly taken to be average of 1.5 for a clear sunny day and this value is used for the calibration of solar cells.

3.5 SOLAR RADIATION GEOMETRY

The position of a point P on the earth's surface with respect to the sun's rays is represented by the latitude, hour angle for the point, and the sun's declination.

As shown in the Fig. 3.7,

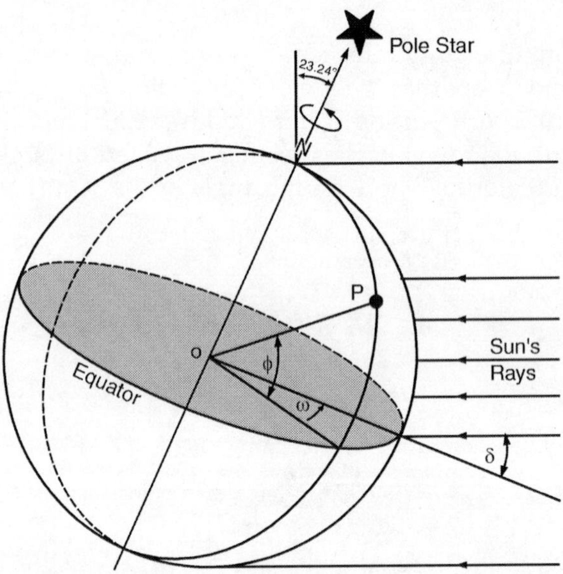

Fig. 3.7 Latitude φ, hour angle ω, and sun's declination d

ϕ is the latitude angle

ω is the hour angle which is the angular displacement of the sun with respect to the local meridian due to the earth's rotation. The hour angle at a point P on the Earth's surface is the angle between the meridian containing point P and the meridian that is parallel to the Sun's rays. The hour angle is negative during the morning, reduces to zero at solar noon (when point P faces the Sun) and becomes increasingly positive as the afternoon progresses.

Note that hour angle at any particular time is the same for all points on any particular meridian (i.e. points with the same longitude). Since the Earth completes one revolution every 24 hours, the hour angle changes by (360/15) 15° every hour.

Solar noon is time of day when the sun appears the highest in the sky compared to its position during the rest of the day.

δ is the declination angle which is the angular position of the sun at solar noon with respect to the plane of the equator.

$$\delta \text{ (in degrees)} = 23.45 \sin\left[\frac{360}{365}(284 + n)\right] \qquad ...(3.5)$$

Where n is the day of the year. The declination angle varies from a maximum value of + 23.45° on June 22 to a minimum value of – 23.45° on Dec. 22 (shown in Fig. 3.8).

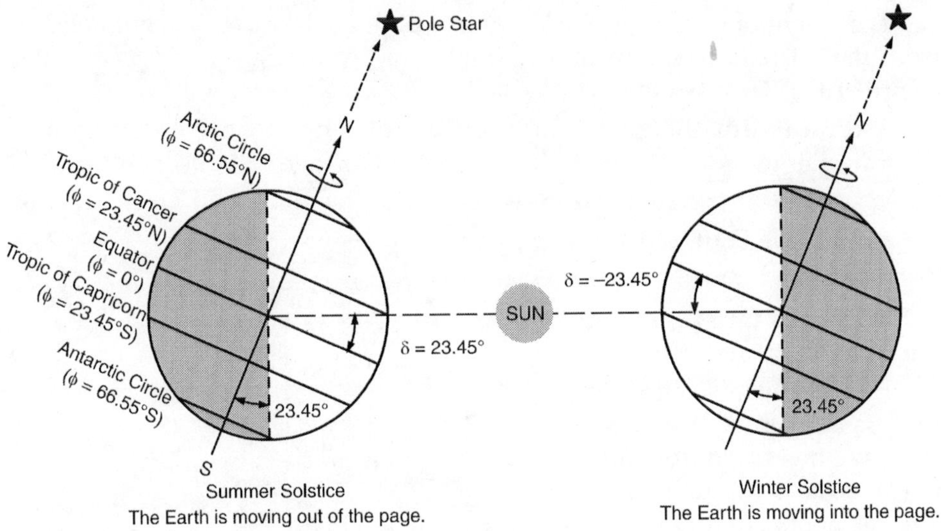

Fig. 3.8 The summer and winter solstices, δ is the declination angle, ϕ is the latitude

More angles are defined by considering the path of the Sun across the sky when viewed from point P on the surface of the Earth. Fig. 3.9 shows the solar zenith angle, θ_z, the solar altitude angle, α, and solar azimuth angle (A_z).

Solar Zenith angle, θ_z: It is complimentary angle of sun's attitude angle. It is a vertical angle between the sun's rays and a line perpendicular to the horizontal plane through the point i.e. the angle between the beam from the sun and the vertical.

$$\theta_z = \frac{\pi}{2} - \alpha$$

Solar Altitude angle, α: It is a vertical angle between the projection of the sun's rays on the horizontal plane and the direction of sun's rays (passing through the point).

Solar Azimuth angle, A_z: It is a solar angle in degrees along the horizon east or west of north or it is horizontal angle measured from north to the horizontal projection of the sun's rays. This angle is positive when measured west wise.

The elevation angle (used interchangeably with altitude angle) is the angular height of the sun in the sky measured from the horizontal. Confusingly, both altitude and elevation are also used to describe the height in meters above sea level. The elevation is 0° at sunrise and 90° when the sun is directly overhead (which occurs for example at the equator on the spring and fall equinoxes). The zenith angle is similar to the elevation angle but it is measured from the vertical rather than from the horizontal, thus making the zenith angle = 90°-elevation. The elevation angle varies throughout the day. It also depends on the latitude of a particular location and the day of the year.

The height of the Sun in the sky at any time can be described either by $\alpha°$ from the horizon or $\theta_z°$ from a normal running though point P from the centre of the Earth (so that $\alpha° + \theta_z° = 90°$).

A formula for the elevation angle at solar noon can be determined according to the formula for locations in the Northern Hemisphere:

$$\alpha = 90 - \phi + \delta \quad ...(3.6)$$

and for the Southern Hemisphere:

$$\alpha = 90 + \phi - \delta \quad ...(3.7)$$

where ϕ is the latitude of the location of interest.

The compass position of the Sun is given by A_z. Fig. 3.9 shows A_z measured from due north, so that it equals 180° at solar noon. An alternative method can be used that measures from due south so that A_z = 0 at solar noon, negative when the Sun is east from this point (i.e. in the morning) and positive when the Sun is west of this point (i.e. in the afternoon, as illustrated in Fig. 3.9).

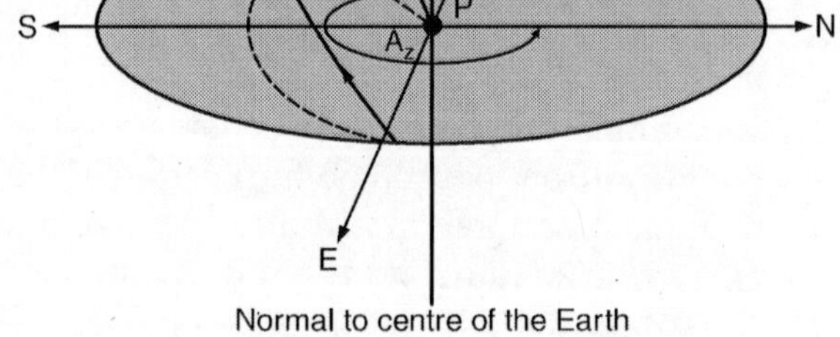

Fig. 3.9 The zenith angle θ_z, the altitude angle α, and the azimuth angle A_z, of the Sun when view from point P on the Earth's surface.

3.6 ESTIMATION OF AVERAGE SOLAR RADIATION

In any solar energy conversion system, the knowledge of global solar radiation is extremely important for the optimal design and the prediction of the system performance. The best way of knowing the amount of global solar radiation at a site is to install pyranometers at many locations in the given region and look after their day-to day maintenance and recording, which is a very costly exercise. The alternative approach is to correlate the global solar radiation with the meteorological parameters at the place where the data is collected. The resultant correlation may then be used for locations of similar meteorological and geographical characteristics at which solar data are not available.

The following relation is the generally accepted modified form of the Angstrom-type regression equation, relating the monthly average daily global radiation to the average daily sunshine hours;

$$H_{av}/H_o = a + b\,(n/N) \qquad \text{...(3.8)}$$

where H_{av} is the monthly average of the daily global radiation on a horizontal surface at a location (MJ/m^2 day),

H_o is the monthly average of the daily global radiation on a horizontal surface at the same location on a clear day (MJ/m^2 day),

n is the monthly average daily bright sunshine hours,

N is the maximum possible monthly average daily sunshine hours or the day length and a and b are regression constants obtained by data fitting.

To determine the daily solar radiation on the horizontal surface H_o, the following equation can be used:

$$H_o = \frac{24.3600 I_{SC}}{\pi}\left[I + 0.034\cos\left(\frac{360n}{365}\right)\right]\left(\cos\phi\cos\delta\sin\omega_s + \frac{2\pi\omega_s}{360}\sin\phi\sin\delta\right) \qquad \text{...(3.9)}$$

Where I_{sc} is the solar constant per hour, n is the day of the year, ϕ is the latitude, δ is the declination angle, and ω is the hour angle; ω_s is the sunrise/sunset hour angle.

The sunrise/sunset hour angle can be determined from equation:

$$\cos\omega_s = -\tan\phi\tan\delta \qquad \text{...(3.10)}$$

N can be calculated from equation shown by using the mean day of the month to calculate the declination angle δ.

$$\text{N (the length of the day)} = \frac{2}{15}\cos^{-1}(-\tan\phi\tan\delta) \qquad \text{...(3.11)}$$

For an inclined surface, facing south,

$$\text{N (the length of the day)} = \frac{2}{15}\cos^{-1}\left[-\tan(\phi-\beta)\tan\delta\right] \qquad \text{...(3.12)}$$

where β is the angle at which the surface is tilted towards an equator from the horizontal surface.

Value for a and b, the climatic constants, are based on regression analysis of solar radiation data for several geographical locations. (Refer Table 3.1)

Table 3.1 Constants *a* and *b* for Some Indian Towns

Location	a	b	Location	a	b
Ahmedabad	0.28	0.48	Manglore	0.27	0.43
Bangalore	0.18	0.64	Shillong	0.22	0.57
Baroda	0.28	0.47	Srinagar	0.35	0.40
Bhavnagar	0.28	0.50	Trivandrum	0.37	0.39
Bhopal	0.27	0.42	Vishakhapatnam	0.28	0.47
Calcutta	0.28	0.48	Nagpur	0.27	0.50
Goa	0.30	0.48	New Delhi	0.25	0.57
Jodhpur	0.33	0.46	Poona	0.31	0.43
Madras	0.30	0.44	Roorkee	0.25	0.56

3.7 LOCAL SOLAR TIME

The solar time is measured with respect to solar noon, which is the time when the sun is crossing the observer's meridian. The difference between two such consecutive solar noons defines a solar day.

Solar time does not coincide with the local clock time because of precession of the earth's axis and orbital and rotational motions. The solar time can be obtained from the standard time observed on the clock by applying two corrections. The first correction arises because of the difference in observer's longitude between a location and the meridian on which the local standard time is based. The correction has a magnitude of 4 minutes for every degree difference in longitude. The (+ve) sign is used if the observer is in east of reference meridian, and the (–ve) sign is used if the observer is in west of reference meridian.

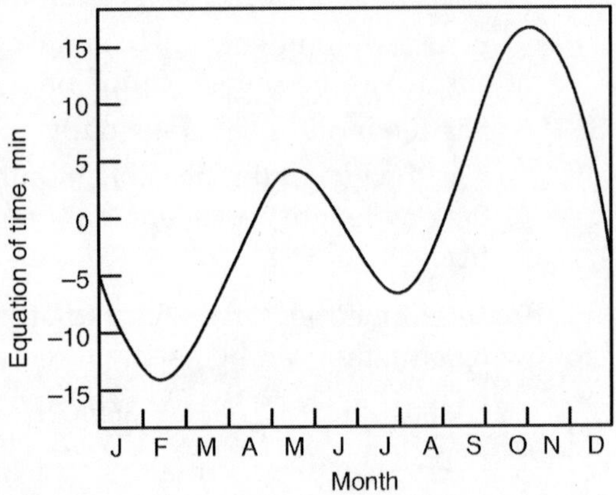

Fig. 3.10 The equation of time E in minutes as a function of time of year

The second correction called the equation of time correction is due to the variation in the length of the solar day through the year.

Thus,

Local Solar Time (LST) = Standard time ± 4 (Standard time longitude – longitude of location) + (Equation of time correction)

The equation of time correction is

$$E = 9.87 \sin 2B - 7.53 \cos B - 1.5 \sin B$$

Where, $B = \frac{360\,(n - 81)}{365}$ and n is the day of the year, $1 \leq n \leq 365$.

The solar noon at a place can be determined from the following equation:

$$\text{Local solar noon} = \frac{\begin{array}{c}12 - \text{equation of time in hours on that day} \pm \text{longitude}\\ \text{of reference meridian} - \text{observer's longitude}\end{array}}{15}$$

3.8 SOLAR RADIATION MEASURING INSTRUMENTS

Determination of the solar radiation and its interaction with the atmosphere and the Earth's surface is important, since solar radiation accounts for almost all of the energy available to the Earth.

There are basically two types of solar radiation measuring instruments: **the Pyranometer and the Pyrheliometer**. The former is used to measure the total (direct or diffuse) radiation within its hemispherical field of view, whereas the latter is an instrument used for measuring the beam radiation at normal incidence.

3.8.1 Pyrheliometers

A Pyrheliometer is an instrument designed specifically to measure the normal incidence direct collimated beam solar irradiance. To exclude sky (diffuse) radiation from the direct normal irradiance (DNI) measurement, baffles and view-limiting apertures are used to restrict the field of view of the sensors. Generally the field of view for Pyrheliometers is between 5.0° and 5.7°, or about 10 times the solar disk angular diameter.

Pyrheliometer helps in assessing the efficiency of solar panels that are installed to tap sun's energy and also to help in meteorological research.

There are mainly three types of Pyrheliometers commonly used for normal incident beam radiation. They are:

3.8.1.1 Angstrom electrical-compensation Pyrheliometers

The electrical-compensation Pyrheliometer of K. Angstrom is one of the best-known instruments for measuring solar intensity and is perhaps the most reliable.

In operation, the absorption of heat by a thin blackened manganin strip A, exposed to the sun's rays, can be determined by measuring the electrical energy necessary to warm a similar but shielded strip B to the same temperature. The strips are placed side by side at the bottom of the collimating tube. The rate of generation of heat in the electrical circuit is then equal to the rate of absorption of heat by the exposed strip. The equality of the temperature of the strips is verified by means of thermocouples attached to the back of the strips and connected in opposition through a sensitive null detector. The thermocouple generates an electrical signal proportional to the temperature difference between "cold" reference junctions at ambient temperature, and the "hot" junctions at the absorber. Fig. 3.11 shows an electrical circuit diagram of the Pyrheliometer.

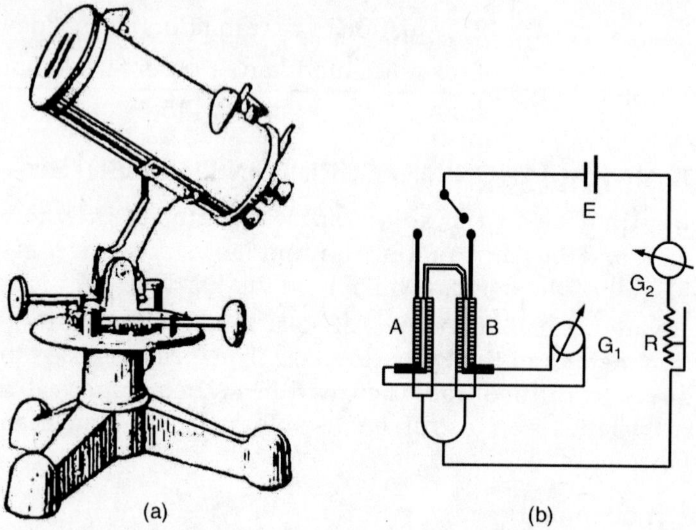

(a) (b)

Fig. 3.11 Angström 11yrheliometer: (a) external view, (b) schematic of the instrument; (G_2) and (G_2) galvanometers, I rheostat regulating the strength of the compensation current

The intensity I_o of direct solar radiation is calculated by means of the formula, $I_o = k\,i^2$, where i is the heating current in amperes and k is a constant typical of each Angstrom Pyrheliometer. When the Pyrheliometer is used absolutely, the constant k is derived as follows:

$$k = r/ba \qquad (I_o \text{ in W cm}^{-2}) \qquad ...(3.15)$$

or

$$k = 60r/Jba \quad (I_o \text{ in cal cm}^{-2}\text{ min}^{-1}) \qquad ...(3.16)$$

where r is the resistance of unit length of strip (Ω cm^{-1}), b is the mean width of strip (cm), a is the absorption coefficient of the blackened surface of the strip (e.g. 0.985 for Eppley-Parsons black lacquer), and J is the electrical heat equivalent (1 cal sec^{-1} = 4.185 W).

3.8.1.2 Abbot silver disc Pyrheliometer

This instrument was developed as a portable version of a water flow Pyrheliometer, which was the former primary standard. In this, a blackened silver disc is positioned at the lower end of the tube with diaphragms to control the limit of the whole aperture upto 5.7°. This Pyrheliometer is mainly used in calibrating pyranometers. The structure of a **silver-disk Pyrheliometer** is shown in Fig. 3.12.

The sensing element is a silver disk measuring 28 mm in diameter with a thickness of 7 mm that is painted black on its radiation-receiving side. It has a hole from the periphery toward the center to allow insertion of the bulb of a high-precision mercury-in-glass thermometer. To maintain good thermal contact between the disk and the bulb, the hole is filled with a small amount of mercury. It is enclosed outside by a heat-insulating wooden container. The stem of the thermometer is bent in a right angle outside the wooden container and supported in a metallic protective tube. A cylinder with diaphragms inside is fitted in the wooden container to let direct solar radiation fall onto the silver disk. There is a metallic-plate shutter at the top end of the cylinder to block or allow the passage of solar radiation to the disk.

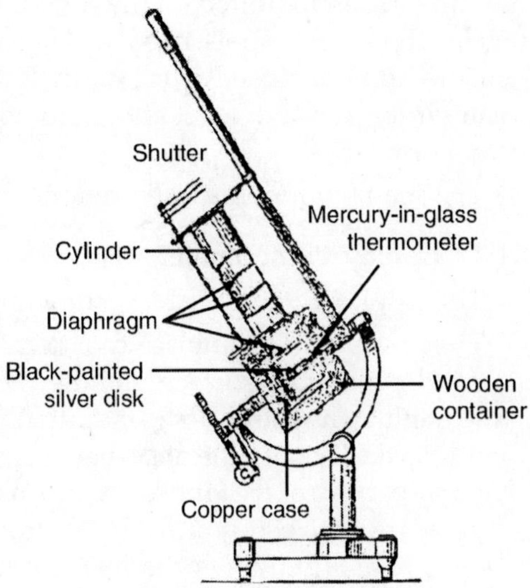

Fig. 3.12 Silver-disk Pyrheliometer

During the measurement phase, the disk is heated by solar radiation and its temperature rises. The intensity of this radiation is ascertained by measuring the temperature change of the disk between the measurement phase and the shading phase with the mercury-in-glass thermometer.

3.8.1.3 Eppley Pyrheliometer

In the case of Eppley Pyrheliometer, there is a bismuth silver thermopile of having temperature compensated 15 junctions connected in series. The limiting diaphragm limits the aperture to 5.7°. It is widely used in USA and many other countries in the world.

The structure of a **thermoelectric Pyrheliometer** instrument uses a thermopile at its sensor, and continuously delivers a thermo-electromotive force in proportion to the direct solar irradiance. While Angstrom electrical compensation Pyrheliometers and silver-disk Pyrheliometers have a structure that allows the outer air to come into direct contact with the sensor portion, this type has transparent optical glass in the aperture to make it suitable for use in all weather conditions. It is mounted on a sun-tracking device to enable outdoor installation for automatic operation by JMA.

3.8.2 Pyranometers

A pyranometer is an instrument which measures total or global radiation over a hemispherical field of view. Pyranometers are radiometers with a 180° field of view that measure the total hemispherical radiation.

It is quite a useful device that helps in meteorological research, solar energy research and also in many scientific applications. It is one instrument that can be seen mounted on the roof of meteorological stations and is placed next to the solar panels used to tap sun's energy. Pyranometers work to measure sun's diffused energy. Since it is sun's diffused energy that is of greater importance to us, it is Pyranometer that has greater significance than Pyrheliometer.

The main commonly used pyranometers are:

3.8.2.1 Eppley Pyranometer

The Eppley Pyranometer is shown in the Fig. 3.13.

They essentially comprise two hemispherical glass domes, a black metal plate as an absorber surface, the thermo-elements located below this, and a white metallic housing. Solar radiation falls through the hemispherical glass domes vertically onto the absorber surface, warming it up. Since the amount of warming directly depends upon the irradiance, the difference in temperature between it and the environment (or, more precisely, the white metallic housing) allows the irradiance to be calculated. The temperature difference is found via thermocouples that are wired in series. These deliver a voltage that is proportional to the difference in temperature. Using a voltmeter, it is then possible to work out the global radiation directly from the voltage and the calibration factor. This emf which is usually in the range of 0 to 10 mV can be read, recorded or integrated over a period of time with regular calibration of about ± 2% can be obtained.

If direct solar radiation is screened out by fitting a shaded ring, the diffuse radiation can be measured.

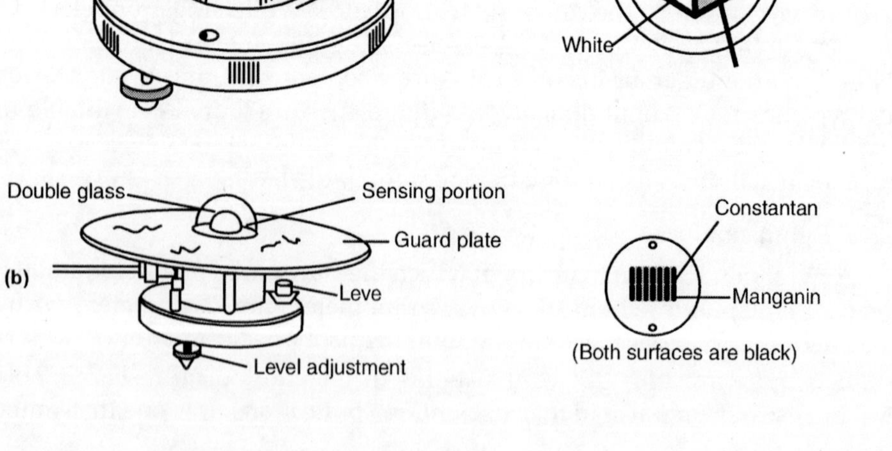

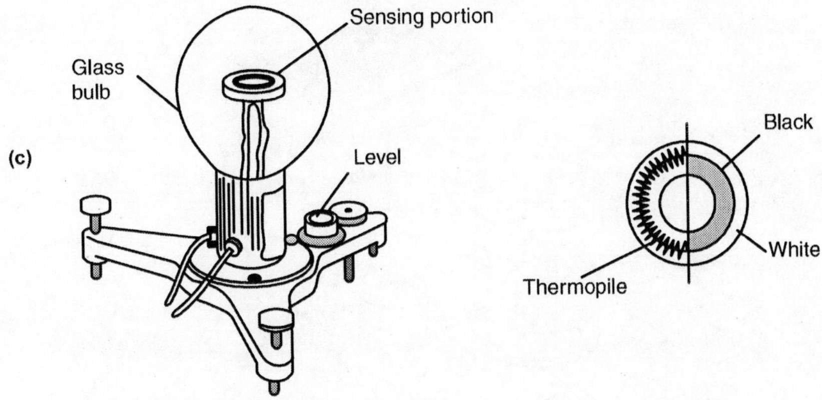

Fig. 3.13 Eppley (thermoelectric) Pyranometers and sensing

3.8.2.2 Bimetallic Pyranograph

A bimetallic pyranograph is shown in Fig. 3.14. The radiation-sensing element (in the upper right of the Fig. 3.14) consists of two pairs of bimetals, one painted black and the other painted white, placed in opposite directions (face up and face down) and attached to a common metal plate at one end. At the other end, the white bimetallic strips are fixed to the frame of the pyranograph, and the black ones are connected to the recorder section via a transmission shaft. The deflection of the free edge of the black strips is transmitted to the recording pen through a magnifying system. When the air temperature changes, the black and white strips attached to the common plate at one end both bend by the same amount but in opposite directions. As a result, only the temperature difference attributed to solar radiation is transmitted to the recording pen.

Thermoelectric pyranometers and bimetallic pyranographs are both hermetically sealed in a glass dome to protect the sensor portion from wind and rain and prevent the sensor surface temperature from being disturbed by wind. A desiccant is placed in the dome to prevent condensation from forming on the inner surface. The glass allows the passage of solar radiation in wavelengths from about 0.3 to 3.0 μm – a range that covers most of the sun's radiation energy. Some models are equipped with a fan to prevent dust or frost, which greatly affect the amount of light received, from collecting on the dome's outer surface. It is necessary to check and clean the glass surface at regular intervals to ensure that the dome wall constantly allows the passage of solar radiation.

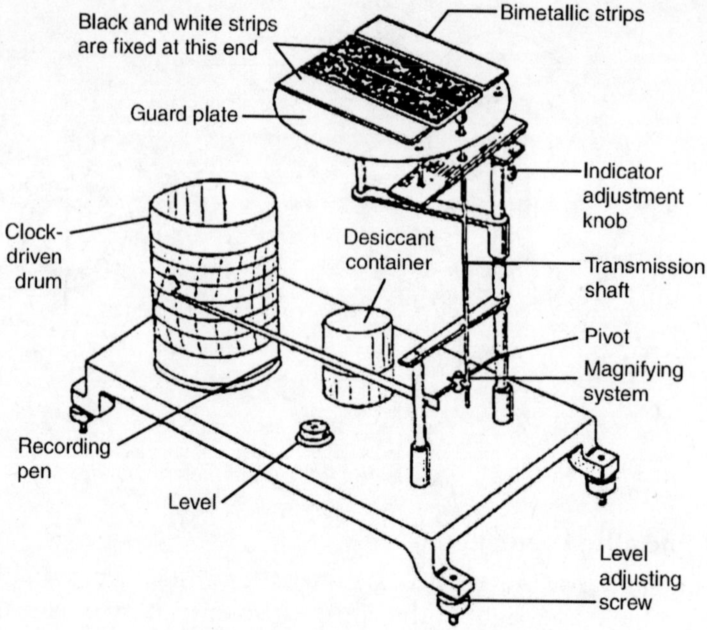

Fig. 3.14 Bimetallic pyranograph

3.9 SUNSHINE RECORDER

The amount of sunshine during the day is measured on a sunshine recorder. The glass ball focuses the sun's rays onto the special card behind it. The rays burn the card so that the times when the sun was shining can be read from this card. We can thus calculate the total hours of sunshine each day. We measure sunshine in hours. Every day a new card is fitted onto the Sunshine recorder. The sunshine recorder is shown in the Fig. 3.15.

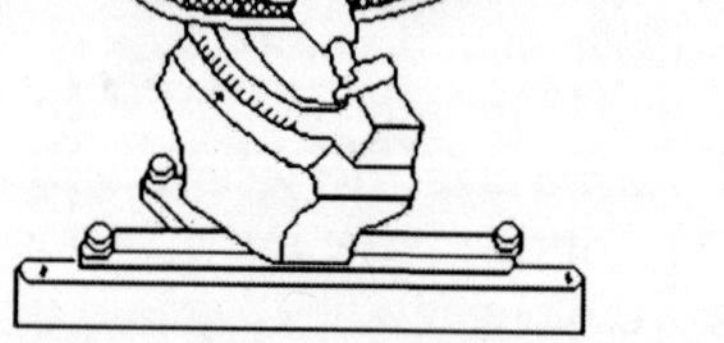

Fig. 3.15 Sunshine Recorder

Campbell-Stokes sunshine recorders and Jordan sunshine recorders have long been used as instruments to measure sunshine duration, and are advantageous in that they have no moving parts and require no electric power. Their disadvantages are that the characteristics of the recording paper or photosensitized paper used in them affect measurement accuracy, differences between observers may arise in determining the occurrence of sunshine, and the recording paper must be replaced after sunset.

3.10 SOLAR RADIATION ON TILTED SURFACES

Generally solar radiation (global as well as diffuse) is measured on a horizontal surface. But, for solar energy applications and thermal environmental designs, the knowledge of radiation on inclined surfaces is required. Several methods have been suggested for obtaining solar radiation on inclined surfaces from the measured values on horizontal surface. The first reliable was given by Liu and Jordan as described below:

$$R_D = \frac{\text{hourly direct radiation incident upon the titled surface } (I_{Dt})}{\text{hourly direct radiation incident upon the horizontal surface } (I_{Th} - I_{dh})} \quad ...(3.17)$$

Where R_D is the conversion factor for direct solar radiation,

I_{Th} is the hourly total radiation incident upon the horizontal surface,

I_{dh} is the hourly diffuse radiation incident upon the horizontal surface,

I_{Dt} is the direct radiation on a tilted surface.

For diffuse radiation, the conversion factor, R_d is defined as;

$$R_d = \frac{\text{hourly diffuse radiation incident upon the titled surface } (I_{dt})}{\text{hourly diffuse radiation incident upon the horizontal surface } (I_{dh})} \quad ...(3.18)$$

A tilted surface will also receive ground reflected radiation also. So, the conversion for ground reflected radiation, R_r is,

$$R_r = \frac{\text{hourly total radiation incident upon the titled surface } (I_{Tt})}{\text{hourly total radiation incident upon the horizontal surface } (I_{Th})} \quad ...(3.19)$$

Thus, the hourly total radiation on a tilted surface I_{Tt}, is given by,

$$I_{Tt} = (I_{Th} - I_{dh})\, R_D + I_{dh}\, R_d + I_{Th}\, R_r\, R \quad ...(3.20)$$

where R is the albedo of the ground.

Now it is well known that $I_{Dh} = I_{DN} \cos \theta_z$ and $I_{Dt} = I_{DN} \cos \theta_t$, where I_{DN} is the direct radiation at normal incidence. Hence,

$$R_D = \frac{I_{Dt}}{I_{Dh}} = \frac{\cos \theta_t}{\cos \theta_z} = \frac{\sin (\varphi - \beta) \sin \delta + \cos (\varphi - \beta) \cos \delta \cos \omega}{\sin \varphi \sin \delta + \cos \varphi \cos \delta \cos \omega} \quad ...(3.21)$$

Where ϕ is the latitude, β is the angle at which the surface is tilted towards an equator from the horizontal surface. (Refer Fig. 3.16)

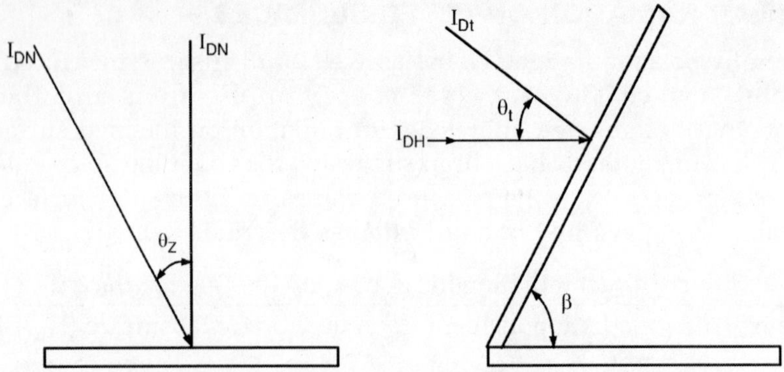

***Fig. 3.16** Radiation on horizontal and tilted surfaces*

Liu and Jordan, while calculating the diffuse radiation on an inclined plane, have assumed as an approximation that the diffuse sky radiation is isotropic i.e. it is uniform in all directions. Then the conversion factor for diffuse radiation, R_d is,

$$R_d = \frac{I_{dt}}{I_{dh}} = \frac{1+\cos\beta}{2} = \cos^2\left(\frac{\beta}{2}\right) \quad ...(3.22)$$

Assuming that the ground which is of infinite horizontal extent reflects the solar radiation diffusely, the conversion factor for the ground reflected radiation will be;

$$R_r = \frac{I_{Tt}}{I_{Th}} = R\left(\frac{1-\cos\beta}{2}\right) = R\sin^2\left(\frac{\beta}{2}\right) \quad ...(3.23)$$

Thus, the hourly hours of total solar radiation on an inclined surface can be determined from the following equation:

$$I_{Tt} = \frac{\cos\theta_t}{\cos\theta_z}(I_{Th} - I_{dh}) + \left(\frac{1+\cos\beta}{2}\right)I_{dh} + \left(\frac{1-\cos\beta}{2}\right)RI_{Th} \quad ...(3.24)$$

The value of reflectivity R (albedo of ground) is generally not known precisely for most situations. A value of ground 0.2, for surfaces of concrete or grass, can be used.

Similarly, the ratio of the monthly average of the daily global radiation falling on a tilted surface (H_t) to the monthly average of the daily global radiation falling on a horizontal surface (H_{av}), called the daily conversion factor, R_T is given by;

$$\overline{R_T} = \frac{H_t}{H_{av}} = \left(1 - \frac{H_d}{H_{av}}\right)\overline{R_D} + \frac{H_d}{H_{av}}\overline{R_d} + \overline{R_r} \quad ...(3.25)$$

Where H_d is the average daily diffuse radiation, R_D, R_d, and R_t, the monthly average values for a south-facing surface ($A_z = 0$), are given by,

$$\overline{R_D} = \frac{\omega_{st} \sin\delta \sin(\varphi - \beta) + \cos\delta \sin\omega_{st} \cos(\varphi - \beta)}{\omega_s \sin\delta \sin\varphi + \cos\delta \sin\omega_s \cos\varphi} \quad \text{...(3.26)}$$

$$\overline{R_d} = R_d = \frac{1 + \cos\beta}{2} \quad \text{...(3.27)}$$

$$\overline{R_r} = R_r = \frac{1 - \cos\beta}{2} \quad \text{...(3.28)}$$

where ω_{st} and ω_s are the sunrise/sunset angles (expressed in radians) for the tilted surface and a horizontal surface respectively.

SOLVED EXAMPLE

Example 1 : Evaluate the monthly average clearness index for 16 March 2001, at a surface located at latitude 30°N. The monthly average daily terrestrial radiation on a horizontal surface is 28.1 MJ/m²/day.

Solution: For 16th March 2001, $n = 75$

$$\delta = 23.45 \sin\left[\frac{360}{365}(284 + 75)\right]$$

$$= -2.4°$$

$$\omega_2 = \cos^{-1}(-\tan\phi \tan\delta)$$

$$= \cos^{-1}[-\tan 30° \tan(-2.4°) = 88.6°]$$

Monthly average of daily extraterrestrial radiation H_o is expressed in joules/m²/day by eqn. Therefore,

$$H_o = \frac{24 \times 3600 \times 1367}{\pi}(1.01 \times 0.832)$$

$$= 31.57 \text{ MJ/m}^2$$

Then, the monthly average clearness index is given as

$$K_T = \frac{H_g}{H_o} = \frac{28.1}{31.57} = 0.89$$

Example 2 : Compute the monthly average hourly solar flux received on a flat-plate collector facing due south ($\gamma = 0°$) having a slope of 12°. The collector is located at a place 15° 00′ N on 20th day of October. The data given are:

Time 11 : 12 h (local apparent time)

$H_g = 2408$ kJ/m²/h

$H_d = 1073$ kJ/m²/h

Ground reflectivity, $\rho = 0.25$, $\omega = 7.5°$

Solution:

Given $\gamma = 0°$ and $n = 293$ for 20th October.

From Copper's equation

$$\delta = 23.45 \sin\left[\frac{360}{365}(284+293)\right]$$

$$= -11.40°.$$

Substituting the given data in eqn., we have

$$R_b = \frac{\sin(-11.4°)\sin(15°-12°)+\cos(-11.40°)\cos 7.5° \cos(15°-12°)}{\sin 15° \sin(-11.4°)+\cos 15° \cos(-11.40°)\cos 7.5°}$$

$$= 1.08$$

From eqns.

$$R_d = \left(\frac{1+\cos 12°}{2}\right) = 0.989$$

$$R_r = 0.2\left(\frac{1-\cos 12°}{2}\right) = 0.0022$$

Equation is valid for evaluating the average daily radiation reaching on an inclined surface if the value of ω is taken at the middle of the hour. Similarly, the monthly average hourly value H_T can be calculated by using a representative day of the month. The modified form of eqn. becomes

$$\frac{H_T}{H_g} = \left(1-\frac{H_d}{H_g}\right)R_b + \frac{H_d}{H_g}R_d + R_r$$

Thus,

$$\frac{H_T}{H_g} = \left(1-\frac{1073}{2408}\right)1.08 + \frac{1073}{2408}0.989 + 0.0022$$

Therefore,

$$H_T = 2508 \text{ kJ/m}^2\text{/h}$$

Example 3 : Determine the local apparent time corresponding to 13:50 IST on July 1, at Delhi (28°35′ N, 77°12′ E). The 'equation of time correction' on July 1 is – 4 minutes. In India, the standard time is based on 82°30′ E.

Solution:

Local apparent time $= 13.50 \text{ h} - 4[(82.50) - (77.2)] \text{ min} + (-4 \text{ min})$

$= 13.50 \text{ h} - 4(82.50 - 77.2) \text{ min} - 4 \text{ min}$

$= 13.50 \text{ h} - 21.20 \text{ min} - 4 \text{ min}$

$= 13.50 \text{ h} - 25.20 \text{ min}$

$$= 13.50 \text{ h} - 0.42 \text{ h}$$
$$= 13.08 \text{ h} = 13 \text{ h } 4 \text{ min } 48 \text{ s}$$

Example 4 : At Nagpur, the following observations were made:
Theoretical maximum possible sunshine hours = 9.5 h
Average measured length of day during April = 9.0 h
Solar radiation for a clear day, H_o = 2100 kJ/m^2/day
Constants: a = 0.27, b = 0.50.
Calculate the average daily global radiation.

Solution:

$$H_g = H_o\left[a + b\left(\frac{D_L}{D_{max}}\right)\right]$$

$$= 2100\left[0.27 + 0.50\left(\frac{9.0}{9.5}\right)\right]$$

$$= 1554 \text{ kJ/m}^2\text{/day}$$

REVIEW QUESTIONS

1. Define the following terms and differentiate between them :
   (*a*) Beam radiation and diffuse radiation
   (*b*) Surface azimuth angle and solar azimuth angle
   (*c*) Local clock time and local apparent time
2. What is a solar radiation? Discuss the following terms:
   (*a*) Diffuse radiation (*b*) Reflected radiation (*c*) Total radiation
3. Explain the following terms:
   (*a*) Solar constant (*b*) Air mass
   (*c*) Average solar radiation (*d*) Solar declination
4. Explain the different types of solar radiation measuring instruments.
5. What is a sunshine recorder? Explain.
6. Explain the method of obtaining solar radiation on inclined surfaces from the measured values on horizontal surface.
7. Write a short note on Terrestrial Şolar radiation.
8. Determine the following :
   (*i*) Solar azimuthal angle (*ii*) Zenithal angle
   (*iii*) Latitude angle (*iv*) Declination angle
   (*v*) Hour angle

❑❑❑

4

SOLAR COLLECTORS

4.1. INTRODUCTION

Solar Collector is a device which absorbs the incoming the solar radiation, converts it into heat, and transfers this heat into fluid (usually air, water or heat transfer oil) flowing through the collector. Solar collectors are the key component of active solar-heating systems.

There are basically two types of solar collectors:

(i) Non-Concentrating or Flat Plate Type Solar Collector

(ii) Concentrating (Focusing) Type Solar Collector

In the non-concentrating type, the collector area (i.e. the area that intercepts the solar radiation) is the same as the absorber area. On the other hand, in concentrating collectors, the area intercepting the solar radiation is greater, sometimes hundred times, than the absorber area.

4.2. FLAT PLATE COLLECTOR (FPC)

Flat-plate collectors are the most common solar collector for solar water-heating systems in homes and solar space heating. Flat plates can collect and absorb both direct and diffuse solar radiation; they are consequently partially effective even on cloudy days when there is no direct radiation. Flat-plate collectors are best suited to applications where the demand temperature is 30-70°C.

Advantages of Flat-plate Collector

(*i*) They have the advantages of using both beam and diffuse solar radiation.

(*ii*) They do not require orientation towards the sun.

(*iii*) They require little maintenance.

(*iv*) They are mechanically simpler than the focusing collectors.

MAIN COMPONENTS OF FLAT PLATE COLLECTOR

1) An absorber plate, treated with a selective surface coating to increase the fraction of incoming radiation absorbed.

2) A transparent cover or glazing, which limits the radiation and convection heat losses.
3) A layer of insulation, which reduces conduction losses.
4) An casing or enclosure to contain the different elements and protects them from the weather.
5) Flow tubes, fins, passages or channels through which the heat transfer fluid circulates.

Flat plate solar collectors may be divided into two main classifications based on the type of heat transfer fluid used:

(i) LIQUID FLAT PLATE COLLECTOR

A typical liquid flat-plate solar collector is shown in Figure 4.1. When solar radiation passes through a transparent cover and impinges on the blackened absorber surface of high absorptivity, a large portion of this energy is absorbed by the plate and then transferred to the transport medium in the fluid tubes to be carried away for storage or use.

The absorber plate is usually made of copper, steel or aluminium material with tubing of copper in thermal contact with the plate is the most commonly used material. The surface finish of the absorber has a flat black paint with an appropriate primer. The coatings on the applied on the absorber plate are called selective coatings. Insulation materials are generally mineral wood or glass wool or fiberglass material. Transparent covers are generally glass (may be one or more) that is transparent to the in-coming radiation and opaque to the infra-red radiation. Plastics can also be used in place of glass but as they are not opaque as glass to the thermal infra-red radiation, so greater loss of heat occurs from the absorber.

The liquid heated is generally water. However sometimes mixtures of water and ethylene glycol are used, if ambient temperatures are below 0°C.

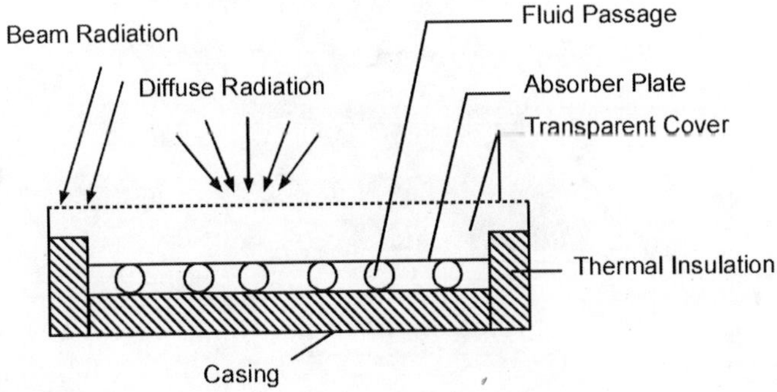

Fig. 4.1 Liquid Flat Plate Collector

Advantages of Liquid Flat Plate Collector

1. Higher transport energy density

2. Better heat transfer properties
3. Water storage has higher energy density
4. Suitable for space heating and cooling
5. Small fluid conduits

Disadvantages of Liquid Flat Plate Collector

1. There is a possibility of freezing in collector tubes in cold climates during cold nights.
2. There occurs a corrosion of metal tubes by the water and water chemistry needs monitoring.
3. Heat exchanger is required for collector storage and storage building loops.
4. Boiling and fluid expansion provisions are required.

(ii) AIR FLAT PLATE COLLECTOR

It is a conventional flat plate collector for heating air. The only difference in its construction from liquid flat plate collectors concerns the passages through which the air flows. For air systems, the space above or below the absorber plate serves as the conduit. Fins are attached to the plate to increase the contact surface.

The most favourable orientation, of a collector, for heating only is facing due south at an inclination angle to the horizontal equal to the latitude plus 15o. The solar air collector is shown in the Figure 4.2.

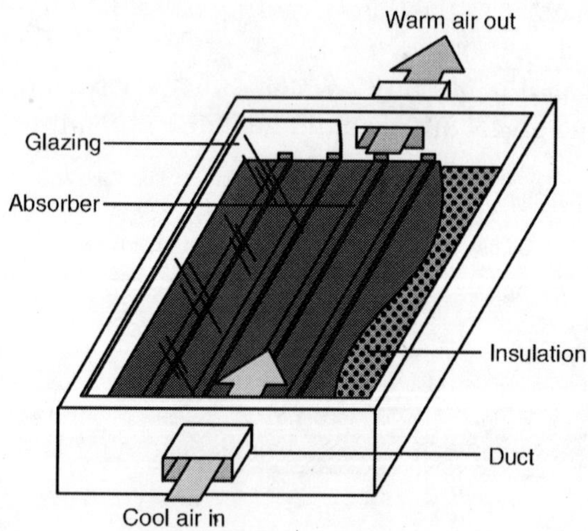

***Fig. 4.2** Air Flat Plate Collector*

Advantages of Air Flat Plate Collector :

1. These collectors usually weigh less than liquid-based collectors because they don't have pressurized piping.

2. The advantages of such a system over a water collector include the absence of problems associated with corrosion and with freezing and overheating.
3. The heated air can be directly for space heating.

Disadvantages of Air Flat Plate Collector

1. Need of handling larger volume of air due to low density of air.
2. Thermal capacity of air is low.
3. Due to lower heat transfer rate efficiencies are lower than liquid solar heater.
4. They have relatively high fluid circulation costs.
5. Relatively larger volume of storage.
6. They have higher noise level.
7. Space is required for ducting.
8. Difficulty of adding conventional absorption air conditioners to air systems.

Application of Air Flat Plate Collector

The solar air heater which supply hot air that could be mainly used for the following purposes:

1. Heating buildings.
2. Drying agricultural products.
3. Heating green house.
4. Space heating.
5. Seasoning of timber.
6. Curing of industrial products.

Classification of Air Flat Plate Collector:

Air heaters are classified in the following two categories:

1. Collectors with Non-porous absorbers

In these absorbers, the air stream does not flow through absorber plate. Air may flow above or behind the absorber plate.

Drawbacks of Non-porous absorber plate

a) Main drawback is the necessity of absorbing all incoming radiation over the projected area from a thin layer the surface, which is in order of a few microns.
b) Unless selective coatings are used, radiative losses from the absorber plate are excessive, therefore collection efficiency cannot be improved.
c) Too many surfaces and too much restriction to air flow will require a large fan and a larger amount of energy to push the air through. Thus, becomes costly.

2. Collectors with Porous absorbers

A porous absorber type collector eliminates the drawbacks of non-porous absorbers. The two ways can be used:

a) The solar radiation penetrates to greater depths and is absorbed gradually depending on the matrix density.

b) The pressure drop for the matrix is usually lower than the non-porous absorber with flow behind the plate since flow per unit cross-section would be much smaller.

THERMAL LOSSES IN A FLAT PLATE COLLECTOR

Heat losses from any solar water heating system take the three modes of heat transfer: radiation, convection and conduction. The conduction heat losses occur from sides and the back of the collector plate. The convection heat losses take place from the absorber plate to the glazing cover and can be reduced by evacuating the space between the absorber plate and the glazing cover and by optimizing the gap between them. The radiation losses occur from the absorber plate due to the plate temperature. Fig. 4.3 shows the heat loss pattern in a typical flat plat collector.

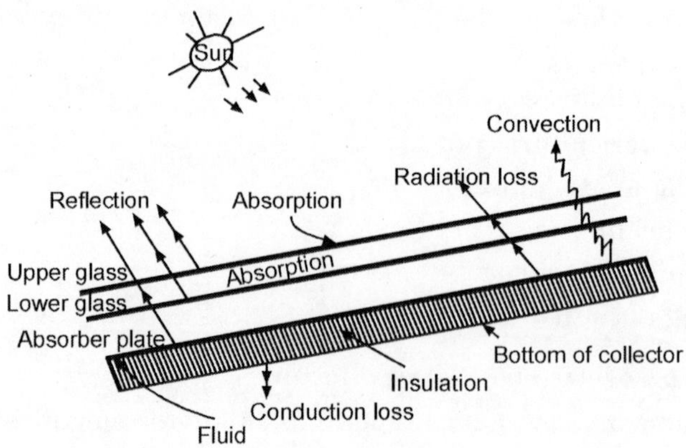

Fig. 4.3 Energy balance of Flat Plate Collector

Convective heat loss of a solar collector receiver is proportional to the surface area of the absorber or receiver, and the difference in temperature between the absorber surface and the surrounding air.

The rate of radiation heat loss is proportional to the emittance of the surface and the difference in temperature to the fourth power.

Conduction loss is generally described in terms of a material constant, the thickness of the material and its cross-section area.

The heat losses from the transparent cover to the ambient air are due to radiative and convective exchanges which are affected by the wind velocity, ground, and surrounding condition and by long wave radiation from the sky. They can be considerably reduced by selective black coatings which have high solar absorptivity and low long wave emmissivity. These coatings prepare surfaces such that their absorption characteristics remain high for wavelength below 2 μm and their emission characteristics low for wavelengths above 2 μm.

Applications of Flat Plate Collector

a) The main use of this technology is in solar water heaters used in residential buildings where the demand for hot water has a large impact on energy bills.

b) Commercial applications include Laundromats, car washes, military laundry facilities and eating establishments.

c) The technology can also be used for space heating if the building is located off-grid or if utility power is subject to frequent outages.

d) Unglazed liquid collectors are commonly used to heat water for swimming pools.

4.3 CONCENTRATING COLLECTOR

In concentrating collectors, temperature can be increased by decreasing the area from which the heat losses occur i.e. absorber area is much less (hundred times) than the area which intercepts the solar radiation. This is done by interposing an optical device between the source of radiation and the energy absorbing surface.

ADVANTAGES OF CONCENTRATING COLLECTOR

1. The working fluid can achieve higher temperatures in a concentrator system when compared to a flat-plate system of the same solar energy collecting surface.
2. The thermal efficiency is greater because of the small heat loss area relative to the receiver area.
3. Reflecting surfaces require less material and are structurally simpler than FPC. For a concentrating collector the cost per unit area of the solar collecting surface is therefore less than that of a FPC.
4. Higher temperatures allow the use of power generation equipment to produce both electricity and heat.

DISADVANTAGES OF CONCENTRATING COLLECTOR

Their disadvantages are:

1. Concentrator systems collect little diffuse radiation depending on the concentration ratio.
2. Some form of tracking system is required so as to enable the collector to follow the sun.
3. Solar reflecting surfaces may lose their reflectance with time and may require periodic cleaning and refurbishing.
4. High initial cost

TYPES OF CONCENTRATING COLLECTORS

(i) Non-Focusing Type

Non-focusing collector is a simple mirror-boosted, flat plate collector. It consists of flat plate facing south with mirrors attached to its north and south edges. If the mirrors are set at the proper angle, they reflect solar radiation on to the absorber plate. Thus, the direct radiation concentration increases which are reaching the absorber plate. Also some part of the diffuse radiations falling on the mirrors will be reflected onto the absorber.

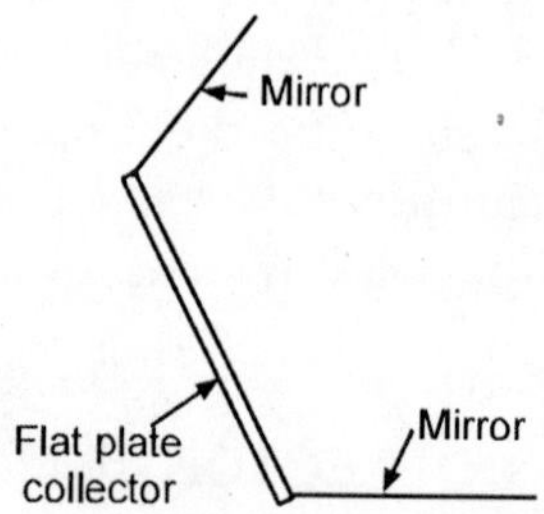

Fig. 4.4 Non-Focusing Type Collector

In order for the mirrors to be effective, the angles should be adjusted continuously as the sun's attitude changes. The Compound Parabolic Concentrator (CPC) is widely used non-focusing type concentrator.

(ii) Focusing Type

Focusing collector is a device to collect solar energy with high intensity of solar radiation on the energy absorbing surface. Such collectors generally use optical system in the form of reflectors or refractors. It is a special form of flat plate collector modified by introducing a reflecting (or refracting) surface (concentrator) between the solar radiations and the absorber.

The important difference between collectors of the non-focusing and focusing type is that focusing collector concentrate only direct radiation coming from a specific direction. Only a very small proportion of diffuse radiations are concentrated.

They are of two types:

(a) **Line Focusing Collectors -** Parabolic Trough Collector, Mirror Strip Reflector, Fresnel Lens Collector

(b) **Point Focusing Collectors -** Paraboloidal Dish Collector, Heliostat Point Focusing Reflector (Central Receiver Collector)

4.4 COMPOUND PARABOLIC CONCENTRATOR (CPC) OR WINSTON COLLECTOR

CPC are non-imaging concentrators. These have the capability of reflecting to the absorber all of the incident radiation within wide limits. Their potential as collectors of solar energy was pointed out by Winston. The necessity of moving the concentrator to accommodate the changing solar orientation can be reduced by using a trough with two sections of a parabola facing each other, as shown in Fig. 4.5.

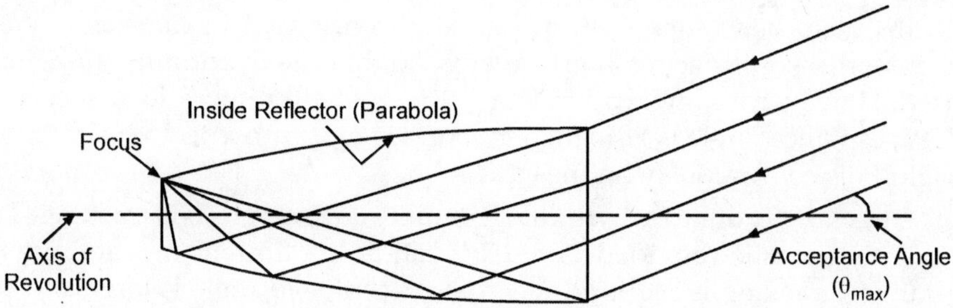

Fig. 4.5. Compound Parabolic Concentrator (CPC)

Compound parabolic concentrators can accept incoming radiation over a relatively wide range of angles. By using multiple internal reflections, any radiation that is entering the aperture, within the collector acceptance angle, finds its way to the absorber surface located at the bottom of the collector. The absorber can take a variety of configurations. It can be flat, bifacial, wedge or cylindrical as shown in the Figure 4.6.

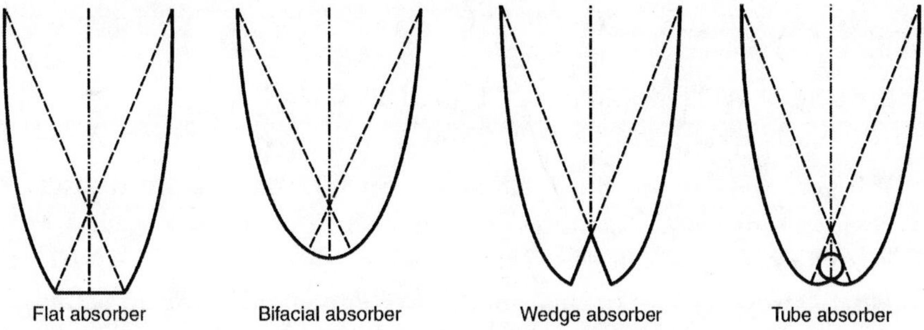

Fig. 4.6. Various types of CPCs

CPCs are usually covered with glass to avoid dust and other materials from entering the collector and thus reducing the reflectivity of its walls. Compound parabolic reflectors should have a small gap between the receiver and the reflector to prevent the reflector from acting as a fin conducting heat way from the absorber.

An advantage of CPC is that it provides moderately good concentration, although less than a focusing collector, in an east-west direction without adjustment for sun tracking. Temperatures of about 200°C are achievable with Winston collectors.

TRACKING REQUIREMENTS

Tracking of a CPC may not be required if the CPC has concentration ratio (i.e. ratio of effective area of the aperture to the surface area of the absorber) of 3 - 5, and high acceptance angle (i.e. limiting angle over which incident ray path may deviate from normal to the aperture plane and still reach the absorber). Also CPC are generally oriented in the East - West direction with south facing aperture area, so that the maximum sunlight is utilized. However for application where the concentration ratio is very high or the acceptance angle is less, than tracking is to be provided to ensure that sunlight falls continuously on the CPC.

The tracking is done by hydraulic circuits and is single axis tracking. The tracking that can be provided for a CPC can be continuous or intermittent. Intermittent tracking is required when the acceptance angle is large and the tracking is required only due to the change in inclination of the earth.

APPLICATION OF CPC

CPC found their application in the following field

1. In solar still (water pasteurization) - to remove impurity or microbes from the water
2. In solar water heating - for domestic water heating purpose in buildings
3. In power generation - in photovoltaic cells
4. In solar cooking

COMPARISON WITH FLAT PLATE COLLECTOR

1. Both are generally used without solar tracking.
2. Receiver area reduces for the same output temperature desired. The cost per unit area of solar collecting surface hence decreases. Also the insolation intensity increases.
3. Heat storage costs are less due to the higher temperature achievable.
4. Temperature up to 300°C - 350°C can be obtained using CPC with vacuum coating. The flat plate collector can deliver heated water up to 90°C. Hence FPC is generally used for domestic solar water heating, while the application of CPC lies even in industrial process and power generation.
6. The radiation losses are less in case of CPC, but optical losses like intercept loss, reflectance losses are present
7. Collector efficiency increase due to reduction in absorber size.
8. Difficult to fabricate and also the maintenance costs are higher as CPC needs frequent cleaning.

4.5 PARABOLIC TROUGH COLLECTOR

The principle of the parabolic trough collector is shown by cross-section in Fig. 4.7. Solar radiation coming from the particular direction is collected over the area of the reflecting surface and is concentrated at the focus of the parabola, if the reflector is in the form of a trough with parabolic cross-section; the solar radiation is focused along a line. Mostly cylindrical parabolic concentrators are used, in which the absorber is placed along focus axis.

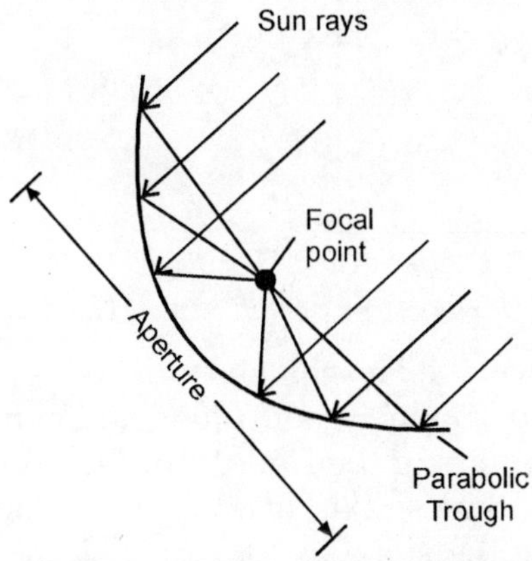

Fig. 4.7 Cross-section of Parabolic Trough Collector

Parabolic trough collectors can effectively produce heat at temperatures between 50°C and 400°C.

PTCs are made by bending a sheet of reflective material into a parabolic shape. A metal black tube, covered with a glass tube to reduce heat losses, is placed along the focal line of the receiver. When the parabola is pointed towards the sun, parallel rays incident on the reflector are reflected onto the receiver tube.

The collector can be orientated in an east-west direction, tracking the sun from north to south, or orientated in a north-south direction and tracking the sun from east to west.

Over the period of one year, a horizontal north-south trough field usually collects slightly more energy than a horizontal east-west one. However, the north-south field collects a lot of energy in summer and much less in winter.

4.6 LINEAR FRESNEL REFLECTOR

It is a refraction type of focusing collector. It utilizes the focusing effect of a Linear Fresnal lens, as shown in Fig.4.8. Solar concentrator linear fresnel lens has been developed for collecting parallel light to a slit form. The solar concentrator linear fresnel lenses are designed such that its plano side face the sun (parallel light source), and the fresnel surface faces photovoltaic cells or heat collector tube (focus) shown in Fig.4.8. In a Fresnal lens collector, the solar radiation is focused into the absorber from the top, rather than from the bottom as in the parabolic (reflection) type.

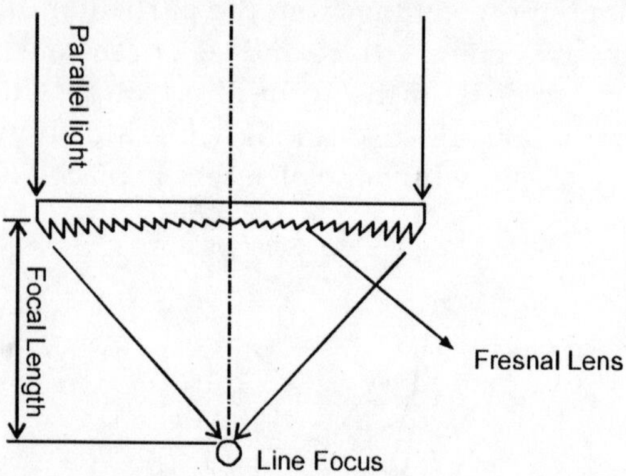

Fig. 4.8 Cross-section of Fresnal Lens Collector

To be fully effective, the Fresnal lens must be continuously aligned with the sun in two directions namely, both along and perpendicular to its length. This is achieved by orienting the troughs in the north-south direction with rotation about the length wise axis; in addition, the north ends of the troughs are raised to increase the slope as the sun's elevation decreases and vice versa. The total solar radiation energy that can be collected annually is about 30% greater than for an east west direction.

The greatest advantage of this type of system is that it uses flat or elastically curved reflectors which are cheaper compared to parabolic glass reflectors. Additionally, these are mounted close to the ground, thus minimizing structural requirements.

One difficulty with the LFR technology is that avoidance of shading and blocking between adjacent reflectors leads to increased spacing between reflectors. Blocking can be reduced by increasing the height of the absorber towers, but this increases cost.

4.7. PARABOLIC DISH REFLECTOR (PARABOLOIDAL DISH COLLECTOR)

A parabolic dish reflector, shown schematically in Figure 4.9, is a point-focus (a small central volume) collector that tracks the sun in two axes (up-down and left-right), concentrating solar energy onto a receiver (absorber) located at the focal point of the dish. The receiver absorbs the radiant solar energy, converting it into thermal energy in a circulating fluid.

The thermal energy can then either be converted into electricity using an engine-generator coupled directly to the receiver, or it can be transported through pipes to a central power-conversion system. Parabolic-dish systems can achieve temperatures in excess of 1500°C.

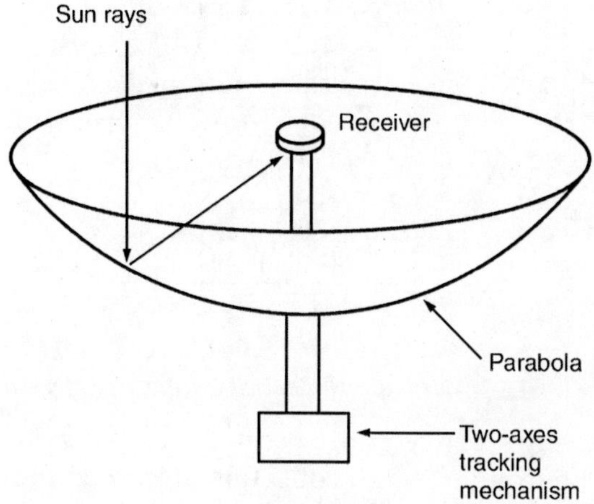

Figure 4.9: Schematic of a parabolic dish collector

A dish 6.6m in diameter is made from about 200 curved mirror segments forming a paraboloidal surface. The absorber, located at the focus, is a cavity made of zirconium-copper alloy with a black chrome selective coating. The heat-transport fuid flows into and out of the absorber cavity through pipes bonded to the interior.

Paraboloids dishes have several important advantages:

1. Because they are always pointing the sun, they are the most efficient of all collector systems.
2. They typically have concentration ratio in the range of 600-2000, and thus are highly efficient at thermal-energy absorption and power conversion systems;
3. Radiation losses are small because of the small area of the absorber at the focus.

4.8 HELIOSTAT FIELD COLLECTOR (CENTRAL RECEIVER COLLECTOR)

The central receiver system consists of an array of flat, movable mirrors sun-tracking mirrors (heliostats) on the ground that reflects the incident sunshine to a receiver (boiler) at the top of a centrally located tower. Typically 80 to 95 percent of the reflected energy is absorbed into the working fluid which is pumped up the tower and into the receiver. The heated fluid (or steam) returns down the tower and then to a thermal demand such as a thermal electrical power plant or an industrial process requiring heat.

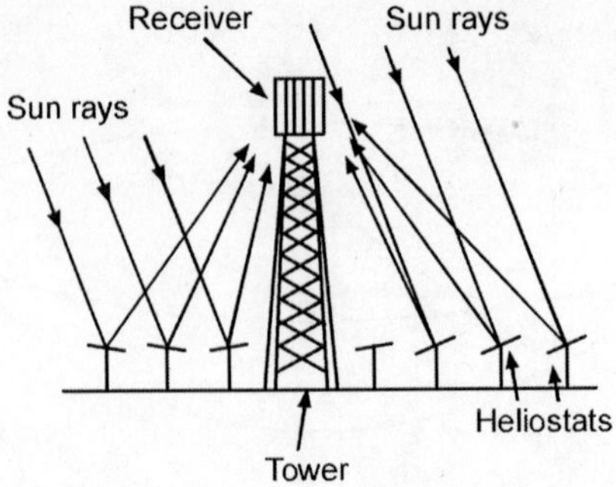

Fig. 4.10 Schematic of Central Receiver System

The basic difference between the central receiver concept of collecting solar energy and the trough or dish collectors discussed previously is that in this case, all of the solar energy to be collected in the entire field is transmitted optically to a small central collection region rather than being piped around a field as hot fluid. Because of this characteristic, central receiver systems are characterized by large power levels (1 to 500 MW) and high temperatures (540 to 840°C).

Central receivers have several advantages:

1. They collect solar energy optically and transfer it to a single receiver, thus minimizing thermal-energy transport requirements;
2. They typically achieve concentration ratios of 300–1500 and so are highly efficient both in collecting energy and in converting it to electricity;
3. They can conveniently store thermal energy;
4. They are quite large (generally more than 10 MW) and thus benefit from economies of scale.

The basic problem associated with the central receiver is that the heliostat mirrors require non-linear drive rate in two coordinates to achieve the requirement of keeping the reflected image point on a fixed receiver. Also with the problem is the requirement that the heliostat be rugged enough to survive storms and operate successfully in a moderate wind.

Each technology has its own characteristics, advantages and disadvantages, some of which are shown in Table 4.1.

Table 4.1. Comparison of Solar Thermal Power Technologies

	Parabolic Trough	Central Receiver	Parabolic Dish
Applications	Grid-connected plants process heat	Grid-connected plants, high temperature process heat	Stand-alone applications or small off-grid power systems

	(Highest solar unit size built to date : 80 MWe)	(Highest solar unit size built to date : 10 MWe)	(Highest solar unit size built to date : 25 kWe)
Advantages	• Commercially available over 10 billion kWh operational experience; operating temperature potential upto 500°C (400°C commercially proven) • Commercially proven annual performance of 40% solar to net electrical output • Commercially proven investment and operating costs • Modularity • Best land use • Lowest materials demand • Hybrid concept proven • Storage capability	• Good mid-term prospects for high conversion efficiencies, with solar collection; operating temperature potential up of 1000°C (565°C proven at 10 MW scale) • Storage at high temperatures Hybrid operation possible	• Very high conversion efficiencies-peak solar to electric conversion of about 30% • Modularity • Hybrid operation possible • Operational experience of first prototypes
Dis-advantages	• The use of oil based heat transfer media restricts operating temperatures to 400°C resulting in moderate steam qualities • Land availabilit; water demand	• Projected annual performance values, investment and operating costs still needs to be proved in commercial operation	• Reliability needs to be improved • Projected cost goals of mass production still need to be achieved

4.9. THERMAL ANALYSIS OF COLLECTORS

In this section the thermal analysis of the two major types of collectors, i.e. flat-plate and concentrating are examined separately. The basic parameter to consider is the collector thermal efficiency. This is defined as the ratio of the useful energy delivered to the energy incident on the collector aperture. The incident solar flux consists of direct and diffuse radiation. While FPC can collect both, concentrating collectors can only utilize direct radiation if the concentration ratio is greater than 10.

4.9.1. Flat Plate Collector Performance

The performance of solar collector is described by an energy balance that indicates the distribution of incident solar radiation into the useful energy gain and various losses.

As it is shown Figure 4.11, a part of incident solar radiation is reflected back to the sky, another component is absorbed by the glazing and the rest is transmitted through the glazing and reaches the absorber plate as short wave radiation.

Therefore the conversion factor indicates the percentage of the solar rays penetrating the transparent cover of the collector (transmission) and the percentage being absorbed.

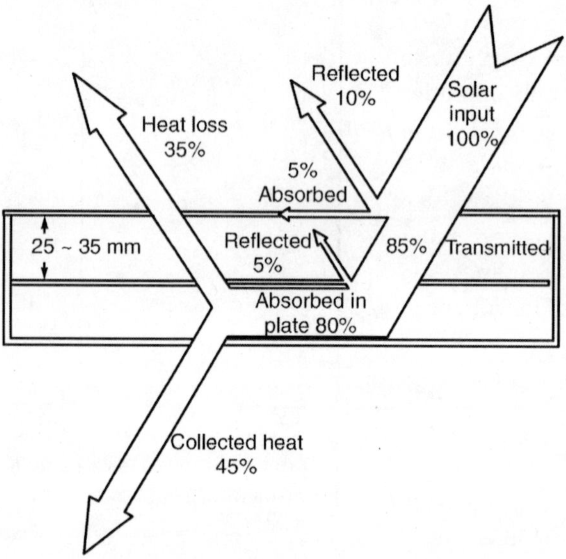

Figure 4.11: Heat flow through a Flat Plate solar collector

Thus, the amount of the energy absorbed in the metal surface is,

$$\text{absorbed energy} = A_c \, [HR \, (\tau \, . \, \alpha)_e]$$

As the collector absorbs heat its temperature is getting higher than that of the surrounding and heat is lost to the atmosphere by convection and radiation. The rate of heat loss depends on the collector overall heat transfer coefficient (UL) and the collector temperature.

Thus, the effective heat loss from the surface directly and indirectly to the surroundings is

$$\text{effective heat loss} = A_c\,[U_L\,(T_p - T_a)]$$

Under steady state conditions, the useful heat delivered by a solar collector is equal to the energy absorbed by the heat transfer fluid minus the direct or indirect heat losses from the surface to the surroundings.

The useful energy collected from the collector can be obtained from the following formula:

$$q_u = \text{absorbed energy} - \text{effective heat loss} = A_c[HR(\tau.\alpha)_e - U_L(T_p - T_a)]$$

It is also known that the rate of extraction of heat from the collector may be measured by means of the amount of heat carried away in the fluid passed through it. The total useful energy collection is given by:

$$q_u = mc_p\,(T_o - T_i)$$

Where

A_c is the collector area, m^2

HR or I is the solar energy received on the upper surface of the sloping collector structure, W/m^2

H is the rate of incident beam or diffuse radiation on a unit area of surface of any orientation

R is the factor to convert beam or diffuse radiation to that on the plane of the collector.

τ is the solar transmittance of the collector glazing, dimensionless

α is the solar absorptance of the collector plate, dimensionless

$(\tau.\alpha)_e$ is the effective transmittance absorptance product of cover system for beam and diffuse radiation

U_L is the collector thermal conductance, normalized to the absorber plate area, $W/m^2\,^oC$

T_p is the average temperature of the upper surface of the absorber plate, °C

T_a is the ambient air temperature, °C

m is the transport fluid mass flow rate, kgs^{-1}

c_p is the specific heat of the transport fluid, $Jkg^{-1}K^{-1}$

T_o is the temperature of the transport fluid flowing out of the collector, °C

T_i is the temperature of the transport fluid flowing into the collector, °C

Equation proves to be somewhat inconvenient because of the difficulty in defining the collector average temperature. It is convenient to define a quantity that relates the actual useful energy gain of a collector to the useful gain if the whole collector surface were at the fluid inlet temperature. This quantity is known as "the collector heat removal factor (FR)" and is expressed as:

$$F_R = \frac{mc_p(T_o - T_i)}{A_c[HR(\tau.\alpha)_e - U_L(T_i - T_a)]}$$

The maximum possible useful energy gain in a solar collector occurs when the whole collector is at the inlet fluid temperature. The actual **useful energy gain** (q_u), is found by multiplying the collector heat removal factor (F_R) by the maximum possible useful energy gain. This allows the rewriting of equation :

$$q_u = A_c F_R[HR\,(\tau.\alpha)_e - U_L(T_i - T_a)]$$

This Equation is a widely used relationship for measuring collector energy gain and is generally known as the "**Hottel-Whillier-Bliss equation**".

A measure of a flat plate collector performance is the **collector efficiency** (η) defined as the ratio of the useful energy gain (q_u) to the incident solar energy over a particular time period :

$$\eta = \frac{\int q_u\,dt}{\int HR\,dt}$$

This instantaneous thermal efficiency of the collector is :

$$\eta = \frac{q_u}{A_c HR} = \frac{A_c F_R[HR(\tau.\alpha)_e - U_L(T_i - T_a)]}{A_c HR} = F_R\left[(\tau.\alpha)_e - U_L\left(\frac{T_i - T_a}{HR}\right)\right]$$

If it is assumed that F_R, τ, α, U_L are constants for a given collector and flow rate, then the efficiency is a linear function of the three parameters defining the operating condition: Solar irradiance (I), Fluid inlet temperature (T_i) and Ambient air temperature (T_a).

Thus, the performance of a Flat-Plate Collector can be approximated by measuring these three parameters in experiment. The result is a single line (ΔT/I-Curve) shown in Fig. 4.12.

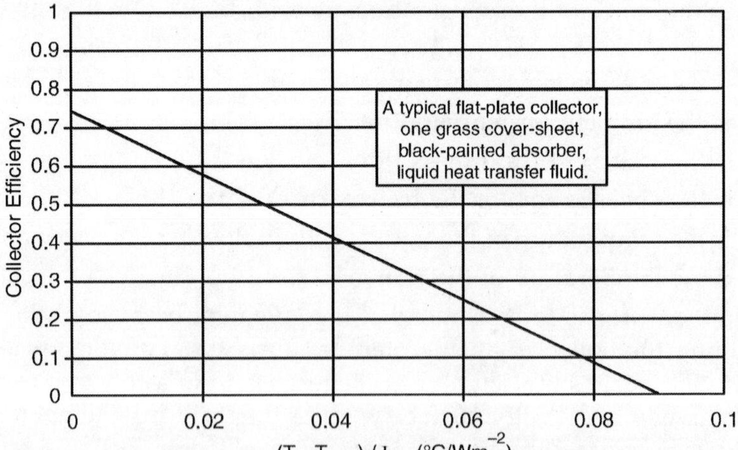

Fig. 4.12. Performance of a typical flat-plate thermal collector (ambient temperature 25 C)

The collector efficiency η is plotted against $(T_i - T_a)/I$. The slope of this line $(-F_R U_L)$ represents the rate of heat loss from the collector. For example, collectors with cover sheets will have less of a slope than those without cover sheets.

There are two interesting operating points on Fig. 4.12 :

1. The first is the maximum collection efficiency, called the optical efficiency. This occurs when the fluid inlet temperature equals ambient temperature $(T_i = T_a)$. For this condition, the ΔT/HR value is zero and the intercept is $F_R(\tau\alpha)$.
2. The other point of interest is the intercept with the ΔT/HR axis. This point of operation can be reached when useful energy is no longer removed from the collector, a condition that can happen if fluid flow through the collector stops (power failure). In this case, the optical energy coming in must equal the heat loss, requiring that the temperature of the absorber increase until this balance occurs. This maximum temperature difference or "stagnation temperature" is defined by this point. For well-insulated collectors or concentrating collectors the stagnation temperature can reach very high levels causing fluid boiling and, in the case of concentrating collectors, the absorber surface can melt.

4.9.2. Concentrating Collectors Performance

Energy balances are used to describe the performance of focusing collector systems as done with flat plate collectors.

The generalized thermal analysis of a concentrating solar collector is similar to that of a FPC. It is necessary to derive appropriate expressions for the collector efficiency factor F; the loss coefficient U_L and the collector heat removal factor F_R. For the loss coefficient standard heat transfer relations for glazed tubes can be used.

The instantaneous efficiency of a concentrating collector may be calculated from an energy balance of its receiver. The useful energy delivered from a concentrator i.e. total energy gain is :

$$q_u = G_b n_o A_a - A_r U_L (T_r - T_a)$$

Where G_b is the beam radiation intensity on a reference surface (generally horizontal) available from solar date of the place, no is the optical efficiency, A_a is the area of aperture, A_r is the area of solar energy absorber, U_L is the surface (receiver) loss coefficient, T_r is the receiver surface temperature and T_a is the ambient temperature.

The useful energy gain per unit of collector length can be expressed in terms of the local receiver temperature T_r as :

$$q'_u = \frac{q_u}{L} = \frac{A_a n_o G_b}{L} - \frac{A_r U_L}{L}(T_r - T_a)$$

In terms of the energy transfer to the fluid at local fluid temperature T_f :

$$q'_u = \frac{\left(\frac{A_r}{L}\right)(T_r - T_f)}{\frac{D_o}{h_{fi}D_i} + \left(\frac{D_o}{2k}\ln\frac{D_o}{D_i}\right)}$$

Where D_o and D_i is outer and inner diameter respectively, h_{fi} is the inside film heat transfer coefficient determined from forced convection (or natural convection) formulae and k is the thermal conductivity of the tube material.

If Tr is eliminated from equations we have :

$$q'_u = F'\frac{A_a}{L}\left[n_o G_b - \frac{U_L}{C}(T_i - T_a)\right]$$

where F′ is the collector efficiency factor given by :

$$F' = \frac{1/U_L}{\frac{1}{U_L} + \frac{D_o}{h_{fi}D_i} + \left(\frac{D_o}{2k} + \ln\frac{D_o}{D_i}\right)}$$

Similarly as for the FPC the heat removal factor can be used and can be written as :

$$q_u = F_R[G_b n_o A_a - A_r U_L(T_i - T_a)]$$

And the collector efficiency can be obtained by dividing q_u by (G_b A_a). Therefore,

$$n = F_R\left[n_o - U_L\left(\frac{T_i - T_a}{G_b C}\right)\right]$$

where C is the concentration ratio [$C = A_a/A_r$]. For the F_R a relation similar to FPC is used by replacing A_c to A_r.

Therefore, the above equation plot as a straight line on a graph of efficiency versus the heat loss parameter $(T_i - T_a)/G_b$ for the case of concentrating collectors. The intercept (intersection of the line with the vertical efficiency axis) equals to $F_R n_o$ for the concentrating ones. The slope of the line, i.e. the efficiency difference divided by the corresponding horizontal scale difference, equals to $2F_R U_L/C$.

4.10 DESIRABLE FEATURES OF SOLAR THERMAL COLLECTOR MATERIALS

1. Transparent cover

Transparent cover acts as a heat trap for infrared (thermal) radiation. Therefore, it reduces radiation losses and convection to the atmosphere. Together with the frame, the cover protects the absorber from adverse weather conditions

The ideal glazing material for solar collectors would have these properties:

1. High temperature capability
2. Transmit light very well
3. Long life when exposed to UV and high temperatures
4. Good impact resistant
5. Light weight and easy to work
6. Opaque to long IR to reduce heat loss
7. Low cost

Some of the solar collectors glazing materials are glass (low iron), Polycarbonate (Corrugated), Polycarbonate (Multiwall), Polycarbonate (Rigid sheet), Polycarbonate (Rigid film), Rigid Acrylic Sheet, Rigid PVC sheet (flat or corrugated), Polyethylene film (greenhouse film), Sun-Light Fiberglass Glazing, corrugated plastic and vinyl.

Low-iron glass has the highest transmission and lowest re?ection of sunlight. The cost premium for low-iron glass is smaller than the increase in ef?ciency, so it is worthwhile.

2. Insulation

Solar collectors are insulated with selective grade of CFC free polyurethane foam (PUF) as insulation material. The use of a PUF-insulated collector and tank ensures superior performance with minimum heat loss.

Insulation must be kept dry otherwise it will lose all or most of its insulating value. To prevent this, quality collectors contain:

(a) Desiccants : A porous bag of silica gel desiccant is used to absorb the moisture. Desiccant is also required for the space between the glazings when two covers are used.

(b) Enclosure : The enclosure is used to contain insulation, provide support for the absorber and glazing, and to protect the collector from heat loss due to wind, plus the important function of keeping moisture out of the insulation from rain and dew. Enclosures are usually may be made from steel, aluminium or fibre glass.

3. Absorber Plates

The primary function of the absorber plate is to absorb as much as possible of the radiation reaching through the glazing, to loose as little heat as possible upward to the atmosphere and downward through the back of the container, and to transfer the retained heat to the circulating fluid.

Factors that determine the choice of absorber material are its thermal conductivity, its durability and ease of handling, its availability and cost, and the energy required to produce it.

Copper, which has high conductivity and is corrosion resistant, is the ideal material for absorber plate but as copper is expensive, steel is also widely used. Absorber plates are usually given a surface coating (which may be a black paint) that increases the fraction of available solar radiation absorbed by the plate (its absorptance α). Black paints, for which $\alpha = 0.92$ to 0.98, are usually applied by spraying and are then heat-treated to evaporate solvents and improve adherence.

4. Phase change materials for solar heat storage

Phase change materials (PCMs) are "latent" thermal storage materials. They use chemical bonds to store and release heat. The thermal energy transfer occurs when a material changes from a solid to a liquid or from a liquid to a solid. This is called a change in state, or "phase". Initially, these solid-liquid PCMs perform like conventional storage materials; their temperature rises as they absorb solar heat

Glauber's salt (sodium sulfate deca-hydrate), calcium chloride hexa-hydrate, and paraf?n wax are the most commonly used PCMs in solar heating systems.

5. Selective Absorber

A surface that has a high absorptance and is a good absorber of solar radiation usually has a high infrared emittance as well and is a good radiator of heat. A flat-black paint that absorbs 96% of the incoming solar energy will also reradiate much of the energy as heat, the exact amount depending on the temperature of the absorber plate and the glazing.

A selective surface is a surface that has a high absorptance for short wave radiation (less than 2.5μm) and a low emmitance of long wave radiation (more than 2.5μm). Selective absorbers often consist of a very thin black metallic oxide coating on a bright metal base. The oxide coating is thick enough to act as a good absorber, with ? = 0.95, but it is essentially transparent to longer wavelength heat radiation, neither absorbing nor emitting much of the 3 to 30 micron radiation. On the other hand, the bright metal base of the absorber surface has a low infrared emittance and radiates very little heat. The combination, in effect, gives a surface that is a good absorber but a poor radiator. As a result, the efficiency of the collector is greater when this type of surface is used.

Table lists properties of some selective coatings where 'α' is absorptance and 'ε' is emittance.

Selective Coatings	α	ε	α/ε
Black Chrome	0.93	0.10	9.3
Black Nickel on polished nickel	0.92	0.11	8.4
Black Nickel on galvanized	0.89	0.12	7.4
Cu on nickel	0.81	0.17	4.7
Co_3O_4 on silver	0.90	0.27	3.3

Cu on aluminium	0.93	0.11	8.5
Cu on anodized aluminu	0.85	0.11	7.7
Black Chrome	0.93	0.10	9.3
Black Nickel on polished nickel	0.92	0.11	8.3

REVIEW QUESTIONS

1. What is a solar collector? Explain the two types of solar collectors.
2. Differentiate between air based and liquid based flat plate collectors.
3. What are sun tracking concentrating collectors? Explain its various types.
4. Differentiate between parabolic trough, central receiver and parabolic dish type collectors.
5. Estimate the performance of flat plate collector along with suitable relations and equations.
6. Estimate the performance of concentrating collectors along with suitable relations and equations.
7. What are applications of flat plate collector?
8. What is a flat plate solar energy collector?
9. Briefly discuss the working principle of Solar-Thermal Central Receiver Systems.
10. Explain the desirable features of solar collector materials.

❑

5

SOLAR THERMAL ENERGY STORAGE

5.1 INTRODUCTION

Energy storage is employed in solar thermal energy systems to shift excess energy produced during times of high solar availability to times of low solar availability such as during night and during cloudy days.

For storing thermal energy, there are three approaches that have been considered over the years for solar thermal systems. These are sensible-heat storage (where a change of temperature occurs), latent heat storage (where a change of phase occurs) and thermochemical energy storage (where a reversible chemical reaction takes place).

However SHS systems possess the following disadvantages :

(*i*) Low heat storage capacity per unit volume of the storage medium and

(*ii*) Non-isothermal behavior during heat storage (charging) and heat release (discharging) processes.

LHS system is particularly attractive due to its ability to provide a high-energy storage density and its characteristics to store heat at a constant temperature corresponding to the phase transition temperature of the heat storage substance.

5.2 THERMAL ENERGY

Thermal energy can be stored in a material as sensible heat by raising its temperature.

The heat storage can be calculated as

$$q = V \rho c_p \, dt$$
$$= m c_p \, dt \qquad ...(5.1)$$

where

q = sensible heat stored in the material (J, Btu)

V = volume of substance (m^3, ft^3)

ρ = density of substance (kg/m^3, lb/ft^3)

m = mass of substance (kg, lb)

c_p = specific heat capacity of the substance (J/kg°C, Btu/lb°F)
dt = temperature change (°C, °F)

The energy released by a material as its temperature is reduced, or absorbed by a material as its temperature is increased, is called the sensible heat.

Latent heat is associated with the changes of state or phase change of a material. For example, energy is required to convert ice to water, to change water to steam, and to melt paraffin was. The energy required to cause these changes is called the *heat of fusion* at the melting point and the *heat of vaporization* at the boiling point. To illustrate, let us consider water, and suppose that we swish to evaporate 1 kg of ice by converting it to liquid and then heating it until it boils. In this case, 80 kcal is required to melt the ice at 0°C to water at 0°C; then, about 100 kcal is needed to raise the temperature of the water to 100°C; finally, 540 kcal is needed to boil the water, giving a total energy need of 720 kcal. The sensible heat for a given temperature change varies from one material to another. The latent heat also varies significantly between differet substances for a given type of phase change.

5.3 BENEFITS OF THERMAL ENERGY STORAGE (TES)

- **Increase generation capacity**
- **Enable better operation of congeneration plants**
- **Shift energy purchases to low-cost periods**
- **Increase system reliability**
- **Integration with other functions**

5.4 METHODS OF THERMAL ENERGY STORAGE

There are three basic methods of storing thermal energy :

1. **Heating a liquid or a solid, without changing phase :** This method is called **sensible heat storage**. The amount of energy stored depends on the temperature change of the material and can be expressed in the form :

$$E = m \int_{T_1}^{T_2} C_p \, dt \qquad ...(5.2)$$

   Where m is the mass, C_p is the specific heat at constant pressure. T_1 and T_2 represent the lower and upper temperature levels between which the storage operates. The difference $(T_2 - T_1)$ is referred to as the temperature swing.

2. **Heating a material which undergoes a phase change (usually melting):** This is called **latent heat storage.** The amount of energy stored (E) in this case depends upon the mass (m) and latent heat of fusion (λ) of the material. Thus,

$$E = m\lambda \qquad ...(5.3)$$

3. **Chemical reactions :** The thermo chemical reactions provide thermal storage capacity. The basic principle is : AB + heat ⇔ A + B; using heat, a compound AB is broken into components A and B which can be stored separately; bringing A and B together AB is formed and heat is released. The storage capacity is the heat of reaction or free energy of the reaction.

The storage systems based on chemical reactions have negligible losses whereas sensible heat storage dissipates the stored heat to the environment and need to be isolated.

For a well-designed short-term storage unit, the value of the efficiency should generally exceed 80 percent. Table 5.1 gives an overview of thermal energy storage methods.

Table 5.1

Overview of thermal energy storage methods

Type of Thermal Energy Storage	**Functional Principle**	**Phases**	**Examples**
Sensible Heat	Temperature change of the medium with highest possible heat capacity	• Liquid • Solid	Hot water, organic liquids, molten, salts, liquid metals Metals, minerals, ceramics
Latent Heat	Essentially heat of phase change	• Liquid-Solid • Solid-Solid	Nitrids, clorides, hydroxides, carbonates, flourides, entectics, Hydroxids
Bond Energy	Large amount of chemical energy is absorbed and released due to shifting of pressureequilibrium by changing and temperature	• Solid-Gas • Gas-Gas • Liquid-Gas	$CaO/H_2O, MgO/H_2O, FeCl_2/NH_3$ CH_4/H_2O $LiBr/H_2O$, $NaOH/H_2O$, H_2SO_4/H_2O

5.4.1 Sensible-heat Storage

In its simplest configuration, cold fluid contained in an insulated tank is heated to some higher temperature by the hot fluid from the field of solar collectors as shown in **Figure 5.1**. In most industrial solar energy systems, the fluid in the collector field and the storage tanks is the same. Thus no heat exchanger is required for sensible-heat storage.

In partially cloudy days, the quantity of thermal energy delivered by the collector field is insufficient to heat the entire storage to a temperature near that of the hot collector fluid and a significant loss in energy quality can occur in the storage subsystem. To avoid this, a two-tank storage system can be used as shown in **Figure 5.2**.

(i) Multitank Storage

The term "multitank storage," refers to the type of sensible-heat storage system illustrated in **Figure 5.2** except more than two tanks can be used. The logic that drives one to consider more than two tanks is that, as the number of tanks increases, the total tank volume decreases.

In a two tank system (**Figure 5.2**), each tank (either the hot or the cold tank) must have the capacity to hold all the fluid. Thus there must be twice as much tankage volume as fluid volume.

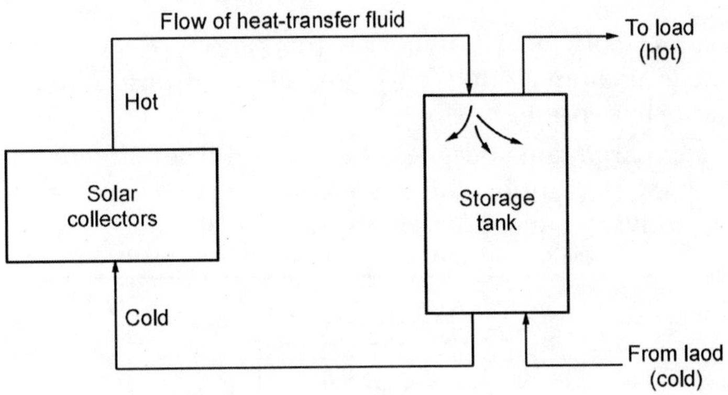

Fig. 5.1 *Single-tank sensible-heat storage*

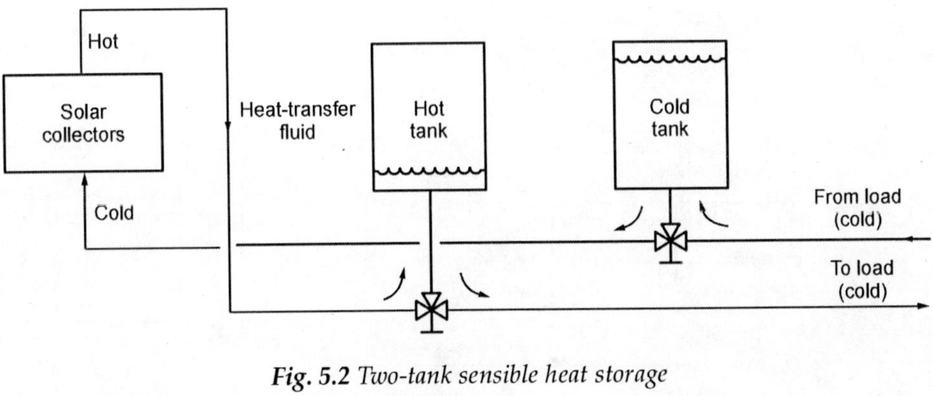

Fig. 5.2 *Two-tank sensible heat storage*

The basic operation of a three-tank system is outlined in Fig. 5.3. At the start of the day, if tanks 1 and 2 are full of cold fluid and tank 3 is empty, the storage of thermal energy from the collector field might proceed as in Fig. 5.3 (*a*). Cold fluid is withdrawn from tank 1, heated in the collector field and placed in tank 3, which is empty. At about midday (see Fig. 5.3 (*b*), tank 3 is full of hot fluid and tank 1 is empty. Cold fluid is then withdrawn from tank 2 and after heating is deposited in tank 1. At the end of the day, the fully charged multitank storage system would appear as in Fig. 5.3 (*c*).

The advantage of the three tank system over the two-tank system is less tank volume. Whereas a two-tank system requires only 1.5 times as much tank volume as fluid volume.

In practice, however, many factors contribute to limit the number of tanks. Such factors include:

Complexity of control: The complexity of controlling liquid levels and automatically switching tanks grows quickly as the number of tanks increases. The control strategy is especially complex on partially cloudy days.

Interconnecting plumbing: The provision of a piping network interconnecting many tanks and provision for automatic valving can become quite expensive.

Heat loss: Large tanks lose less heat per unit volume of hot fluid than do small tanks. In addition, the interconnecting piping network (especially the control valves) is a source of increased heat loss.

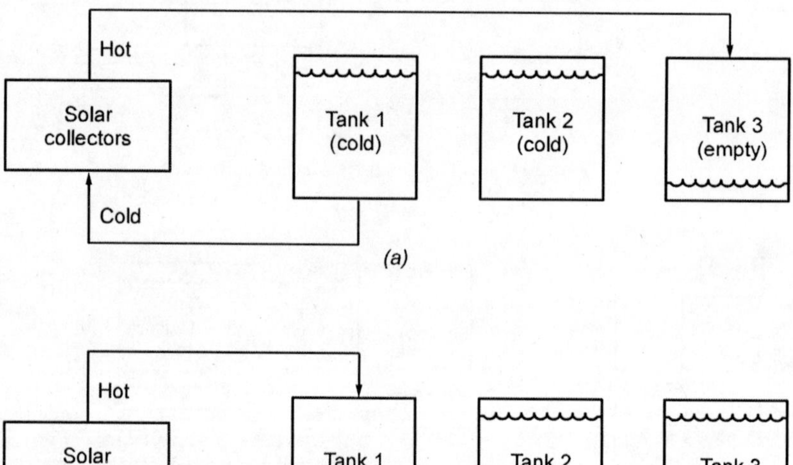

(*a*)

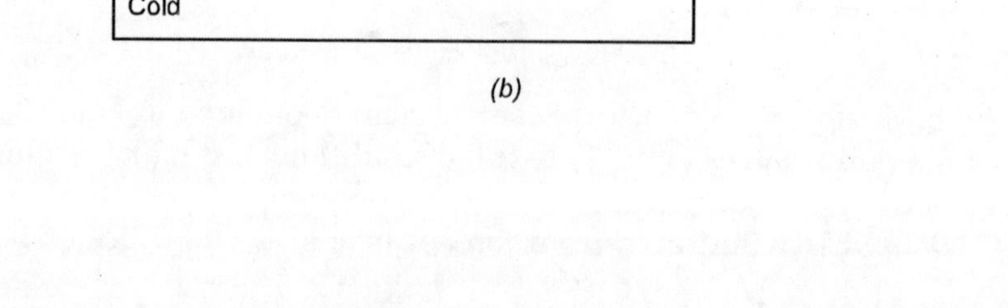

(*b*)

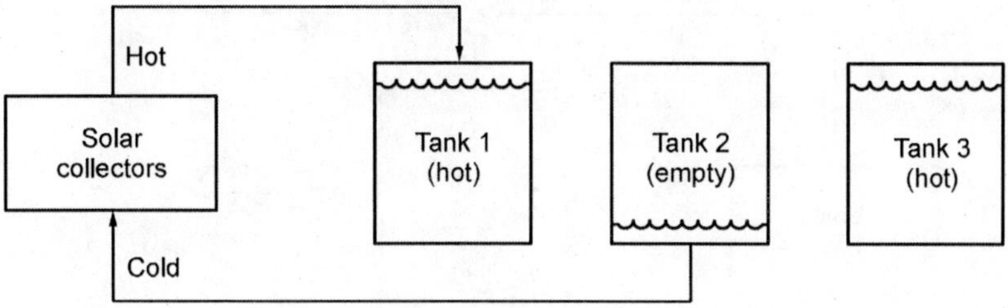

(c)

Fig. 5.3 *Three-tank sensible-heat storage operation: (a) startup; (b) midday; (c) end of day*

(ii) Thermocline Energy Storage

In a thermocline system both the hot and cold storage fluids occupy the same tank, thus storage tank volume is reduced. Conceptually, the operation of a thermocline sensible-heat storage system is illustrated in **Figure 5.4**

At the start of operation, the storage tank is full of cold fluid. As thermal energy, in the form of hot collector fluid, becomes available, cold storage fluid is withdrawn from the bottom of the storage tank and heated. The hot storage fluid is then put back into the top of the storage tank. If properly done, the less dense hot storage fluid will "float" on top of the cold storage fluid, creating what is termed a *thermocline.*

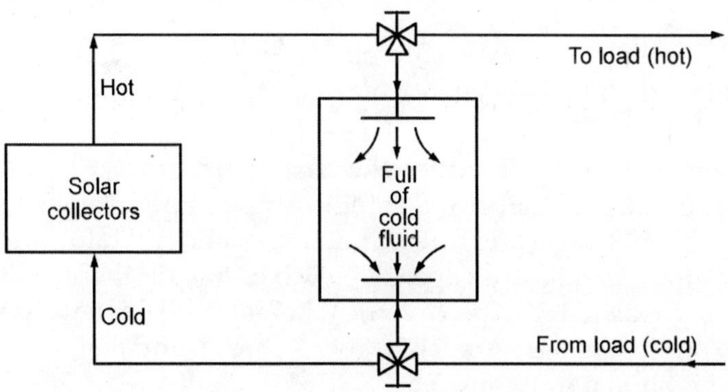

(a)

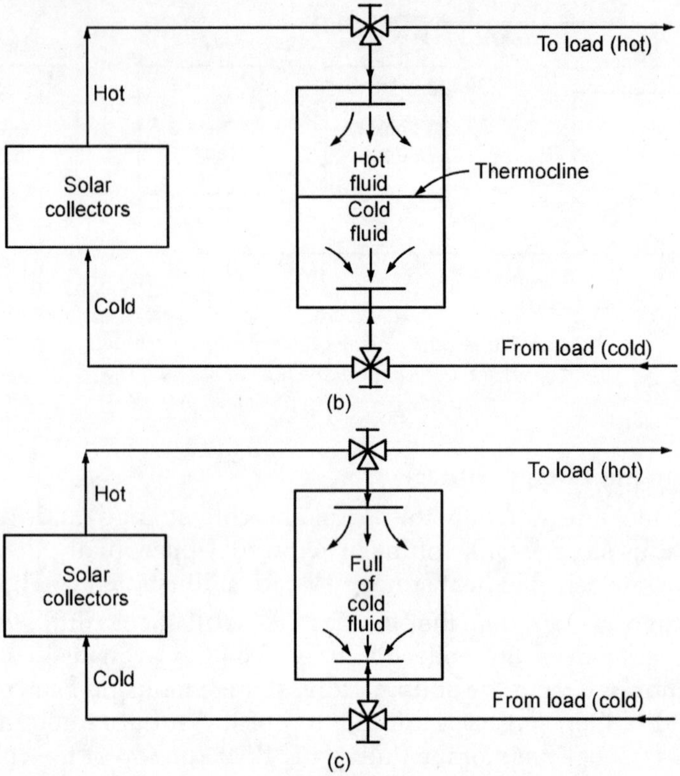

Fig. 5.4 Thermocline sensible-heat storage operation: (a) startup; (b) midday; (c) end of day

(iii) Mixed-Media Thermocline Storage

Once the tank volume has been reduced to a minimum through use of, for example, a thermocline system, the next step in reducing the capital cost of the storage system is to reduce the cost of the storage fluid. Organic heat-transfer oils are typically used in high-temperature solar energy systems to avoid the cost of high-pressure plumbing systems. Unfortunately, most organic heat-transfer oils are expensive. Mixed-media thermocline storage systems seek to displace expensive heat-transfer oil inventory in storage with less expensive materials such as rock. One example of a mixed-media thermocline is shown in **Figure 5.5.**

An important question in the design of a mixed-media storage system is the stability of the hot storage fluid in the presence of the rock.

A second question in the design of a mixed-media storage system is the strength of the tank with respect to so-called *thermal ratcheting.* As the tank heats up, its internal volume increases and the solid media settles. When the tank cools, stress builds up at the bottom of the tank as the solid media is compressed. Thus careful consideration must be paid to the tank design to prevent tank rupture due to these stresses.

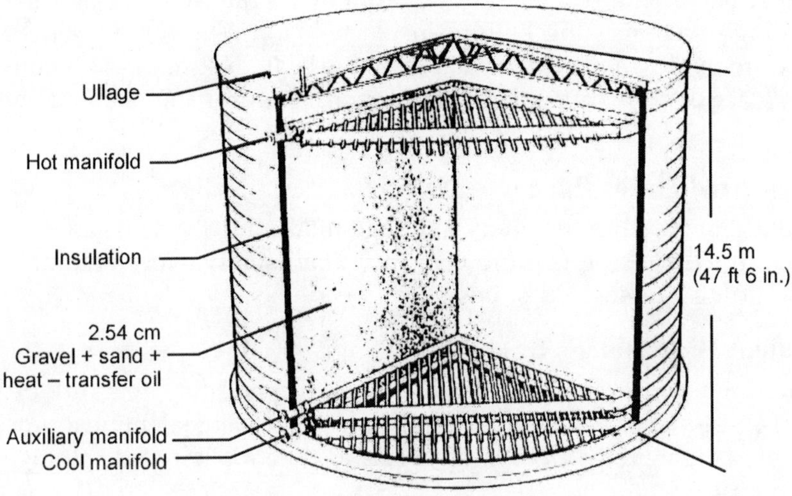

Fig. 5.5 Mixed-media thermal storage unit, central receiver installation at Barstow, CA

(iv) High-Temperature Sensible Heat Storage

The ability to store high temperature thermal energy is basically limited by the availability of heat-transfer fluids. Above about 400°C (752°F), most organic heat-transfer fluids tend to thermally decompose. For electric power generation and other high-temperature applications, therefore, fluids such as molten salts, liquid metals, and air (with air-rock storage medium) are typically considered.

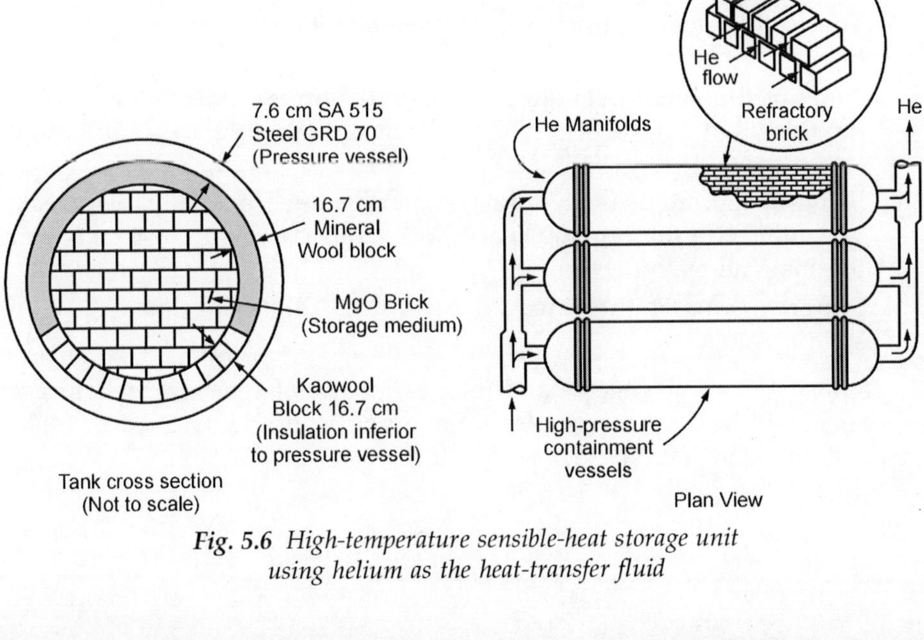

Fig. 5.6 High-temperature sensible-heat storage unit using helium as the heat-transfer fluid

Figure 5.6 illustrates a conceptual design for a high-temperature sensible heat storage system using helium in place of air. The hot gas flows over magnesium oxide (MgO) bricks that store the heat. Helium gas is commonly used in place of air because of the rather poor heat-transfer characteristics of air.

(i) Pressurized Fluids (Steam or Water)

The use of water or steam as a storage medium represents another way in which to reduce storage fluid costs but it is usually overwhelmed by the expense of the pressurized storage tank needed.

5.4.2 Latent Heat Storage Systems

One limitation of a sensible-heat system is that the capability of most materials to store heat sensibly is small. By comparison, latent heat processes can provide high energy density storage and potentially reduce storage tank size and cost.

A "latent heat storage system" refers to a storage system in which the energy is stored or released during the freeze - thaw cycle of a material. As an example of a latent heat process, consider the melting of sodium hydroxide (NaOH). The latent heat of fusion (melting) of NaOH is 156 kJ/kg (68 Btu/1b). This means that when 1 kg of NaOH melts, 156 kJ of thermal energy is absorbed.

Latent heat storage systems require heat exchanger within the storage system. Thus results in increased system costs compared to systems that use sensible heat storage.

Other characteristics that adversely affect design of a latent heat storage system include :

1. The cost of many of the more effective latent heat storage materials is high.
2. Some of the latent heat storage materials are not pure materials but mixtures that tend to separate into their component parts on repeated freeze-thaw cycling.
3. Some of the latent heat storage materials such as NaOH can react violently with the organic heat-transfer oils commonly used in solar thermal energy collectors.
4. Supercooling of the latent heat storage material can occur on solidification.

Because of these problems and the availability of sensible heat storage systems, latent heat storage systems have not been widely used in high-temperature solar thermal energy systems.

(i) Storage In Phase Change Materials (PCM)

Phase change materials (PCMs) are "latent" thermal storage materials. They use chemical bonds to store and release heat. The thermal energy transfer occurs when a material changes from a solid to a liquid or from a liquid to a solid. This is called a change in state, or "phase." Initially, these solid-liquid PCMs perform like conventional storage materials; their temperature rises as they absorb solar heat. Unlike conventional (sensible) storage materials, when PCMs reach the temperature at which they change phase (their melting point) they absorb large amounts of heat without getting hotter. When the ambient temperature in the space around the PCM material drops, the PCM solidifies, releasing its stored latent heat.

Types of PCMS

The PCMs fall in three categories:

- Salt hydrates
- Paraffins
- Non paraffin organics

Salt Hydrates

Salt hydrates are characterized by $X(Y)_n.m\ H_2O$, where $X(Y)_n$ is an inorganic compound. These materials are preferred because of their high latent heat storage density. Salt hydrates such as sodium sulphate decahydrate and calcium chloride hexahydrate have suitable phase change temperatures for use as storage in space heating systems. These have the advantage of larger energy density.

Paraffins

Paraffins qualify as heat-of-fusion storage materials due to their availability in large temperature range and their reasonably high heat of fusion. Paraffins like other mineral oil products are complicated mixtures of several organic compounds and contain one major component called alkanes. The desirable characteristics that make them suitable to be used as PCMs are:

- Congruent melting
- Good nucleating properties

Non-Paraffin Organic Solids

This is the largest category of candidate materials for phase change storage. Some features of these organic materials are :

- High heat of fusion
- Inflammability
- Low thermal conductivity
- Varying levels of toxicity
- Instability at high temperatures
- Low flash points

Inorganic Compounds And Eutectics

Apart from many inorganic salt hydrates there are many inorganic compounds, which undergo solid liquid phase transformation with high latent heat of fusion at higher temperature. Also apart from the pure compounds, eutectics of organic or inorganic compounds can be used to obtain the desired melting point .It is possible to get a fixed melting or freezing point eutectic mixture of inorganic salts.

Heat Storage Capacities

Non paraffin organics 125-200 kJ/dm^3

Salt hydrates 250 -400 kJ/dm^3

5.4.3 Thermochemical Energy Storage

A thermochemical energy storage system is one in which thermal energy is used to rupture chemical bonds in a reversible fashion. The rupture of the chemical bond requires large quantities of energy input, thus resulting in thermal energy storage. The product or products of the thermochemical reaction are typically unreactive at ambient temperatures. At elevated temperatures the energy storing reaction reverses, forming the original chemical system with the release of heat.

An example of such a reversible energy storage system is the thermal dissociation of water. At temperatures in excess of 2000°C (3632°F), water begins to dissociate into hydrogen and oxygen :

$$2H_2O + \text{thermal energy} = 2H_2 + O_2 \quad ...(5.5)$$

The reverse reaction,

$$2H_2 + O_2 = 2H_2O + \text{thermal energy} \quad ...(5.6)$$

will not proceed at low temperatures without a catalyst. Thus a mixture of hydrogen and oxygen in a jar at room temperature will not react. If the mixture of hydrogen and oxygen is heated (e.g., if a match were placed in the jar), however, the reaction proceeds explosively.

The advantages of thermochemical energy storage systems:

1. Chemical reactions are typically very energetic, thus allowing large quantities of energy to be stored in small quantities of material.
2. The reverse, the energy-releasing chemical reaction, seldom proceeds at room temperature. Thus the energy can be stored indefinitely, without energy loss, at ambient temperatures.
3. Because of very high energy density and stability at low temperatures of some thermochemical energy storage systems, the stored thermal energy can be transported. An extreme case of transportability is the formation of a chemical fuel, such as hydrogen, which can be piped around the country and then burned (i.e., reacted with oxygen) to provide thermal energy.

5.5 DESIGN CONSIDERATIONS

Some of the considerations, which determine the selection of the method of storage and its design, are as follows :

1. The temperature range, over which the storage has to operate.
2. The capacity of the storage has a significant effect on the operation of the rest of the system. A smaller storage unit operates at a higher mean temperature. This results in a reduced heat transfer equipment output as compared to a system having a larger storage unit.
3. Heat losses from the storage have to be kept to a minimum. Heat losses are particularly important for long-term storage.
4. The rate of charging and discharging.
5. Cost of the storage unit: This includes the initial cost of the storage medium, the containers and insulation, and the operating cost.

A figure of merit that is used occasionally for describing the performance of a storage unit is the storage efficiency, which is defined by equation as:

$$\eta = \frac{mC(T - To)}{mC(T\infty - To)} \qquad ...(5.7)$$

where mC is the total heat capacity of the storage medium and T , To are the maximum and minimum temperatures of the storage during discharging respectively, and $T\infty$, is the maximum temperature at the end of the charging period. Heat losses to environment between the end of discharging and the beginning of the charging periods, as well as during these processes are neglected. The first law efficiency can have only values less than one.

The time period over which this ratio is calculated would depend upon the nature of the storage unit. For a short-term storage unit, the time period would be a few days, while for a long-term storage unit it could be a few months or even one year.

5.6 SOLAR POND

A solar pond is a large-area collector of solar energy resembling a pond that stores heat, which is then available to use for practical purposes. It stores the energy in the incoming solar radiation in the heated depths of the pond, and suppresses the convection currents that would otherwise lead to heat loss to the surroundings.

Solar ponds are an alternative source of harnessing the suns energy to heat water that can be converted to electricity. This technology is very basic and easy to use with adequate land space and proper design. For residential use, ponds need to be at least 12x12 feet and 3 feet deep and for commercial use ponds must be sized according to their functionality. Solar ponds require lots of sunlight and salt water.

Working of Solar Pond:

Solar ponds can be naturally occurring; however, most ponds are man-made. Once the pond is dug, the pond must be lined with an impermeable lining, preferable one that is insulating. Then the pond is filled with salty water. Once the sun hits the pond the water warms and divides into three layers. The top layer, known as the surface zone, is composed of primarily freshwater due to the fact that salt typically settles at the bottom of water. The middle layer is known as the insulation zone. The insulation zone has a higher salt concentration than the surface zone. Crucial to a solar pond is the bottom layer known as the storage zone. The storage zone is where all the hot water is held and this is what is converted into electricity. The hot salt water produced is similar in chemical characteristics to brine.

In a typical freshwater pond, when the sun penetrates the water the layers that are heated up rise to the top of the pond and release the heat into the atmosphere. This is how a pond maintains a constant temperate. The oxygen in warm water is greater than cold water. This causes warm water to rise to the top of the water body and this heat is then released.

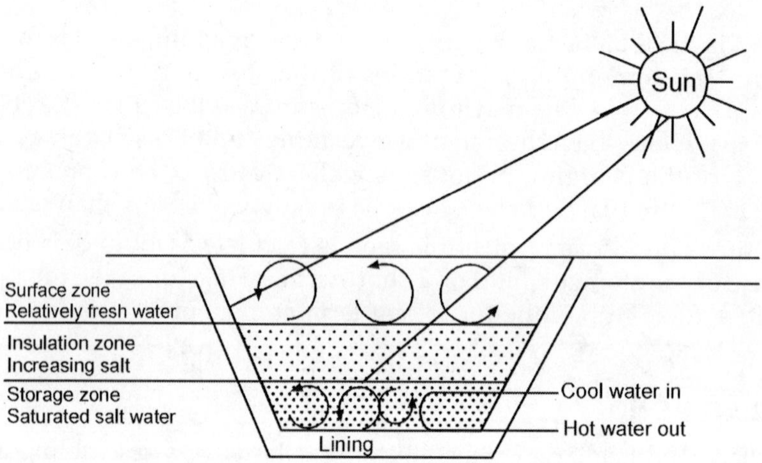

Fig. 5.7 Diagram of differents layers of solar pond

However, in a solar pond this process does not happen. Instead the water that is warmed is unable to rise to the top due to the salt concentration. Therefore, the warm water stays at the bottom of a pond and gets hotter and hotter with the more sunlight it receives. The bottom layer of a solar pond can reach 178 degrees Fahrenheit.

Solar pond can be used as an energy source as a pipe is placed at the bottom of the pond and draws the warm/ hot water out of the pond by a pump and is circulated through a piping system that utilizes the heat. It is similar to how radiant heat, or solar hot water heaters use the warm water. Once the water has run through the pipe it is deposited back into the pond in the storage zone so this water can be heated again. This system is a close system so is quite efficient in terms of water retention. Typically this is how a solar pond is used for heating purposes.

Solar ponds can be used in all climates as Long as there is plenty of sun. Even when a pond is frozen over, a salient gradient solar pond still produces hot water.

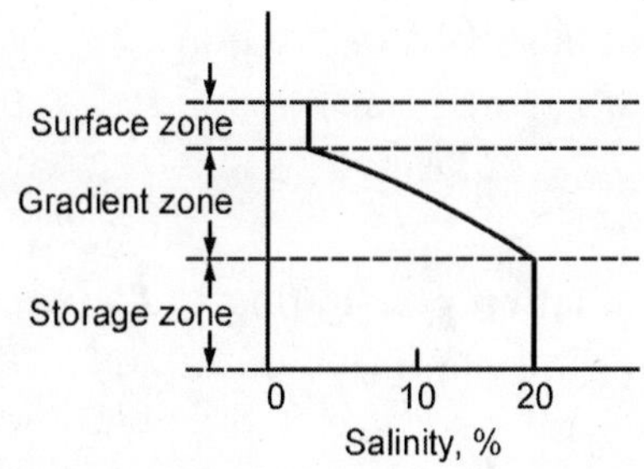

Fig. 5.8 *Salinity profile in a solar pond*

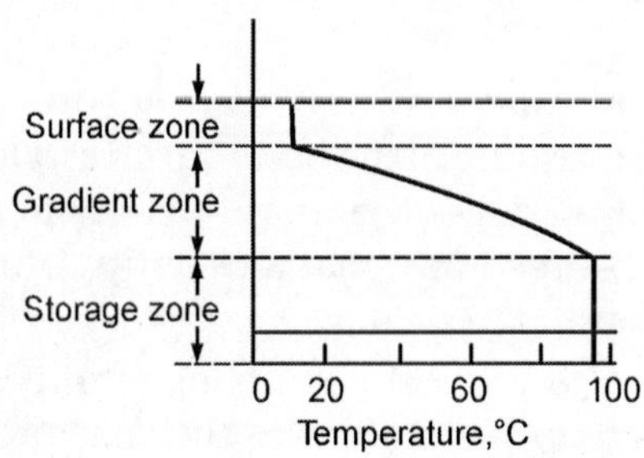

Fig. 5.9 *Temperature profile in a solar pond*

Benefits of a solar pond

(i) A solar pond produces heat or electricity with little to no carbon emissions.

(ii) For desalinization, no energy is required to produce potable water; instead the clean water is a result of the separation of water according to salt concentration.

(iii) Solar ponds are not only an effective way for producing solar heat for industrial processes, but also quite cost effective:

5.6.1 Temperatures and Efficiencies of Solar Ponds

If the width and length of a solar pond are sufficiently large with respect to its depth, then the temperature in the non-convecting zone of the solar pond in one dimensional form can be written as:

$$\frac{\delta}{\delta z}\left(K\frac{\delta T}{\delta z}\right) = \rho c\frac{\delta T}{\delta z} - H(z,t) \qquad ...(5.8)$$

where K = thermal conductivity,

c = heat capacity,

ρ = density,

$H(z, t)$ = heat absorbed in the pond

= heat absorbed in the pond

$= -\frac{dl}{dz}$

$l(z, t)$ = irradiation penetrating to the depth z in the pond.

Equation is subject to boundary conditions at the surface of the pond and the pond bottom. At the surface of the pond, heat gets exchanged with the atmosphere due to convection, evaporation, and long wave surface radiation. The accurate calculation of the heat transfer from a pond's surface is a difficult problem.

For the purpose of analysis it is sufficient to assume, as a boundary condition, that the temperature of the pond surface follows closely the ambient temperature. The boundary condition at the bottom of the pond is that the irradiation $I(z, t)$ is absorbed and that a quantity $U(h, t)$ of heat is extracted from the pond's bottom.

Parameters K, ρ, and c are functions of salinity and temperature and, consequently, a function of depth. The thermal properties of the ground beneath the pond can be considerably different from the thermal properties of the saline solution.

5.6.2 Applications of Solar Pond

1. **Process heat** : Studies have indicated that there is excellent scope for process heat applications (i.e. water heated to 80 to 90 deg. C.), when a large quantity of hot water is required, such as textile processing and dairy industries. Hot air for industrial uses such as drying agricultural produce, timber, fish and chemicals and space heating are other possible applications.
2. **Desalination :** Drinking water is a chronic problem for many villages in India. In remote coastal villages where seawater is available, solar ponds can provide a cost-effective solution to the potable drinking water problem. Desalination costs in these places work out to be 7.5 paise per litre, which compares favourably with the current costs incurred in the reverse osmosis or electrodialysis/desalination process.
3. **Refrigeration** : Refrigeration applications have a tremendous scope in a tropical country like India. Perishable products like agricultural

produce and life saving drugs like vaccines can be preserved for long stretches of time in cold storage using *solar pond* technology in conjunction with ammonia based absorption refrigeration system.

5.6.3 Solar Pond Electric Power Plant

A solar pond electric power plant is shown in Fig. 5.13. The solar pond serves the purpose of a large flat plate collector as well as thermal storage. In a large area brine pond approximately 1 m deep, vertical gradient of salt concentration is maintained such that most concentrated and dense solutions are at the bottom. Solar radiation penetrates through water up to the backened bottom, where it gets absorbed and increases the temperature near bottom. In spite of the temperature rise of the bottom layers of the brine, its specific gravity remains higher than that at the top because of concentration gradient and thus, convection mixing is minimized. The bottom layers of the brine reach 70-80°C, while the top remains at 25°C. The hot brine from the bottom is slowly withdrawn in a laminar flow pattern from the pond and used to evaporate an organic working fluid in a heat exchanger and returned to the pond. The organic working fluid produces mechanical power in a Rankine cycle, which in turn generates electrical power using alternator. A 2,000 sq. m solar pond equipped with a 20 kW turbine has been constructed in Australia.

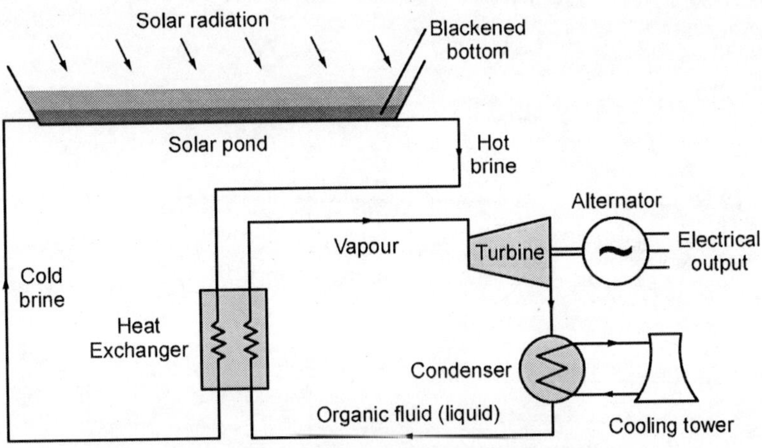

Fig. 5.10 Solar pond electric power plant

REVIEW QUESTIONS

1. What is a thermal energy? What are the benefits of thermal energy storage?
2. What are the different methods of thermal energy storage? Explain them.
3. Explain the sensible heat storage system in detail
4. How PCMs are used to store thermal energy of solar power? Explain.
5. Explain thermo chemical energy storage systems in detail.
6. What are the various considerations which determine the selection of the method of storage and its design? Explain.

7. What is a solar pond? How they are used to store solar energy? Explain.
8. What are the various applications of solar pond?
9. Explain the solar pond electrical power plant.
10. Discuss the solar energy storage in a fully stratified water tank.
11. What is the problem with salt hydrates for solar energy storage?
12. Explain the principle of solar pond.

❑❑❑

6

Solar Thermal Power

6.1. INTRODUCTION

Solar thermal power generation systems also known as Solar Thermal Electricity (STE) generating systems are emerging renewable energy technologies and can be developed as viable option for electricity generation in future.

In solar thermal power plants the incoming radiation is tracked by large mirror fields which concentrate the energy towards absorbers. They, in turn, receive the concentrated radiation and transfer it thermally to the working medium. The heated fluid operates as in conventional power stations directly (if steam or air is used as medium) or indirectly through a heat exchanging steam generator on the turbine unit which then drives the generator.

To make solar high flux, with high equivalent temperatures of approximately 5800 K usable for technical processes and commercial applications, different concentrating technologies have been developed. Such solar thermal concentrating systems will undoubtedly provide within the next decade a significant contribution to efficient and economical, renewable and clean energy supply.

6.2. SOLAR THERMAL POWER GENERATION TECHNOLOGIES

Solar Thermal Power systems, also known as Concentrating Solar Power systems, use concentrated solar radiation as a high temperature energy source to produce electricity using thermal route. Since the average operating temperature of stationary non-concentrating collectors is low (max up to 120°C) as compared to the desirable input temperatures of heat engines (above 300°C), the concentrating collectors are used for such applications. These technologies are appropriate for applications where direct solar radiation is high. The mechanism of conversion of solar to electricity is fundamentally similar to the traditional thermal power plants except use of solar energy as source of heat.

There are four recognized CST system designs for converting the sun's thermal energy into utility-scale or grid-quality electrical power.

1. Parabolic trough mirror solar thermal plants (trough mirror)
2. Power-tower solar thermal plants (power tower)
3. Linear Fresnel reflector solar thermal plants (Fresnel reflector)
4. Parabolic dish Stirling solar thermal plants (dish Stirling)

6.2.1. Parabolic Trough Mirror Solar Thermal (CST) Plants

The parabolic trough mirror solar thermal plant (Fig. 6.1) is one of three CST systems requiring many acres of movable linear parabolic mirrors to produce grid-compatible power. Each installation has thousands of feet of mirrors shaped as parabolic troughs or flat plates, both arranged in straight parallel rows. The parabolic mirrors are contoured to permit them to focus solar thermal radiation on thousands of feet of black-painted steel pipe located in front of them.

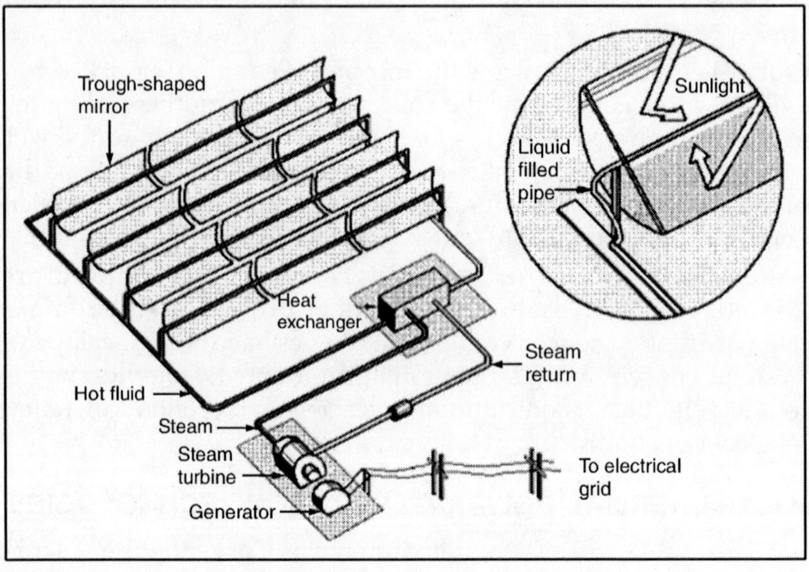

Fig. 6.1 Parabolic Trough Mirror Solar Thermal Power Plant

Heat-absorbing mineral oil in the pipes acts as the intermediate heat transfer medium in an extensive closed-loop plumbing system. The pipes, positioned at the focal points of all of the mirrors, gather heat which is then delivered to a common heat exchanger. Solar radiation can keep the circulating oil at 750°F (400°C) over thousands of feet before it reaches the heat exchanger where its heat is transferred to a separate hot-water plumbing system. The water in that system is converted to steam, which spins a turbine to drive an electric generator. After the steam is condensed to water, it is returned to the heat exchanger.

Each of these mirror sections is continuously repositioned on its yaw (vertical) axis by computer control to keep the sunlight focused on the pipe sections during daylight hours.

6.2.2. Power-Tower Solar Thermal (CST) Plants

The power-tower solar thermal power plant (Fig. 6.2) is an alternative design for a CST plant. It uses large arrays of flat rectangular mirrors or heliostats to track the sun throughout the day. Each mirror or heliostat is individually moved around both its pitch or lateral axis and its yaw or vertical axis under computer control to keep the sun's thermal radiation focused on a *receiver* or steam boiler positioned on top of a tower designed to be tall enough to receive the reflections from even the most distant heliostats thousands of feet away from it. As in trough mirror systems, all power-tower heliostats are aligned along the east-west axis.

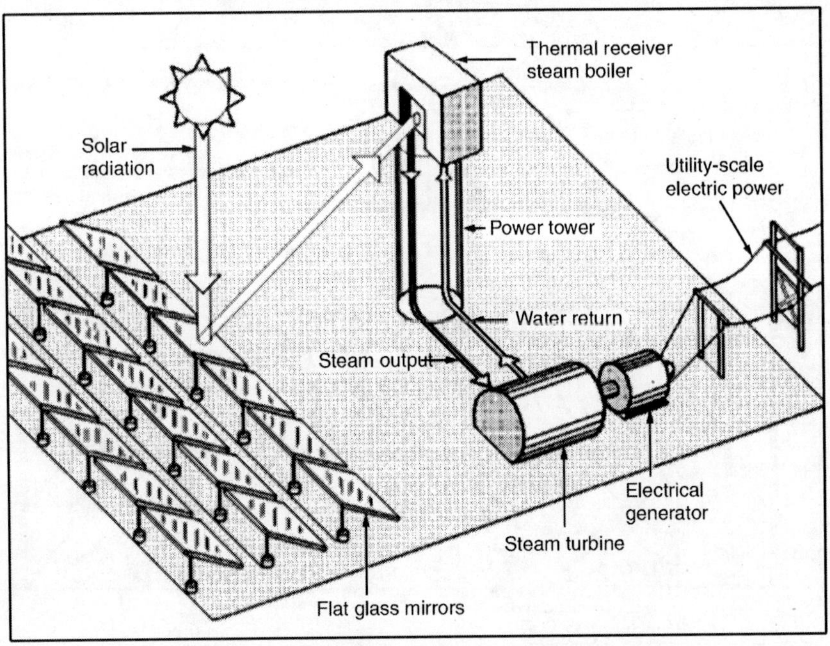

Fig. 6.2 Power Tower Solar Thermal Power Plant

Water circulating in pipes within the receiver at top of the tower is converted directly into steam by the high temperature of the solar heat concentrated on it from the thousands of heliostats. This steam is piped down to the ground and sent thousands of feet to a common turbine which, in turn, drives a generator capable of producing utility-grade, grid-compatible electric power. The steam from the turbine is condensed back to water, which is then pumped back up to the receiver on the tower to maintain a continuous flow of steam to keep the process operational during daylight hours.

The mirrors or heliostats for this technology are smaller than those used in other CST installations; they measure only about 10 ft^2 (1 m^2). Their lower profile and smaller size make them easier to install and maintain.

The power-tower system is considered to be more cost-effective than the parabolic trough system because water is the only heat transfer medium being used.

6.2.3. Linear Fresnel Reflector Thermal (CST) Plants

A linear Fresnel reflector (LFR) plant (Fig. 6.3) is a CST facility consisting of an array of long, narrow mirrors, typically curved, to reflect solar radiation onto steam-filled miled steel pipes mounted on 50 ft (15 m) high posts above the mirrors. These pipes, called linear receivers or absorbers, are heated by solar radiation reflected from the mirrors below them and convey the hot water and steam mixtures to a heat exchanger where the steam drives a turbine generator to produce utility-grade electric power as in the other CST systems.

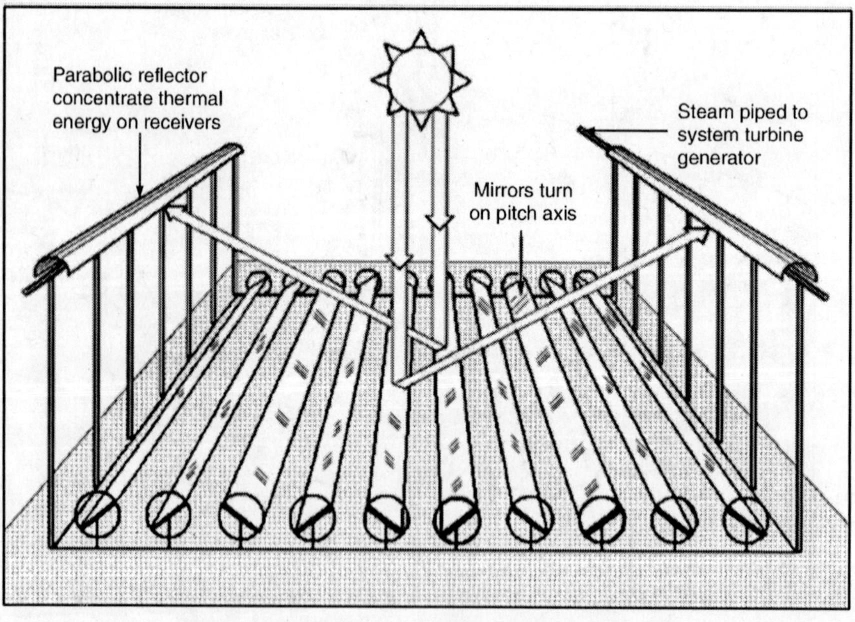

Fig.6.3 Linear Fresnel Reflector Thermal Plant

The slightly curved mirrors, laminated with a composite metal backing, will be arranged in three 200 m segments. Each LFR mirror segment will be rotated by a single motor and gearbox around its pitch or lateral axis. As in other CST systems, mirrors and receiver pipes will be oriented along the east-west direction.

As in the power tower systems, LFR systems use only fresh water as the heat transfer medium, eliminating the cost of an intermediate heat transfer fluid. Because their mirror mounting frames do not have to support the receiver pipes, they can be lighter, simpler, and closer to the ground.

6.2.4 Parabolic Dish Stirling Solar Thermal Power (CST) Plant

The parabolic dish system uses a parabolic dish shaped mirror or a modular mirror system that approximates a parabola and incorporates two-axis tracking to focus the sunlight onto receivers located at the focal point of the dish, which absorbs the energy and converts it into thermal energy. This can be used directly as heat for thermal application or for power generation. The thermal energy can either be transported to a central generator for conversion, or it can be converted directly into electricity at a local generator coupled to the receiver (Figure 6.4).

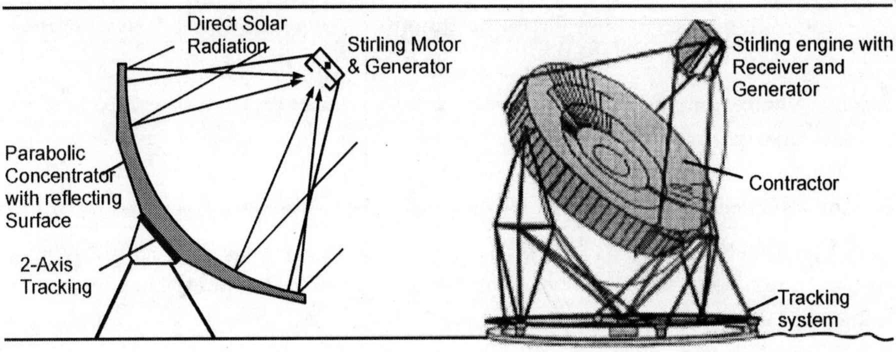

Fig. 6.4. Schematic of Parabolic Dish Solar Thermal Power Plant

The mirror system typically is made from a number of mirror facets, either glass or polymer mirror, or can consist of a single stretched membrane using a polymer mirror of thin metal stretched membrane.

The parabolic dish collector track the sun on two axes, and thus they are the most efficient collector systems. Their concentration ratios usually range from 600 to 2000, and they can achieve temperatures in excess of 1500°C.

A major benefit of parabolic dish/engine systems is that they have a hybrid capability in that the Brayton cycle can get its heat from either the concentration of solar energy from the parabolic dish or from a combustion chamber within the Brayton cycle burning a fossil fuel, such as natural gas. Depending on the availability of sunlight, the parabolic dish/engine system has a very high reliability as a power source, since it can produce power using two types of fuels almost directly eliminating the need for a second entire separate cycle for generating power.

Unlike parabolic trough systems or power towers, parabolic dish arrangements are not able to produce large-scale power needs and are intended for small power generation in the range of kilowatts of power instead of the megawatts of power produced by the other two systems. Parabolic dish/engine system also can have high operations and maintenance costs, since moving parts are needed for the two-axis tracking of the dish and in the Brayton cycle for producing the electricity, a turbine and compressor are needed.

6.2.5 Comparison Between Different Types

Table 6.1 below shows a comparison between the three major types of solar thermal electric power plants. Both the power tower and parabolic trough systems are used for large grid-connected utility power project on the scale of tens to hundreds of megawatts, while the parabolic dish systems are used on a much smaller scale for small villages or remote applications on the scale of tens of kilowatts.

Table 6.1 : Characteristics of solar thermal electric power system

	Parabolic Trough	Power Tower	Dish/Engine
Size	30-320 MW*	10-200 MW*	5-25*
Operating Temperature (°C/°F)	390/734	565/1,049	750/1,382
Annual Capacity Factor	23-50%*	20-77%*	25%
Peak Efficiency	20%(d)	23%(p)	29.4%(d)
Net Annual Efficiency	11(d')-16%	7(d')-16%	12-25%(p)
Commercial Status	Commercially Available	Scale-up Demonstration	Prototype Demonstration
Technology Development Risk	Low	Medium	High
Storage Available	Limited	Yes	Battery
Hybrid Designs	Yes	Yes	Yes
Cost			
$\$/m^2$	630-275*	475-200*	3,100-320*
\$/W	4.0-2.7*	4.4-2.5*	12.6-1.3*
$\$/W_p{}^?$	4.0-1.3*	2.4-0.9*	12.6-1.1*

* Values indicated changes over the 1997-2030 time frame.

? $\$/W_p$ removes the effect of thermal storage (or hybridization for dish/engine).

(p) = predicted; (d) = demonstrated; (d') = has been demonstrated, out years are predicted values.

6.3 AREAS OF OPERATION

The areas where photovoltaic systems and solar thermal power plants can operate overlap only in a narrow range (Figure 6.5).

Due to their modularity, photovoltaic operation covers a wide range from less than one Watt to several megawatts. Solar thermal power plants can work in both areas as well. Dish/Stirling systems are small units in the kilowatt range. The parabolic trough and solar tower power plants operate only in the megawatt range.

Global solar irradiance consists of direct and diffuse irradiance. When skies are overcast, only diffuse irradiance is available. While solar thermal power plants can only use direct irradiance for power generation, photovoltaic systems can convert the diffuse irradiance as well. That means, they can produce some electricity even with cloud-covered skies.

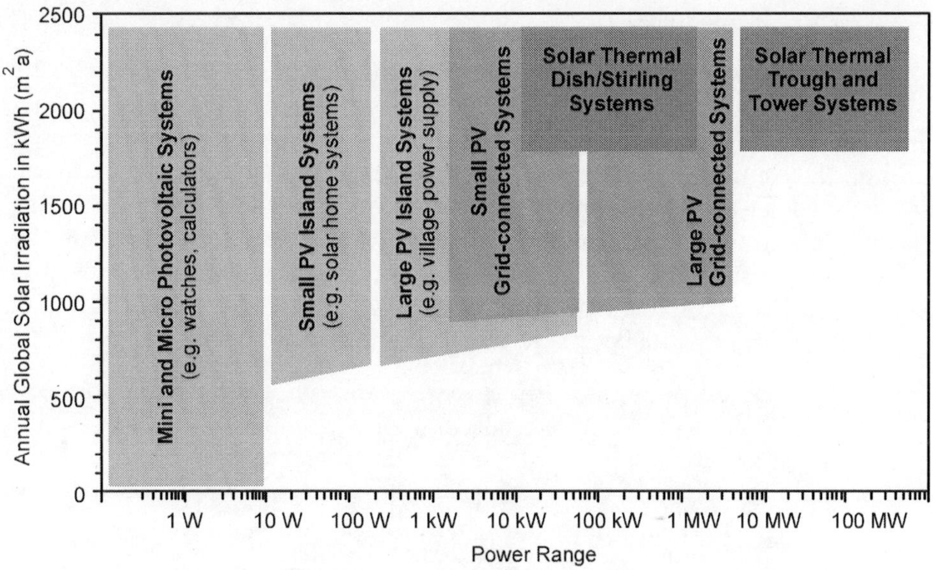

Figure 6.5: Operational areas for solar thermal power plants and photovoltaic systems depending on the installed capacity and the annual global solar irradiation

6.4 OPPORTUNITIES IN INDIA

Solar thermal power generation can play a significant important role in meeting the demand supply gap for electricity. Three types of applications are possible:

1. Rural electrification using solar dish collector technology. Typically these dishes are of 10 to 25 kW capacity each and use stirling engine for power generation. These can be developed for village level distributed generation by hybridizing them with biomass gasifier for hot air generation.
2. Integration of solar thermal power plants with existing industries such as paper, dairy or sugar industry, which has cogeneration units. Many

industries have steam turbine sets for cogeneration. These can be coupled with solar thermal power plants. Typically these units are of 5 to 250 MW capacities and can be coupled with solar thermal power plants. This approach will reduce the capital investment on steam turbines and associated power-house infrastructure thus reducing the cost of generation of solar electricity.

3. Integration of solar thermal power generation unit with existing coal thermal power plants. The study shows that savings of upto 24% is possible during periods of high insolation for feed water heating to 241 ^{0}C.

6.5. SOLAR CHIMNEY

This is a fairly simple concept. The solar chimney has a tall chimney at the center of the field, which is covered with glass. The solar heat generates hot air in the gap between the ground and the wall cover which is then passed through the central tower to its upper end due to density difference between relatively cooler air outside the upper end of the tower and hotter air inside tower. While traveling up this air drives wind turbines located inside the tower. These systems need relatively less components and were supposed to be cheaper. However, low operating efficiency, and need for a tall tower of height of the order of 1000m made this technology a challenging one.

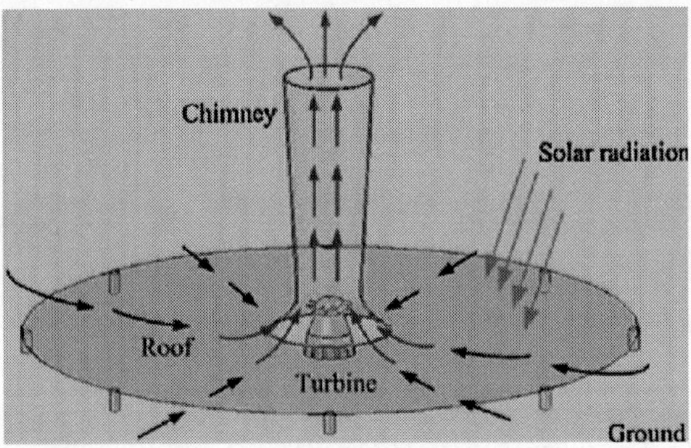

Figure 6.6: Principle of Solar Chimney

6.6 SOLAR COOKERS

A solar cooker is a device which uses solar energy for cooking food. Cooking with solar cookers is an energy efficient, pollution free way to help fight global warming and take advantage of nature's free, inexaustible energy supply. It is a simplest, safest, most convenient way to cook food without consuming fuels.

6.6.1 Types of Solar Cooker

1. BOX TYPE SOLAR COOKER

This type of solar cooker, consists of a well insulated box, the inside of which is painted dull black and is covered by one or more transparent covers. The purpose of these transparent covers is to trap heat inside the solar cooker. These covers allow the radiation from, the sun to come inside but do not allow the heat from the absorbing plate to come out of the box. Because of this the temperature of the blackened plate inside the box increases and can heat up the space inside to temperature up to 140°C which is adequate for cooking. The box type solar cooker is illustrated in Fig. 6.7. The important parts of a simple box type solar cooker are:

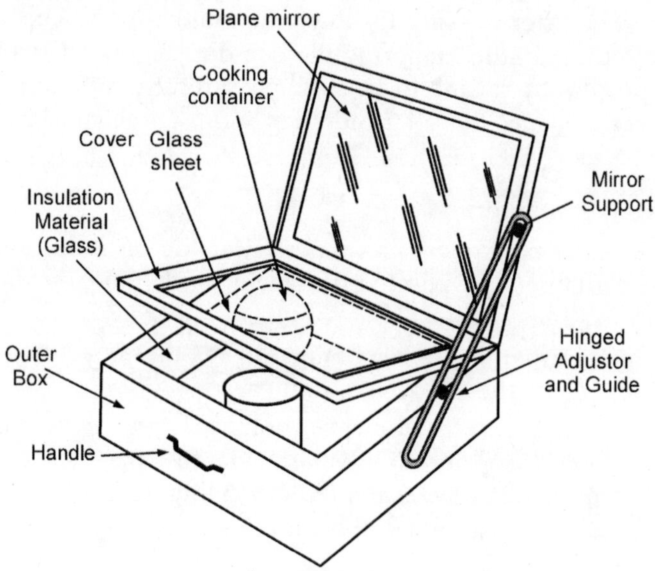

Fig. 6.7 Schematic view of box type solar cooker.

(1) Outer box

The outer box of a solar cooker may be made of wood, iron sheet or fiber reinforced plastic with suitable dimensions.

(2) Inner box

The Inner box can be made from galvanized iron or mild steel or aluminium sheet. All four sides and the bottom of the inner box which are exposed to the sun are coated with black paint which absorbs solar radiation.

(3) Thermal insulation

The space between the outer box and the inner box is filled with insulating material such as glass wool, etc. This prevents heat losses from the cookers.

(4) Double glazing

Generally a double glass cover is provided for a solar cooker. These covers have length and breadth slightly greater than the inner box and can be fixed in a wooden frame maintaining a small spacing between the two glasses. This space contains air which acts as an insulator and prevents heat escaping from inside. The wooden frame is attached to the outer box by means of hinges. A rubber strip is affixed all around on the edges of this frame to prevent any heat leakage.

(5) Mirror

A mirror is used in a solar cooker to increase the radiation input on the absorbing surface. Sunlight incident on the mirror gets reflected from it and enters the box after passing through the glass covers. This radiation is in addition to the radiation entering the box directly and helps to quicken the cooking process by raising the inside temperature of the cooker. The use of a mirror can enhance the solar radiation input to the cooker by about 50 per cent.

(6) Cooking containers

The cooking containers are generally made of aluminium or stainless steel. The containers are painted dull black on the outer surface so that they also absorb radiation directly.

Maximum air temperature obtained inside the cooker box (without load) is 140oC in winter and 160oC in summer.

It is an ideal device for domestic cooking during most of the year, except for the monsoon season and cloudy days. A family size solar cooker is sufficient for 4 to 5 members and saves about 3 to 4 cylinders of LPG every year, while the life of this cooker is 10 to 20 years.

2. PARABOLIC DISH SOLAR COOKER

These solar cookers are the concentrating devices with a dish type reflector directing most of the intercepted solar radiation to the point focus. A typical dish solar cooker has an aperture diameter of 1.4 meter and focal length 0.28 meter. The cooking utensil is supported at its focal point. The temperature of the focal point vary between 150oC to 400oC depending upon the solar irradiance conditions and the load. The temperature achieved at the bottom of the vessel could be around 350 to 400oC which is sufficient for roasting, frying and boiling.

The solar cooker requires frequent orientation towards the sun, thus tracking of the cooker has to be adjusted in 15 to 20 minutes during cooking time. The cooker having a thermal efficiency of around 40% can meet the needs of 10 to 15 people and can save upto 10 LPG cylinders per year on full use at small establishments. It can be used from one hour after sunrise to one hour before sunset on clear days.

The paraboloid concentrator solar cooker works based on collection of only beam (direct) component of the solar radiation since it is only the direct solar rays which can be reflected from focal point.

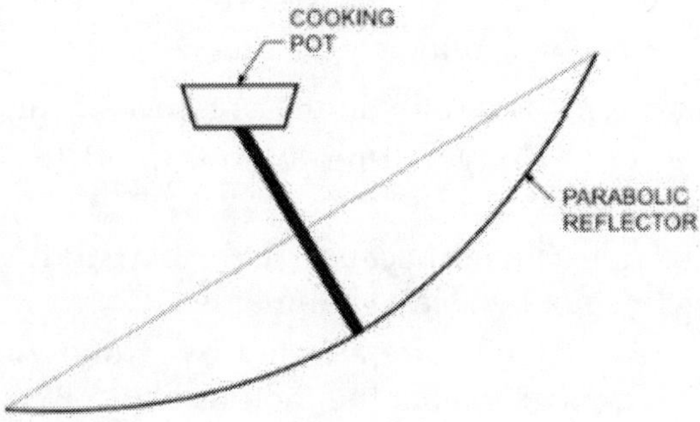

Fig. 6.8 Parabolic Dish Solar Cooker

3. PANEL TYPE SOLAR COOKER

A panel-type solar cooker is a very simple and inexpensive form of solar cooker. It uses reflective panels to direct sunlight towards a transparent, plastic bag containing the cooking vessel (painted black). It uses the same heat trapping principle as the box cooker, except that instead of a box, the cooking vessel is kept in a tightly closed transparent bag. A panel cooker relies on focusing sunlight towards the transparent bag by using multifaceted reflective panels. It can reach temperatures as high as 121°C.

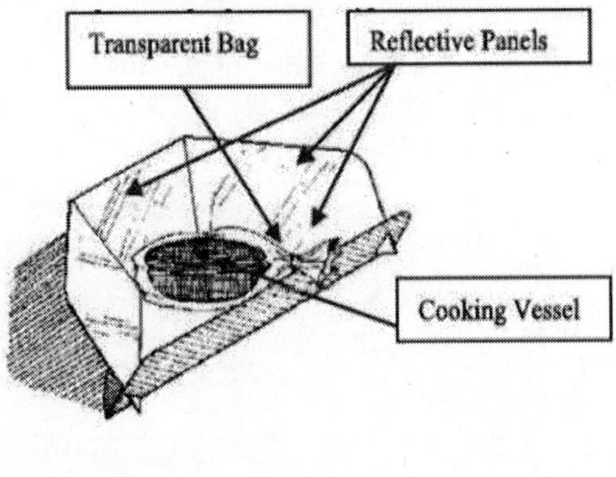

Fig. 6.9 Panel Type Solar Cooker

6.6.2. Benefits of Solar Cooking

1. The use of solar cooker for cooking food saves fuel.
2. The use of solar cooker does not produce smoke and does not cause any pollution.

3. When food is cooked in solar cooker, its nutrients do not get destroyed due to low heating.
4. Negligible maintenance cost
5. No attention is needed during cooking as in other devices.

6.6.3. Limitations of Solar Cooking

1. Solar cooking can be done only in the presence of sun.
2. Solar cooking takes longer time to cook food than conventional methods.
3. Chapaties are not cooked because high temperature for baking is required which is not be able to maintained.
4. Some solar cooker designs are affected by strong winds, which can slow the cooking process, cool the food due to convective losses, and disturb the reflector. It may be necessary to anchor the reflector, such as with string and weighted objects like bricks.

REVIEW QUESTIONS

1. What is concentrating solar thermal systems? What is the main principle used to store solar energy?
2. Explain parabolic trough mirror solar thermal plant.
3. Explain parabolic tower solar thermal plant.
4. Explain linear Fresnel thermal plant.
5. Explain parabolic dish system.
6. Compare the various solar thermal electric power systems.
7. Explain the concept of solar chimney.
8. What are the various areas of operation of solar thermal power plants?
9. Explain in brief 'Solar Cooker'.

❑

7

GEOTHERMAL ENERGY

7.1 INTRODUCTION

The word geothermal comes from the Greek words geo (earth) and therme (heat). Geothermal energy is heat from within the Earth. This heat comes from deep inside our planet, and we can use its power to work machines, as well as to heat our homes, offices and factories.

Much of the Earth's surface is covered by the water of the oceans. The surface temperature of the oceans varies from a warm 86°F (30°C) near the equator to freezing near the North and South poles. Just beneath Earth's surface, the water temperature also varies in different places. Inside a deep cave, the water might be very cold. But in places where underground water comes in contact with hot rocks, it heats up. This hot water can be used to generate geothermal power.

If we could travel to the center of our planet, the temperature would keep rising throughout the journey. Beneath Earth's crust, which forms its hard outer surface, is a much thicker layer called the mantle. At the bottom of the crust, the temperature is about 1800°F (1000°C), and this increases by about 2.9°F (1.6°C) per mile (1.6 km) as we go down through the mantle. This layer is about 1,800 miles (2900 km) thick and much of it is molten rock. At the planet's center is the core. This is made up of an outer layer of red-hot, molten iron and nickel, and a solid inner sphere. In the inner

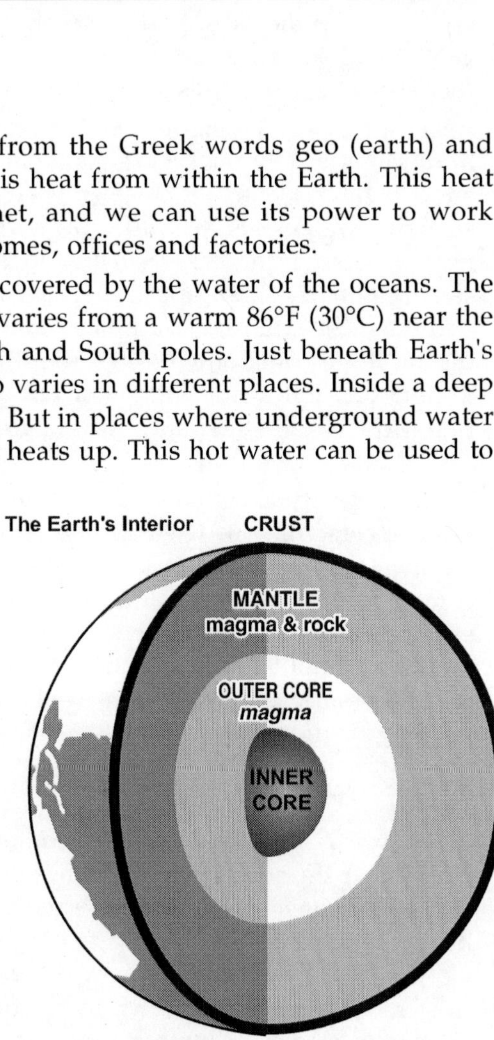

Fig. 7.1 Different layers inside Earth

core, the pressure is enormous and the temperature climbs to about 12,600°F (7000°C), which is hotter than the surface of the sun. We are able to use a tiny amount of this geothermal heat at Earth's surface.

The crust is not a solid piece, like the shell of an egg, but is broken into pieces called plates, which fit together like a giant puzzle. As heat from the mantle rises up into the crust, it makes the solid plates move very slowly, just a few inches every year. As the plates move, they rub against each other, and their squeezing and buckling can cause volcanoes. These are openings where molten rock, called magma, forces its way through cracks in the crust. The volcanic regions of the world are generally near the edge of plates, where one plate is forced beneath another. These areas are useful for geothermal power, because Earth's heat comes right up to the surface. Molten rock that reaches Earth's surface called as 'lava'.

In areas where magma lies just below the surface of the earth, there are hot springs and thermal pools. Rainwater seeps underground through cracks and reaches rocks that have been heated up by the molten magma. The hot, steaming water rises back up to the surface, where it may form a pool or just give off steam from rocks. Some springs build up such a force that water and steam regularly shoot up through a hole or crack. These are called geysers, and the most explosive examples shoot water more than 300 feet (95 m) into the air. If the water only reaches the surface in the form of steam, it is called a fumarole; and if the water is mixed with mud and clay, it is called a mud pot. Most of the water stays below ground. It collects to make geothermal reservoirs.

Hydrothermal activity occurs around the world, but it is most abundant (and spectacular) in Iceland, the North Island of New Zealand, and in Yellowstone National Park. In these areas, water underground comes in contact with heated rocks and magma, and then travels up to the planet's surface through a maze of cracks and fractures, an underground plumbing system. Without this water and this heat, and a way for their creation to reach the surface, these boiling, bubbling, hissing, spewing, spouting, and gushing landforms would never exist.

7.2 GEOTHERMAL FIELD

Figure 7.2 shows a typical geothermal field. The hot magma (molten mass) near the surface (A) solidifies into igneous rock (B). Igneous is Latin word, igneous meaning "of fire" specially formed by volcanic action or great heat. The heat of the magma is conducted upward to this igneous rock. Ground water that finds its way down to this rock through fissures (a long fine crack) in it will be heated by the heat of the rock or by mixing with hot gases and steam emanating from the magma. The heated water will then rise convectively upward and into a porous and permeable reservoir (C) above the igneous rock. The reservoir is capped by a layer of impermeable solid rock (D) that traps the hot water in the reservoir. The solid rock, however, has fissures (E) that acts as vents of the giant underground boiler. The vents show up at the surface as geysers or fumaroles (F) or hot spring (G). A well (H) taps steam from the fissures for use in a geothermal power plant.

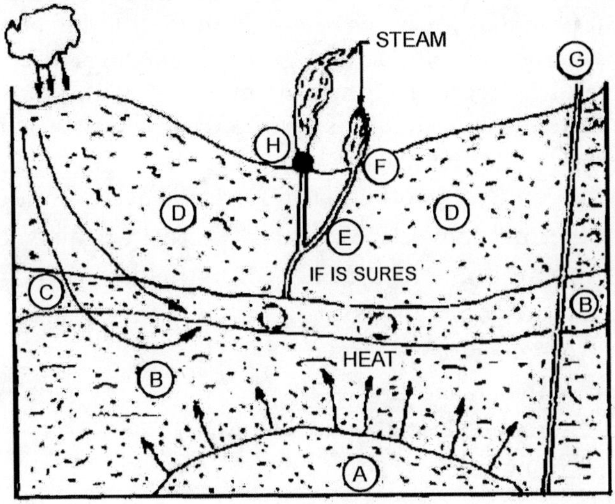

Fig. 7.2 Geothermal Field

It is convenient to classify earth's surface into three broad groups.

1. **Non-thermal areas** having a temperature gradient of 10 - 40°C per km depth.
2. **Semi-thermal areas** having a temperature gradient of 70°C per km depth.
3. **Hyper-thermal areas** where the temperature gradients are many times greater than in non-thermal areas.

Geothermal fields may further be classified into three types:

(A) Hyper-thermal Fields

(*i*) ***Wet fields*** where the water is pressurized and temperatures are above 100°C. When they are led to the surface a fraction will be splashed into steam and a major part remains as the boiling water.

(*ii*) Dry fields. They produce dry saturated steam or superheated steam at pressure above atmospheric.

(B) Semi-thermal Fields

These are capable of producing hot water at temperatures above 100°C.

7.3 GEOTHERMAL RESOURCES

Geothermal resources are classified based on the thermodynamic state (temperature, pressure, and enthalpy) of the resource. Commercial geothermal resources that are being utilized today use a hydrothermal resource (normally between 100°C and 300°C), meaning that geothermal energy comes from a resource containing mostly water, whether it exists in the form of a liquid or a vapour or a mixture of both. The geothermal resources with the most potential for power generation tend to be located in regions with a high geothermal temperature gradient and high tectonic activity. A high geothermal temperature gradient means that the rate at which the temperature changes with depth below the Earth's surface is relatively high when compared with the global average.

Five general kinds of geothermal resources have been identified:

(*i*) Hydrothermal convective systems. These are again sub-classified as:
- (*a*) Vapour-dominated or dry steam fields
- (*b*) Liquid-dominated system or wet steam fields
- (*c*) Hot-water fields

(*ii*) Geopressured resources

(*iii*) Petro-thermal or Hot Dry Rocks (HDR)

(*iv*) Magma resources

(*v*) Volcanoes

7.4 HYDROTHERMAL (CONVECTIVE) RESOURCES

These are wet reservoirs at moderate depths containing steam and/or hot water under pressure at temperatures up to about 350°C. These systems are further subdivided, depending upon whether steam or hot water is the dominant product. Hydrothermal resources arise when water has access to high temperature rocks, this account for the description as "hydrothermal".

In order to utilize the hydrothermal energy, wells are drilled either to intercept a fissure or, more commonly, into the formation containing the water (i.e. the hydrothermal reservoir). Most hydrothermal wells range in depth from about 600 m to 2100 m, although there are some shallower and deeper production wells.

In vapour dominated systems, the wells deliver steam, with little or no liquid water, usually at temperatures of about 150°C to 250°C but occasionally higher. Liquid dominated systems, on the other hand produce a mixture of steam and hot water. In liquid dominated systems the hot water circulating and trapped underground is at a temperature range of 174°C to 315°C.

7.4.1 Vapour Dominated Systems (or Dry Steam Power Plant)

As indicated by the name, dry steam power plants utilise dry steam resources emerging from production wells. Dry steam is steam that is either saturated or superheated, with no liquid present. The main challenge with operation of dry steam plants is to maintain the dry steam resource. Dry steam plants account for 12% of geothermal plants by number and generate

26% of worldwide geothermal power capacity, however only an estimated 5% of hydrothermal resources are dry steam resources.

The dry-steam power plant has several processes and requires different components in order to operate effectively. Figure 7.3 showing the components of the dry-steam geothermal power plant.

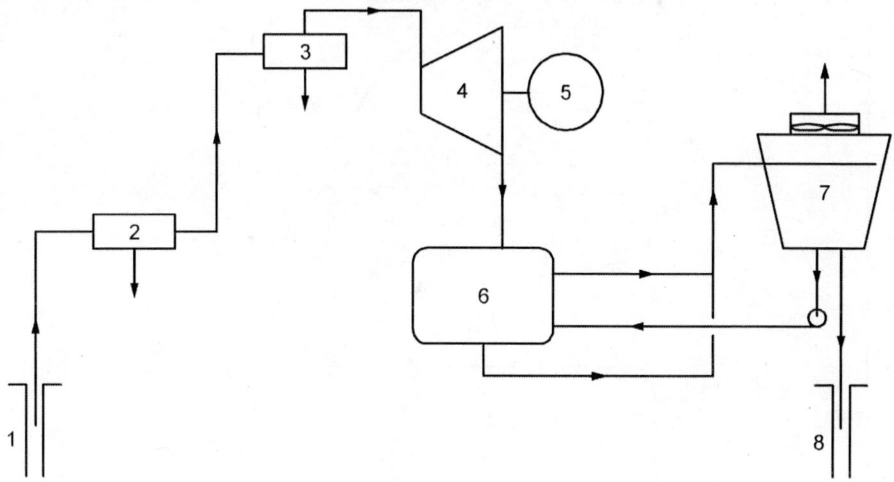

Fig. 7.3 Schematic diagram of a Dry Steam Power Plant

Where in the above Figure 7.3:

1. Production well, 2. Particle remover, 3. Moisture remover, 4. Steam turbine, 5. Electrical generator, 6. Condenser, 7. Cooling tower, 8. Injection well

The processes which occur in the power plant can be described by referring to the different points which represent components in Figure 7.3. As the geothermal fluid is extracted from the production well (Point 1) at a specific pressure, it passes through the particle and moisture removers (Points 2 and 3 respectively). These are important components which protect the turbine from damage from entrained particles and moisture, however not as important in flash steam plants where the geothermal resource is more "liquid-dominated". After the steam exits the moisture and particle removers it is ready for admission to the steam turbine. In the steam turbine, the thermal energy of the steam (some of the thermal energy is converted to kinetic energy in the nozzle or stator of the turbine) is converted to mechanical energy in the rotation of the turbine shaft which turns an electrical generator shaft (Electrical generator is at Point 5) which converts this mechanical rotation into electrical energy. At the exit of the steam turbine the steam is cooled and condensed by the condenser (Point 6) and cooling tower (Point 7) in tandem. The purpose of the cooling tower is to transfer heat from the cooling water exiting the condenser to the atmosphere. The geothermal fluid is often reinjected to the geothermal reservoir underground via the injection well (Point 8) in order to maintain the resource for sustainable power generation.

The T-S diagram describing energy conversion in dry steam geothermal power plants is shown in Figure 7.4.

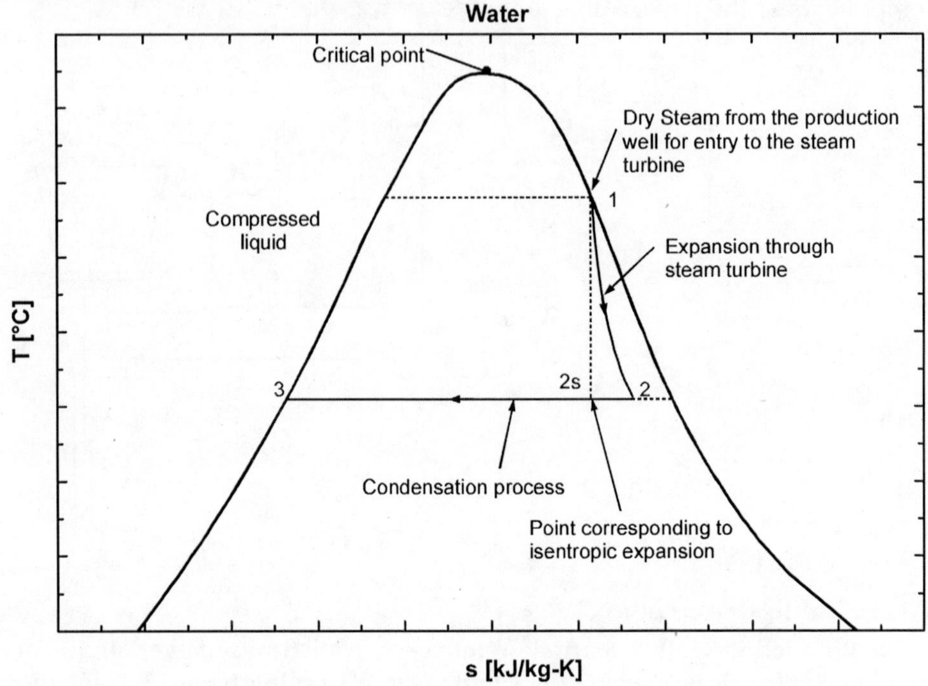

Fig. 7.4 *T-S diagram of Vapour Dominated System*

Where in the diagram,

- 1-Dry Steam is extracted from the geothermal production well
- 1-2 -Expansion of the steam in the turbine, power is extracted in this stage which corresponds to the change in the enthalpy multiplied the mass flow and the turbine efficiency
- 1-2s -The case of ideal expansion, where there are no losses, in other words if it is an isentropic expansion process
- 2-3-The steam and liquid mixture passes through the condenser, which condenses the geothermal steam to liquid
- 3-The liquid is then injected underground; returning it to the geothermal reservoir where it is heated and the cycle can be started at the production well.

The Geysers installation in California (U.S.A.), Larderello in Italy and Motsukawa, Japan are good examples of dry steam fields.

7.4.2 Liquid Dominated Systems (Wet steam fields)

For liquid dominated (high temperature) systems two methods which will be covered are:

(*a*) **Flashed steam system,** suitable for water in the high temperature range

(*b*) **Binary-cycle system,** suitable for water at moderate temperatures

(*c*) **Total Flow system**

(a) **Flashed-Steam System**

Flash steam power plants are the most commonly used geothermal power plant that utilise water-dominated geothermal resources. They require that the geothermal fluid be "flashed" to a steam and water mixture and that the steam be separated from the water. By "flashing" it is meant that the geothermal fluid is taken to a lower pressure by expansion causing it to flash into steam.

Flashed system is preferred for high temperature mixture of geothermal water, steam with low dissolved impurities. Flashed systems make use of hot water available from the geothermal reservoir, with temperatures above approximately 180°C. This hot water flows up to the production well due to pressure difference. As it flows upward, the pressure decreases and some of the hot water boils into steam. This process is called 'flash evaporation'. Flash evaporation is allowed to happen inside one or more flash tanks, which are large vessels allowing a portion of liquid to expand to steam.

(*i*) Liquid-dominated Single Flash Steam System

Flash steam power plants have similar structure and components to dry steam power plants, the major differences are that the flash steam power plant utilises a liquid dominated resource above 180°C and the flash steam power plant requires a steam separator (and provide a way for the liquid to be flashed to steam).

The schematic diagram of a liquid-dominated single flash steam system is shown in Figure 7.5.

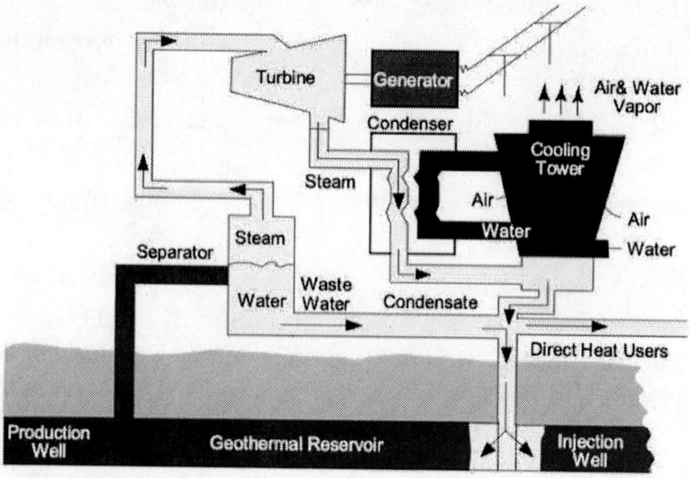

Fig. 7.5 Schematic of a liquid dominated single-flash steam system

The hot water from the underground reservoir reaches the well head at lower pressure. This process is essentially a constant enthalpy throttling process which results into two phase mixture having the steam of low quality. The mixture is further throttled in the flash chamber cum brine separator which results into dry saturated steam and saturated brine (hot, saline water). The separated brine is collected from bottom and the hot brine is re-injected into the ground. The dry steam is expanded in a turbine and generates electricity. Turbine exhaust is run through a condenser, where the steam is turned back into liquid form to facilitate reinjection into the geothermal reservoir. Heat is rejected from the condenser via either wet or dry cooling towers. The leftover water and condensate (condensed steam) provide heat to the direct heat users, and the rest is reinjected back into the geothermal reservoir via the injection well.

T-S diagram showing the characteristics of the geothermal fluid (assumed to be water) as it goes through the flash geothermal power plant is shown in Figure 7.6.

From point 1 the compressed liquid in the well is flashed (isenthalpic process) to a liquid vapour mixture at point 2. The liquid vapour mixture at point 2 enters a separator which separates it into saturated steam (point 4) and saturated liquid (point 3). The saturated steam enters a steam turbine (point 4) which facilitates energy conversion from thermal energy eventually into mechanical rotation of the turbine shaft. After exiting the turbine at point 5 the fluid mixture passes through a condenser which condenses the turbine exhaust. At point 6 and point 3, the utilised geothermal liquid is often reinjected into the geothermal reservoir in order for disposal of the liquid and increasing the useful life of the geothermal resource. Point 5s represents the ideal case of turbine expansion, where expansion is isentropic (without losses). Point 7 is the thermodynamic state if the turbine exhaust to the condenser was saturated vapour (at the same condenser temperature and pressure).

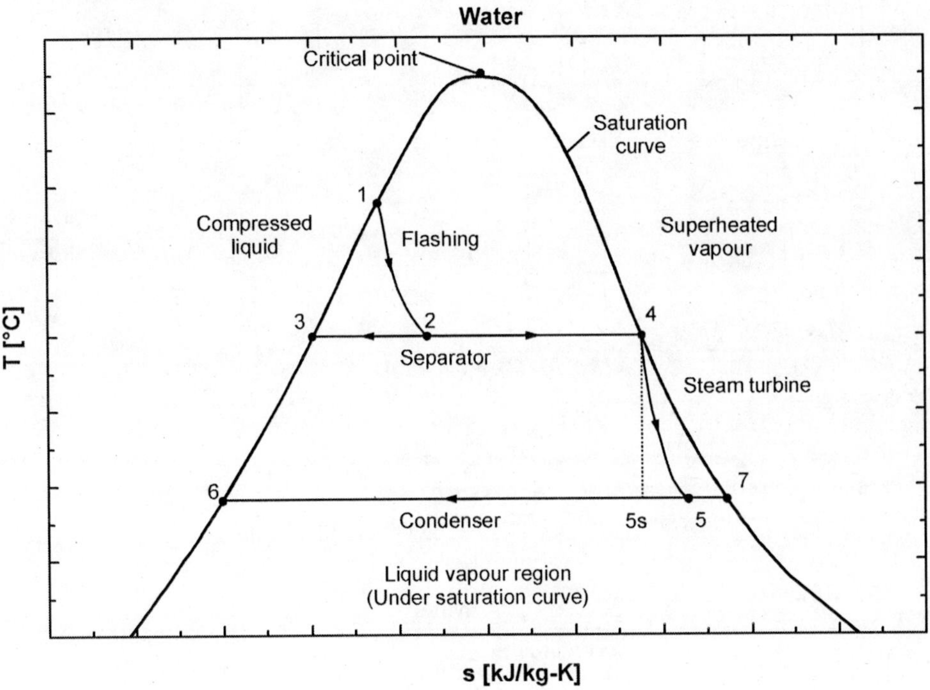

Fig. 7.6

Drawbacks

1. This system requires much larger total mass flow rates through the well.
2. Due to the large amount of flow there is a greater degree of surface subsidence.
3. Greater corrosion of piping, well casing and other conduits.
4. Many times temperature and pressure of the water may not sufficient to produce flash steam.

(*ii*) Liquid Dominated Double Flash Steam System

Double flash geothermal power plants utilise the separated geothermal fluid for a second flash and separation process. The advantage of the double flash geothermal power plant is that it uses a larger portion of the resource extracted for power generation when compared to single flash geothermal power plants which translates to a greater efficiency.

Double flash power plants use the same technology as the single flash power plants, however the efficiency is increased since the initially separated water is utilised by flashing to a lower pressure (see Figure 7.7).

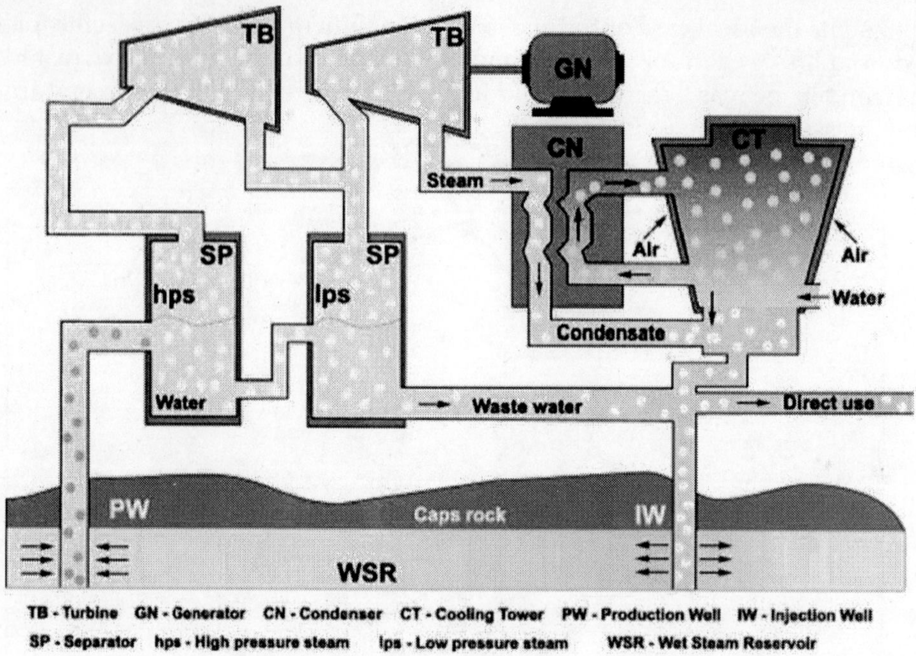

Fig. 7.7 *Illustration of the major components involved in the double flash geothermal power plant*

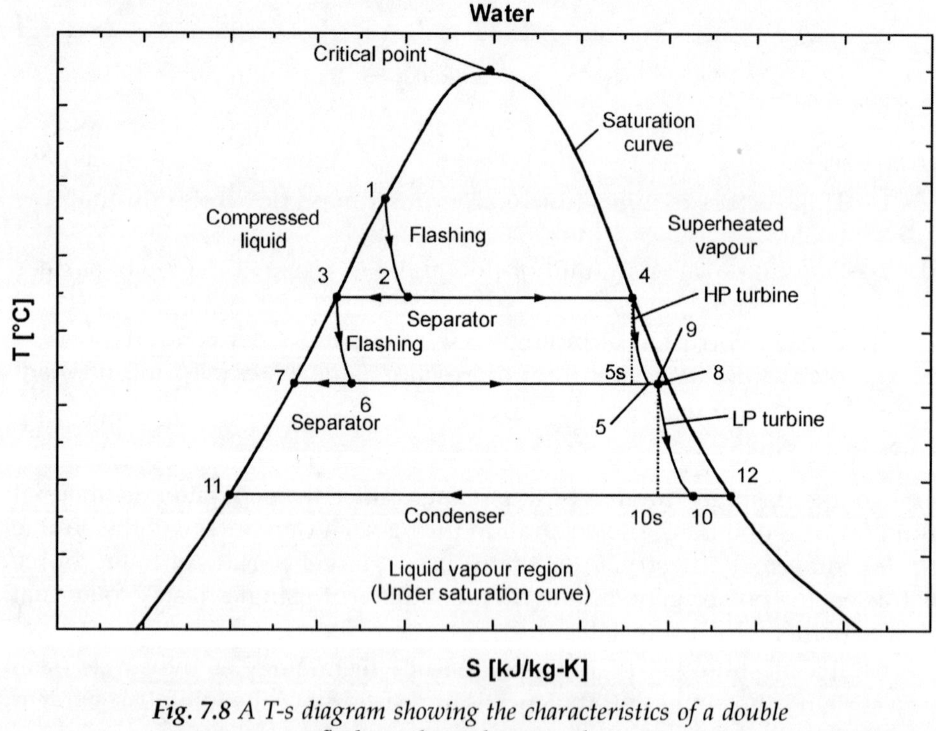

Fig. 7.8 *A T-s diagram showing the characteristics of a double flash geothermal power plant*

The process begins in a similar way to the single flash geothermal power plant. Referring to Figure 7.8, compressed geothermal liquid (point 1) is flashed (point 2) and then separated into saturated steam (point 4) and saturated water (point 3). The saturated steam passes through a high pressure steam turbine, while the saturated liquid at point 3 is flashed a second time (point 6) and then separated into saturated water (point 7) and saturated steam (point 8). From this point the saturated steam at point 8 as well as the high pressure turbine exhaust at point 5 are combined (point 9) and pass through the low pressure turbine, with the turbine exhaust being point 10. The low pressure turbine exhaust is condensed in the condenser and saturated water at points 7 and 11 are removed, most times for reinjection to the geothermal reservoir.

The increase in efficiency associated with the use of a double flash power plant related to single flash power plants is estimated at between 20 and 30%. If the cost of additional components and equipment is justified then the double flash power plant is recommended since the efficiency is increased.

(*b*) Liquid Dominated Systems: Binary Cycle

Geothermal binary cycle power plants utilize geothermal fluid as an external heat source to power a thermodynamic cycle which uses a separate working fluid. Both the geothermal fluid and energy conversion system are in their own closed loop with a heat exchanger between them (see Figure 7.9). The closed circuit of geothermal fluid is represented as the loop including points A and B in Figure, where geothermal fluid is extracted from the production well at point A and passes through a heat exchanger before being reinjected at point B. The closed circuit for working fluid in the power generation cycle is represented by points 1-4 in Figure 7.9, where between point 1 and 2 the working fluid passes through the heat exchanger which acts as an evaporator for the working fluid. Between points 2 and 3 the working fluid is expanded in a turbine before passing through a condenser and (3-4) and a pump (4-1). After going through the pump the working fluid completes the cycle and begins another by entering the heat exchanger. Binary cycle plants are generally suited for lower geothermal resource temperatures and cases where the geothermal brine is difficult to handle due to high corrosiveness.

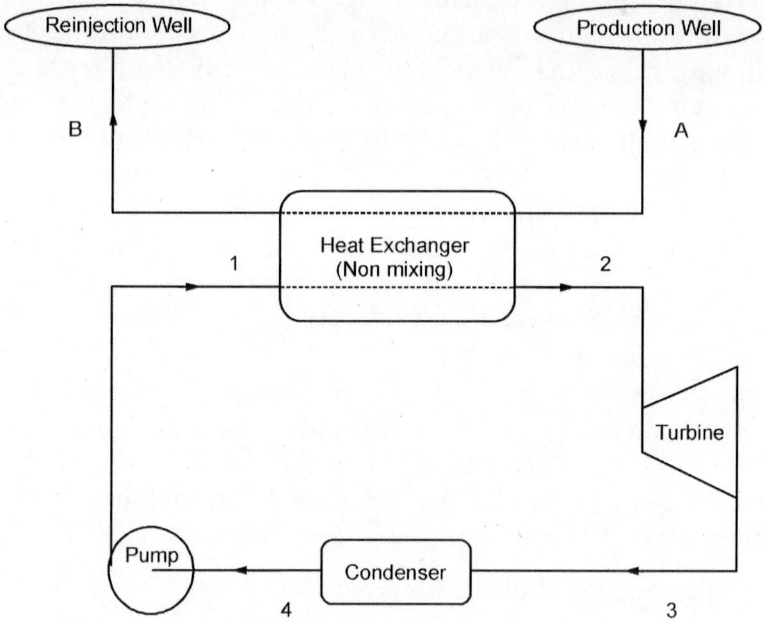

***Fig. 7.9** Flow diagram describing the basic processes involved in a binary cycle power plant*

The schematic diagram of a Binary fluid geothermal power system is shown in Figure 7.10. Hot water or brine from the underground reservoir, either as unflashed liquid or as steam producing by flashing is circulated through a primary heat exchanger. In the heat exchanger the hot brine transfer its heat to the organic fluid thus converting it to a superheated vapour that is used in a standard closed Rankine cycle. The vapour drives the turbine-generator .The exhaust vapour from the turbine is cooled in the regenerative heat exchanger and then condensed, using either and air-cooled condenser or a water-cooled condenser and cooling tower. The condensed liquid organic fluid is returned to the primary heat exchanger by way of the regenerative heat exchanger. The hot geothermal fluid and the organic fluid, constitute the two fluids of the binary-fluid system.

The condenser is cooled by water from a natural source, if available, or a cooling tower circulation system. The blow down from the tower may be reinjected to the ground with the cooled brine. Make-up of the cooling tower must be provided however.

If the temperature and salinity of the geothermal brine are not high, the tendency of solids to deposit on surfaces in the heat exchanger is not too great. However, where the temperature and salinity of the brine are high, this procedure may not be practical because the heat exchangers may soon be rendered ineffective by scale deposition.

The first binary cycle was installed in the Soviet Union on the Kamchatka Peninsula in 1967. It has a gross output of 680 kW using a low temperature water reservoir at 80°C and Freon-12 as working fluid. The first to be built in the United States is an 11 MW plant built by the Magma Company in California. The site has a potential of 10,000 MW. Isobutene was chosen in preference to Freon-12 primarily because of its lower cost. A second U.S. binary cycle plant is being built at Raft River-Idaho. It is a 10 MW plant.

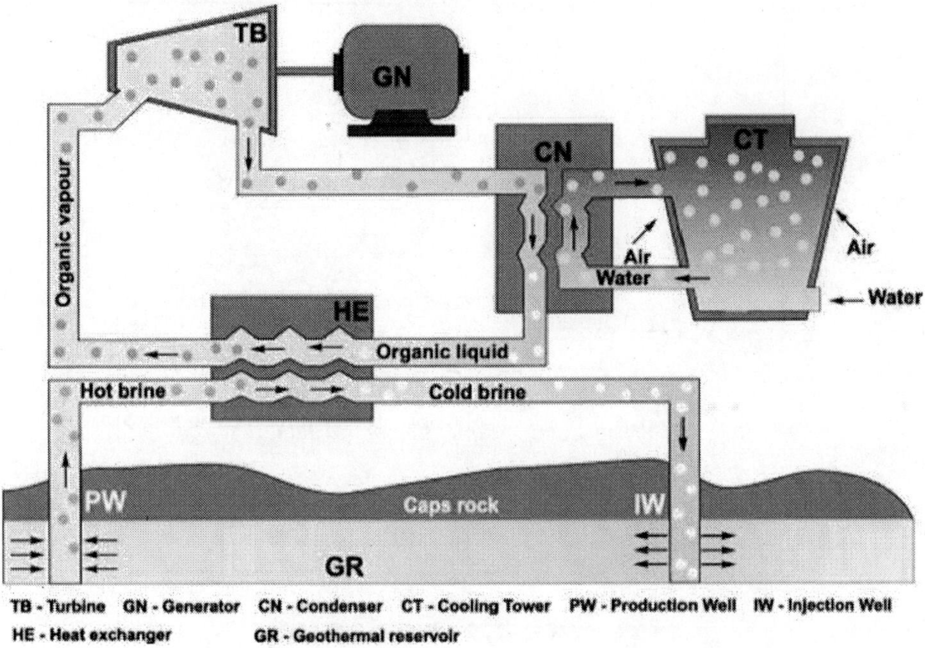

Fig. 7.10 Schematic diagram of Binary Cycle Power Plant

(*c*) Liquid Dominated Systems: Total Flow Concept

In the flashed-steam system, some useful energy is discarded with the separated brine regardless of how many stages of separation are used. Thermodynamically, therefore, direct expansion of the fluid from the well head to the condenser has the potential of converting the greatest fraction of available energy in the fluid to mechanical work. This means that the total well-head flow is to be expanded to the condenser pressure, hence the name total-flow concept. In principle this concept is simple, as can be seen from the flow and T-S of Figures 7.11 and 7.12. Again, hot brine from the well at 1 is throttled to 2, where it becomes a two phase mixture of low quality. Instead of separating the two phases at this point, the full flow is expanded to 3, condensed to 4, and reinjected into the ground at 5.

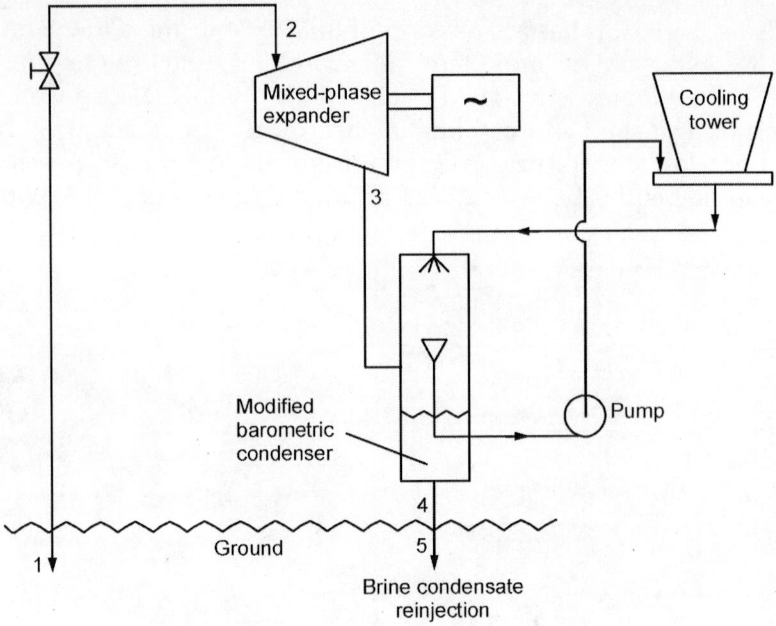

Fig. 7.11 Schematic of a liquid-dominated total flow concept

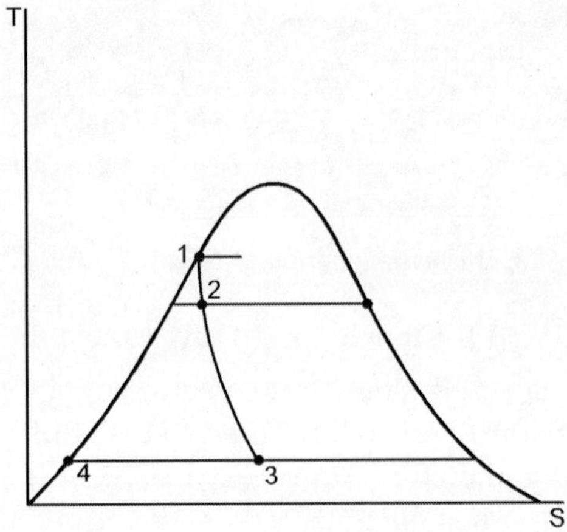

Fig. 7.12 T-S diagram of cycle shown in Fig. 7.11

Problems to be solved before the total-flow concept can be a commercial success include brine management; inhibition of precipitation and scale; turbine material selection for maximum erosion resistance; the handling of the condensate, which is in form of a slurry (solids in suspension rather than in solution in a liquid); and the carryover into the coolant system. The condenser, for example, would be a modified direct-contact barometric condenser designed to separate the vapour fraction from the brine fraction to prevent fouling of the circulating-water system. No water makeup in the cooling tower is required as that can be supplied from the condensed steam before reinjection into the ground.

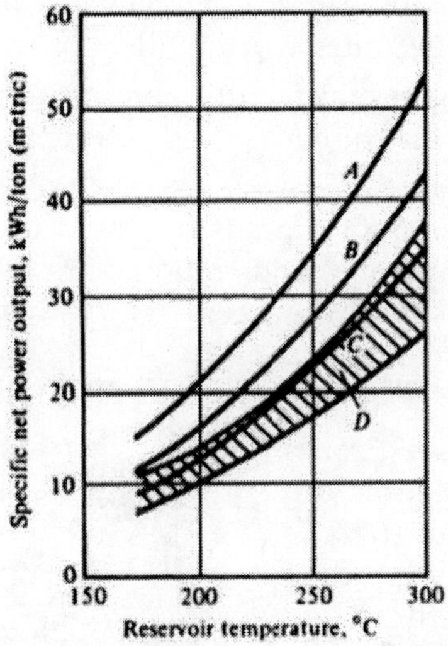

Fig. 7.13 Comparison of various liquid-dominated systems: (A) total-flow concept, (B) double flash steam, (C) single flash steam, (D) binary cycle

Figure 7.13 shows the results of an analytical comparison of various liquid-dominated systems. The curves indicate that the total-flow concept produces the highest specific power per unit mass-flow rate at the well head. The calculations are based on the same condenser temperatures of 120°F, the same turbine efficiencies of 85%, and the same in-plant power requirements of 30 percent of the gross. Differences in these would naturally change the differences between the curves.

7.5 GEOPRESSURED RESOURCES

Geopressured resources are deep reservoirs of high-pressured hot water that contain dissolved natural gas. A geopressured reservoir is formed in sedimentary formations when water percolates into the pores of a layer of sand. When non-porous shale settles on top, it traps the fluid into the sand layer at very high pressures. Over millions of years, this pressure increases even more as additional sedimentary layers build on top of the reservoir. If the sand body in which the water is trapped is large enough, the reservoir can economically produce energy for quite a long time. An important characteristic of geopressured reservoirs, at least from an energy perspective, is that they contain dissolved methane, or natural gas. This, therefore, yields three sources of energy that can be utilized from the reservoir:

- Hydraulic energy from extreme pressure
- Heat energy from the fluid
- Dissolved natural gas

Comparing to other natural gas reservoirs, the amount of dissolved methane in these types of reservoirs is very small. For the natural gas alone, the reservoir would be uneconomical. However, with two more sources of energy, their utilization becomes worthwhile.

A geopressured geothermal facility operates on both natural gas and geothermal fuel. It could also be considered as a geothermal-fossil fuel hybrid system.

A successful demonstration plant operated in US in the 1980's. The Department of Energy built a demonstration plant in Texas which produced electricity from geopressured resources.

7.6 PETRO-THERMAL RESOURCES OR HOT DRY ROCKS

These are very hot solid rocks occurring at moderate depths but to which water does not have access, either because of absence of ground water or the low permeability of the rock (or both). The temperature of these dry rocks varies between 150-300°C and this energy of rocks is called as petro thermal energy and it represents by far the largest resources of geothermal energy.

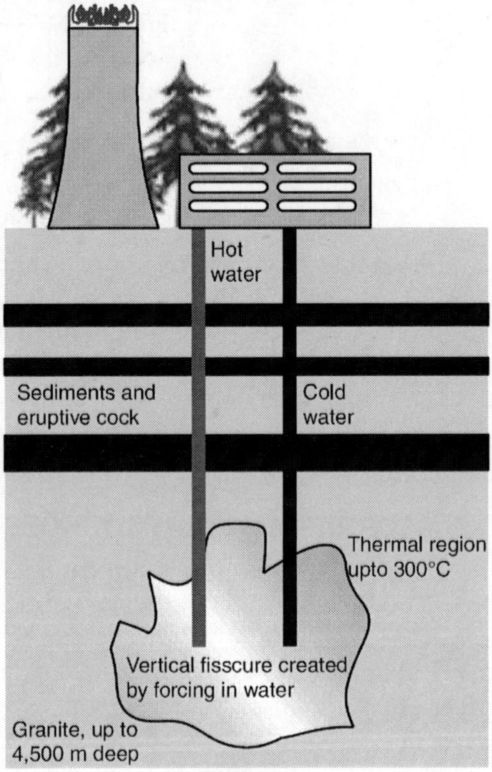

Fig. 7.14

In principle the recovery of heat from such dry rocks involves breaking up or cracking of rock to make it permeable and then introducing water from the surface, circulating it through the cracks and then collecting the water back for utilizing in various applications. Rocks are fractured detonating explosives at the bottom well drilled into the rock or by using hydraulic fracturing techniques. Heat is then extracted by circulating the water through the cracks. Extraction of petro thermal energy is shown in the following Figure 7.14.

7.7 MAGMA RESOURCES

These consist of partially or completely molten rock with temperatures in excess of 650°C, which may be encountered at moderate depths, especially in a recently active volcanic region. These resources have large geothermal energy content, but restricted to some places and this high temperature will make difficulty to extract.

7.8 GEOTHERMAL APPLICATIONS

Geothermal energy can be used for electricity production, for commercial, industrial, and residential direct heating purposes, and for efficient home heating and cooling through geothermal heat pumps.

(*a*) **Geothermal Electricity:** To develop electricity from geothermal resources, wells are drilled into a geothermal reservoir. The wells bring the geothermal water to the surface, where its heat energy is converted into electricity at a geothermal power plant.

(*b*) **Heating Uses:** Geothermal heat is used directly, without involving a power plant or a heat pump, for a variety of applications such as space heating and cooling, food preparation, hot spring bathing and spas (balneology), agriculture, aquaculture, greenhouses, and industrial processes.

(*c*) **Geothermal Heat Pumps (GHPs):** Geothermal heat pumps take advantage of the Earth is relatively constant temperature at depths of about 10 ft to 300 ft.

Geothermal heat pump systems consist of basically three parts: the ground heat exchanger, the heat pump unit, and the air delivery system (ductwork). The heat exchanger is basically a system of pipes called a loop, which is buried in the shallow ground near the building. A fluid (usually water or a mixture of water and antifreeze) circulates through the pipes to absorb or relinquish heat within the ground.

In the winter, the heat pump removes heat from the heat exchanger and pumps it into the indoor air delivery system. In the summer, the process is reversed, and the heat pump moves heat from the indoor air into the heat exchanger. The heat removed from the indoor air during the summer can also be used to heat water, providing a free source of hot water.

Geothermal heat pumps use much less energy than conventional heating systems, since they draw heat from the ground. They are also more efficient when cooling your home. Not only does this save energy and money, it reduces air pollution. GHPs reduce electricity use 30% to 60% as compared with traditional heating and cooling systems, because the electricity which powers them is used only to collect, concentrate, and deliver heat, not to produce it.

Geothermal energy has the ability to:

(*a*) provide reliable electricity at a stable price;

(*b*) help states diversify the mix of fuels they use to produce electricity;

(*c*) generate electricity in a manner that produces minimal environmental impacts and emissions;

(*d*) help states meet renewable portfolio standards;

(*e*) generate economic development opportunities, especially in rural areas;

(*f*) Provide heat for agricultural, industrial and space heating applications.

7.9 ENVIRONMENTAL CONSIDERATIONS

The environmental effects mainly depend strongly on the physical, thermodynamic, and chemical properties of the reservoir, and will therefore be site-specific. Impacts can be expected from drilling, reservoir development, surface collection system construction and operation and conversion plant construction and operation. Since reservoirs will continually need replacement or stimulation, reservoir development impacts would continue through the life of the facility.

(i) Land Use : About an acre of land is required for drilling and reservoir development operations at each well. This land can be compatible with limited other uses (forestry, crops, grazing) once equipment is in place.

(ii) Noise : Noise problems arise from several operations, including drilling and testing of wells and the release of vented steam, Mufflers can be placed on wells to reduce steam discharge noise.

(iii) Air Pollutants : Hydrothermal reservoirs typically contain a variety of dissolved gases which can be released to the atmosphere when vapor or liquid-dominated sources are utilized. Some of these, such as mercury and radon, could accumulate in the environment of geothermal facilities. Others, such as methane, hydrogen, carbon dioxide, nitrogen, ammonia and hydrogen sulfide, do not accumulate but can be irritating or require removal.

(iv) Water Pollutants : Water pollutants are naturally dissolved in hydrothermal systems and can be leached by the circulating water of hot dry rock technology. These pollutants pose problems in several ways. During reinjection of fluids, existing groundwater supplies may be contaminated. If pollutants such as mercury or arsenic are present, a hazard may be created. Scaling and deposition of materials such as silica or calcium carbonate can occur in the geothermal system. When these materials are discarded leaching into the groundwater may occur.

(v) Heat Discharges : Geothermal plants are less efficient than conventional technologies and therefore reject more heat into the environment per unit of electricity produced. Counteracting this problem is the smaller size of typical geothermal facilities, resulting in wider dispersal of heat discharges.

Use of conventional cooling technologies can avoid the need for discharging heat into rivers or lakes, where even relatively small temperature rises can upset the ecosystem. Also hot dry rock systems, which have closed cycle circulation of water, may be able to reject some heat by reinjecting cool water. This may even prolong reservoir life.

(vi) Seismic and Subsidence Effects : The removal of water from aquifers for irrigation has been known to produce micro-earthquakes and surface subsidence. Similarly, open loop (no reinjection) geothermal systems might produce instabilities as water is removed from rock formations and internal pressures are reduced.

Dry hot rock systems and systems employing reinjection should experience fewer seismic and subsidence effects.

7.10 BENEFITS OF GEOTHERMAL ENERGY

(*a*) Geothermal power plants provide steady and predictable base load power.

(*b*) New geothermal power plants currently generate electricity for between $0.05 per kWh and $0.08 per kWh, which can decrease below $0.05 per kWh after capital investment has been recovered.

(*c*) Direct use applications and power plants can generate tax revenue and royalty payments for federal, tribal, state and local governments and create construction, operation, administrative and maintenance jobs.

(*d*) Responsibly managed geothermal resources can deliver energy and provide power for decades.

(*e*) Geothermal power plants in the United States are reliable, capable of operating about 98 percent of the time.

(*f*) Power plants are small, require no fuel purchase and are compatible with agricultural land uses.

(*g*) Geothermal plants produce a small amount of pollutant emissions compared to traditional fossil fuel power plants.

7.11 CHALLENGES OF GEOTHERMAL ENERGY

(*a*) Many of the best potential resources are located in remote or rural areas, often on federal or state lands.

(*b*) Developing projects on federal or state lands can be a challenge. The leasing process can be very cumbersome, especially when a proposed project might conflict with other land uses, ESA, and historical or cultural resources.

(*c*) Although costs have decreased in recent years, exploration and drilling for power production remain expensive.

(*d*) Using the best geothermal resources for electricity production may require an expansion or upgrade of the transmission system.

(*e*) The success rate for discovering geothermal resources in new, untapped areas is approximately 20 percent. In areas where wells already are producing, the chance of locating more wells increases to about 80 percent.

(*f*) The productivity of geothermal wells may decline over time. As a result, it is crucial that developers manage the geothermal resource efficiently.

7.12 NON-ELECTRICAL USES OF GEOTHERMAL ENERGY

(i) Industrial Applications

1. Wood and Paper Industry
   - A. Pulp and Paper
   - B. Veneer Factory
   - C. Timber Drying
2. Chemicals
   - A. Salt Plant
   - B. Soda Ash
   - C. Caustic Soda (By Product : Chlorine)
   - D. Alcohol (By Product : Ethylene)

     Chlorine + Ethylene will Produce VCM (Vinyl-Chlorine-Monomer) Which can be turned into PVC (Poly-Vinyl-Chloride)
   - E. Dry Ice
   - F. Boric Acid
   - G. Calcium and Potassium Chlorides
3. Beer Brewery and Distillation Industries
4. Confectionary Industry

(ii) Agricultural Applications

1. Drying purposes (Grains, Copra, Seaweeds, Etc.)
2. Food Processing
   - A. Canning Industry
   - B. Conversion of Organic Waste to Protein.
   - C. Leaf-Protein Extraction
3. Aquaculture
   - A. Alligator Crocodile Breeding
   - B. EEL Breeding

7.13 GEOTHERMAL WELL DRILLING

Geothermal drilling is the process of creating boreholes in the earth to extract the earth's heat. Typical rock types in geothermal reservoirs include granite, granodiorite, quartzite, greywacke, basalt, volcanic tuff. Compared to the sedimentary formations of most oil/gas reservoirs, geothermal formations are, by definition:

(i) Hot (production intervals from 160°C to above 300°C)
(ii) Often hard (240+ MPa compressive strength), abrasive (quartz content above 50%)
(iii) Highly fractured (fracture apertures of centimeters)
(iv) Underpressured
(v) Often contain corrosive fluids
(vi) Some formation fluids have very high solids content

Drilling is usually difficult, with problems that include:

(i) Rate of penetration and bit life are typically low
(ii) Corrosion is often a problem
(iii) Lost circulation is frequent and severe
(iv) These problems are often compounded by high temperature

Some of the geothermal drilling technologies are:

1. **Drilling mud :** Clay-based muds, such as bentonite, are the most commonly used in geothermal drilling at low temperatures (~150°C). At higher temperatures, ordinary clay-based muds tend to gel and therefore chrome-lignite/chrome-lignosulphonate (CL-CLS)-based mud is generally used.
2. **Drilling bits :** Roller bits with hardened steel teeth or tungsten carbide insers are commonly used in geothermal drilling. Since the steel used in roller bits is drawn at temperatures of about 200–250°C, these bits lose much of their strength when operated at temperatures in excess of 250°C.

   Diamond drills can drill at temperatures in excess of 500°C.
3. **Casing :** To obtain a sustained flow of steam from a reservoir, it is necessary to choose an appropriate diameter fro the production well. Additionally, it is necessary to provide adequate casing at correct depths to prevent hot water from higher formations from entering into the well. When the pH water from higher formations from entering into the well. When the pH value of the hot water produced with the steam is low, it tends to corrode the casing and reduce the life span of the well.
4. **Cementing :** To prevent circulation losses of drilling mud, cementing is sometimes done at the horizons where losses occur. This is usually a permanent measure against such losses.

   Proper cementing of geothermal wells requires that the cement slurry should rise uniformly and continuously from the casing shoe to the ground level.

   Ordinary cement is adequate for temperatures up to 150°C, but to resist higher temperatures, silica is often mixed with it. In geothermal wells where steam is accompanied by low-pH hot water, it is necessary to use acid-resistant cement.

5. Drilling with air : Two important advantages of air drilling over mud drilling are : (1) the production zone is not damaged by the circulating mud, and (2) compared to mud drilling, the drilling speed is 3 to 4 times faster and the bit life is 2 to 4 times longer.

Few examples of new drilling technologies are hydrothermal spallation, chemical plasma, erosion, laser, electric discharge, electrical plasma and direct transfer of heat.

7.14 PROSPECTS OF GEOTHERMAL ENERGY IN INDIA

India has huge potential to become a leading contributor in generating eco-friendly and cost effective geothermal power. Around 6.5 per cent of electricity generation in the world would be done with the help of geothermal energy and India would have to play a bigger role in the coming years in this direction.

Geological Survey of India has identified about 340 geothermal hot springs in the country. Most of them are in the low surface temperature range from 37°C-90°C which is suitable for direct heat applications. These springs are grouped into seven geothermal provinces i.e. Himalayan (Puga, Chhumathang), Sahara Valley, Cambay Basin, Son-Narmada-Tapi (SONATA) lineament belt, West Coast, Godavari basin and Mahanadi basin. Some of the prominent geothermal resources include Puga Valley and Chhumathang in Jammu and Kashmir, Manikaran in Himachal Pradesh, Jalgaon in Maharashtra and Tapovan in Uttarakhand. A new location of geothermal power energy has also been found in Tattapani in Chhattisgarh. In addition, Gujarat is set to tap geothermal electricity through resources which are available in Cambay between Narmada and Tapi River.

Puga, which is located at a distance of about 180 km from Leh in the Ladakh region of Jammu and Kashmir across the great Himalayan range, is considered to be a good potential of geothermal energy. In Puga valley, hot spring temperatures vary from 30°C to 84°C (boiling point at Puga) and discharge up to 300 liters /minute.

Chhumathang spring is another geothermal area located about 40 km north of Puga. The thermal water from Chhumathang is quite similar to the thermal waters at Puga except the difference that its water has relatively higher pH and sulphate.

Geothermal activity at Manikaran occurs in the form of hot springs over a distance of about 1.25 km on the right bank of Parvati river with a temperature range of 34°C-96°C whereas on the left bank over a distance of about 450 m with a temperature range of 28°C-37°C.

At Tapovan geothermal area, the highest temperature recorded is 65°C. The discharge from this spring varies between 0.83-9.2 litre/second. Similarly, Tattapani is a promising geothermal resource in Peninsular India.

Sixty thermal water springs occur at eighteen localities in the West Coast hot spring belt. One geothermal power project has a capacity of 25MW. Himurja, Himachal Pradesh has decided to select some geothermal resources in Beas valley, Parvati valley, Satluj valley and Spiti valley in Himachal Pradesh for deep drilling up to 2 km for exploitation of geothermal energy.

Thus, geothermal energy has great potential as a clean, green and naturally occurring renewable source of energy.

REVIEW QUESTIONS

1. What is geothermal energy? Explain the structure of Earth.
2. What are the various types of geothermal resources? Explain them.
3. Explain the various applications of geothermal energy.
4. What is the environmental impact of using geothermal energy as a renewable resource?
5. What are the benefits and challenges of geothermal energy?
6. Explain the working of geothermal power plant. Discuss the various technical developments.
7. What are the essential criteria of selecting site for Geothermal power plant?
8. Write a short note on Geothermal Field.
9. Explain Dry Steam Power Plant with T-S diagram.
10. Explain liquid dominated single-flash steam system with T-S diagram.
11. Explain liquid dominated double-flash steam system with T-S diagram.
12. Explain binary cycle power plant with T-S diagram.
13. Explain Geopressured resources.
14. Explain Petro-thermal resources.

❑

8

MAGNETO-HYDRO-DYNAMIC (MHD) POWER GENERATION

8.1 INTRODUCTION

Magneto hydrodynamics (MHD) (magneto fluid dynamics or hydro magnetics) is the academic discipline which studies the dynamics of electrically conducting fluids. Examples of such fluids include plasmas, liquid metals, and salt water. The word magneto hydro dynamics (MHD) is derived from magneto- meaning magnetic field, and hydro- meaning liquid, and -dynamics meaning movement. The field of MHD was initiated by Hannes Alfvén, for which he received the Nobel Prize in Physics in 1970.

80 % of total electricity produced in the world is hydal, while remaining 20% is produced from nuclear, thermal, solar, geothermal energy arid from magneto hydro dynamic (MHD) generator.

MHD power generation is a new system of electric power generation which is said to be of high efficiency and low pollution. In advanced countries MHD generators are widely used but in developing countries like INDIA, it is still under construction, this construction work in progress at TRICHI in TAMIL NADU, under the joint efforts of BARC (Bhabha atomic research center), Associated Cement Corporation (ACC) and Russian technologists.

As its name implies magneto hydro dynamics (MHD) is concerned with the flow of a conducting fluid in the presence of magnetic and electric field. The fluid may be gas at elevated temperatures or liquid metals like sodium or potassium.

Principle of MHD Power Generation

In magnetohydrodynamic power generation heat is directly converted into electrical energy. The basic principle of MHD generation is same as that of conventional electrical generation i.e. the motion of a conductor through a magnetic field induces an emf in it. In steam power plant the heat released by the fuel is converted into mechanical energy by means of a thermo-cycle and mechanical energy is then used to drive the electric generation.

In MHD generation, electrical energy is directly generated from hot combustion gases produced by the combustion of the fuel without moving parts.

So an MHD generator is a device for converting heat energy of a fuel directly into electrical energy with to a conventional electric generator. (see Fig. 8.1)

In an MHD generator electrically conducting gas at a very high temperature is passed at high velocity through a strong magnetic field at right angle to the direction of flow therefore generating electrical energy. The electrical energy is then collected from stationary electrodes placed on the opposite side of channel. The current so obtained is direct current d.c. which can be converted into a.c. by using an inverter.

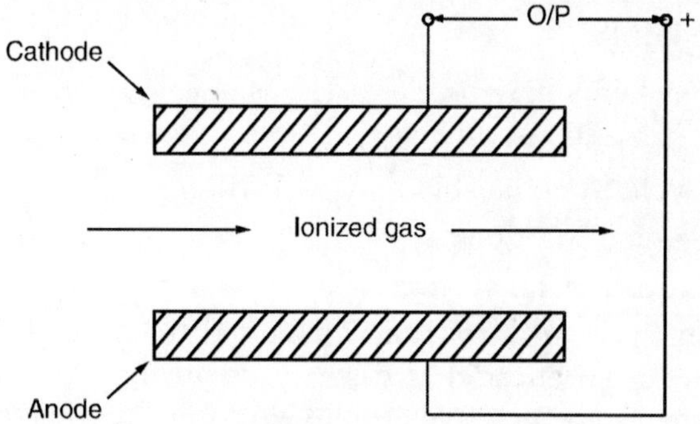

Fig. 8.1

In MHD generator, the solid conductors are replaced by a gaseous conductor, ionized gas plasma.

The induced EMF is given by

$$E_{ind} = \vec{u} \times \vec{B}$$

where u = velocity of the conductor, B = magnetic field intensity.

The induced current density is given by,

$$\overrightarrow{J_{ind}} = \sigma \overrightarrow{E_{ind}}$$

where σ = electric conductivity

The retarding force on the conductor is the Lorentz force given by

$$\overrightarrow{F_{ind}} = \overrightarrow{J_{ind}} \times \vec{B}$$

In this method ionized gas is produced by heating the gas to high temperature. On heating of a as, the outer electron escape out from its atoms or molecules. The particles acquire an electric charge and the gases passes into the state of plasma. To achieve thermal ionization of products of combustion of fossil fuels or inert gases, extremely high temperatures are necessary. Air become highly ionized at temperature of 5000°C to 6000°C. The gases are selected with additive of easily ionizing materials such as cesium or potassium.

Ionization is also produced either by seeding with substance like cesium or potassium vapors which ionizes at relatively low temperatures. The atoms of seed element split off electrons. The presence of the negatively charged electrons makes the gas an electrical conductor.

8.2 MHD SYSTEMS

The MHD systems may be classified as:

(*i*) Open Cycle System

(*ii*) Closed Cycle System. This may be further sub-classified as:

- (*a*) Seeded inert gas system
- (*b*) Liquid metal system

In an open cycle system, the working fluid after doing useful work (generating electrical energy) is discharged to the atmosphere through a stack while in a closed cycle system the working fluid is recycled to the heat source and used again and again. In open cycle system air used as a working fluid and in closed cycle system gases used as a working fluid is helium or argon.

8.2.1 Open Cycle MHD System

In open cycle MHD system a high pressure, high temperature combustion gas is forced through a strong magnetic field. (see Fig. 8.2)

Coal is processed and burnt in the combustor at a high temperature of about 2600°C and pressure of about 12 atmosphere is applied with preheated air to form the plasma. Then a seeding material such as potassium carbonate is injected to the plasma in order to increase the electrical conductivity.

The resulting mixture is passed through the strong magnetic filed of about 5-7 Tesla of the MHD generator. During the expansion of gas at high temperature the positive and negative ions move to the electrode and so constitute an electric current. This current is d.c. and an inverter is employed for its conversion into a.c. The gas leaving the MHD generator is still very hot. The heat from the exhaust gases of the MHD generator is utilized in preheating the air supplied to the combustor. The seed material is recovered from the gas for successive use and harmful emissions (such as nitrogen and sulphur) are removed from the gas, for pollution control and the gas finally discharged to the atmosphere through the state.

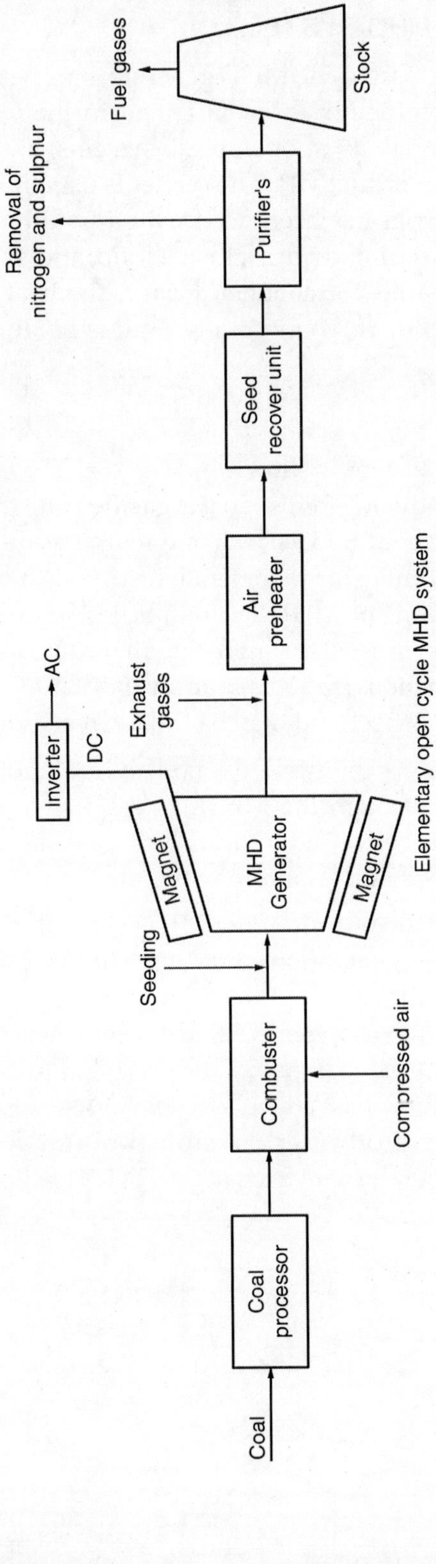

Fig. 8.2 *Elementary open cycle MHD system*

8.2.2 CLOSED CYCLE MHD SYSTEM

Two general types of closed cycle MHD generators are being investigated. In one type, electrical conductivity is maintained in the working fluid by ionization of a seed material, as in open cycle systems; and in the other, a liquid metal provides the conductivity. The carrier is usually a chemical inert gas, although a liquid carrier has been used with a liquid metal conductor. The working fluid is circulated in a closed loop and is heated by the combustion gases using a heat exchanger. Hence, the heat source and the working fluid are independent. The working fluid is helium or argon with cesium seeding.

(*i*) Seeded Inert Gas System

A closed cycle MHD system is shown in Fig. 8.3a. The complete system has three distinct but introducing loops. Coal is gasified and the gas produced has a high peak value of about 5.35 MJ/ kg and temperature of about 520°C. This gas is burnt in the combustor to generate heat. This heat is transferred to the working fluid (argon) of MHD cycle in a heat exchanger HX1. The combustion products are passed through the air pre-heater (to recover a part of the heat of combustion products) and purify it and then discharged to the atmosphere. This is loop 1 and may be called an external heating loop.

The loop in the centre is the MHD loop. The hot argon gas is seeded with cesium and passed through the MHD generator that produces direct current. This d.c. output is converted into a.c. by means of inverter and then supplied to the grid. This is loop-2 and may be called an MHD loop.

Now the argon gas at the output of the MHD generator is still very hot. So this heat is used in the generation of steam. The working fluid (argon gas) is slowed down in a diffuser, and then this fluid is passed through the heat exchanger HX2. Heat exchanger HX2, serves as a waste heat boiler to generate steam. This steam is used partly for driving a turbine which runs the argon (or helium) compressor and partly expanded for driving turbine generator. The working fluid after passing through compressor and intercooler returned back to the heat exchanger HX1. This is loop 3 and may be called a steam loop.

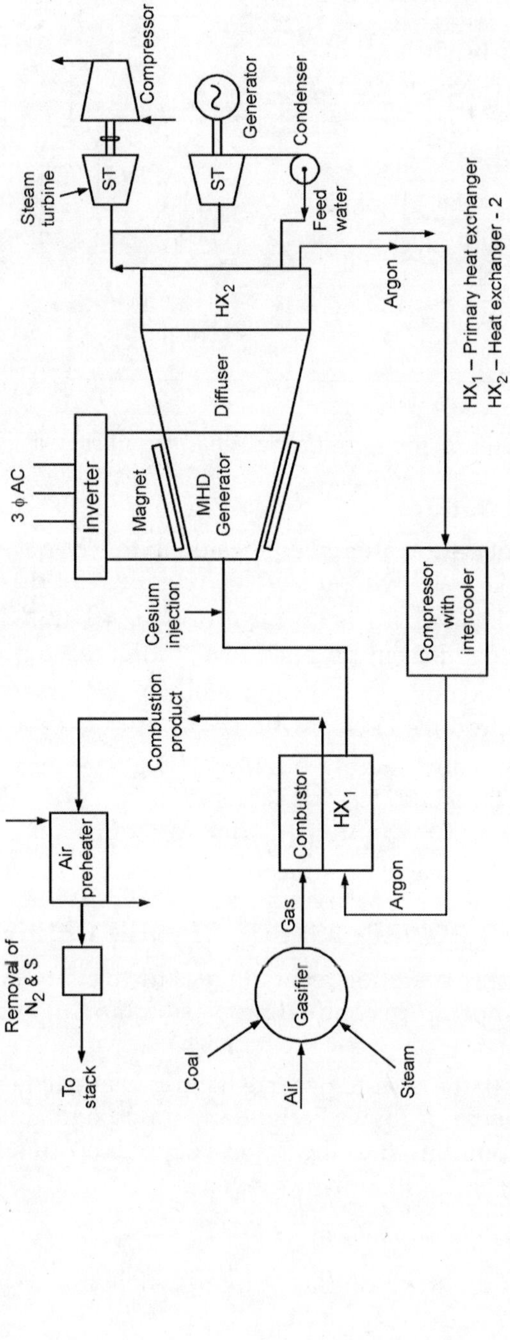

*Fig. 8.3 **(a)** Seeded Insert Gas System*

(ii) Liquid Metal System

Fig. 8.3(*b*) shows the schematic of a *closed-cycle liquid metal system.* In this system, a liquid metal (*Potassium*) is used *as a working fluid.*

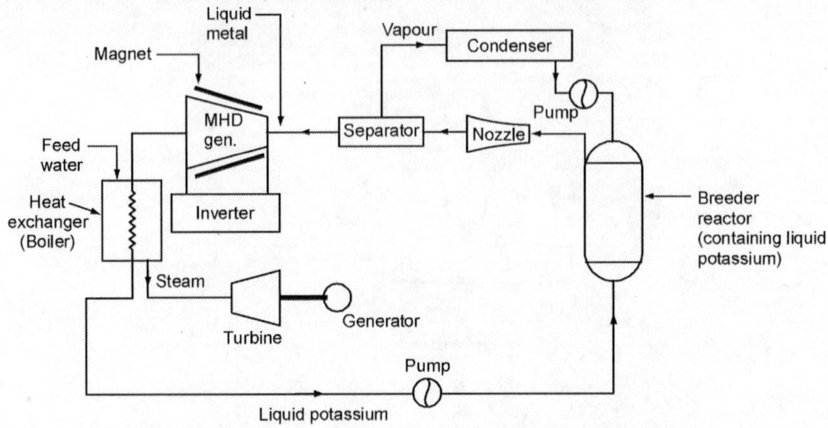

Fig. 8.3(b) Closed-cycle (liquid metal) system

Construction and working

- The liquid potassium after being heated in the *'breeder reactor'* is passed through the 'nozzle' where its velocity is increased.
- The vapours formed due to nozzle action are separated in the *'separater'* and *condensed* and them pumped back to the reactor.
- Then the liquid metal with high velocity is passed through *'MHD generator'* to produce D.C. power.
- The liquid possium coming out of MHD generator is passed through the *heat exchanger'* (boiler) to use its remaining heat to run a turbine-generator set and then pumped back to the reactor.
- The *system entails many constructional and operational difficulties.*

8.3 VOLTAGE AND POWER OUTPUT OF MHD GENERATOR

The MHD power generation technology is the production of electric poer utilizing a high temperature conducting plasma moving through an intense magnetic field.

Let us assume that a charge particle having charge q (a positive charge), moving with a velocity v' towards right and a perpendicular magnetic field of flux density B, pointing into the paper is applied. A magnetic orce F acts on the charged particle. This force is given by.

$$\vec{F} = q(\vec{v}' \times \vec{B}) \qquad ...(8.1)$$

Fig. (8.4) gives the force on the charge particle moving in the magnetic field.

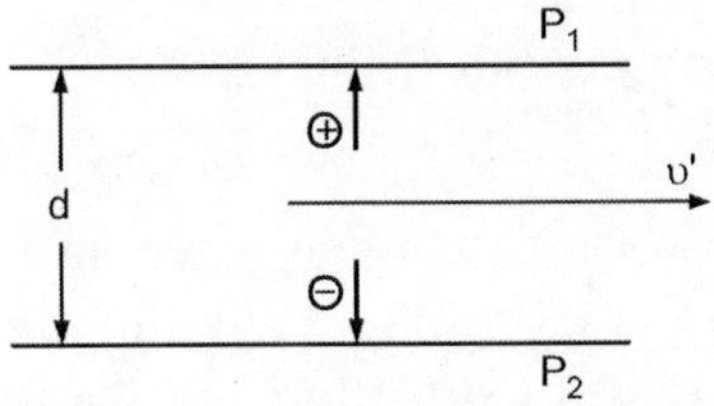

Fig. 8.4 Force on the charge particle

Force F, velocity v', and magnetic flux density B are vectors. A positively charge particle is forced upwards and negatively charge particle is forced downward. If the particle is replaced by a mass of ionised gas molecules, moving at a velocity v', the positive ions would be accelerated towards the upper plate P_1 and the negative ions would be accelerated towards the plate P_2. If the pates $P_1$and P_2 are externally connected through a resistance, a current would flow through the resistance. Thus mechanical energy is extracted from the gas and converted into electrocal energy. This is the principle of MHD generation. It is a reversible process. If an emf is applied, in place of resistance, in a direction opposite to the direction of above current, energy would be supplied to gas and the gas particles would be accelerated.

If an electric field of strength E is also operate in the region, the total force experienced as

$$\vec{F} = q\vec{E} + q(\vec{v}' \times \vec{B})$$

$$= q(\vec{E} + \vec{v}' \times \vec{B}) \qquad ...(8.2)$$

Throughout the following analysis, the symbol q denotes a positive charge. If in the final experessions, the solutions for electrons are required, then all that is needed is the subatitution $q = -e$, where e is equal to 1.602×10^{-19} Coulomb. Equation (8.1) defines the direction of force.

In the case of the MHD generator, the velocity v' in equation (8.2) is the vector sum of the gas velocity u, and the particle drift velocity (heing driven by current) v *i.e.*

$$v' = \vec{u} + \vec{v} \qquad ...(8.3)$$

Equation (8.2) now become

$$\vec{F} = q\vec{E} + (q\vec{u} \times \vec{B}) + (q\vec{v} \times B)$$

$$= q(\vec{E} + \vec{u} \times \vec{B} + \vec{v} \times \vec{B}) \qquad ...(8.4)$$

Equation (8.4) can be written as

$$\vec{F} = q\vec{E} + q(\vec{v} \times \vec{B}) \qquad ...(8.5)$$

where $E' = (E + \vec{u} \times \vec{B})$, is the effective field seen by the moving particle. The draft velocity is related to the force on the particles through the mobility, μ *i.e.*

$$F = \frac{qv}{\mu} \qquad ...(8.6)$$

Equation (8.4) then becomes

$$\vec{v} = \mu\vec{E} + \mu(\vec{u} + \vec{B}) + \mu(\vec{v} + \vec{B}) \quad ...(8.7)$$

This is the general equation.

Referring to Fig. (8.5), the motion of the gas is in x direction, magnetic field B is in y direction and the force on the particle is in x direction. When the current I is flowing across load resistance R_L, with voltage V across the load, then electric intensity between the plates will be given by

$$\vec{E}_a = -\frac{V}{d} \quad ...(8.8)$$

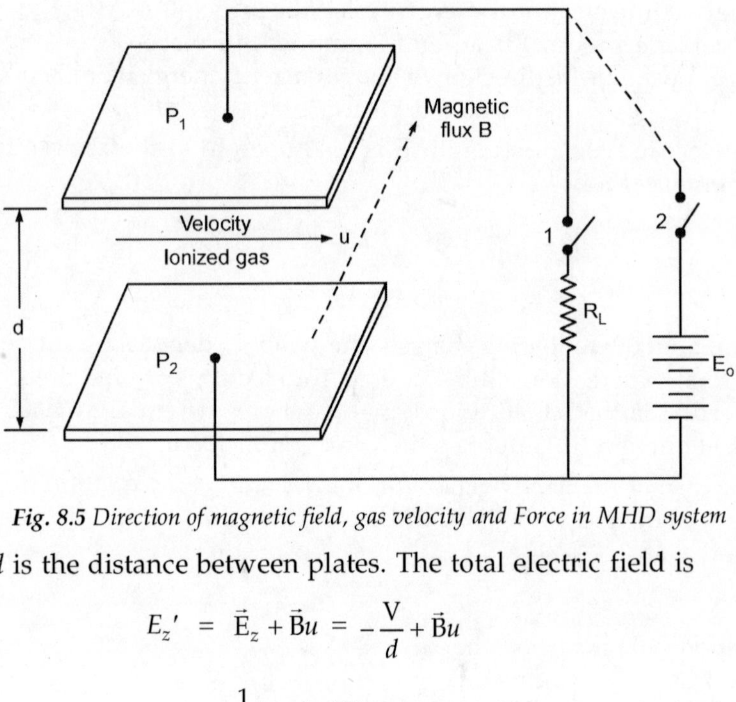

***Fig. 8.5** Direction of magnetic field, gas velocity and Force in MHD system*

where d is the distance between plates. The total electric field is

$$E_z' = \vec{E}_z + \vec{B}u = -\frac{V}{d} + \vec{B}u$$

$$= \frac{1}{d}(Bud - V) \quad ...(8.9)$$

The electromagnetic field E_z and B acting on the moving gas produce the same force on the ions as the electromagnetif fields. E_x' and B produce on a gas with zero average velocity. Evidently the open circuit voltage

$$E_0 = Bud \quad ...(8.10)$$

The R_g = internal resistance of the generator

$$= \frac{d}{\sigma A} \quad ...(8.11)$$

where σ = conductivity of the gas

A = plate area

Maximum power output (P_{max}) is obtained when internal resistance and total resistance are equal *i.e.*

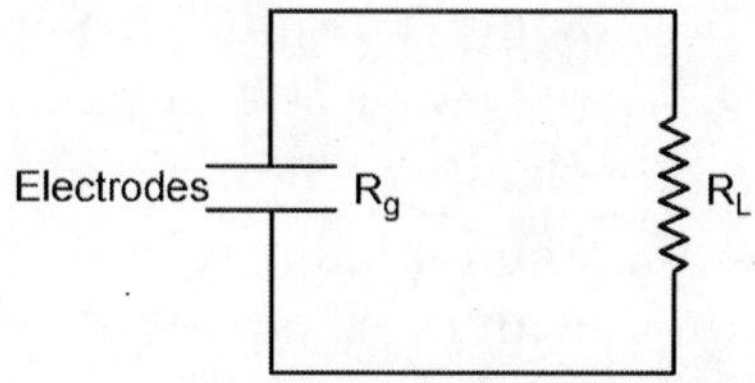

Fig. 8.6 Electrical circuit of MHD generator

$$R_g = R_L$$

$$P_{max} = E_0 I$$

$$= I R_g I = I^2 R_g$$

$$= \left(\frac{E_0}{R_L + R_g} \right)^2 R_g$$

$$= \frac{E_0^2}{4R_g} \quad ...(8.12)$$

$$= \frac{B^2 u^2 d^2}{4R_g} \quad (\because \; E_0 = Bud)$$

Putting the value of R_g from equation (8.11)

$$P_{max} = \frac{B^2 u^2 d^2}{4d} \sigma A$$

$$= \frac{1}{4} \sigma u^2 B^2 dA$$

$\therefore$ Maximum Power per unit volume

$$= \frac{1}{4} \sigma u^2 B^2 \quad ...(8.13)$$

It can be shown with the help of Fig. (8.5). that if an external voltage greater than B*ud* (or E_0) be connected instead of Load by putting the switch to position 2, then the directions of current and force acting on ions are reversed. The system tends to speed up the gas velocity. The velocity of the ejected gas is higher than the velocity of inlet gas. The reaction force acting on the magnet tends to push the MHD generator in the negative *x* direction. Electrical energy is converted in mechanical energy.

8.4 ADVANTAGE OF MHD POWER GENERATION

MHD power generation offers several advantage over other conventional methods of power generation.

1. In MHD power generation high temperatures are involved, operation efficiency is high.
2. In MHD power generations there is no moving part, so it is more reliable
3. Lesser thermal pollution.
4. In MHD power generations, there is no limitation to the size of the durt, so high capacity generations are possible.

5. Direct conversion of heat into electrical energy results in elimination of the gas turbine (compared with a gas turbine power plant) and both the boiler and turbine (compared with a conventional steam power plant) and thus in reduction of energy losses.
6. The capital cost of the MHD plants are estimated to be competitive with those of coal fired steam power plant
7. The overall costs of the MHD power generation are also estimated to be lower (20%) than those of conventional power plants. This is because of higher efficiency of MHD power generating.
8. All kinds of heat sources such as coal oil, gas, solar and nuclear can be used with MHD generator.
9. MHD generators have low specific weight, rapid start, high power density and compact.

8.5 PROBLEMS ENCOUNTERED IN DESIGN OF MHD

1. The combustor, MHD-generator channel, electrodes, and air preheater are exposed to corrosive combustion gases at very high temperatures, materials must be developed to permit an adequate operating life for the components.
2. Another problem is separation of the seed material (as potassium sulphate) from the flyash and its reconversion into its original (carbonate) form. Otherwise seed material potassium sulphate attacks insulating materials and make them conducting.
3. The power output of an MHD generator is theoretically proportional to the square of the magnetic field strength (Equation 8.13). Hence a strong magnetic field is desirable. Thus, for large scale MHD power generation, instead of conventional electro-magnets which require very large currents, the superconducting magnets, which use very little current, will be necessary.
4. The major problem forced by this generator is the economics. Although the overall thermal efficiency is 60% against 40% for conventional thermal plant, additional investment in the magnet, generator, duct, compressors, scrubbers, seed recovery plant and DC to AC converters may increase the plant cost and it may be much higher than conventional plant.

8.6 MATERIALS FOR MHD GENERATORS

Owing to high temperature of plasma (2700°C), refractory materials are requiredin various partsof MHD generator like electrodes, channel or duct wall.

The materials for various parts are given in Table below:

Table Materials for MHD generators

S. No.	Components	Required properties	Materials
1.	*Electrodes*	High conductivity, stable at high temperature.	Zirconia based, materials, chromite based materials, Aluminate based materials, Nickel oxide based materials.
2.	*Channel or duct*	Thermal and electrical insulator	$MgAl_2O_3$, Beta alumina ($KAl_{11}O_{17}$), MgO
3.	*Magnet*	Stronger than permanent magnet	Tin, Niobium, Niobium 33, Niobiumtitanium
4.	*Insulator*	Withstand high temperature	Oxides, Nitrides, Zirconates, etc.

8.7 GAS CONDUCTIVITY

This is the most important parameter in the power generation. A reasonable conductivity refers to a value between about 10 to 100 mhos/m. Most metals have conductivities of the order of 107 mhos/m and even transistor materials have conductivities exceeding 100 mhos/m. The gas has to be sufficiently conducting, in order that it may be utilized as a working fluid. In other words, it has to be ionized - processes in which electrons are removed from an atom. Conduction is due to the free electrons and positive ions which move under the effect of a magnetic field.

There are several types of ionization:

1. Thermal ionization : This is the most important method of ionizing plasma. Ionization is obtained by imparting enough thermal energy to the gas. It depends upon the temperature.
2. Magnetically Induced Ionisation : A dc voltage is applied across a gas at reduced pressure to create an electric field which will supply energy to electrons.
3. Radio-frequency wave induced ionization : It is used to produce a low amount of ionization in a gas. This is not effectively enough for MHD generation.

Other methods of Ionisation

1. Seeding

One way of increasing the conductivity of gas withou the need of exceedingly high temperature, is to introduce into the gas a material whose ionisation potential is lower than of the gas.

This means that the addition of seeding agent will ionize more readily than the gas itself & will thus enhance the electrical conductivity.

Main seeding materials are alkali metals like caesium, potassium etc. the addition of the seeding material allows the attainment of suitable conductivites at very much lower temperature.

However owing to the difficulties incurred, alternative methods of increasing the conductivity are intensively studied.

2. Non-thermal ionization

An alternative approach to the problem of achieving adequate conductivity is to obtain the required electron density by a non-equilibrium process.

This non-equilibrium state must then be maintained for a long time to allow the gas to pass through the generator duct in non-equilibrium ionisation systems, the carrier is a monoatomic gas this is usually the chemically inert gas argon, although helium is possible alternatives.

Adequate electrical conductivity for MHD application can thus be attained in a monoatomic gas with a cesium seed at temperture below 2000 degree Celsius.

8.8 APPLICATION OF MHD GENERATION

1. MHD generators are used to power submarines and aircrafts.
2. Electrical power production for domestic applications.
3. They can be used as power plants in industry and uninterrupted power supply system.
4. Plasma physics applications
5. Hypersonic wind tunnel experiments

8.9 PERFORMANCE OF MHD GENERATION

Of all the emerging power generation technologies, MHD offers one of the most promising performance efficiency. Overall efficiencies of MHD systems may exceed 50% as compared to 34-37% projected for conventional coal-fired plants with FGD now scheduled for construction. Using MHD conversion as a topping cycle for a conventional steam turbine, an overall efficiency of 50 to 60 percent should be possible. This may be compared with about 40% for the most efficient steam turbine. Since coal-fired steam power plants currently supply about half of the nation's electrical energy, merely adding MHD as a topping system to existing plants could conceivably increase the nation's generating capacity by as much as 25% with the same fuel consumption.

8.10 ENVIRONMENTAL ASPECTS OF MHD GENERATION

Reduced atmospheric contamination is one of the most significant aspects in favour of MHD generation. Burning the same grade coal as conventional steam power plants, MHD plants reduce particulate pollutants by 91 percent, sulfur oxide pollutants by 99.3 percent and nitrogen oxide pollutants by 92 percent. The MHD process requires all exhaust gases to be treated before going up the stack.

Thermodynamically, MHD operates more efficiently than present power plants. An MHD plant can produce the same amount of power as a conventional steam-generating plant with 30 percent less fuel. If MHD replaces conventional coal-fired generating plants as the primary power production method, power demands could be met and the degree of air pollution would actually decline.

MHD not only reduces air pollution but reduces thermal pollution as well. The process develops more power per pound of coal burned, therefore less energy is lost as heat carried away by a cooling system. Although MHD does have definite environmental advantages over conventional power production methods the system contains potential dangers to our environment which must be acted upon and eliminated.

Effluents resulting from the MHD processes, seed regeneration, and solid waste disposal need to be characterized and assessed to ensure that they do not contain any unexcepted hazardous pollutants or excessively high potassium levels, and that they will meet applicable water quality standards. Also in order for open-cycle MHD to be acceptable both environmentally and economically, it is expected that the seed material containing potassium compounds must be recovered, probably regenerated and recycled.

Large scale MHD power production will necessitate accelerated coal mining operations. Adequate safeguards must be instituted to insure that coal mining operations do not damage the environment in the future as they have in the past.

SOLVED EXAMPLES

Example 8.1 : An MHD duct has an inlet pressure of 10 atm and discharges into the atmosphere.

(*a*) Find its volume for a length 20 m and inlet diameter of 2 m, if the duct is of circular cross-section throughout, as well as theoutlet diameter.

(*b*) Repeat for a square cross-section, if the inlet dimension is 1.5 m and duct lengthof 25 m.

Solution : For both cases, outlet area = 10 × inlet area.

(*a*) $$\text{Outlet dia} = \sqrt{10} \times \text{inlet dia} = 2\sqrt{10} = 6.235 \text{ m}$$

$$\text{Volume} = \pi(2 + 6.325)^2 \times 10/16 = 272.2 \text{ m}^3$$

$$\text{Inlet area} = \pi 2^2/4 = 3.1416 \text{ m}^2$$

(*b*) $$\text{Outlet dimension} = 1.5\sqrt{10} = 4.4743 \text{ m}$$

$$\text{Outlet area} = 10 \times \text{inlet area} = 10 \times 1.5^2 = 22.5 \text{ m}^2$$

$$\text{Volume of duct} = [(1.5 + 4.743)/2]^2 \times 25 = 243.6 \text{ m}^3$$

Example 8.2 : With the following specifications for an MHD generator, calculate the open circuit voltage and maximum power output.

Plate are = 0.25 m^2

Distance between plates = 0.50 m

Flux density = 2 Wb/m^2

Average gas velocity = 10^3 m/second

Gaseour conductivity = 10 Mho/m.

Solution : We have open circuit voltage

$$E_0 = Bud$$

where B = flux density

u = Average gas velocity

d = distance between plates.

$$E_0 = 2 \times 1000 \times 0.50 = 1000 \text{ volts.} \quad \textbf{Ans.}$$

Generator resistance

$$R_g = \frac{d}{\sigma A} = \frac{0.50}{10 \times 0.25} = 0.20 \text{ ohm}$$

Maximum power

$$= \frac{E_0^2}{4R_g} \text{ watts}$$

$$= \frac{(1000)^2}{4 \times 0.20} = \frac{1000 \times 1000}{0.80}$$

$$= \frac{10}{0.80} \times 10^5 \text{ watts} = 1250 \text{ kW.} \quad \textbf{Ans.}$$

REVIEW QUESTIONS

1. Explain the basic principle of MHD power generation with suitable diagrams.
2. How the MHD systems are classified? Explain them in brief.
3. Explain the working principle of MHD power generation in detail. Derive the suitable relations.
4. What are the advantages of MHD power generation?
5. Explain Open cycle MHD system with suitable diagrams.
6. Explain Seeded Inert Gas System with suitable diagrams.

7. Explain Liquid Metal System with suitable diagrams.
8. Derive the equations for the voltage and power output of an MHD generator.
9. What are the problems encountered in designing of MHD?
10. An MHD generator has the following parameters:

    Plate area = 0.20 m^2

    Distance between plates = 0.4 m^2

    Flux density = 2 Wb/m^2

    Average gas velocity = 1000 m/s

    Conductivity of the gas = 10 mho/m

    Calculate the open circuit voltage and maximum power output. [Ans. 800 volts, 800 kW]
11. What are the materials used for MHD generator.

❑

9

Fuel Cells

9.1 INTRODUCTION

A fuel cell is a electrochemical device that converts chemical energy into electrical energy and heat without combustion.

Fuel cell system generally operate on pure hydrogen and air to produce water and heat as the bi-product; in the process electrons are released and flow through an external circuit as an electric current. A catalyst is often used to speed up the reactions at the electrodes.

A fuel cell requires continuous supply of a fuel and oxidant to produce d.c. electric power.

The basic difference between battery and fuel cell is batteries stores electrical charges and after discharge it needs recharging but in fuel cell recharging is not required.

In fuel cell, the fuel and oxidant are combined in the form of ions rather than neutral molecules.

In fuel cells the chemical energy of the reactants is converted into electrical energy as an isothermal process.

9.2 WORKING PRINCIPLE OF FUEL CELLS

The two permeable nickel electrodes are immersed in a well conducting electrolyte (a solution of H_2SO_4 for acidic fuel cell and KOH for alkali fuel cells).

Negative electrode (anode) is fed with hydrogen and positive electrode (cathode) is fed with oxygen. The electrodes are connected together through an external circuit. Then for every molecule of hydrogen consumed, two electrons pass from negative to positive electrodes where they react with absorbed oxygen.

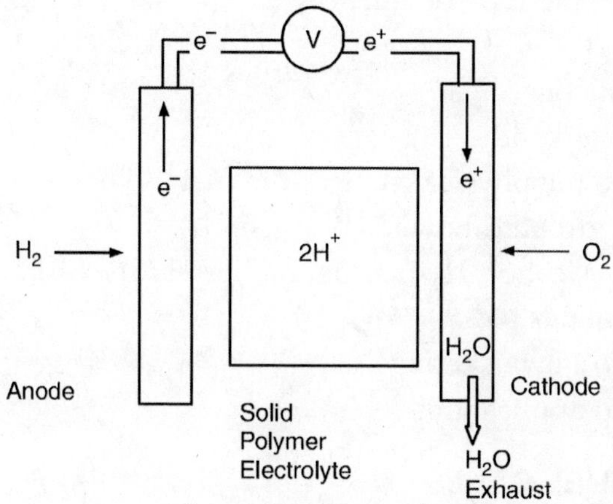

Fig. 9.1 A hydrogen-oxygen fuel cell

At anode, hydrogen gas is ionized, producing free electrons and H+ ions.

Every hydrogen molecule brought to the electrode surface is dissociated into two atoms by virtue of the catalytic property of the surface. These enter the solution as hydrogen ions leaving behind two electrons which pass through the external circuit to the positive electrode (cathode). The oxygen supplied to the positive electrode reacts with hydrogen ions from the electrolyte and the electrons to give water. Thus water is the waste product of the cell, which is formed at cathode.

The reaction are :

At anode

$$H_2(g) \longrightarrow 2H^+(aq) + 2e^-$$

At cathode

$$\frac{1}{2}O_2(g) + 2H^+(aq) + 2e^- \longrightarrow H_2O(l)$$

The Overall reaction is

$$H_2(g) + \frac{1}{2}O_2(g) \longrightarrow H_2O(l)$$

9.3 CLASSIFICATION OF FUEL CELLS

Fuel cell may be classified in the various ways :

1. According to the temperature range in which they operate
   - (*a*) Low temperature 25-100°C
   - (*b*) Medium temperature 100-500°C
   - (*c*) High temperature 500-1000°C
   - (*d*) and very high temperature above-1000°C

2. According to the type of electrolyte
   (*a*) aqueous
   (*b*) Non aqueous
   (*c*) Molten or solid
3. According to the physical state of the fuel
   (*a*) Gas–Hydrogen, Lower Hydrogen
   (*b*) Liquid–Alcohol, Hydrozine, higher Hydro carbon
   (*c*) Solid–Metals etc.
4. According to Power Ratings
5. According to applications.

9.4 TYPES OF FUEL CELLS

9.4.1 Alkaline Fuel Cell (AFC)

In this type of cell Potassium hydroxide (KOH) is used as a electrolyte. In this type of cell wide range of electro-catalyst can be used eg. nickel, nobel metal etc.

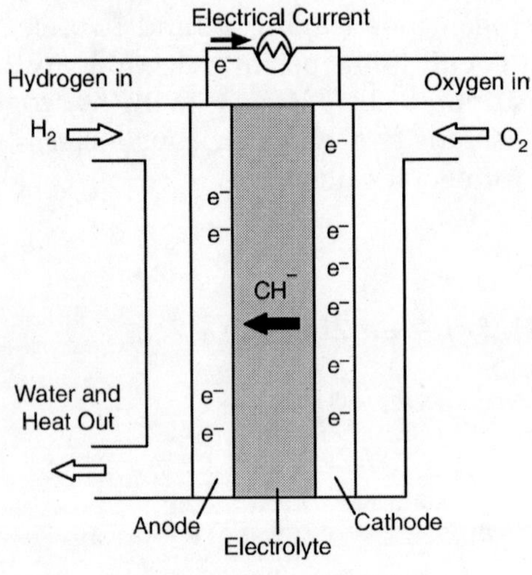

Fig.9.2 Alkaline Fuel Cell

In Alkali fuel cell:

At the anode, hydrogen gas reacts with the OH- ions producing water and releasing electrons. The reaction is

$$\text{Anode : } \quad 2H_2 + 4OH^- \longrightarrow 4H_2O + 4e^- \qquad ...(9.3)$$

Now the e^- reaches to the cathode through electrical circuit attached to the fuel cell. Then at cathode e- react with the oxygen and water producing more OH^- to be used at the anode.

Cathode : $O_2 + 2H_2O + 4e^- \longrightarrow 4OH^-$ ...(9.4)

Now the OH^- ions move through the electrolyte and the electrons move round the circuit.

Water is produced at the anode as fast as it is used up at the cathode.

The net reaction in the fuel cell is hydrogen and oxygen supplied to the fuel cell produce electrical energy, water and heat.

AFCs are high-performance fuel cells having efficiencies of 60 percent in space applications. Cost is less of a factor for remote locations such as space or under the sea.

The disadvantage of this fuel cell type is that it is easily poisoned by carbon dioxide (CO_2). CO_2 can combine with KOH to form potassium carbonate which will increase the resistance.

9.4.2 Proton Exchange Membrane Fuel Cell (PEMFC)

The electrolyte in this fuel cell is an ion exchange membrane (fluorinated sulfonic acid polymer or other similar polymer) that is an excellent proton conductor. They are also called polymer electrolyte membrane fuel cells (PEFC). It uses a platinum-based catalyst on both electrodes.

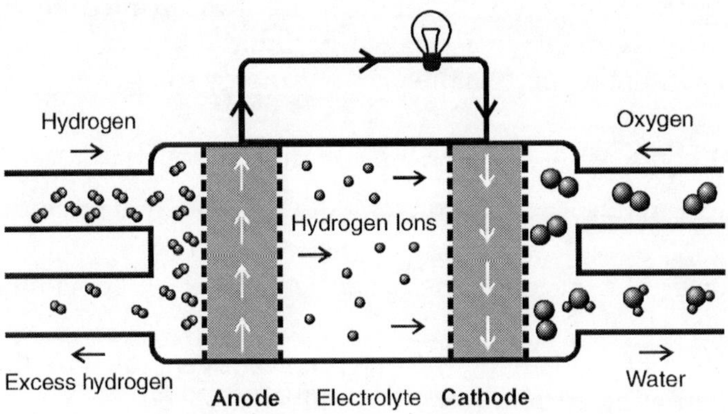

Fig.9.3 Proton Exchange Membrane Fuel Cell

At Anode : $2H_2 \longrightarrow 4H^+ + 4e^-$ ...(9.5)

At Cathode : $O_2 + 4H^+ + 4e^- \longrightarrow 2H_2O$ ...(9.6)

Total Reaction $2H_2 + O_2 \longrightarrow 2H_2O$ ...(9.7)

In PEMFC, the fuel is hydrogen and charge carriers are hydrogen ion (Proton). At anode, the hydrogen molecule is split into hydrogen ions and electrons. The hydrogen ions permeate across the electrolyte to cathode while the e- flow through an external circuit and produce electric power oxygen is supplied to the cathode and com bines with electrons and the hydrogen ions to produce water.

Advantages

1. Proton exchange membrane fuel cell generates more power for a given volume i.e. has high power density.
2. Operating temperature is less than 100°C
3. Rapid start
4. Less Expensive
5. Larger life.
6. Because of solid electrolyte, PEMFC cells has fewer problems with corrosion.

The main disadvantage of this type cell is that due to low operating temperature these are not enough to perform useful co-generation. These cells are suitable for transportation application.

Water management in the membrane is critical for efficient performance; the fuel cell must operate under conditions where the by-product water does not evaporate faster than it is produced because the membrane must be hydrated.

9.4.3 Fossil Fuels Cells

The most interesting fuel cells for the near future are modified hydrogen-oxygen (or air) cells, in which a gaseous or liquid hydrocarbon is the source of hydrogen. Coal may serve as the primary energy source for fuel cells. (see Fig. 9.3)

Cell based on fossil fuels have three main components :

1. The fuel processor which converts the fossil fuel into a hydrogen-rich gas.
2. The power section consisting of the actual fuel cell (or combination of cells)
3. The inverter for changing the direct current generated by the fuel cell into alternating current to be transmitted to user.

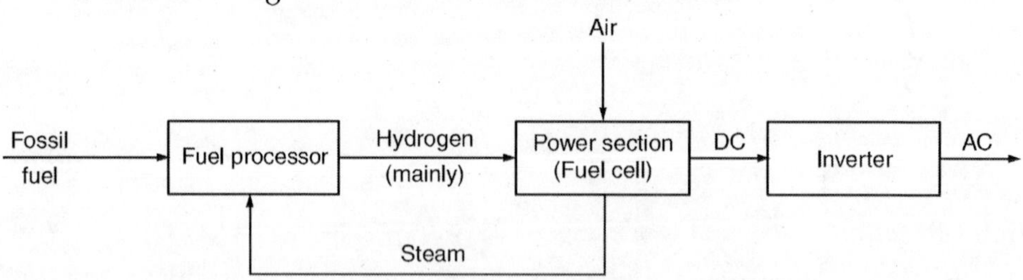

Fig. 9.4 Fossil fuel cell

The most highly developed fossil fuel cells are phosphoric acid cells, molten carbonate cell, solid oxide electrolyte cell.

9.4.4 Phosphoric Acid Fuel Cells (PAFC)

The electrolyte in this fuel cell is 100% concentrated phosphoric acid (H_3PO_4). It uses a finely dispersed platinum catalyst on carbon.

The ionic conductivity of phosphoric acid is low at low temperature.

PAFC is similar in operation to PEMFC.

PAFC are operated at 150°C to 220°C. The PAFC operates at greater than 40% efficiency in generating electricity when operating in co-generation applications, the overall efficiency is approximately 85%.

PAFC offer the lowest cost per KW and are used mainly for plants of 50 to 200 KW capacity.

In addition, the use of concentrated acid (100 percent) minimizes the water vapor pressure so water management in the cell is not difficult.

PAFCs are much less sensitive to CO than PEFCs and AFCs. In addition, the waste heat from PAFC can be readily used in most commercial and industrial cogeneration applications, and would technically allow the use of a bottoming cycle.

9.4.5 Molten Carbonate Fuel Cells (MCFC)

Molten carbonate fuel cells use an electrolyte, which is a molten mixture of carbonate salt. Two minutes are used : Lithium carbonate and potassium carbonate, or lithium carbonate and sodium carbonate. These salt can act as electrolytes only in liquid phase, the operating temperature should be as high as 650°C. (see Fig. 9.5)

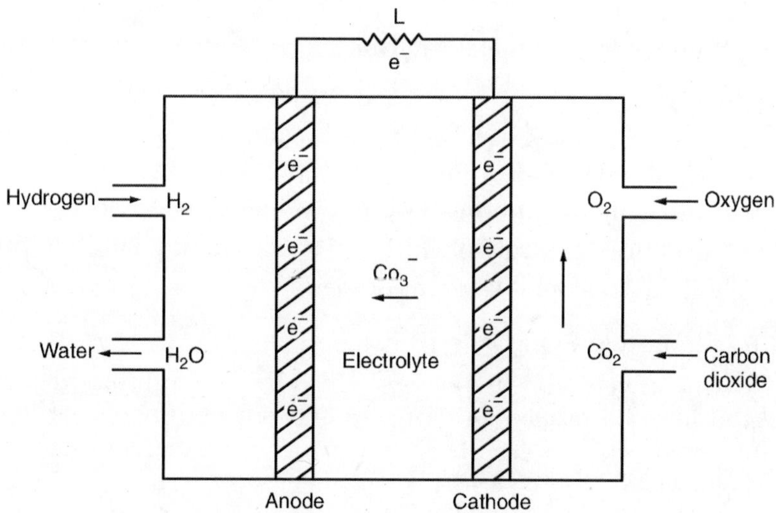

Fig. 9.5 Molten carbonate fuel cell

At anode $$CO_3^{--} + H_2 \longrightarrow H_2O + CO_2 + 2e^-$$

At cathode $CO_2 + \frac{1}{2}O_2 + 2e^- \longrightarrow CO_3^{--}$

Total Reaction $H_2(g) + \frac{1}{2}O_2(g) + CO_2 \text{ (cathode)} \rightarrow H_2O + CO_2 \text{ (anode)}$

When heated to a temperature of around 650°C, then salts melt and became conductive to carbonate ions (CO_3^{--}).

There ions flow the cathode to anode where they combine with hydrogen to give water, carbon dioxide and e^-. The e^- flow through external circuit and reaches to cathode generating electricity and by product heat.

The cathode process combines oxygen and CO_2 from the oxidant stream with electrons from the cathode to produce carbonate ions which enter the electrolyte. The need for CO_2 in the oxidant stream requires a system for collecting CO_2 from the anode exhaust and mixing it with the cathode feed stream.

Efficiency of MCFC is more than PAFC around 60%. The by product heat from MCFC can be used to generate high pressure steam that can be used in many industries and commercial applications.

Advantages

1. Support spontaneous internal reforming of light hydro-carbon fuels.
2. Generate high-grade waste heat
3. Have a fast reaction kinetics (react quickly)
4. Have high efficiency
5. Do not need noble metal catalyst.

Disadvantages

1. Have a high intolerance to sulfur. The anode in particular cannot tolerate more than 1-5 ppm of sulfur compounds (primarily H_2S and COS) n the fuel gas without suffering a significant performance loss.
2. Have a liquid electrolyte which introduces liquid handling problems.
3. Require a considerable warm up period.

9.4.6 Regenerative Fuel Cells (RFC)

A regenerative fuel cell is one in which the fuel cell product (water) is recovered into the reactants (hydrogen and oxygen) by one of the several possible methods - thermal, chemical, photochemical, electrical and radiochemical.

There are two stages in a regenerative fuel cell:

1. Conversion of fuel cell reactants into products while producing electrical energy, and
2. Reconversion of fuel cell products into reactants.

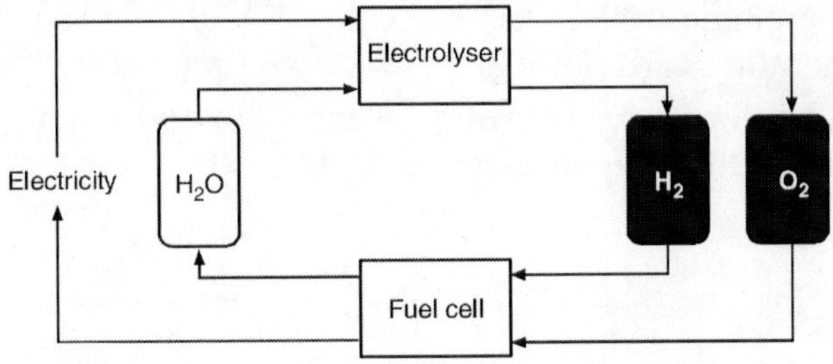

Fig.9.6 A Regenerative Fuel Cell System

A hydrogen fueled Proton exchange membrane fuel cell, for example, uses hydrogen gas (H_2) and oxygen (O_2) to produce electricity and water (H_2O); a regenerative hydrogen fuel cell uses electricity and water to produce hydrogen and oxygen.

When the fuel cell is operated in regenerative mode, the anode for the electricity production mode (fuel cell mode) becomes the cathode in the hydrogen generation mode (reverse fuel cell mode), and vice versa. When an external voltage is applied, water at the cathode side will undergo electrolysis to form hydrogen and oxide ions; oxide ions will be transported through the electrolyte to anode where it can be oxidized to form oxygen. In this reverse mode, the polarity of the cell is opposite to that for the fuel cell mode. The following reactions describe the chemical process in the hydrogen generation mode:

At cathode : $H_2O + 2e^- \rightarrow H_2 + O^{2-}$

At anode : $O^{2-} \rightarrow 1/2O_2 + 2e^-$

Overall : $H_2O \rightarrow 1/2O_2 + H_2$

9.4.7 Direct Methanol Fuel Cells (DMFC)

In direct Methanol fuel cells (DMFC) Polymer is used as electrolyte and charge carrier is the hydrogen ion.

It uses a platinum-ruthenium catalyst on the anode and a platinum catalyst on the cathode. This catalyst can draw hydrogen atoms from liquid methanol, which is used as fuel instead of hydrogen, giving the cell its name.

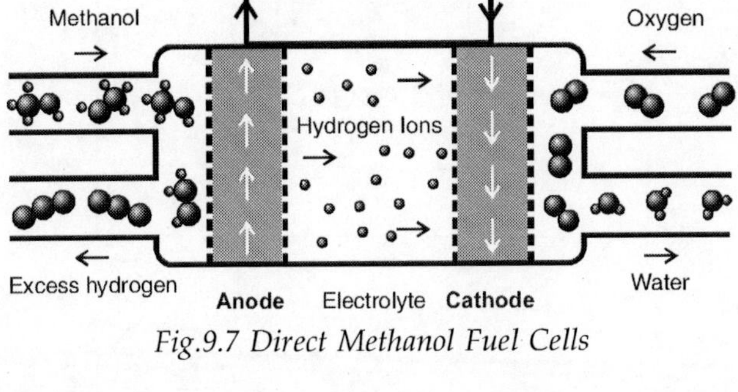

Fig.9.7 Direct Methanol Fuel Cells

The liquid methanol (CH_3OH) is oxidized in the pressure of water at anode and generating carbon dioxide, Hydrogen ions and electrons.

The hydrogen ions travel through electrolyte and react with oxygen. The electrons travel through the external circuit and form water at the anode.

Anode Reactions $$CH_3OH + H_2O \longrightarrow CO_2 + 6H^+ + 6e^-$$

Cathode Reaction $$\frac{3}{2}O_2 + 6H^+ + 6e^- \longrightarrow 3H_2O$$

Total Reactions $$CH_3OH + \frac{3}{2}O_2 \longrightarrow CO_2 + 2H_2O$$

Efficiency of these cells is approximately 40% at operating temperature 50°C-120°C. The main disadvantage of this cell is that at low temperature oxidation of methanol to hydrogen. ions and carbon dioxide requires more active catalyst, which increase the cost and weight.

DMFC are convenient for portable power applications with outputs generally less than 250 W.

9.4.8 Solid Oxide Fuel Cell (SOFC)

Solid oxide fuel cells (SOFC) (see Fig. 9.8) operate at high temp^r between 650°C to 1000°C. The electrolyte in this cell is a solid non porous metal oxide that is conductive to oxygen ions. The charge carrier is SOFC is oxygen ion. At the cathode, the oxygen molecule from the air are split into oxygen ion with the addition of four electrons. The oxygen ions are conducted through the electrolyte and combine with hydrogen at the anode releasing four e^-. The electrons move through the internal circuit producing electric power and by product heat.

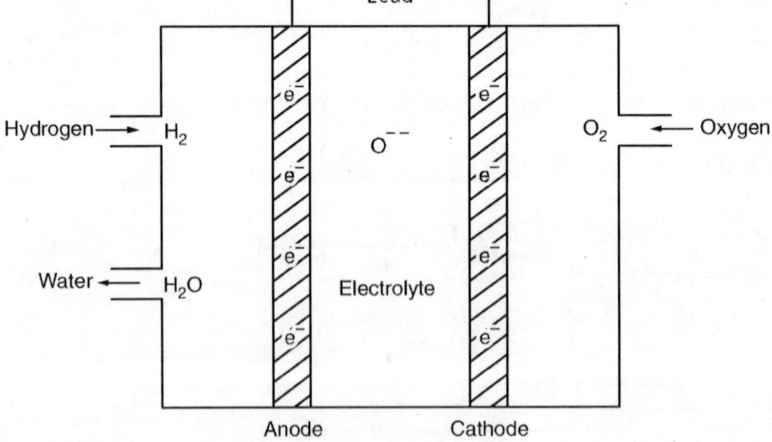

Fig. 9.8 Solid oxide fuel cell

At anode $2H_2 + 2O^{--} \longrightarrow 2H_2O + 4e^-$

At cathode $4e^- + O_2 \longrightarrow 2O^{--}$

Advantages

1. Since all the components are solid, as a result, there is no need for electrolyte loss maintenance and also electrode corrosion is eliminated.
2. Since SOFCs are operated at high temperature, expensive catalysts such as platinum or ruthenium are totally avoided.
3. Low cost
4. Due to high-quality waste heat for cogeneration applications and low activation losses, the efficiency for electricity production is greater than 50%.

Disadvantages

SOFCs operate high temperature, so the materials used as components are thermally challenged.

Applications

They can be used as power systems for trains, ships and vehicles; supplying electrical power for residential or industrial utility.

9.5 PERFORMANCE ANALYSIS OF A FUEL CELL

In a fuel cell a chemical reaction takes place whereby the reactants are converted into products in a steady flow process.

From the first law of thermodynamics for a steady flow process,

$$\Delta Q - \Delta W = \Delta H + \Delta(KE) + \Delta(PE)$$

Where ΔQ = heat transferred to the steady flow stream from the surroundings

ΔW = workdone by the flow stream on the surroundings

ΔH = change in enthalpy of the flow stream from entrance to exit and

$\Delta(KE)$ and $\Delta(PE)$ denote changes in kinetic and potential energy of the stream, which in this case is negligible.

Hence,

$$\Delta W = \Delta Q - \Delta H$$

If ΔW is to be maximum, the process must be reversible. For a reversible process,

$$\Delta Q\text{reversible} = T\Delta S \quad \text{(from 2}^{\text{nd}}\text{ law of thermodynamics)}$$

Thus,

$$\Delta W_{max} = T\Delta S - \Delta H = -(\Delta H - T\Delta S)$$

Gibbs free energy G is given by

$$G = H - TS \qquad \text{where H is enthalpy}$$

Therefore, $\Delta G = \Delta H - T\Delta S - S\Delta T = \Delta H - T\Delta S$ as T is constant.

Hence, $\Delta W_{max} = -\Delta G$

It states that the maximum useful workdone by a steady flow system during a process equals the negative of the change in Gibbs free energy of the system.

In order to determine the reversible voltage or emf of the cell the following equation is considered.

$$\Delta W_{rev} = E\,\Delta q = nFE$$

Where Δq is charge transported which is equal to nF.

Thus,

$$E = \frac{\Delta W_{rev}}{nF} = \frac{-\Delta G}{nF} \qquad ...(9.21)$$

The ideal efficiency of an electrochemical energy converter is defined as:

$$\eta_i = \frac{\Delta G}{\Delta H} = -\frac{nFE}{\Delta H}$$

Where

n = number of electrons transferred per molecule of the reactant

F = Faraday's constant = 96500 coulombs per gram-mole

E = Emf of cell

9.6 ADVANTAGES OF FUEL CELL

Fuel cell having following advantages:

1. Efficiency of fuel cell are high, approximately 90%.
2. Fuel cells are compact, noiseless.
3. Fuel cells are pollution free.
4. The unit is lighter, smaller and requires little maintenance because of absence of mechanical part.
5. A fuel cell is quick start in nature, even in sub-freezing temperature down to (–40°C).
6. They require less space for installation as compared to conventional power plants.

9.7 LIMITATION OF FUEL CELLS

1. The development cost of fuel cell is very high.
2. The fuel cells are low voltage and low service life.

9.8 APPLICATIONS OF FUEL CELLS

1. Fuel cells generate direct current which can be used for electric lamps and some small applications such as heat pumps, motors etc.

2. Low cost fuel cells can be used by electric utilities for load leveling.
3. Fuel cells can be used in central-station power plant in which coal is gasified and the gas is used to generate electricity directly by means of fuel cells. Such an installation is expected to have a higher efficiency for fuel utilization than a conventional steam -electric plant.
4. Fuel cells are used in remote or rural areas for mobile and emergency power sources and for vehicle propulsion.
5. Hydrogen-oxygen and hydro-carbon oxygen fuel cells will be used to an increasing extent in special military and space projects.

REVIEW QUESTIONS

1. What is a fuel cell? Explain the working principle and operation of a fuel cell.
2. Comment on the classification of fuel cell. Also explain them.
3. List the advantages and disadvantages of fuel cell.
4. Comment on the applications of fuel cell.
5. Discuss the working of hydrogen-oxygen fuel cell.
6. Describe Regenerative fuel cells. What are the various performance limiting factors of a fuel cell?

❑

10

THERMOELECTRIC AND THERMOIONIC CONVERSIONS

10.1 THERMOELECTRIC CONVERSION SYSTEMS

Thermoelectric conversion system also known as thermo-electric power generator is a device which converts heat energy (thermal energy) into electrical energy through semi-conductor or conductor.

10.1.1 Basic Principles of Thermoelectric Power Generation

(i) Seebeck (thermoelectric) Effect

The German Scientist Seebeck (in 1822) discovered that if two dissimilar materials are joined to form a loop and the two junctions maintained at different temperatures, an e.m.f. will be set up around the loop. This effect has long been used in thermocouples to measure temperatures.

This phenomenon offers one method of producing electrical energy directly from the heat to combustion, but its thermal efficiency is very low, of the order of 1 to 3 per cent.

Consider two dissimilar materials joined together in the form of a loop so that there are two junctions. Such a system is illustrated in Fig. 10.1. If a temperature difference is maintained between these two junctions, an electric current will flow round the loop.

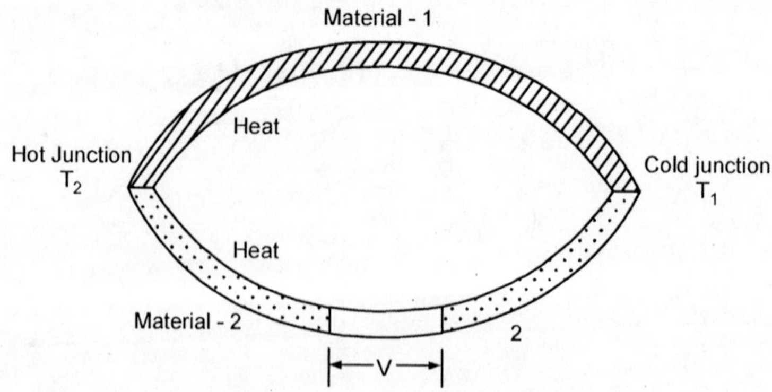

Fig. 10.1 Seebeck Effect Principle

The magnitude of the current will depend on both the materials used and the temperature difference of the junction ($\Delta T = T_2 - T_1$). If the circuit is broken an open circuit voltage 'V' appears across the terminals of the break as shown in Fig. 10.1. The thermo emf, V produced by the device is given by,

$$V = \alpha_{S_{1-2}} \Delta T \qquad ...(10.1)$$

where $\alpha_{S_{1-2}}$ is the seebeck coefficient. The subscript 1 – 2 indicates that the value is particular to the materials composing the loop. In most cases $\alpha_{S_{1-2}}$ is depend on temperature, so that for larger temperature difference it is more accurate to express equation (10.1) in the form,

$$V = \int_{T_1}^{T_2} \alpha_{S_{1-2}} dT \qquad ...(10.2)$$

where T_2 will be throughout to denote the temperature of the hot junction and T_1 that of the cold one. From equation (10.2) it will be seen that the Seebeck coefficient is the temperature coefficient of thermo emf or the rate of change of thermo emf with temperature i.e.

$$\alpha_{S_{1-2}} = \lim_{\Delta T \to 0} \frac{\Delta V}{\Delta T} = \frac{dV}{dT}$$

The Seebeck coefficient depends upon the choice of the materials and cannot be attributed to either material above. It has unit of volt per degree. Depending upon the choice of materials, the drop in the potential may be either positive or negative in the direction of the drop of temperature.

(ii) Peltier Effect

When an electric current flows across an isothermal junction of two dissimilar materials, there is an either an evolution or absorption of heat at the junction. This effect is called the peltier heat. The Peltier effect ia a reversible effect because if heat is evolved when current flows in one direction, the same amount of heat is absorbed at the junction if the current flow is reversed.

The Peltier Coefficient $\alpha_{p1\text{-}2}$ is defined as the heat evolved or absorbed at the junction per unit current flow, per unit time.

$$\alpha_{S_{1-2}} = \alpha_{p1} - \alpha_{p2} = \frac{q_p}{I}$$

Where I is the electric current.

(iii) Thomson Effect

When an electric current flows through on material having a temperature gradient, there is an evolution or absorption of heat. This phenomenon is called the Thomson Effect. The Thomson heat is reversible because reversing the direction of current flow reverses the direction of heat transfer without change in magnitude. The Thomson Coefficient is defined as the Thomson heat absorbed or evolved per unit time per unit electric current and per unit temperature gradient.

$$\sigma = \frac{\frac{d_{qT}}{d_x}}{\frac{d_T}{d_x}}$$

Where $\frac{d_{qT}}{d_x}$ is heat interchange per unit time per unit length of conductor

and $\frac{d_T}{d_x}$ is temperature gradient.

10.1.2 Principle of Working

A thermoelectric converter is a form of heat engine. Heat is taken up at an upper temperature (i.e the hot junction) and part is converted into electrical energy; the remainder is discharged (or removed) at a lower temperature (i.e. the cold junction).

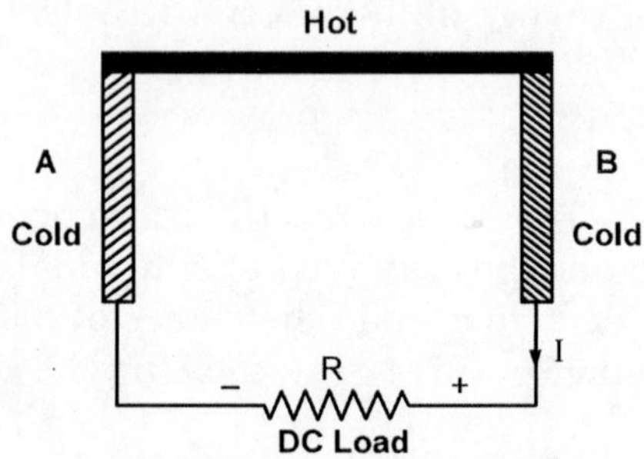

Fig. 10.2 Simple Thermocouple Arrangement

A simple thermocouple arrangement is shown in Fig. 10.2. The thermocouple material A and B are joined at the hot end, but the other ends are kept cold; an electric voltage or emf is then generated between the cold ends. A direct current will flow in a circuit or load (e.g. resistor) connected between these ends. The current will continue to flow as long as the heat is supplied at the hot junction and removed from the cold ends. For a given thermocouple, the voltage and electric power output are increased by increasing the temperature difference between the hot and cold ends.

The operation of a thermoelectric generator is shown in Fig. 10.2. The net useful power output is given by

$$W = I^2R \text{ [W]}$$

where I = current [A]

R = External load resistance [Ω]

The current in the circuit is given by

$$I = \frac{\alpha \Delta T}{(R_i + R)} \text{[A]}$$

where α = Seebeck coefficient (V/K]

ΔT = Temperature difference between hot and cold junction [K]

R_i = Internal resistance of thermoelectric generator [Ω]

The magnitude of potential difference depends on the pair of conductor materials and on the temperature difference between the junctions.

For a loop made of copper and constant wires, the value of Seebeck coefficient a is 0.04 mV/K. For a temperature difference of 600 K between the junctions, a voltage of 24 mV will be developed. In order to achieve higher potential difference many generators have to be connected in parallel.

For increasing the useful power output, parallel and series connections are used.

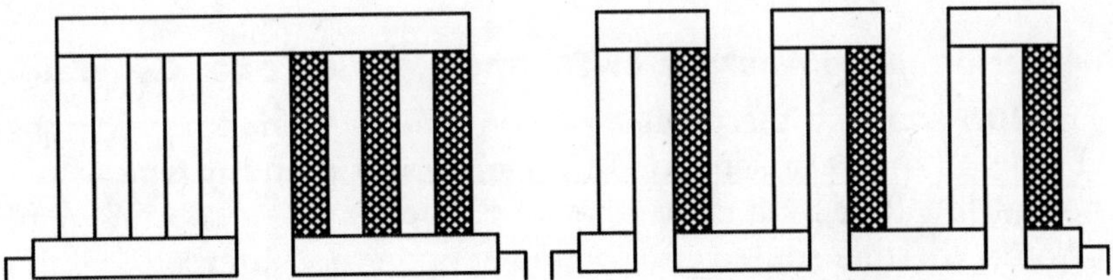

Fig. 10.3 Cascading of Thermoelectric Generators

10.1.3 Construction of Thermoelectric Generators

Thermoelectric power generators consist of three major components: thermoelectric materials, thermoelectric modules and thermoelectric systems that interface with the heat source.

(i) Thermoelectric materials

Thermoelectric materials generate power directly from heat by converting temperature differences into electric voltage. These materials must have both high electrical conductivity (σ) and low thermal conductivity (K) to be good thermoelectric materials. Having low thermal conductivity ensures that when one side is made hot, the other side stays cold, which helps to generate a large voltage while in a temperature gradient.

The main three semiconductors known to have both low thermal conductivity and high power factor were bismuth telluride (Bi_2Te_3), lead telluride (PbTe), and silicon germanium (SiGe).

(ii) Thermoelectric module

A thermoelectric module is a circuit containing thermoelectric materials that generate electricity from heat directly. A thermoelectric module consists of two dissimilar thermoelectric materials joining in their ends: an n-type (negatively charged); and a p-type (positively charged) semiconductors.

The junctions and materials must be selected so that they survive in tough mechanical and thermal conditions. Also, the module must be designed such that the two thermoelectric materials are thermally in parallel, but electrically in series. The efficiency of thermoelectric modules is greatly affected by its geometrical design.

(iii) Thermoelectric system

Using thermoelectric modules, a thermoelectric system generates power by taking in heat from a source such as hot exhaust flue. In order to do that, the system needs a large temperature gradient, which is not easy in real-world applications. The cold side must be cooled by air or water. Heat exchangers are used on both sides of the modules to supply this heating and cooling.

10.1.4 Performance Analysis of Thermo-electric Power Generator

Fig. 10.4 shows a thermoelectric converter schematically. It consists of two blocks A and B of semiconductor materials p and n type respectively, connected together by a conductor (e.g. copper). The conductor receives heat from a thermal source and the lower open (not conducted) ends of the blocks reject heat to a low temperature sink. The two junctions are kept at a temperature difference T. The sides of the blocks are insulated. Hence, heat flow occurs along the length of the blocks only, supplying heat to the hot junction causes the electrons in the n type block and holes in the p type block to flow away from the hot junction, thereby producing a potential difference between the two open ends. If the circuit is completed at the cold junction, an electric current will flow through the load.

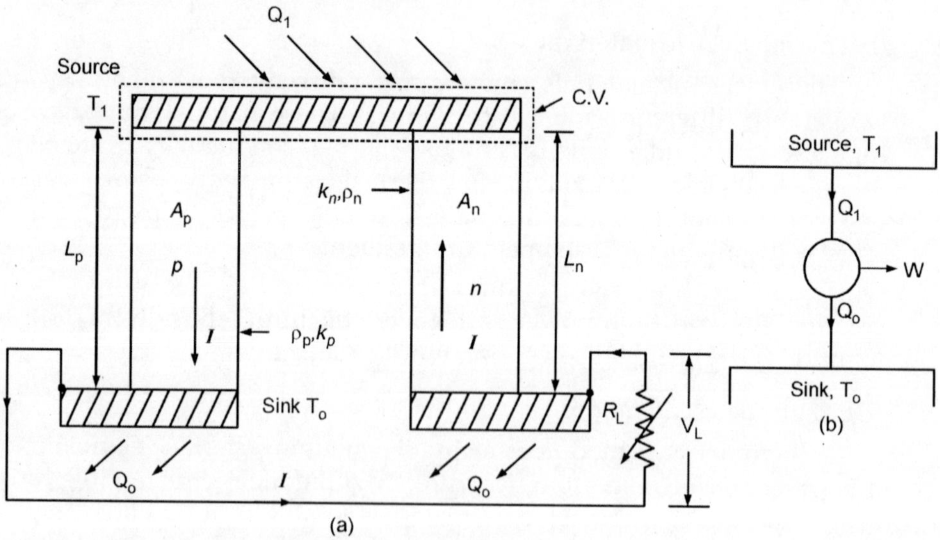

Fig. 10.4 Circuit Diagram of Thermo-electric Power Generator

Let us now apply the first law energy balance to the hot plate for which during a unit time the energy effects are:

(*a*) An amount of energy Q_1, is supplied to the plate from the source.

(*b*) An amount of heat Q_K, is conducted away from the plate through the two blocks

(*c*) The Peltier heat, Q_P, is absorbed at the junction due to current flowing in the circuit.

(*d*) An amount of heat, $Q_j/2$ (Joule heat) is transferred to the plate. This amount represents one half of the Joule heat generated by the current flow. The remaining one half of the Joule heat is transferred to the cold junction.

The energy balance equation (for hot plate) is given by,

$$\dot{Q}_1 + \frac{1}{2}\dot{Q}_j = \dot{Q}_P + \dot{Q}_K$$

where

$$\dot{Q}_P = \pi_{p,n} I = \alpha_{p,n} I T_1$$

$$Q_j = (R_p + R_n) I^2 = \left[\frac{\rho_p L_p}{A_p} + \frac{\rho_n L_n}{A_n}\right] I^2$$

$$\dot{Q}_k = (K_p + K_n)(T_1 - T_0) = \left[\frac{k_p A_p}{L_p} + \frac{k_n A_n}{L_n}\right](T_1 - T_0)$$

Here,

T_1 = temperature of the source (K)

T_0 = temperature of the sink (K)

L_p, L_n = length of thermoelectric elements (*n*)

A_p, A_n = cross-sectional area of thermoelectric elements (m^2)

k_p, k_n = thermal conductivity of the element (W/mk)

ρ_p, ρ_n = electric resistivity of the elements (ohm-m)

K_p, K_n = thermal conductance of the elemtns, kA/L (W/K)

R_p, R_n = electrical resistance ot the elements, $\rho L/A$ (ohm)

α_p, α_n = Seebeck coefficient (V/K)

π_p, π_n = Peltier coefficient (V)

On substitution,

$$\dot{Q}_1 = \alpha_{p,n} IT_1 - \frac{1}{2}\left[\frac{\rho_p L_p}{A_p} + \frac{\rho_n L_n}{A_n}\right] I^2 + \left[\frac{k_p A_p}{L_p} + \frac{k_n A_n}{L_n}\right](T_1 - T_0)$$

The useful power generated is

$$W_L = I^2 R_L = \frac{V_L^2}{R_L}$$

where the voltage output across the load is given by

$$V_L = \alpha_{p,n}(T_1 - T_0) - I(R_p + R_n)$$

By Kirchoff's law,

$$I = \frac{\alpha_{p,n}(T_1 - T_0)}{R_L + R_p + R_n}$$

Let m be the resistance ratio defined by

$$m = \frac{R_L}{R_p + R_n}$$

so that
$$1 + m = \frac{R_p + R_n + R_L}{R_p + R_n}$$

and
$$I = \frac{\alpha_{p,n}(T_1 - T_0)}{(R_p + R_n)(1 + m)}$$

The useful power is then

$$W_L = \frac{\alpha_{p,n}^2 (T_1 - T_0)^2}{(R_p + R_n)^2 (1 + m)^2}(R_p + R_n)m = \frac{m}{(1+m)^2}\frac{\alpha_{p,n}^2 (T_1 - T_0)^2}{R_p + R_n}$$

and the heat input

$$\dot{Q}_1 = \alpha_{p,n}^2 \frac{T_1(T_1 - T_0)}{(R_p + R_n)(1 + m)} - \frac{1}{2}\frac{\alpha_{p,n}^2 (T_1 - T_0)^2}{(1 + m)^2 \, R_p + R_n} + (K_p + K_n)(T_1 - T_0)$$

The efficiency of the thermoelectric generator is given as

$$\eta = \frac{\dot{W}_L}{Q_1} = \frac{\dfrac{m}{(1+m)^2}\cdot\dfrac{\alpha_{p,n}^2}{R_p + R_n}(T_1 - T_0)^2}{\alpha_{p,n}^2 \dfrac{T_1(T_1 - T_0)}{(R_p + R_n)(1+m)} - \dfrac{1}{2}\dfrac{(T_1 - T_0)^2 \alpha_{p,n}^2}{(1+m)^2 (R_p + R_n)} + (K_p + K_n)(T_1 - T_0)}$$

$$= \frac{T_1 - T_0}{T_1}\,\frac{m}{(1+m) - \dfrac{1}{2}\dfrac{T_1 - T_0}{T_1} + \dfrac{(K_n + K_p)(R_n + R_p)(1+m)^2}{\sigma_{p,n}^2 \cdot T_1}}$$

Let z, called the figure of merit, be defined by

$$z = \frac{\alpha_{p,n}^2}{(K_n + K_p)(R_n + R_p)}$$

It consists of only material properties of the two semiconductors. It can be seen that as z increases, η will increase. If $R = R_n + R_p$ and $K = K_n + K_p$, for a pair of materials when the product (R . K) is minimum, z(and hence η) is maximum.

$$R \cdot K = \left[\frac{\rho_p L_p}{A_p} + \frac{\rho_n L_n}{A_n}\right]\left[\frac{k_p A_p}{L_p} + \frac{k_n A_n}{L_n}\right]$$

Let $A_P/L_P = \gamma_p$ and $A_n/L_n = \gamma_n$, so that

$$R \,.\, K = \left[\frac{\rho_p}{\gamma_p} + \frac{\rho_n}{\gamma_n}\right](k_p\gamma_p + k_n\gamma_n)$$

$$= k_p\rho_p + k_p\rho_n\frac{\gamma_p}{\gamma_n} + k_n\rho_p\frac{\gamma_n}{\gamma_p} + k_n\rho_n$$

Once the materials have been selected, the variables are γ_n and γ_p, the area-to-length ratios of thelegs. To minimise R · K,

$$\frac{d(R \cdot K)}{d(\gamma_n/\gamma_p)} = 0 \Rightarrow k_n\rho_p - k_p\rho_n\left(\frac{\gamma_n}{\gamma_p}\right)^{-2} = 0$$

$$\therefore \qquad \frac{\gamma_n}{\gamma_p} = \left[\frac{k_p\rho_n}{k_n\rho_p}\right]^{1/2}$$

On substitution

$$R \cdot K_{min} = k_p\rho_p + k_p\rho_n\left[\frac{k_n\rho_p}{k_p\rho_n}\right]^{1/2} + k_n\rho_p\left[\frac{k_p\rho_n}{k_n\rho_p}\right]^{1/2} + k_n\rho_n$$

$$= [\sqrt{(\rho_p k_p)} + \sqrt{(\rho_n k_n)}]^2$$

and the maximum figure of merit is given by

$$z_{max} = \left[\frac{\alpha_{p,n}}{\sqrt{(\rho_p k_p)} + \sqrt{(\rho_n k_n)}}\right]^2$$

Thus,

$$\eta = \frac{T_1 - T_0}{T_1}\,\frac{m}{(1+m) - \frac{1}{2}\frac{T_1 - T_0}{T_1} + \frac{(1+m)^2}{zT_1}}$$

For given values of T_1 and T_0, and with the maximum z for a given pair of materials, η depends on m, and to find the optimum value of m,

$$\frac{d\eta}{dm} = 0, \text{ which gives}$$

$$m_{opt} = \left[1 + z_{max}\frac{T_1 + T_0}{2}\right]^{1/2} = m_0, \text{ say}$$

By rearrangement,

$$m_0 + 1 = \frac{z_{max}}{m_0 - 1}\frac{T_1 + T_0}{2}$$

$$\eta_{zmax} = \left(\frac{T_1 - T_0}{T_1}\right)\frac{m_0}{(1 + m_0) - \frac{1}{2}\left(\frac{T_1 - T_0}{T_1}\right) + \frac{(1 + m_0)^2}{z_{max}T_1}}$$

$$= \left(\frac{T_1 - T_0}{T_1}\right)\frac{m_0}{(1 + m_0) - \frac{1}{2}\left(\frac{T_1 - T_0}{T_1}\right) + \frac{(1 + m_0)(T_1 - T_0)}{2T_1(m_0 - 1)}}$$

$$= \left(\frac{T_1 - T_0}{T_1}\right)\left(\frac{m_0 - 1}{m_0 + \frac{T_0}{T_1}}\right)$$

This is expression for maximum efficiency of a thermoelectric generator, which can never achieve the efficiency allowed by the second law of thermodynamics.

Now,

$$\dot{W}_L = \frac{m}{(1 + m)^2}\frac{\alpha_{p,n}^2 (T_1 - T_0)^2}{R_p + R_n}$$

To find the optimum resistance ratio m for a given pair of elements,

$$\frac{d\dot{W}_L}{dm} = 0, \text{ which gives } m = 1.$$

Therefore, $$\dot{W}_L = \frac{1}{4}\frac{\alpha_{p,n}^2(T_1 - T_0)^2}{R_p + R_n}$$

The corresponding efficiency is

$$\eta_{max\ power} = \frac{T_1 - T_0}{T_1}\frac{1}{2 - \frac{1}{2}\frac{T_1 - T_0}{T_1} + \frac{4}{zT_1}} \quad \text{when m = 1}$$

10.1.5 Thermoelectric Materials

The following materials have been found suitable for use in thermoelectric elements:

(*a*) Lead Telluride (Pb Te) in *n*-type and *p*-type forms

(*b*) Bismuth Telluride (Bi_2 Te_3)

(*c*) Bismuth Sulphide (Bi_2 S_3)

(*d*) Antimony Telluride (Sb_2 Te_3)

(*e*) Tin Telluride (Sn Te)

(*f*) Germanium Telluride (Ge Te)

(*g*) Cesium Sulphide (CeS)

10.1.6 Properties Of Thermoelectric Materials

1. **High Seebeck Coefficient:** The See-back coefficient of n-type bismuth telluride is –287μV/°C. The Seebeck coefficient of n-type bismuth telluride is 81 μV/K .
2. **High Electrical Conductivity:** The n-type electrical conductivity of n-type bismuth telluride is 1.1 × 105 siemens per meter.
3. **Low Thermal Conductivity:** The thermal conductivity of bismuth telluride is 1.20 W/mK giving the compound a thermal insulation value similar to ordinary glass.

10.1.7 Application of Thermoelectric Generators

(*i*) For increasing the fuel efficiency of cars, thermoelectric generators are used. These generator use heat produced when the vehicle is running.

(*ii*) Seebeck Power Generation is used to supply power to spacecrafts.

(*iii*) These generators are used to supply power to remote stations like weather stations, relay stations etc.

10.1.8 Advantages of Thermoelectric Power Generators

(*i*) **Easy maintenance :** They works electrically without any moving parts so they are virtually maintenance free.

(*ii*) **Environment friendly :** Thermoelectric generators product no pollution. Therefore they are eco friendly generators.

(*iii*) **Compact and less weight :** The overall thermoelectric cooling system is much smaller and lighter than a comparable mechanical system.

(*iv*) **High Reliability :** Thermoelectric modules exhibit very high reliability due to their solid-state construction.

(*v*) **No noise :** They can be used in any orientation and in zero gravity environments. Thus they are popular in many aerospace applicatons.

(*vi*) **Convenient Power Supply :** They operate directly from a DC power source.

10.1.9 Limitations of Thermoelectric Power Generators

(*i*) "High output resistance required - For getting high output voltage and power several thermoelectric generators are connected in series, which in turn increases the total output resistance. Therefore for transferring high power efficiently large resistances is needed. This problem can be overcome by connecting more thermoelectric elements in parallel rather in series because it causes decrease in effective resistance.

(*ii*) "Thermoelectric power generators generate less electric power for the same heat flow i.e they have low efficiency as compared to other mechanical generators.

(*iii*) "Low thermal characteristics - The heat dissipation of any device depends upon its thermal conductivity. Thermoelectric power generator has low thermal conductivity and hence poor heat dissipation. So, these generators are efficient only when small power is required.

(*iv*) "Thermoelectric generators are costly as compare to other generators.

10.2 THERMOIONIC CONVERSION SYSTEMS

Thermionic converter transforms heat directly into electrical energy by utilizing thermionic emission effect, that is the emission of electrons from heated metal (and some oxide) surfaces. All metals and some oxides have free electrons which are released on heating. These electrons can travel through a space and collected on a cooled metal. These electrons can return to hot metal through an external load thereby producing electrical power.

The energy required to extract an electron from the metal is an important parameter, known as the work function of the metal. The value of work function varies with the nature of the metal and its surface condition.

A thermionic converter is a sealed and evacuated device (refer Fig. 10.5) having two electrodes with different work function enclosed in a tube. The cathode is called an emitter and is heated enough to release electrons from its surface. The electrons cross a small gap and accumulate on a cooled metal anode called the collector. The space between the electrodes is maintained at high vacuum or filled with a highly conducting plasma liked ionised cesium vapour to minimal energy losses. The external load R is connected through anode to cathode. The electrons return to cathode through the external load and electrical power is produced.

Thermionic conversions is a sealed and evacuated device comprising of

1. A heated cathode (electron emitter)
2. An anode (electron collector)
3. Vacuum gap between 1 and 2 (with ionised vapour to neutralise space charge.

The gap is only about a mm. External electrical circuit is connected between anode and cathode. (Ref. Fig. 10.5). The thermionic converter converts thermal energy directly to electrical energy by virtue of flow of electrons through the vacuum gap.

Heat is supplied to emitter. Electrons released from emitter flow through small vacuum gap seeded with ionising substance. Heat is rejected from collector. Electrical energy is tapped from the terminals.

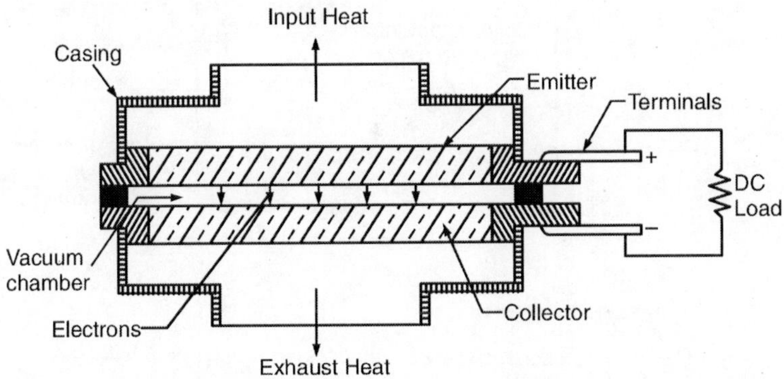

***Fig. 10.5** Principle of Thermoionic Converter*

Because electrons cannot travel far in air, thermionic converters require that the electrodes be in a vacuum. This limits the size of the converter so that only small scale power production is feasible.

The emission of electrons from the hotter electrode is inhibited by a space charge resulting from the accumulation of electrons in its vicinity. To reduce the space charge, small quantity of cesium metal is introduced into the evacuated vessel containing, the electrodes. At this existing high temperature, the cesium vaporizes and ionizes; that is to say, it forms a mixture a positive ions and electrons. By combining with the electrons in the vicinity of the emitter electrode, the possible ions help to decrease the space charge.

Deposition of solid cesium on the colder electrode (collector) is also beneficial in decreasing the work function and thus increasing the output voltage. A common thermionic electrode combination is a tungsten emitter and a cesium-coated tungsten collector.

10.2.1 Analysis of Thermionic Generator

Fig. shows the characteristic curve of thermionic converter.

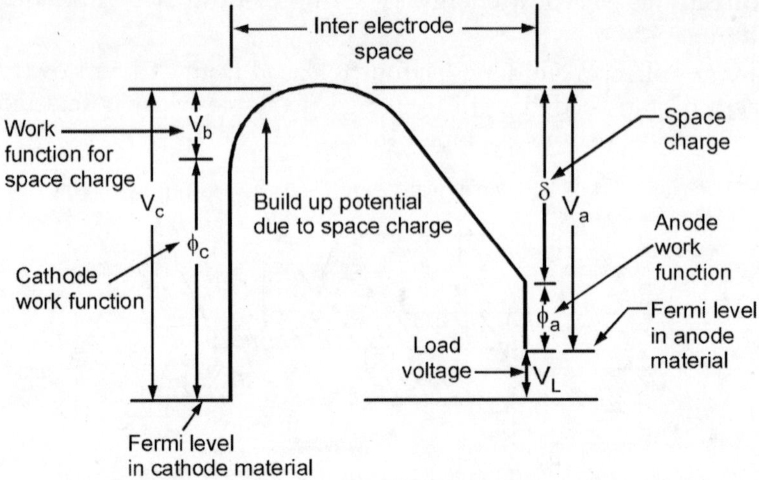

Fig. 10.6 Characteristic curve of thermionic converter.

Let, ϕ_c = Cathode work function,

ϕ_a, = Anode work function,

V_b = Kinetic energy barrier at cathod (work function for space charge)

V_L = Load voltage,

δ = Space charge,

T_c = Temperature of cathode, and

T_a = Temperature of anode.

The total energy required at cathode = $\phi_c + V_b$

Current densityof cathode (J_c is given by:

$$J_c = AT_c^2 \exp\left(\frac{-V_c}{kT_c}\right)$$

Similarly, current desnityof *anode* (J_a) is given by:

$$J_a = AT_a^2 \exp\left(\frac{-V_a}{kT_a}\right)$$

Load voltage (output),

$$V_L = V_c - V_a = \phi_c - \phi_a$$

Energy required for the electrons to reach at *anode*,

$$Q_1 = (\phi_c + V_b) \times J_c = V_c J_c$$

The electrons also carry the energy in the form of *kinetic energy* (2 KT_c), given by:

$$Q_2 = J_c \cdot \frac{2KT_c}{e}$$

∴ Total energy needed for electrons to reach at anode,

$$Q_c = Q_1 + Q_2$$

$$= J_c V_c + J_c \cdot \frac{2KT_c}{e}$$

or, $$Q_c = J_c\left(V_c + \frac{2kT_c}{e}\right)$$

Similarly *back emission from anode carries the energy,* given by:

$$Q_a = J_a V_a + J_a \frac{2kT_a}{e}$$

i.e. $$Q_a = J_a\left(V_a + \frac{2kT_a}{e}\right)$$

The *net energy* supplied to the *cathode,*

$$Q_{net} = J_c\left(V_c + \frac{2kT_c}{e}\right) - J_a\left(V_a + \frac{2KT_a}{e}\right)$$

Power output, *P* $= V_L(J_c - J_a)$

Efficiency of converter,

$$\eta = \frac{P}{Q_{net}}$$

$$= \frac{V_L(J_c - J_a)}{J_c\left(V_c + \frac{2KT_c}{e}\right) - J_a\left(V_a + \frac{2KT_a}{e}\right)}$$

$$\eta = \frac{(V_c - V_a)(J_c - J_a)}{J_c\left(V_c + \frac{2KT_c}{e}\right) - J_a\left(V_a + \frac{2KT_a}{e}\right)}$$

$(\because\ V_L = V_c - V_a)$

Let, $$\frac{V_c}{KT_c} = \gamma_c;\ \frac{V_a}{KT_a} = \gamma_a;\ \frac{T_a}{T_c} = \beta$$

Substituting the valued and similifying, we get:

or $$\eta = \frac{(\gamma_c - \beta\gamma_a) \times [1 - \beta^2 \exp(\gamma_c - \gamma_a)]}{(\gamma_c + 2) - \beta^2(\gamma_a + 2\beta)\exp(\gamma_c - \gamma_a)}$$

if $\gamma_a = \gamma_c = \gamma$, then

$$\eta_{max} = (1 - \beta)\frac{\gamma}{\gamma + 2}\left[\frac{1 - \beta^2}{1 - \frac{\beta^2(\gamma + 2\beta)}{\gamma + 2}}\right]$$

$$\text{But, } \frac{1-\beta^2}{1-\frac{\beta^2(\gamma+2\beta)}{\gamma+2}} \simeq 1$$

$$\therefore \qquad \eta_{max} = (1-\beta)\frac{\gamma}{\gamma+2}$$

10.2.2 Advantages, Disadvantages and Applications of Thermionic Generators

Following are the *advtanges, disadvantages/limitations and applications* of thermionic converter:

Advantages

1. Compact device.
2. High conversion efficiency.
3. Quiet in operationand durable.
4. Low cost and less maintenance required.
5. Absence of rotating parts.
6. Can be developed for very low power to very high power generation.
8. Can operate in remote areas and harsh environments.

Disadvantages/Limitations

1. Metal is ostly as it has to withstand high temperatures.
2. Needs high operating temperatures at anode.
3. Needs special seal to protect the cathode from corrosive gases.
4. Needs cesium vapour in the tube to reduce the space charge.

Applications

1. Power generation in both centralised and distributed systems.
2. Residential and Commercial purposes.
3. Automobiles, marine and air vehicles.
4. Electronics and telecommunications.

REVIEW QUESTIONS

1. What is a thermoelectric effect? Explain the working principle of thermoelectric generator. Derive an expression for power output.
2. Explain the performance analysis of thermoelectric generator.
3. List the various types of thermoelectric materials. Also list the various properties of thermoelectric materials.
4. What are thermionic conversion systems? Explain the basic principle of thermionic converter.

5. Explain vapour filled thermionic converter in detail.
6. How the ideal and actual efficiency of thermionic converter is calculated. Explain.

7. Show that the maximum thermal efficiency of a thermionic generator is approximately given by:

$$\eta_{max} = \frac{T_c - T_a}{T_c} \cdot \frac{\beta}{\beta + 2}$$

where, $\beta_e = \beta_a = \beta ; \frac{eVc}{kTc} = \frac{eVa}{kTa}$, the symbols having their usual names.

❑❑❑

11

WIND ENERGY

11.1 INTRODUCTION

Wind is simply air in motion. It is caused by the uneven heating of the Earth's surface by radiant energy from the sun. Since the Earth's surface is made of very different types of land and water, it absorbs the sun's energy at different rates. Water usually does not heat or cool as quickly as land because of its physical properties.

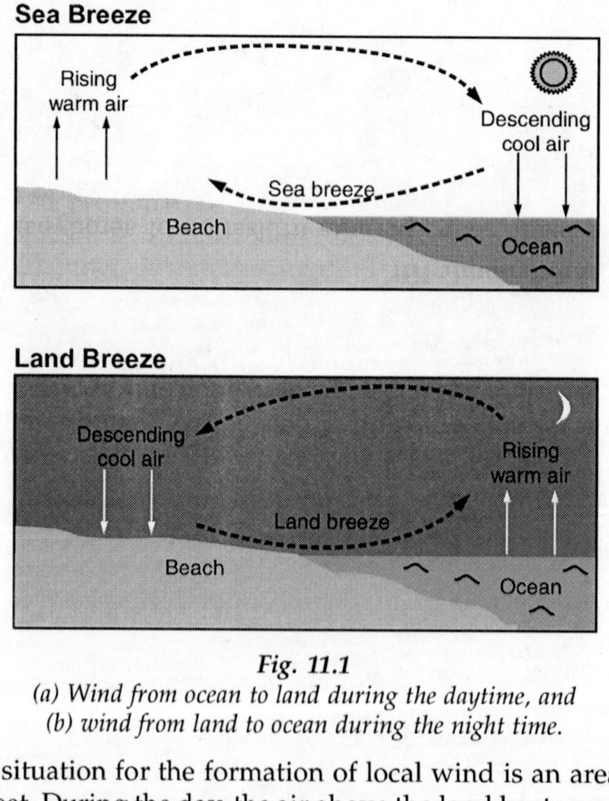

Fig. 11.1
(a) Wind from ocean to land during the daytime, and
(b) wind from land to ocean during the night time.

An ideal situation for the formation of local wind is an area where land and water meet. During the day, the air above the land heats up more quickly than the air above water. The warm air over the land expands, becomes less dense and rises.

The heavier, denser, cool air over the water moves into replace it. Thus, creating wind which flows from the water to the land. At night, the direction of the wind is reversed because the land surface cools more rapidly than the water.

In the same way, the atmospheric winds that circle the Earth are created because the land near the equator is heated more by the sun than land near the North and South Poles.

Today, people use wind energy to make electricity. Wind is called a **renewable** energy source because the wind will blow as long as the sun shines.

Wind energy conversion devices are commonly known as wind turbines or wind energy conversion systems (WECS) or wind turbine generators because they convert the energy of the windstream into energy of rotation: the component which rotates is called the rotor. Because wind turbines produce rotational motion, wind energy is readily converted into electrical energy by connecting the turbine to an electric generator. The combination of wind turbine and generator is sometimes referred to as aero generator.

A weather vane, or wind vane, is used to show the direction of the wind. A wind vane points toward the source of the wind. Wind direction is reported as the direction from which the wind blows, not the direction toward which the wind moves. A north wind blows from the north toward the south.

11.2 TERMS USED IN WIND ENERGY

Airfoil (Aerofoil): A streamlined curved surface designed for air to flow around it in order to produce low drag and high lift forces.

Angle of attack: It is the angle between the relative air flow and the chord of the airfoil (Fig. 11.2 (*a*)).

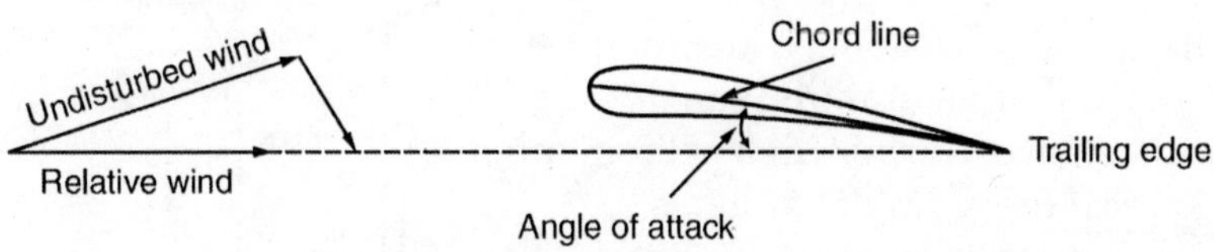

(a) Angle of attack of a wind turbine airfoil.

Fig.11.2. (a) Angle of attack of a wind turbine airfoil.

Blade: An important part of a wind turbine that extracts wind energy.

Leading edge: It is the front edge of the blade that faces towards the direction of wind flow (Fig.11.2 (*b*)).

Trailing edge: It is the near edge of the blade that faces away from the direction of wind flow (Fig.11.2 (*b*)).

Chord line: It is the line joining the leading edge and the trailing edge (Fig.11.2 (*b*)).

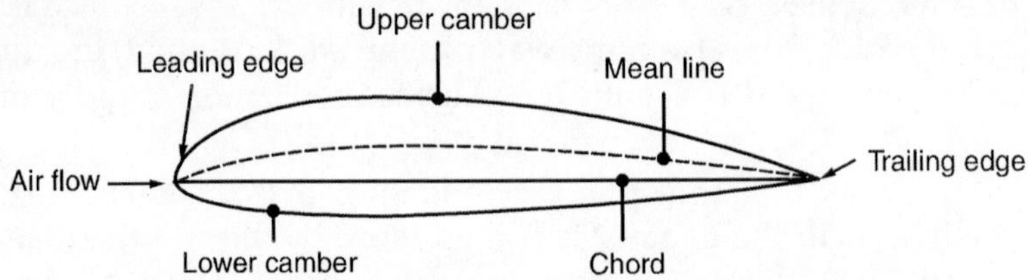

Fig.11.2. (b) Airfoil showing edges, camber and cord.

Mean line: A line that is equidistant from the upper and lower surfaces of the airfoil.

Camber: It is the maximum distance between the mean line and the chord line, which measures the curvature of the airfoil.

Rotor: It is the prime part of the wind turbine that extracts energy from the wind. It constitutes the blade-and-hub assembly.

Hub: Blades are fixed to a hub which is a central solid part of the turbine.

Propeller: It is the turbine shaft that rotates with the hub and blades and is called the propeller. Blades are twisted as per design. The outer profile of the blades conforms to aerodynamic performance while the inner profile meets the structural requirements.

Tip speed ratio: It is the ratio of the speed of the outer blade tip to the undisturbed natural wind speed.

Pitch angle: It is the angle made between the blade chord and the plane of the blade rotation.

Pitch control of blades: A system where the pitch angle of the blades changes according to the wind speed for efficient operation (Fig.11.2(*c*)).

Stall-regulated system: When the turbine blades are fixed at an optimum angle and the machine is stalled during high winds either by mechanical or hydraulic systems.

Swept area: This is the area covered by the rotating rotor.

Solidity: It is the ratio of the blade area to the swept area.

Drag force: It is the force component which is in line with the velocity of wind.

Lift force: It is the force component perpendicular to drag force.

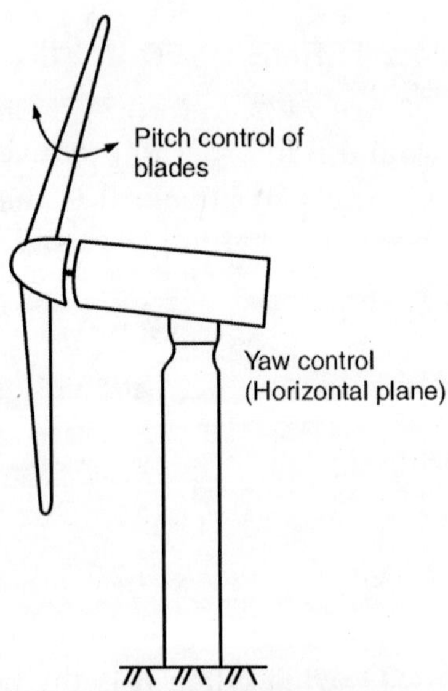

Fig.11.2. (c) Pitch and yaw control of wind turbine.

Nacelle: The nacelle houses the generator, the gear box, the hydraulic system and the yawing mechanism.

Yaw control: As the direction of the wind changes frequently, the yaw control is provided to steer and axis of the turbine in the direction of the wind. It keeps the turbine blades in the plane perpendicular to the wind, either in the upward wind direction or in the downward wind direction.

Cut-in speed: It is the wind speed at which a wind turbine starts to operate.

Rated wind speed: It is the wind speed at which the turbine attains its maximum output.

Cut-out speed: It is the wind speed at which a wind turbine is designed to be shut down to prevent damage from high winds. It is also called the *furling wind speed*.

Down wind: It is the opposite side of the direction from which the wind is blowing.

Up wind: It is the side of direction from which the wind is blowing (in the path of the oncoming wind).

Wind rose: It is the pattern formed in a diagram illustration vectors that represent wind velocities occurring from different directions.

Wind vane: A wind vane monitors the wind direction. It sends a signal to the controlling computer which activates the yaw mechanism to make the rotor face the wind direction.

11.3 AERODYNAMIC OPERATION OF WIND TURBINES

Aerodynamics deals with the movement of solid bodies through the air. In wind turbines, aerodynamics provides a method to explain the relative motion between airfoil and air. Airfoil is the cross-section of the wind turbine blade. When the wind passes over the surface of the rotor blade, it automatically passes over the longer or upper side of the blade, creating a low pressure area above the aerofoil as shown in Figure 11.3(a).

The pressure difference between the top and the bottom surfaces results in a force called the aerodynamic lift that causes the airfoil to rise. As the blades can only move in a plane with the hub as their centre, the lift force causes rotation about the hub (Figure 11.3(b)). The turbine thus extracts energy from the wind stream by converting the wind's linear kinetic energy into rotational motion. In addition to the lift force, a drag force perpendicular to the lift force also acts on the blade which impedes rotor rotation. The prime objective in wind turbine design is the desired lift-to-drag ratio of the blade (airfoil structure).

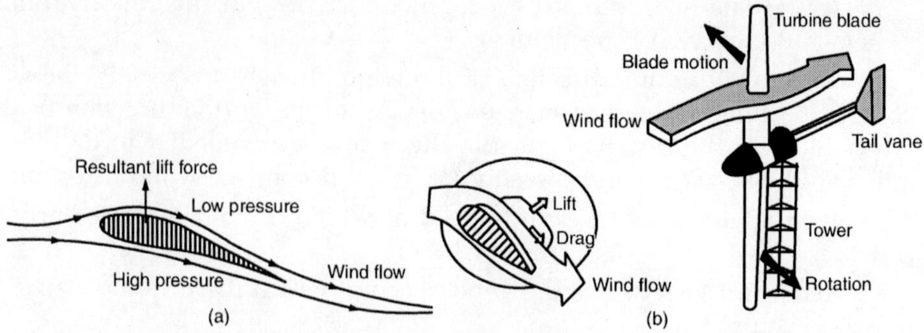

Fig.11.3. *(a) Aerodynamic lift force on blade cross-section of wind turbine, and (b) the basic operation principle of wind turbine aerodynamic lift*

When air flows over solid bodies, several physical phenomenon are noticed such as drag force acting on objects like trees and electric towers, the lift force developed by airplane wings, the lift force experienced by dust particles in a wind storm and the blade motion developed by a turbine. Either the fluid moves over a stationary body or a body moves through a standstill fluid; aerodynamically both activities are the same. The approach is to study the relative motion between the fluid and the body.

Drag

It is the resistance which a body experiences when a fluid moves over it. Flood water washes away animals, vehicles and buildings. Wind storm and hurricane knocks down transmission towers, trees, sweeps away catamaran and ships. These are a few undesirable examples of drag forces. The force that a flowing fluid exerts on a body in the direction of flow is called 'drag force'. Drag may bring an undesirable effect of friction, such as burning of space vehicles on entering into the earth's atmosphere. Reduction of drag is the basic engineering approach, associated with the reduction in fuel consumption in automobiles, aircraft and submarines. However, in certain engineering activities the drag produces a useful effect. A meteor from outer space burns due to friction with the earth's atmosphere, saving the inhabitants on earth from catastrophic impact.

Friction acts to help us as a 'life saver' in brakes of automobiles. Similarly, the drag force is useful in safe landing with a parachute.

Lift

When a body is immersed in a standstill fluid, only the normal pressure force is exerted on it. A flowing fluid in addition exerts tangential shear forces on the surface. Both these forces have two components, one is drag in the flow direction, the other is perpendicular to the fluid flow called 'lift'. It causes the body to move in the upward direction. The relative magnitudes of drag and lift forces depend completely on the shape of the object. Streamlined objects experience a smaller drag force than that experienced by blunt objects. Generation of lift always creates a certain amount of drag force.

Airfoils of a wind turbine are especially shaped to produce lift force on coming in contact with the moving air. It is achieved by fabricating the top surface of the airfoil as curved and the bottom surface nearly flat. Air flowing over the airfoil travels a longer distance to reach the tip-end of airfoil, in contrast to air flowing under the foil (Fig.11.4). It creates a pressure difference that generates an upward force which tends to lift the airfoil causing rotation of the wind turbine rotor. Good airfoils can have lift 30 times greater than drag.

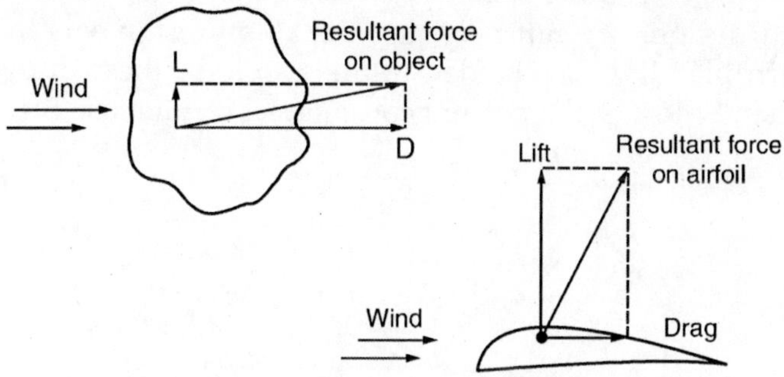

Fig.11.4. Relative magnitudes of lift and drag forces on a blunt and a streamlined airfoil

11.4 CLASSIFICATION OF WIND TURBINES

Since the inception of the wind energy technology, machines of several types and shapes were designed and developed around different parts of the world. Some of these are innovative designs which are not commercially accepted. Although there are several ways to categorize wind turbines, they are broadly classified into horizontal axis machines and vertical axis machines, based on their axis of rotation.

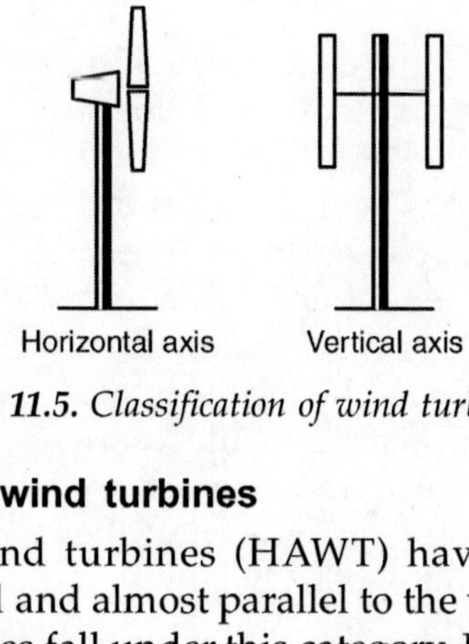

Fig. 11.5. Classification of wind turbines

11.4.1 Horizontal axis wind turbines

Horizontal axis wind turbines (HAWT) have their axis of rotation horizontal to the ground and almost parallel to the wind stream. Most of the commercial wind turbines fall under this category. Horizontal axis machines have some distinct advantages such as low cut-in wind speed and easy furling. In general, they show relatively high power coefficient. However, the generator and gearbox of these turbines are to be placed over the tower which makes its design more complex and expensive. Another disadvantage is the need for the tail or yaw drive to orient the turbine towards wind.

Depending on the number of blades, horizontal axis wind turbines are further classified as single bladed, two bladed and multi bladed, as shown in Fig.11.6 Single bladed turbines are cheaper due to savings on blade materials. The drag losses are also minimum for these turbines. However, to balance the blade, a counter weight has to be placed opposite to the hub. Single bladed designs are not very popular due to problems in balancing and visual acceptability. Two bladed rotors also have these drawbacks, but to a lesser extent. Most of the present commercial turbine used for electricity generation have three blades.

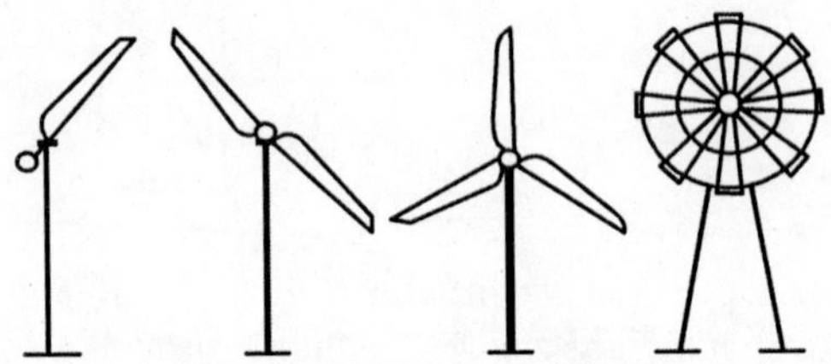

Single bladed, two bladed, three bladed and multi bladed turbines

Fig. 11.6.

They are more stable as the aerodynamic loading will be relatively uniform Machines with more number of blades (6, 8, 12, 18 or even more) are also available. The ratio between the actual blade area to the swept area of a rotor is termed as the solidity. Hence, multi-blade rotors are also called high solidity rotors. These rotors can start easily as more rotor area interacts with the wind initially. Some low solidity designs may require external starting.

Based on the direction of receiving the wind, HAWT can be classified as upwind and down wind turbines as shown in Fig.11.7 Upwind turbines have their rotors facing the wind directly. As the wind stream passes the rotor first, they do not have the problem of tower shadow. However, yaw mechanism is essential for such designs to keep the rotor always facing the wind. On the other hand, down-wind machines are more flexible and may not require a yaw mechanism. But, as the rotors are placed at the lee side of the tower, there may be uneven loading on the blades as it passes through the shadow of the tower.

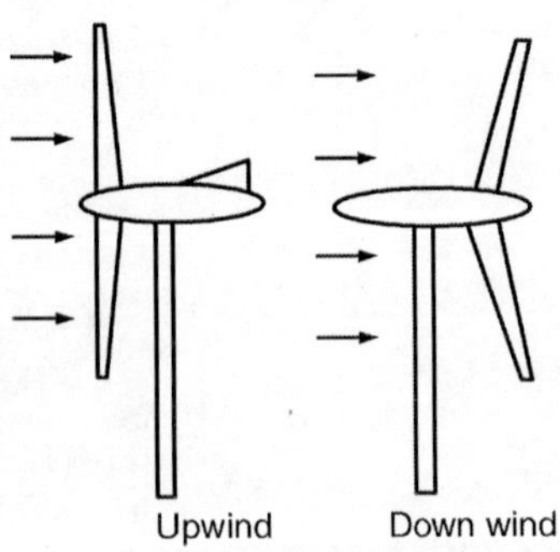

***Fig.11.7.** Upwind and downwind turbines*

11.4.2. Vertical axis wind turbines

The axis of rotation of vertical axis wind turbine (VAWT) is vertical to the ground and almost perpendicular to the wind direction as seen from Fig.11.5 The VAWT can receive wind from any direction. Hence complicated yaw devices can be eliminated. The generator and the gearbox of such systems can be housed at the ground level, which makes the tower design simple and more economical. Moreover the maintenance of these turbines can be done at the ground level. For these systems, pitch control is not required when used for synchronous applications.

The major disadvantage of some VAWT is that they are usually not self starting. Additional mechanisms may be required to 'push' and start the turbine, once it is stopped. As the rotor completes its rotation, the blades have to pass through aerodynamically dead zones which will result in lowering the system efficiency. There are chances that the blades may run at dangerously high speeds causing the system to fail, if not controlling properly. Further, guy wires are required to support the tower structure which may pose practically difficulties. Features of some major vertical axis designs are discussed below.

(i) Darrieus rotor

Darrieus rotor, named after its inventor Georges Jeans Darrieus, works due to the lift force generated from a set of airfoils. In the original design the blades are shaped like egg beaters or *troposkein* (turbine rope) and are under pure tension while in operation. This typical blade configuration helps in minimizing the bending stress experienced by the blades. There are several variations in the Darrieus design of which some are with straight vertical blades, usually called Giromills. Darrieus rotor usually works at high tip speed ratio which makes it attractive for wind electric generators. However, they are not self-starting and require external 'excitation' to cut-in. Moreover, the rotor produces peak torque only twice per revolution. (Refer Fig. 11.8)

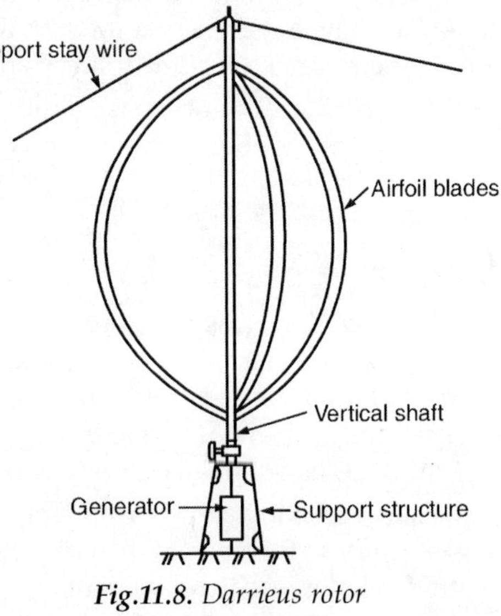

Fig.11.8. Darrieus rotor

(ii) Savonius rotor

The Savonius wind turbine, invented by S.J. Savonius, is a vertical axis machine consisting of two half cylindrical (or elliptical) blades arranged in 'S' shape.

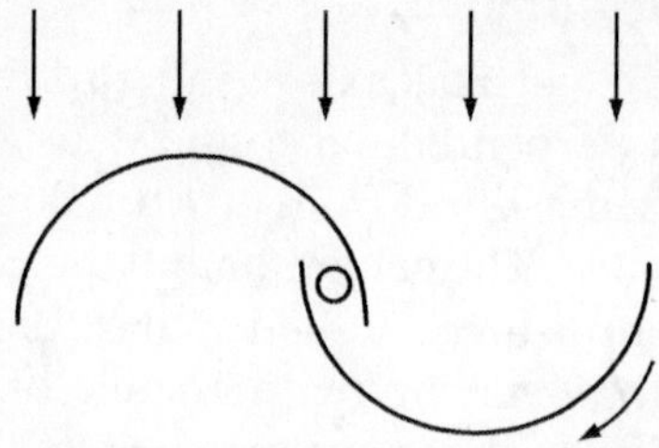

Fig.11.9 Principle of Savonius rotor

Convex side of one of the half cylinder and the concave side of the other are facing the wind at a time as shown in Fig. 11.9. The basic driving force of Savonius rotor is drag. The drag coefficient of a concave surface is more than the convex surface. Hence, the half cylinder with concave side facing the wind will experience more drag force than the other cylinder, thus forcing the rotor to rotate. Some times two or more rotors fixed one over the other at 90° offset may be used to smoothen the torque fluctuations during rotation. Another way to improve the performance is to attach deflector augmenters with the rotor. The augmenter shades the convex half facing the wind and directs the flow to the concave half thus enhancing the performance.

Being drag machine, Savonius rotors have relatively lower power coefficient. However, some experimental rotors have shown power coefficient upto 35 per cent. These rotors have high solidity and thus high starting torque.

They work at low tip speed ratios, with the maximum of about 1. They are very simple in construction-even can be made from oil barrels cut in two halves length-wise. Hence they are preferred for high torque-low speed applications like water pumping.

(iii) Musgrove rotor

Musgrove rotor was developed by a research team under Prof. Musgrove at the Reading University, UK. It is basically a vertical axis lift machine having 'H' shaped blades and a central shaft (Fig.(11.10)). At high wind speeds the rotor feathers and turn about a horizontal point due to the centrifugal force. This eliminates the risk of higher aerodynamic forces on the blades and the structure.

Based on driving aerodynamic force, wind turbines are classified as lift and drag machines. Turbines that work predominantly by the lift force are called the lift machines and that by the drag force are called drag turbines. It is always advantageous to utilize the lift force to run the turbine. Wind turbines are available in various sizes ranging from a fraction of kW to several MW. Based on the size, the turbines may be classified as small (< 25 kW) medium (25-100 kW), large (100-1000 kW) and very larve (> 1000 kW) machines.

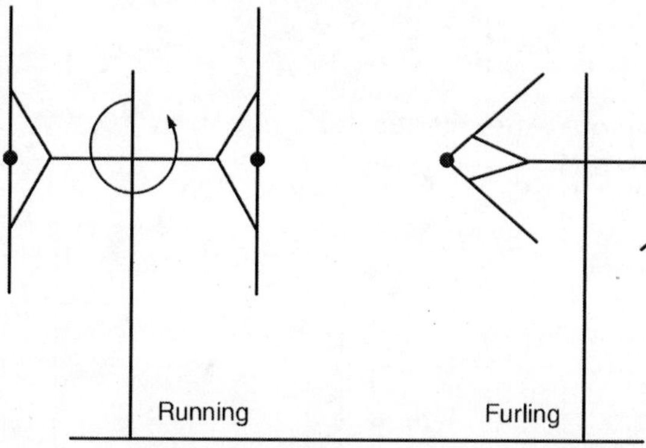

Fig.11.10 Principle of Musgrove turbine

11.5 BETZ'S ELEMENTARY MOMENTUM THEORY

The kinetic energy of an air mass m moving at a velocity v can be expressed as:

$$E = \frac{1}{2}mv^2 \text{ (Nm)}$$

Considering a certain cross-sectional area A, through which the air passes at velocity v, the volume V flowing through during a certain time unit, the so-called volume flow, is:

$$V = v\text{A (m}^3\text{/s)}$$

and the mass flow with the air density ρ is:

$$m = \rho v\text{A (kg/s)}$$

The equations expressing the kinetic energy of the moving air and the mass flow yield the amount of energy passing through cross-section A per unit time. This energy is physically identically to the power P:

$$P = \frac{1}{2}\rho v^3\text{A (W)}$$

The question is how much mechanical energy can be extracted from the free-stream airflow by an energy converter. As mechanical energy can only be extracted at the cost of the kinetic energy contained in the wind stream, this means that, with an unchanged mass flow, the flow velocity behind the wind energy converter must decrease. Reduced velocity, however, means at the same time a windering of the cross-section, as the same mass flow must pass through it. It is thus necessary to consider the conditions in front of an behind the converter (Fig.11.11).

Here, v_1 is the undelayed free-stream velocity, the wind velocity, before it reaches the converter, whereas v_2 is the flow velocity behind the converter.

The mechanical energy which the disk-shaped converter extracts from the airflow corresponds to the power difference of the air stream before and after the converter:

$$P = \frac{1}{2}\rho A_1 v_1^3 - \frac{1}{2}\rho A_2 v_2^3 = \frac{1}{2}\rho(A_1 v_1^3 - A_2 v_2^3) \text{ (W)}$$

Maintaining the mass flow (continuity equation) requires that:

$$\rho v_1 A_1 = \rho v_1 A_1 \text{ (kg/s)}$$

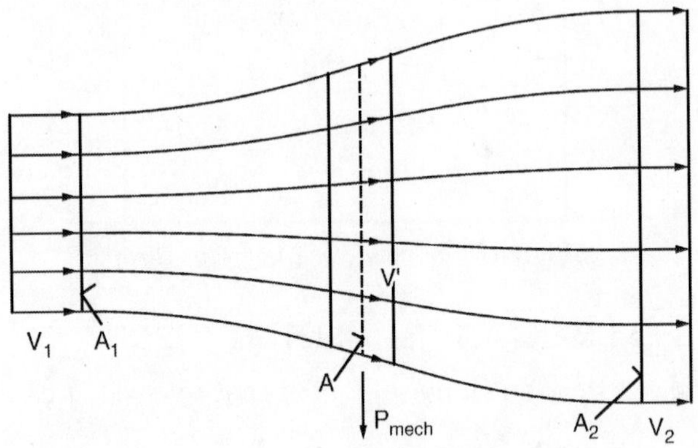

Fig.11.11. *Flow conditions due to the extraction of mechanical energy from a free-stream air flow, according to the elementary momentum theory*

Thus,

$$P = \frac{1}{2}\rho v_1 A_1 (v_1^2 - v_2^2) \text{ (W)}$$

or

$$P = \frac{1}{2}m(v_1^2 - v_2^2) \text{ (W)}$$

From this equation it follows that, in purely formal terms, power would have to be at its maximum when v_2 is zero, namely when the air is brought to a complete standstill by the converter. However, this result does not make sense physically. If the outflow velocity v_2 behind the converter is zero, then the inflow velocity before the converter must also become zero, implying that there would be no more flow through the converter at all. As could be expected, a physically meaningful result consists in a certain numerical ratio of v_2/v_1 where the extractable power reaches its maximum.

This requires another equation expressing the mechanical power of the converter. Using the law of conservation of momentum, the force which the air exerts on the converter can be expressed as:

$$F = m(v_1 - v_2) \text{ (N)}$$

According to the principle of "action equals reaction", this force, the thrust, must be counteracted by an equal force exerted by the converter on the airflow. The thrust, so to speak, pushes the air mass at air velocity v', present in the plane of flow of the converter. The power required for this is:

$$P = Fv' = m(v_1 - v_2)\, v' \ \text{(W)}$$

Thus, the mechanical power extracted from the air flow can be derived from the energy or power difference before and after the converter, on the one hand, and, on the other hand, from the thrust and the flow velocity. Equating these two expressions yields the relationship for the flow velocity v':

$$\frac{1}{2} m(v_1^2 - v_2^2) = m(v_1 - v_2)\, v' \ \text{(W)}$$

$$v' = \frac{1}{2}(v_1 - v_2) \ \text{(m/s)}$$

Thus the flow velocity through the converter is equal to the arithmetic mean of v_1 and v_2:

$$v' = \frac{v_1 + v_2}{2} \ \text{(m/s)}$$

The mass flow thus becomes:

$$m = \rho A v' = \frac{1}{2}\rho A(v_2 + v_1) \ \text{(kg/s)}$$

The mechanical power output of the converter can be expressed as:

$$P = \frac{1}{4}\rho A(v_1^2 - v_2^2)(v_1 + v_2) \ \text{(W)}$$

In order to provide a reference for this power output, it is compared with the power of the free-air stream which flow through the same cross-sectional area A, without mechanical power being extracted from it. This power was:

$$P_o = \frac{1}{2}\rho v_1^3 A \ \text{(W)}$$

The ratio between the mechanical power extracted by the converter and that of the undisturbed air stream is called the "power coefficient" c_P:

$$c_P = \frac{P}{P_o} = \frac{\frac{1}{4}\rho A(v_1^2 - v_2^2)(v_1 + v_2)}{\frac{1}{2}\rho A v_1^3}$$

After some re-arrangement, the power coefficient can be specified directly as a function of the velocity ratio v_2/v_1:

$$c_P = \frac{P}{P_o} = \frac{1}{2}\left|1 - \left(\frac{v_2}{v_1}\right)^2\right|\left|1 + \frac{v_2}{v_1}\right|$$

The power coefficient, i.e. the ratio of the extractable mechanical power to the power contained in the air stream, therefore, now only depends on the ratio of the air velocities before and after the converter. If this interrelationship is plotted graphically—naturally, an analytical solution can also be found easily—it can be seen that the power coefficient reaches a maximum at a certain velocity ratio (Fig. 11.12).

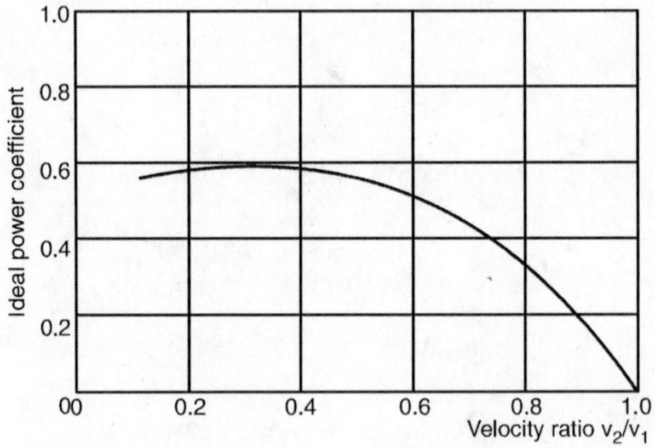

Fig.11.12. *Power coefficient versus the flow velocity ratio of the flow before and after the energy converter*

With $v_2/v_1 = 1/3$, the maximum "ideal power coefficient" c_P becomes

$$c_P = \frac{16}{27} = 0.593$$

Betz was the first to drive this important value and it, therefore, frequently called the "Betz factor".

Knowing that the maximum, ideal power coefficient is reached at $v_2/v_1 = 1/3$, the flow velocity v'

$$v' = \frac{2}{3}v_1$$

and the required reduced velocity v_2 behind the converter can be calculated:

$$v_2 = \frac{1}{3}v_1$$

Fig.11.13 shows the flow conditions through the wind energy converter once again, in greater detail. In addition to the flow lines, the variations of the associated flow velocity and the static pressure are indicated. When approaching the converter plane the air is retarded, it flows through and is then slowed down further to a minimum value behind the turbine. The flow lines show a widening of the stream tube to a maximum diameter at the point of lowest air velocity. Approaching the turbine, the static pressure increases, and then jumps to a lower value, to level out again at the ambient pressure behind the converter due to pressure equalisation. The flow velocity then also increases again to its initial value far behind the converter and the widening of the stream tube disappears.

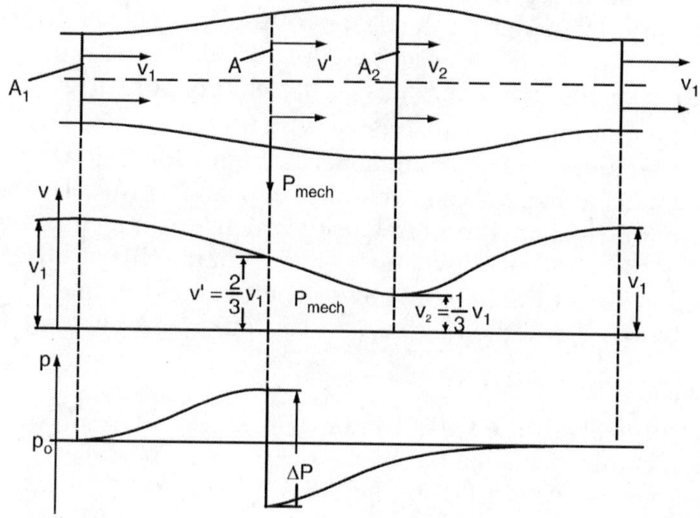

Fig.11.13. *Flow conditions of the stream an ideal disk-shaped energy converter with the maximum possible extraction of mechanical power*

It is worthwhile to recall that these basic relationships were derived for an ideal, frictionless flow, and that the result was obviously derived without having a close look at the wind energy converter. In real cases, the power coefficient will always be smaller than the ideal Betz value. The essential findings derived from the momentum theory can be summarised in words as follows:

- The mechanical power which can be extracted from a free-stream airflow by an energy converter increases with the third power of the wind velocity.
- The power increases linearly with the cross-sectional area of the converter traversed; it thus increases with the square of its diameter.
- Even with an ideal airflow and lossless conversion, the ratio of extractable mechanical work to the power contained in the wind is limited to a value of 0.593. Hence, only about 60% of the wind energy of a certain cross-section can be converted into mechanical power.
- When the ideal power coefficient achieves its maximum value $c_P = 0.593$, the wind velocity in the plane of flow of the converter amounts to two thirds of the undisturbed wind velocity and is reduced to one third behind the converter.

11.6 WIND ENERGY CONVERTERS USING AERODYNAMIC DRAG OR LIFT

The momentum theory by Betz indicates the physically based, ideal limit value for the extraction of mechanical power from a free-stream airflow without considering the design of the energy converter. However, the power which can be achieved under real conditions cannot be independent of the characteristics of the energy converter.

The first fundamental difference which considerably influences the actual power depends on which aerodynamic forces are utilised for producing mechanical power. All bodies exposed to an airflow experience an aerodynamic force the components of which are defined as aerodynamic drag in the direction of flow, and as aerodynamic lift at a right angle to the direction of flow. The real power coefficients obtained vary greatly in dependence on whether aerodynamic drag or aerodynamic lift is used.

Drag devices

The simplest type of wind energy conversion can be achieved by means of pure drag surfaces (Fig.11.14). The air impinges on the surface A with velocity v_W, the power capture P of which can be calculated from the aerodynamic drag D, the area A and the velocity v with which it moves:

$$P = Dv_r$$

The relative velocity $v_r = v_W - v$ which effectively impinges on the drag area is decisive for its aerodynamic drag. Using the common aerodynamic drag coefficient c_D, the aerodynamic drag can be expressed as:

$$D = c_D \frac{\rho}{2}(v_W - v_r)^2 F$$

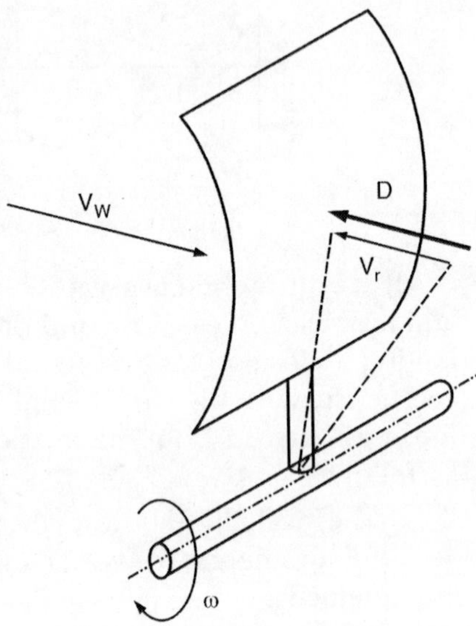

Fig.11.14 Flow conditions and aerodynamic forces with a drag-device

The resultant power is

$$P = \frac{\rho}{2} c_D (v_W - v_r)^2 A v_r$$

If power is expressed again in terms of the power contained in the free-strain airflow, the following power coefficient is obtained:

$$c_P = \frac{P}{P_o} = \frac{\frac{\rho}{2} c_D A (v_W - v_r)^2 v_r}{\frac{\rho}{2} v_W^3 A}$$

Analogously to the approach it can be shown that c_P reaches a maximum value with a velocity ratio of $v/v_W = 1/3$. The maximum value is then

$$c_P = \frac{4}{27} c_D$$

The order of magnitude of the result becomes clear if it is taken into consideration that the aerodynamic drag coefficient of a concave surface curved against the wind direction can hardly exceed a value of 1.3. Thus, the maximum power coefficient of a pure drag-type rotor becomes:

$$c_{P\,max} \approx 0.2$$

It thus achieves only one third of Betz' ideal c_p value of 0.593. It must be pointed out that, strictly speaking, this derivation only applies to a translatory motion of the drag surface. Fig.11.19 shows a rotating motion, in order to provide a more obvious relationship with the wind rotor.

Rotors using aerodynamic lift

If the rotor blade shape permits utilisation of aerodynamic lift, much higher power coefficients can be achieved. Analogously to the conditions existing in the case of an aircrafts airfoil, utilisation of aerodynamic lift considerably increases the efficiency (Fig.11.15).

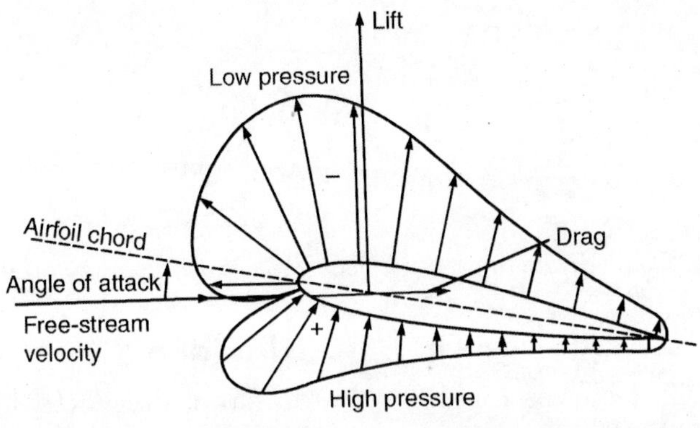

***Fig.11.15.** Aerodynamic forces acting on an airfoil exposed to an air stream*

All modern wind rotor types are designed for utilising this effect and the type best suited for this purpose is the propeller type with a horizontal rotational axis (Fig.11.16). The wind velocity v_W is vectorially combined with the peripheral velocity u of the rotor blade. When the rotor blade is rotating, this is the peripheral velocity at a blade cross-section at a certain distance from the axis of rotation. Together with the airfoil chord the resultant free-stream velocity v_r form the aerodynamic angle of attack. The aerodynamic force created is resolved into a component in the direction of the free-stream velocity, the drag D, and a component perpendicular to the free-stream velocity, the lift L. The lift force L, in turn, can be resolved into a component L_{torque} in the plane of rotation of the rotor, and a second component perpendicular to its plane of rotation. The tangential component L_{torque} constitutes the driving torque of the rotor, whereas L_{thrust} is responsible for the rotor thrust.

Modern airfoils developed for aircraft wings and which also found application in wind rotors, have an extremely favourable lift-to-drag ratio (E). This ratio can reach values of up to 200.

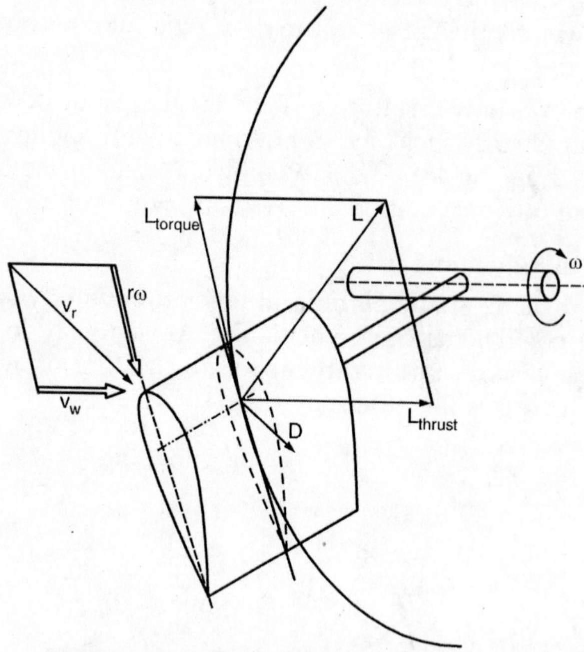

Fig. 11.16. *Flow velocities and aerodynamic forces acting on a propeller-like rotor*

11.7 CHARACTERISTICS OF WIND TURBINES

Typical C_P-λ curves for different rotors are presented in Fig.11.17. In general, initially the power coefficient of the turbine increases with the tip speed ratio, reaches a maximum at a typical λ, and then decreases with further increase in the tip speed ratio. These variations in C_P with λ depend on several design features of the rotor. American multi-bladed rotors show the lowest power coefficient and work at low speed ratio with the wind. A typical value for its peak power coefficient may be 14 per cent at a tip speed ratio of 0.8. However they have high solidity and hence high starting torque which make them attractive for water pumping. Two and three bladed propeller turbines and the Darrieus design work at higher tip speed ratios and show better efficiency. Hence they are suitable for wind-electric generators.

Savonius rotors, with its high solidity, work at lower tip speed ratio. Although, theoretically it is shown that the peak efficiency of such rotors cannot cross the limit of 20 per cent, Savonius reported a peak efficiency of 31 per cent under the wind tunnel test and 37 per cent in the free air stream. Efficiencies ranging from 25 to 35 per cent are reported under various investigations on this rotor. These values are quite impressive as these rotors are easier to fabricate and cost effective.

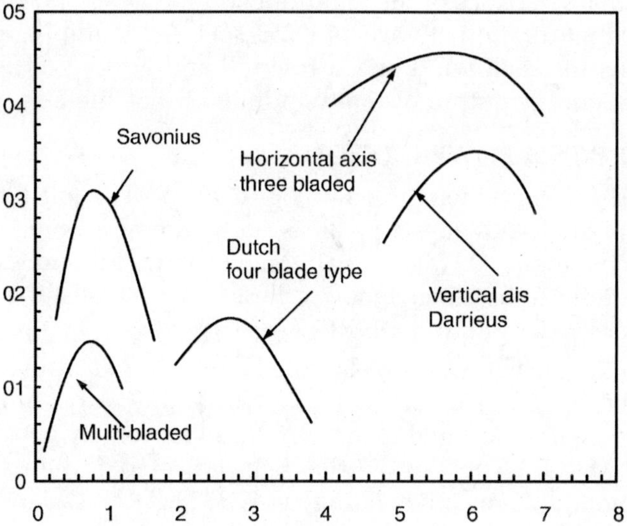

Fig.11.17. *Performance characteristics of wind rotors*

Consequently there is a maximum value of C_P of 59.3% (known as the Betz limit), although in practice real wind rotors have maximum C_P values in the range of 25%-45%.

11.8 WINDMILL PERFORMANCE

Although the power available is proportional to the cube of wind speed, the power output has a lower order dependence on wind speed. This is because the overall efficiency of the windmill (the product of rotor C_P, transmission efficiency and pump or generator efficiency) changes with wind speed. There are four important characteristic wind speeds:

- the cut-in wind speed: when the machine begins to produce power
- the design wind speed: when the windmill reaches its maximum efficiency
- the rated wind speed: when the machine reaches its maximum output power
- The furling wind speed: when the machine furls to prevent damage at high wind speeds.

Performance data for windmills can be misleading because they may refer to the peak efficiency (at design wind speed) or the peak power output (at the rated wind speed). The data could also refer to the average output over a time period (e.g. a day or a month).

Because the power output varies with wind speed, the average output over a time period is dependent in the local variation in wind speed from hour to hour. Hence to predict the output for a given windmill one needs to have output characteristics of the windmill and the wind speed distribution curve of the site (duration at various wind speeds). Multiplying the values of both graphs for each wind speed interval and adding all the products gives the total energy output of that windmill at that site.

ESTIMATED WIND POWER RESOURCE

The Centre for Wind Energy Technology16 (C-WET) published the Indian Wind Atlas in 2010, showing large areas with annual average wind power densities of more than 200 Watts/m^2 at 50 meter above ground level (MAGL). This is considered to be a benchmark criterion for establishing wind farms in India as per CWET and the MNRE17.

The potential sites have been classified according to annual mean wind power density ranging from 200 W/m^2 to 500 W/m^2. Most of the potential assessed sites have an annual mean wind power density between 200-250 W/m^2 at 50 MAGL. The Wind Atlas has projected Indian wind power installable potential (name plate rating) as 49,130 MW at 2% land availability 18. This is seen as a conservative estimate of wind power potential in India. Comparative wind power development across some of the Indian states is shown in Table.

Table 11.1 : Comparison of State Level Wind Power Development in India

Particulars	STATES							
	Andhra Pradesh	Gujarat	Karnataka	Kerala	Madhya Pradesh	Mahara -shtra	Rajas -than	Tamil Nadu
1. Total number of identified sites	32	40	26	17	7	39	8	45
2. Identified numberof potential districts	7	9	9	3	5	13	5	11
3. Annual mean wind speed spped (m/sec) at 50 m mast height	4.86–6.61	4.33–6.97	5.19–8.37	4.41–8.12	5.0–6.25	4.31–6.58	4.02–5.73	4.47–7.32
4. Number of wind monitoring stations established till October 2010	63	69	49	27	37	112	36	68
5. Number of wind monitoring stations operating (as of December 2010)	2	6	5	-	4	22	1	1
7. Installable wind potential (MW)	5,394	10,609	8,591	790	920	5,439	5,005	5,374
8. Presently installed capacity (MW) till Dec. 2010	176.8	2,005.30	1,576.20	28	230.8	2,201.60	1,353.40	5,502.90
9. Untapped installable potential (MW) as in Dec. 2010	5,217.20	8,603.80	7,014.90	762	689.2	3,237.40	3,641.70	-128.9*

** Note : Basedon government estimated potential for wind power. Currently at least anotehr 3000 MV of projects are inthe pipeline in Tamil Nadu.*

11.9 WIND POWER GENERATION

A basic wind power-generating plant converts motional wind energy into electrical energy. The schematic representation of the wind power-generating system is shown in Fig.11.18.

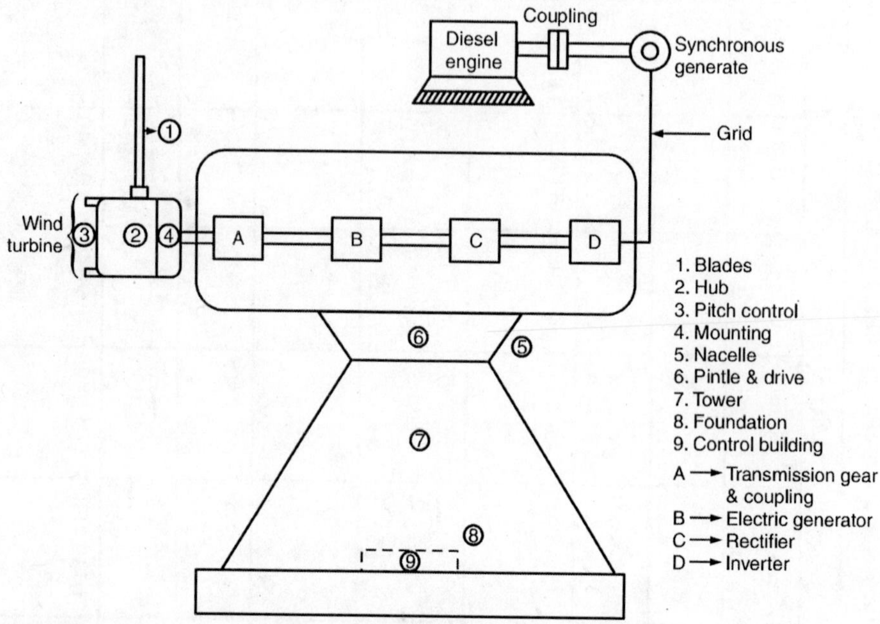

Fig.11.18. Wind power generating plant

In wind energy-generation system, wind turbine converts kinetic energy of wind motion into mechanical energy with the help of blades. The direction of wind flow control, i.e., pitches and yaw control is required for the proper operation. A suitable mechanical transmission gear is provided to transmit the mechanical energy from the wind turbine to electrical generator.

An electric generator converts mechanical energy into electrical energy and is fed to the rectifier thereby converting fixed AC to variable DC supply. Further DC is fed to an inverter, which converts DC into variable AC supply, transmitted to grid system for utility purpose.

A diesel engine is used to drive a synchronous machine when there is no wind energy as input to the aero turbine.

11.10 SITE SELECTION FOR WIND ENERGY FARM

An area where a number of wind electric generators are installed is known as a wind farm. The essential requirements for establishment of a wind farm for optimal exploitation of the wind are the following:

- High wind resource at particular site.
- Adequate land availability

- Suitable terrain and good soil condition
- Maintenance access to site
- Suitable power grid nearby
- Techno-economic selection of specific turbines
- Scientifically prepared layout

11.11 ADVANTAGES AND DISADVANTAGES OF WIND ENERGY SYSTEMS

Wind energy offers may advantages, which explains why it is fastest-growing energy source in the world. Research efforts are aimed at addressing the challenges to increase the use of wind energy.

Advantages

- Wind energy systems are energized by the naturally flowing wind, therefore it can be considered as a clean source of energy. Wind energy does not pollute the air like power plants that rely on combustion of fossil fuels, such as coal or natural gas. Wind turbines do not produce atmospheric emissions that cause acid rain or greenhouse gases.
- Wind energy is available as a domestic source of energy in many countries worldwide and not confined to only few countries, as in case of oil.
- Wind energy is one of the lowest-priced renewable energy technologies available today.
- Wind turbines can also be built on farms or ranches, thus benefiting the economy in rural areas, where most of the best wind sites are found. Farmers and ranchers can continue to use their land because the wind turbines use only a small fraction of the land. Wind power plant owners make rent payments to the farmer or rancher for the use of the land.

Disadvantages

- Wind power has to compete with conventional power generation sources on a cost basis. Depending on the wind profile at the site, the wind farm may or may not be as cost competitive as a fossil fuel based power plant. Even though the cost of wind power has decreased in the past 10 years, the technology requires a higher initial investment than fossil-fueled solutions for power supply.
- The major challenge to using wind as a source of power is that the wind is intermittent and it does not always blow when electricity is needed. Wind energy cannot be stored; and not all winds can be harnessed to meet the timing of electricity demands. The option of energy storage in battery banks is much beyond economically feasible limits for large wind turbines.

- Good wind sites are often located in remote locations, far from cities where the electricity is needed. In developing countries, there is always the extra cost of laying grid for connecting remote wind farms to the supply network.
- Wind resource development may compete with other uses for the land and those alternative uses may be more highly valued than electricity generation.
- Although wind power plants have relatively little impact on the environment compared to other conventional power plants, there is some concern over the noise produced by the rotor blades, and aesthetic (visual) impacts. Most of these problems have been resolved or greatly reduced through technological development or by properly siting wind plants.

11.12 ENVIRONMENTAL CONCERNS

Wind power is a clean renewable energy source. There are, however some environmental considerations to keep in mind when planning a wind power scheme. They include the following:

- Electromagnetic interference - some television frequency bands are susceptible to interference from wind generators.
- Noise - wind rotors, gearboxes and generators create acoustic noise when functioning; this needs to be considered when siting a machine.
- Visual impact - modern wind machines are large objects and have a significant visual impact on their surroundings. Some argue that it is a positive visual impact, others to the contrary.

11.13 WIND ENERGY STORAGE

The storage of electrical energy can take place in different way, i.e. it can be stored as chemical, mechanical or electrical energy. In the following, the main characteristics of flywheels, capacitors, superconducting magnetic energy storages, batteries, compressed air energy storages, hydro pump stations and hydrogen will be made.

(i) Flywheel

The energy is being stored with the help of a rotating mass (rotor) in a form of rotating energy. This rotor is over one motor-generator unit connected to the power grid. Conventional flywheels are made of metal (steel or titanium). By introducing new materials (glass or carbon fibre reinforced plastics) substantially higher peripheral speeds can be achieved and thus higher energy quantities can be stored. The self discharge rate of a flywheel is high and depending on design lies between 1% and 10% per hour. Therefore, the use of flywheels for longer period can not be recommended. Flywheels are characterised by long life time, high energy density, large maximum power output, short access time, high efficiency and small environment impact.

(ii) Capacitors

The capacitors are particularly characterised by their high power density. Double layer capacitors, as compared to conventional capacitors have higher storage capacity and also known as super capacitors. They can charge or discharge a large amount of power within very short access time of a few milliseconds.

However, this power is only for a short time at disposal. The self discharge rate of the double-layer capacitors, which amounts to about 10% per day, leads to the fact that they are less suitable for a long-term storage. Also they still can not store large amounts of energy.

(iii) Superconducting Magnetic Energy Storage (SMES)

SMES store energy in the magnetic field of a coil. Within few milliseconds a very high power can be released. However, this is possible only for few seconds, i.e. they are not suitable for the energy storage yet. Frequent charging and discharging have no influence on their life time. In case of large SMES the resulting magnetic field can have an impact on the environment. The disadvantages are small energy density and stability problems for large systems caused by the strong magnetic field.

(iv) Batteries

Due to their very good technical characteristics (large energy density, fast access time, pulse power...) the sodium sulphur batteries (NAS) have been chosen as battery storage of the large amount of wind energy. They can supply the system with a large amount of the power in a short time, or large amount of energy for a longer period. A higher power capacity can be achieved by connecting more modules.

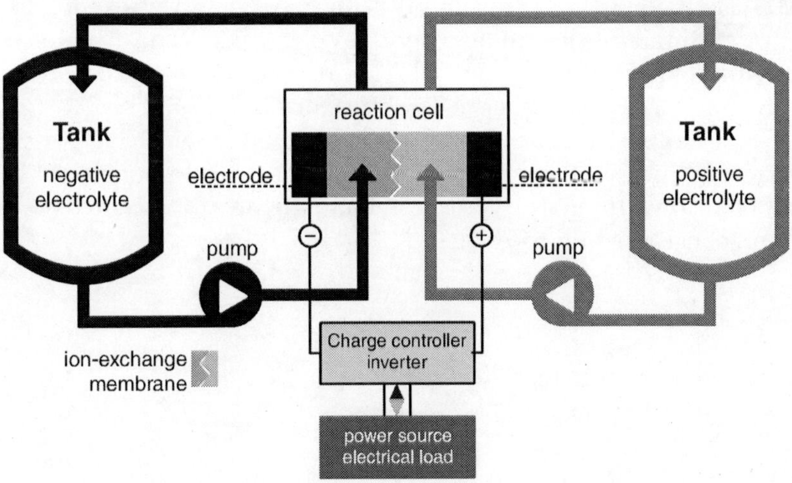

Fig. 11.19. Schematic Representation of a Flow Battery

(v) Pump Hydro Stations

During the off-peak periods (nights) and weekends water is pumped from lower into upper basin and stored as potential energy. In peak load periods this water is used to drive the generator and produce electricity which is being fed into the system. The efficiency is app. 75%. These stations have a life time of app. 50 years. The largest problems for building these stations are: the lack of suitable places and the impact in the nature environment.

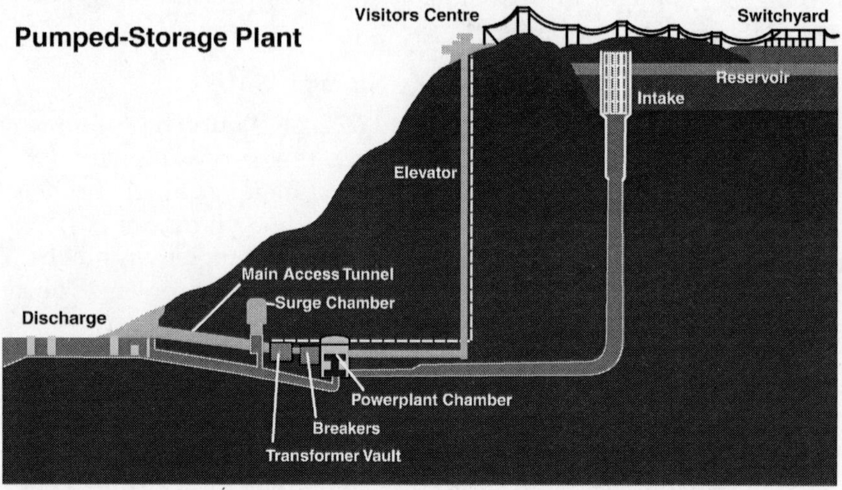

Fig. 11.20. Pumped-Storage Plant (Pumps could operate from wind power)

(vi) Compressed Air Energy Storage (CAES)

CAES use the electricity during off-peak periods and weekends to store and compress the air into the underground cavities (salt cavern, abandon mines, rock structures, artificial reservoirs...). At peak load times the compressed air is used to produce electrical energy. The efficiency is app. 42% to 52% (exhaust gases). Very actual and interesting are the adiabatic CAES which have additional heat storage. In this case the waste heat is stored in this additional heat storage and later used to warm up the compressed air. Therewith the efficiency of the CAES can be increased up to 70%.

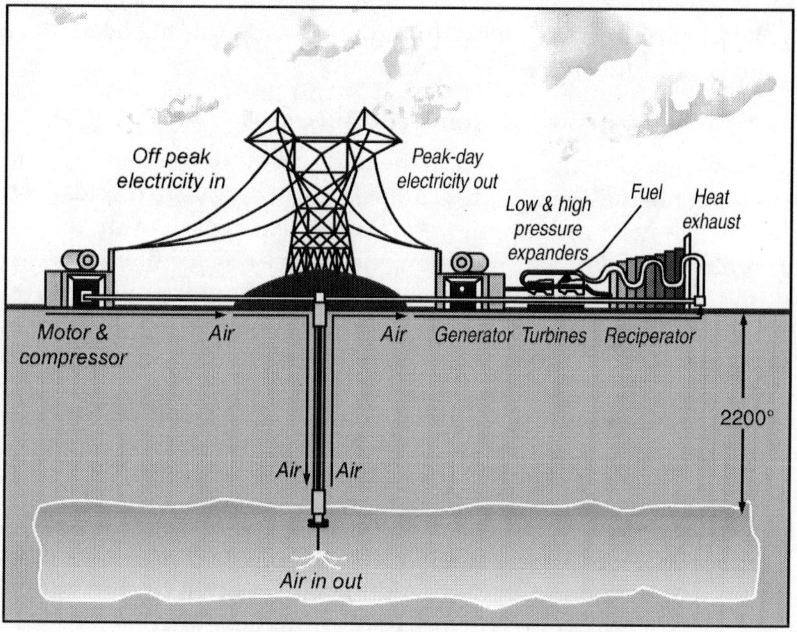

Fig. 11.21. Compressed Air Energy Storage (Compressor could operate from wind power)

(vii) Hydrogen

Hydrogen is being gained with the help of electrolysis and, afterwards, stored into a gas tank. When required, the fuel cells can use stored hydrogen and produced electricity which is supplied into the system. During the transformation the fuel cell develops pure water and no emissions are set free. They can store large amount of the power, but with low efficiency (25%).

11.14 MAJOR APPLICATIONS OF WIND POWER

1. Water Pumping

The livelihood and well-being of people, animals, and crops depends on a reliable, cost-effective supply of clean water. A wind electric pumping system overcomes some of the problems with the simple mechanical wind water pumper. This system generates electricity, which, in turn, runs an electric pump. Wind electric pumping systems allow greater siting flexibility, higher efficiency of wind energy conversion, increased water output, increased versatility in use of output power, and decreased maintenance and life-cycle costs.

The size of the wind turbine required for water delivery depends on the average daily volume of water required, the total pumping head, the average wind speed, and the system efficiency.

2. Stand-Alone Systems for Home and Business

In many places, wind power is the least-cost option for providing power to homes and businesses that are remote from an established grid. Researchers estimate that wind produces more power at less cost than diesel generators at any remote site with an average wind speed greater than about 4 meters per second. The applications for electricity in households range from operating small household appliances to refrigeration and freezing, heating, cooling, and lighting.

3. Systems for Community Centers, Schools, and Health Clinics

A larger system can provide power to a centralized community center, health clinic, or school. A power system for a health center can enable the storage of vaccines and radio communication for emergency calls. A power system for a school can provide electricity for computers and educational television, video, and radio. Community centers often find that, in addition to the benefits of the power, such as lighting and cooling, the "waste energy" can be used to charge batteries or make ice for sale to households.

Extending the distribution lines to individual homes and creating"mini-grid" increases the convenience of the power system to the community.

4. Industrial Applications

Wind power is currently being used for the applications such as telecommunications, radar, pipeline control, navigational aids, cathodic protection, weather stations/seismic monitoring and air-traffic control.

11.15 GENERATING SYSTEMS

In the wind electric system, several schemes have been developed for electric generation. These schemes can be divided into three categories:

(i) Constant Speed Constant Frequency systems (CSCF)

The constant speed, constant-frequency system requires that the rotor speed be maintained constant by controlling the pitch angle of the turbine blades. This in turn will result in a constant electrical frequency if the blade adjustment is correct for the various wind speeds that are encountered. This arrangement may be necessary in installations employing very large blades where allowing the rotor speed to vary over a wide range might risk mechanical resonance. Unfortunately, the mechanical efficiency of the wind turbine, owing to the varying of the blade pitch, cannot be kept at its maximum value.

(ii) Variable Speed Constant Frequency systems (VSCF)

The variable-speed, constant-frequency system permits the turbine speed to vary with the wind speed, but at the same time requiring that a constant electrical frequency be maintained. In such arrangements, the generated alternating current is converted or rectified into direct current, and the direct current in turn inverted or reconverted to alternating current, the frequency usually being 60 Hz so that this type of system can be synchronized with and connected to existing power lines.

Other attempts have been made as far as producing systems having a constant frequency. However, they have all, as far as we know, required rectification and inversion in order to provide the requisite alternating current frequency.

(iii) Variable Speed Variable Frequency systems (VSVF)

The variable-speed, variable-frequency system is ideal where frequency insensitive heating loads are to be supplied with power. Since the frequency of the power furnished to resistive loads is not a factor to contend with, wind-generated alternating current, whatever its frequency due to the wind velocity at that particular moment, can be supplied directly to a heating load of this character. Studies, it might be pointed out, have indicated that in a residential home, a significant portion of the energy that is used is consumed for space heating and hot water heating. In such cases, wind energy is expected to find greater and greater economical application for supplementing the normal utility supplied power (or the thermal power derived directly from fuel oil or propane gas, as the case may be) as fossil fuel costs continue to rise. Since the amount of wind energy is not constant at all times, reliance on fossil fuels cannot be entirely eliminated by utilizing wind power, but an appreciable reduction in their consumption can be achieved.

REVIEW QUESTIONS

1. What is a wind? How this energy can be used a renewable resource of energy?
2. Explain the basic principle of wind energy conversion system.
3. How the wind turbines are classified? Explain.
4. What is a wind concentrator? Explain.
5. Comment on aerodynamic operation of wind turbines.
6. Comment on wind energy extraction.
7. Explain Betz's Elementary Momentum Theory.
8. Comment on the characteristics of wind turbines in detail.
9. Differentiate between Horizontal axis and Vertical axis rotors.
10. Describe the working of wind power generating plant in detail.
11. What are the various factors to select a site for setting the wind power plant? List the factors.

12. What are the advantages and disadvantages of wind energy systems?
13. Comment on the environmental impact of wind power plants.
14. Discuss the following parameters used in rotor design:
    (*a*) Pitch
    (*b*) Solidity
    (*c*) Tip-speed ratio
15. Discuss various designs of rotors along with their merits and demerits.
16. Discuss the prospects and status of wind energy in India.

❑

12

BIOMASS ENERGY

12.1 INTRODUCTION

Biomass is a regenerative (renewable) organic material obtained from sources which includes aquatic or terrestrial vegetation, residues from forestry or agriculture, animal waste and municipal waste etc. that can be used to produce energy. It can be used as a solid fuel, or converted into liquid or gaseous forms for the production of electric power, heat, chemicals, or fuels.

12.1.1 Photosynthesis Process

Photosynthesis is the fundamental process in biomass energy whereby energy in sunlight is captured and stored in the chemical bonds of the tissues of living plants. In the process of photosynthesis, plants convert radiant energy from the sun into chemical energy in the form of glucose (or sugar). The chemical reaction involved is:

$$6\,H_2O + 6\,CO_2 + \text{sunlight (radiant energy)} = C_6H_{12}O_6\ \text{(glucose)} + 6O_2 \quad ...(12.1)$$

12.1.2 Important Characteristics of Biomass

1. Biomass is one of the most abundant resources in the world and can readily be available as it is created from waste products.
2. Biomass can be used directly (e.g., burning wood for heating and cooking) or indirectly by converting it into a liquid or gaseous fuel (e.g., alcohol from sugar crops or biogas from animal waste).
3. The cost of producing biomass for use as fuels and energy sources is very cheap compared to the cost of finding and extracting fossil fuels.
4. Biomass provides a potential benefit to the environment as it reduces carbon emissions if produced, transported and used in a sustainable manner.
5. Accumulation, harvesting and storage of raw biomass materials is quite expensive compared to fossil fuels.
6. Recycling of biomass wastes requires large amount of water.

12.1.3 Using Biomass Energy

Usually we burn wood and use its energy for heating. Burning, though, is not the only way to convert biomass energy into a usable energy source. There are four ways:

(i) Burning : We can burn biomass in special plants to produce steam for making electricity, or we can burn it to provide heat for industries and homes.

(ii) Bacterial Decay : Bacteria feed on dead plants and animals, producing a gas called methane. This is a natural process that happens whenever waste decays.

(iii) Fermentation : Adding yeast to biomass produces an alcohol called ethanol. This is how wine, beer, and liquor are made. Wine is just fermented grape juice.

(iv) Conversion : Biomass can be converted into gas or liquid fuels by using chemicals or heat. In India, cow manure is converted to methane gas to produce electricity. Methane gas can also be converted to methanol, a liquid form of methane.

12.2 BIOMASS RESOURCES

Biomass is an important source of energy and the most important fuel worldwide after coal, oil and natural gas. Bio-energy, in the form of biogas, which is derived from biomass, is expected to become one of the key energy resources for global sustainable development. Biomass resources include primary, secondary, and tertiary sources of biomass.

(*a*) **Primary biomass resources** are produced directly by photosynthesis and are taken directly from the land. They include woody crops and herbaceous crops, the seeds of oil crops, and residues resulting from the harvesting of agricultural crops and forest trees (e.g., wheat straw, corn stover, and the tops, limbs, and bark from trees).

(*b*) **Secondary biomass resources** result from the processing of primary biomass resources either physically (e.g., the production of sawdust in mills), chemically (e.g., black liquor from pulping processes), or biologically (e.g., manure production by animals).

(*c*) **Tertiary biomass resources** are post-consumer residue streams including animal fats and greases, used vegetable oils, packaging wastes, and construction and demolition debris.

Some other Biomass Resources

12.2.1 Types of Biomass

(*a*) Wood Fuel

Wood can be continually replenished, which leads to a sustainable and dependable supply. Wood fuels are fuels derived from natural forests, natural woodlands, and forestry plantations. These fuels include sawdust and other residues from forestry and wood processing activities. Advantages of wood biomass fuel are renewability, little carbon emissions, lower heavy metals and sulfur, minimal ash with some utilization possibility, and lower cost in economic aspect.

(*b*) Agriculture Residues

Agricultural residues are basically biomass materials that are byproducts of agriculture. This includes cotton stalks, wheat and rice straw, coconut shells, maize and jowar cobs, jute sticks, rice husks, and so on.

(*c*) Urban wastes

Urban wastes include municipal solid waste (MSW) generated by household and commercial activities and liquid waste or sewage.

(*d*) Landfill Gas and Biogas

Bacteria and fungi are not picky eaters. They eat dead plants and animals, causing them to rot or decay. A fungus on a rotting log is converting cellulose to sugars to feed itself. Although this process is slowed in a landfill, a substance called methane gas is still produced as the waste decays. Landfills can collect the methane gas, purify it, and use it as fuel. Methane can also be produced using energy from agricultural and human wastes.

Biogas digesters are airtight containers or pits lined with steel or bricks. Waste put into the containers is fermented without oxygen to produce a methane-rich gas. This gas can be used to produce electricity, or for cooking and lighting.

(*e*) Alcohol Fuels

Ethanol is an alcohol fuel (ethyl alcohol) made by fermenting the sugars and starches found in plants and then distilling them.

Biodiesel is a fuel made by chemically reacting alcohol with vegetable oils, animal fats, or greases, such as recycled restaurant grease. Biodiesel contains virtually no sulfur, so it can reduce sulfur levels in the nation's diesel fuel supply.

Table 12.1 Examples of biomass energy sources

Sources	**Examples**	**Uses/Products**	**Comments**
Forest products	Wood chips	Direct burning, charcol	Major source today in developing countries
Agricultural waste	Coconut husks, sugarcane waste,	Direct burning,	Minor source

	corncobs, peanut shells		
Energy crops	Sugarcane corn, sorghum	Ethanol (alcohol) gasification	Ethanol is major source of fuel in brazil for automobile
Trees	Palm oil	biodiesel	Fuel for vehicles
Animal residues	manure	methane	Use to run farm machinery
Urban waste	Waste paper, organic household waste	Direct burning of methane from wastewater treat-ment of from landfills	minor source

12.3 BIOMASS CONVERSION PROCESSES

The main three biomass conversion processes to produce energy or biofuels are:

12.3.1 Direct Combustion

The simplest and most common way of extracting energy from biomass is by direct combustion of solid matter. Majority of the developing countries especially in rural areas obtain the majority of their energy needs from the burning of wood, animal dung and other biomass. Biomass is burned to produce steam, the steam turns a turbine and the turbine drives a generator, producing electricity. Because of potential ash build-up (which fouls boilers, reduces efficiency and increases costs), only certain types of biomass materials are used for direct combustion.

12.3.2 Thermo-Chemical Conversion of Biomass

(i) PYROLYSIS

Pyrolysis, or destructive distillation, is the thermal conversion process of biomass in complete absence of oxygen or an oxidant. Products of this process include medium calorific value gas (MCV), liquid condensates (bio-oil, water and tar), and char (carbonaceous solid products with greater than 2 percent carbon).

The pyrolysis of biomass can be simply described as the following formula:

$$\text{Pyrolysis}: (C_6H_{12}O_6)m \xrightarrow{\text{Heat}(500\sim600°C)} \underset{\text{Gas}}{(H_2 + CO + CH_4 + ... + C_5H_{12})} \uparrow$$

$$+ \underset{\text{Liquid}}{(H_2O + ... + CH_3OH + CH_3COOH + ...)} + \underset{\text{Char}}{C}$$

Types of pyrolysis

The distribution of pyrolysis products varies depending on the feedstock composition, heating rate, temperature, and pressure, see Table 12.2.

Table 12.2 : Different types of pyrolysis

Pyrolysis	Heating rate [K/s]	Residence time [s]	Temperature [°C]	Product
Slow	<<1	300 – 800	400	char
			600	gas, oil, char
Fast	500 – 10^5	0.5 – 5	500 – 650	70% oil 15% char 15% gas
Flash	> 10	<1	< 650	oil
		< 1	> 650	gas
		< 0.5	1000	gas

(ii) Gasification

Gasification is thermal conversion with limited amounts of oxidant. Products of the process are very similar to those of the pyrolysis process. Gasification is an endothermic reaction and, thus, would not need supplemental fuels or heating once the process had begun.

Biomass gasification means incomplete combustion of biomass resulting in production of combustible gases consisting of carbon monoxide (CO), Hydrogen (H_2) and traces of Methane (CH_4). This mixture is called producer gas. Gasification is carried out in gasifier (air tight close container).

Types of Gasifiers

There are three types of gasifiers:

(i) Updraft gasifier

In this gasifier (Fig. 12.1) air enters below the combustion zone and producer gas leaves near the top of the gasifier. This type of gasifier is easy to build and operate. The gas produced has no ash content but is contains tar and water vapour because of the fact that the gas is passing through the unburnt fuel wood. They are suitable for tar free fuels like charcoal.

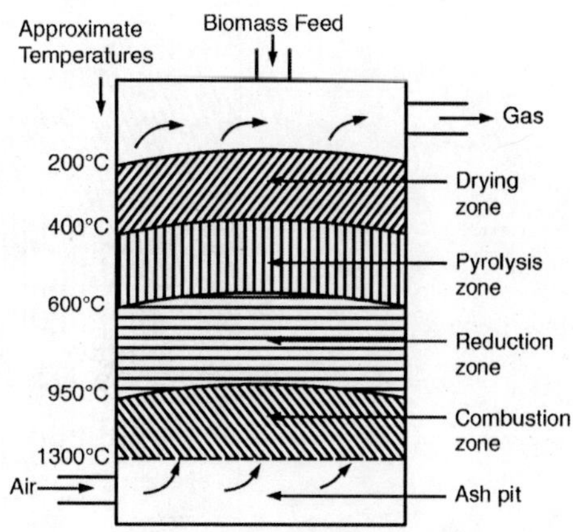

Fig. 12.1 Updraft gasifier.

(ii) Downdraft gasifier

In this gasifier (Fig. 12.2) air enters at the combustion zone through the air tuyers. Combustion of wood takes place in front of air tuyers. Heat produced during combustion pyrolysis the wood fuel and the hot producer gas is passed downwards. Producer gas leaves near the bottom of the gasifier through the grate.

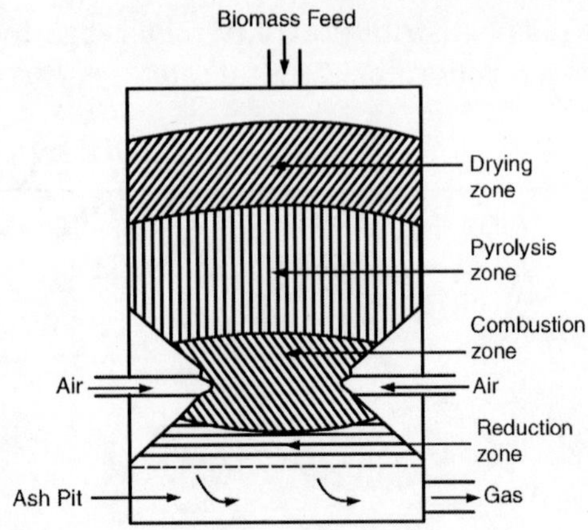

Fig. 12.2 Downdraft gasifier.

The volatile material and the tar produced during the combustion moves down to the reduction zone where they are further heated to become hydrocarbons and produce ash. The gas produced is nearly clean gas.

The ash is collected at the bottom. The gas produced is passed through the ash pit. Hence it contains less tar and more ash. These gasifiers are more suitable to wood and agriculture residues. They can generate electricity up to 10kW.

(iii) Crossdraft gasifier

In a cross flow gasifier (Fig. 12.3) the feed moves downwards while the air is introduced from the side, the gases being withdrawn from the opposite side of the unit at the same level of air entry. A hot combustion or gasification zone is formed around the entrance of the air, with the pyrolysis and drying zones being formed higher up in the vessel.

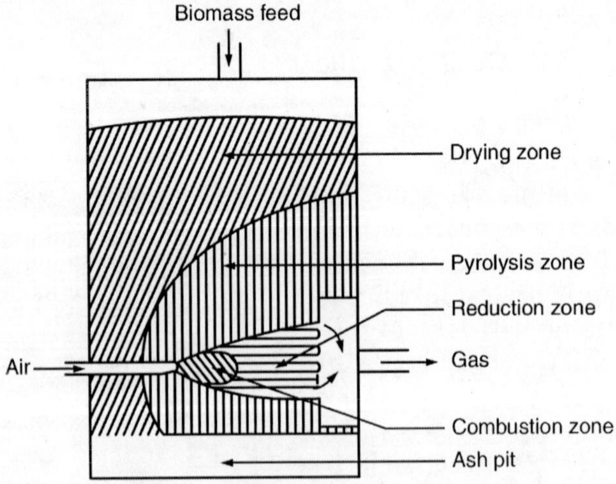

Fig. 12.3 Crossdraft gasifier.

Ash is removed at the bottom and the temperature of the gas leaving the unit is about 800-900oC; as a consequence this gives low overall energy efficiency for the process and a gas with high tar content.

In this type of gasifier, the path length of travel of air into producer gas is very less. This type of gasifier is not commonly used.

ZONES OF GASIFIER

1. **Drying Zone :** Biomass enters the gasification reactor into the drying zone whereby heat from the combustion section promotes evaporation of any remaining moisture in the feedstock. This section typically ranges in temperature from 70-200°C.
2. **Pyrolysis Zone :** As the biomass nears the combustion region, the temperature increases until it reaches the point at which pyrolysis begins. Pyrolysis is the vaporization of the volatile components in the fuel caused by the high temperatures and absence of oxygen. Temperatures in this section typically range from 300-600°C. Pyrolysis drives tar and gases such as CO, H_2, CH_4, CO_2, H_2O and other light hydrocarbons from the solid fuel only leaving behind char.
3. **Combustion Zone:** Some of the combustible gas (CO, H_2, CH_4) and char generated from pyrolysis are oxidized in the combustion zone where a controlled amount of air is allowed to enter the reactor. The exothermic reactions of oxidation in this section provide the heat required for the endothermic reactions in the drying, pyrolysis, and reduction zones. This section typically ranges from 700-1200°C. The product gases from this section are CO_2 and H_2O.
4. **Reduction Zone :** In the reduction zone, char that has made it through the combustion zone from the pyrolysis zone is reacted with the CO_2 and H_2O from the previous steps. The CO_2 and H_2O react with the carbon in the char which causes these gases to reduce to CO, H_2, and CH_4 leaving behind the minerals of the char as ash Gas then exits the reactor typically in the range of 200-300°C.

The following major reactions take place in various zones:

$$\begin{aligned}
C + O_2 &= CO_2 && (+\ 393\ \text{MJ/kg mole}) \\
2H_2 + O_2 &= 2H_2O && (-\ 242\ \text{MJ/kg mole}) \\
C + CO_2 &= 2CO && (-\ 164.9\ \text{MJ/kg mole}) \\
C + H_2O &= CO + H_2 && (-\ 122.6\ \text{MJ/kg mole}) \\
CO + H_2O &= CO + H_2 && (+\ 42\ \text{MJ/kg mole}) \\
C + 2H_2 &= CH_4 && (+\ 75\ \text{MJ/kg mole}) \\
CO_2 + H_2 &= CO + H_2O && (-\ 42.3\ \text{MJ/kg mole})
\end{aligned}$$

The average energy conversion efficiency of wood gasifiers is about 60-70% and is defined as

$$\eta_{Gas} = \frac{\text{Calorific value of gas/kg of fuel}}{\text{Avg. calorific value of 1kg of fuel}}$$

(iii) Hydrothermal liquefaction

Hydrothermal liquefaction is pyrolysis in hot compressed water of around 300°C and 10 MPa. It is suitable for high moisture content biomass, such as aquatic biomass, garbage, organic sludge, and so on.

Simple reaction scheme is shown in Figure 12.4. At first step, biomass can be degraded into water-dissolved materials. Then the water-dissolved materials are polymerized to form oil. When reaction is prolonged, the formed oil is polymerized into char.

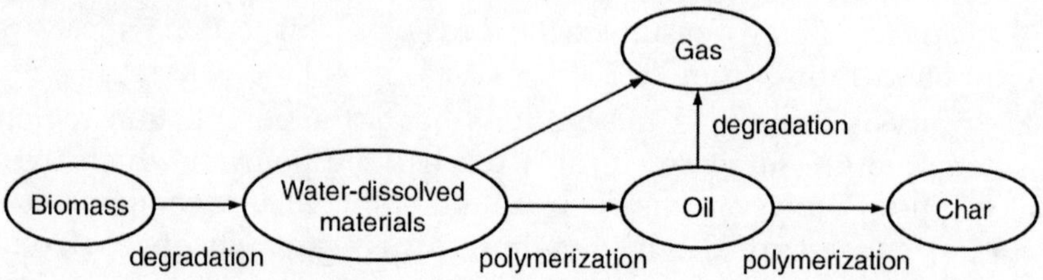

Fig. 12.4 Simple reaction scheme of liquefaction

Properties of obtained oil by liquefaction are shown in Table 12.3.

Table 12.3 Properties of obtained oil by liquefaction

Biomass	Wood	Sewage sludge
Elemental composition [wt%]		
Carbon	72	71
Hydrogen	6	9
Nitrogen	–	6
Oxygen	22	16
H/C	1.00	1.52
Higher heating value (MJ/kg)	29 – 30	33 – 34
Viscosity [mPa.s]	$> 10^6$	$10^3 - 10^4$

The energy yield (= calorie in the obtained oil / calorie in the feedstock biomass) is around 70%.

12.3.3 Biochemical Conversion of Biomass

(i) Alcohol (Ethanol) Fermentation

Fermentation is the breakdown of complex molecules in organic compound under the influence of ferment such as yeast, bacteria, enzymes, etc.

Ethanol is produced by fermentation of sugar solution by natural yeasts. After about 30 hours of fermentation the brew (or beer) contains 6-10% alcohol and this can readily be removed by distillation.

The overall process is as follows:

$$\underset{\substack{\text{Sugar}\\ \text{(Glucose)}}}{C_6H_{12}O_6} \rightarrow \underset{\substack{\text{Alcohol}\\ \text{(Ethyl alcohol)}}}{2(CH_3CH_2OH)} + \underset{\text{Carbon dioxide gas}}{2(CO_2)}$$

Sugar compounds, such as sweet sorghum or sugarcane juices, only need ethanol-producing yeasts for conversion. However, starchy materials need amylase-producing microbes to convert the starch into sugar, followed by the use of yeast to convert the resulting sugar into ethanol. Cellulosic biomass such as wood, paper waste or straw needs an additional step to convert the cellulosic materials into organic acids, sugars, and ethanol.

(ii) Anaerobic Digestion

Anaerobic digesters produce conditions that encourage the natural breakdown of organic matter by bacteria in the absence of air. Anaerobic digestion (AD) provides an effective method for turning residues from livestock farming and food processing industries into :

- Biogas (rich in methane) which can be used to generate heat and/or electricity
- Fibre which can be used as a nutrient-rich soil conditioner, and
- Liquor which can be used as liquid fertiliser.

AD is a process which manages farm and food processing residues. The digestion process takes place in a warmed, sealed airless container (the digester) which creates the ideal conditions for the bacteria to ferment the organic material in oxygen-free conditions. The digestion tank needs to be warmed and mixed thoroughly to create the ideal conditions for the bacteria to convert organic matter into biogas (a mixture of carbon dioxide, methane and small amounts of other gases).

There are two types of AD process :

- **Mesophilic Digestion**

The digester is heated to 30-35°C and the feedstock remains in the digester typically for 15-30 days. Mesophilic digestion tends to be more robust and tolerant than the thermophilic process, but gas production is less, larger digestion tanks are required and sanitisation, if required, is a separate process stage.

- **Thermophilic Digestion**

The digester is heated to 55°C and the residence time is typically 12-14 days. Thermophilic digestion systems offer higher methane production, faster throughput, better pathogen and virus 'kill', but require more expensive technology, greater energy input and a higher degree of operation and monitoring.

12.4 URBAN WASTE TO ENERGY CONVERSION

Municipal solid waste (MSW) is typically known by the public as "trash" or "garbage." Basically MSW consists of product packaging, grass clippings, furniture, clothing, bottles, food scraps, newspapers, appliances, and batteries. Half of the energy content in MSW is from biogenic material. Consequently, this energy is often recognized as renewable energy according to waste input. 1 ton of MSW combustion produce approximately 1 ton of CO2. If 1 ton of MSW is landfilled, it will produce 45kgs of methane.

Waste to energy is the conversion of non-recyclable waste materials into electricity, useable heat, or fuel through a variety of processes, including combustion, pyrolysis, gasification, anaerobic digestion and landfill gas recovery.

Table 12.4 Sources of MSW

Sources and Examples	Example Products
Residental : single and multifamily homes.	**Newspapers,** clothing, disposable tableware, food packaging, cans and bottles, food scraps, yard trimmings.
Commercial : office buildings, retail and papers, wholesale establishments, restaurants.	**Corrugated boxes,** food scraps, office disposable tableware, paper napkins, yard trimmings.
Institutional : school, libraries, hospital, prisons.	**Cafeteria** and restroom trash can wastes, office papers, classroom wastes, yard trimmings.
Industrial : packaging and administrative; not process wastes.	**Corrugated boxes**, plastic film, wood pallets, lunchroom wastes, office papers.

MSW TO ENERGY PROCESS:

The steps are:

(*i*) Waste Reception – The MSW trucks (Compactors) dump the waste into an enclosed reception hall which is under 'negative pressure' to prevent bad smell to the neighbourhood.

- The 'sucked' air is being 'refused' to enhance the combustion process. The tippng and bunker area is maintained under negative pressure to prevent odour.

(*ii*) Waste Segregation – Waste is transferred to a separation/segregation process where inerts, plastics, rubber, glass and metals will be removed and sent back to the recycling industry.

(*iii*) Storage of Waste – The residual waste (RDF) is then stored in a MSW Pit/Bunker whre large hydraulic cranes will be mixing the fuel to a homogenous fuel.

(*iv*) Leachate Removal & Treatment – The waste is stored for 2 to 5 days to remove moisture. With mixing pressure, the moisture is reduced and the leachate is removed to a sophisticated 'leachate treatment facility'.

(*v*) A crane grabs the waste and places it into the feed hopper. It then drops down a feed chute on to the Grate in the Combustion chamber.

(*vi*) The action of the moving grates turns the waste to allow it to burn fully with minimum combustion temperature of 850 degree. Celsius and residence time of 2 seconds.

(*vii*) The burnt out grate ash passes through the ash discharger on to an ash handling system.

(*viii*) Hot flue gases produced in the combustion process pass through a boiler where heated water becomes steam.

(*ix*) A turbo-generator uses the steam to produce electricity for export to the local power grid. The heat can also be used for industrial processes or residential district heating/industry near the WTE plant.

(*x*) The polluted flue gases from the boiler go through an extensive flue gas cleaning process. The cleaned flue gases & water vapours are finally released to the atmosphere through the chimney.

(*xi*) Incineration of MSW generates large volumes of flue gases. the flue gases carry a wide range of pollutants and residues from incomplete combustion.

(*xii*) The flue gas cleaning means optimal removal of Dust, Acidic components (NOx, SOx HCL, HF), Heavy Metals (Hg, Cd, Cr, Pb, Zn, Cu, Ni) Polyaromatic compounds, Dioxins and Furans.

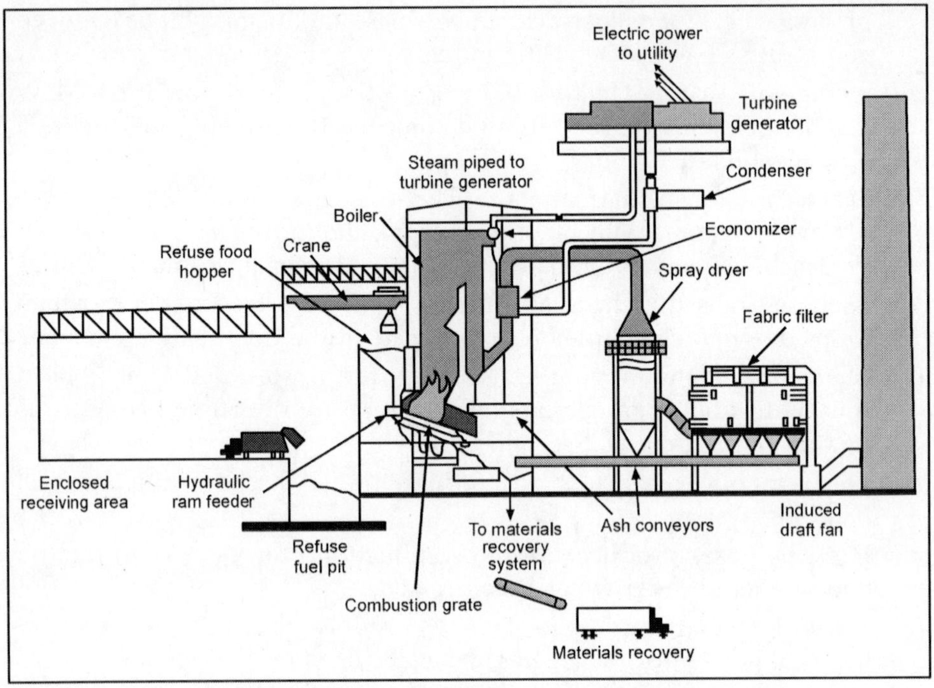

Fig. 12.5 MSW to Energy Process

12.5 BIOMASS TO ETHANOL PRODUCTION

Bio-ethanol is derived from alcoholic fermentation of sucrose or simple sugars, which are produced from biomass. Absolute and 95% ethanols are good solvents and are used in many industrial products such as paints, perfumes and tinctures. Solutions of ethanol (70-85%) are used as disinfectants in medicine. Except for the uses in motor fuels, synthesic ethanol got the largest market share in industrial applications, as it is cheaper than ethanol derived from biomass. Bi-ethanol however captures the alcoholic beverages market and a small share of the vehicle fuels market.

Some ethanol production ways from different types of biomass are:

1. Natural Sugars such as sugarcane or sugar beet juice

Ethanol is produced by fermentation of sugar solution by natural yeasts. After about 30 hours of fermentation the brew (or beer) contains 6-10% alcohol and this can readily be removed by distillation.

The overall process is as follows:

$$\underset{\text{(Glucose)}}{\underset{\text{Sugar}}{C_6H_{12}O_6}} \longrightarrow \underset{\text{(Ethyl alcohol)}}{\underset{\text{Alcohol}}{2(CH_3CH_2OH)}} + \underset{\text{gas}}{\underset{\text{Carbon dioxide}}{2(CO_2)}}$$

2. Disaccharide or Sucrose

Sucrose is composed of glucose of fructose. Fermentation of surcose is performed using commercial yeast such as *Saccharomyces ceveresiae.* Chemical reaction is composed of enzymatic hydrolysis of sucrose followed by fermentation of simple sugars. First, invertase (an enzyme present in the yeast) catalyzes the hydrolysis of sucrose to convert it into glucose and fructose.

$$\underset{\text{Sucrose}}{C_{12}H_{22}O_{11}} + H_2O \xrightarrow{\text{invertase}} \underset{\text{Glucose}}{C_6H_{12}O_6} + \underset{\text{Fructose}}{C_6H_{12}O_6}$$

Then, another enzyme (zymase), also present in the yeast, converts the glucose and the fructose into ethanol and CO_2.

$$\underset{\text{Glucose or Fructose}}{C_6H_{12}O_6} \xrightarrow{\text{zymase}} \underset{\text{Ethanol}}{2CH_3CH_2OH} + 2CO_2$$

Theoretically, 1 ton of hexose (glucose or fructose) yields 511 kg of ethanol.

3. Starch

Starch stored in grains is long chains of α-glucose monomers, 1000 or more monomers for one amylose molecule and 1000 to 6000 or more monomers for amylopectin. To convert starch to ethanol, polymer of α-glucose is broken into glucose through a hydrolysis reaction with gluco-amylase enzyme.

$$(C_6H_{10}O_6)_n + n\ H_2O \xrightarrow{\text{gluco-amylase}} n\ C_6H_{12}O_6$$

The resulting sugar is known as dextrose or D-glucose that is an isomer of glucose. The enzymatic hydrolysis is then followed by fermentation, distillation and dehydration to yield anhydrous ethanol.

Main steps in Biomass-to-Ethanol Processes

Once the biomass is delivered to the ethanol plant, it is sotred in the warehouse and conditioned to prevent from early fermentation and bacterial contamination (Fig. 12.6). Through pre-treatment, carbohydrates are extracted or made more accessible for further extraction. During this steps, simple sugars may be made available in proportions depending on the biomass and the pre-treatment process. A large portion of fibres may remain for saccharification through hydrolysis reactions or other techniques, in order to obtain simple sugars, which are then fermented.

In the batch fermentation, the hydrostate, the yeasts, nutrients and other ingredients are added from the beginning of the step. In case of a fed batch process, one or more inputs are added as fermentation progresses. Continuous processes, in which ingredients are constantly input and products removed from the fermentation vessels, are also used. In efficient processes, the cell densities are made high by recycling or immobilising the yeasts in order to improve their activity and increase the fermentation productivity. The fermentation reaction occur at 25-30°C and last 6-72 h depending on the composition of the hydrolysate, the type, the density and activity of the yeast. The broth typically contains 8-14% v/v ethanol. Abote this concentration, inhibition of yeast may occur that reduces their activity. Distillation yields an azeotropic mixture (95.5% alcohol, 4.5% water) often termed "hydrous" or "hydrated" ethanol, which is then dehydrated to give "anhydrous" ethanol (99.6% alcohol, 0.4% water).

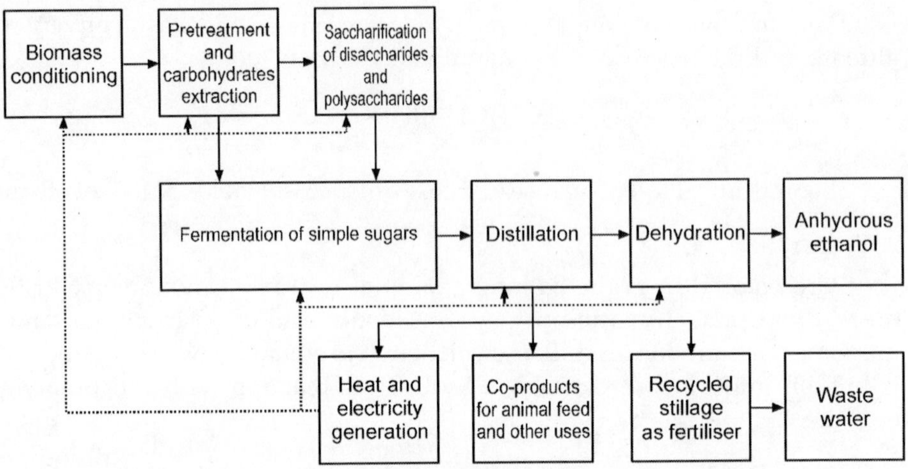

Fig. 12.6 Schematic outline of biomass to ethanol process

The remaining flow from the distillation column, known as vinasse or stillage, can be valorised to produce co-products, which may include process steam and electricity, products for feeding animals, more or less concentrated stillage used as fertiliser and other valuable by products.

12.6 BIOGAS

Biogas originates from bacteria in the process of bio-degradation of organic material under anaerobic (without air) conditions.

12.6.1 Composition and Properties of Biogas

Biogas is a mixture of gases that is composed chiefly of:

1. Methane (CH_4) : 40-70 vol.%
2. Carbon dioxide (CO_2) : 30-60 vol.%
3. Other gases : 1-5 vol.% including
   hydrogen (H_2): 0-1 vol.%
   hydrogen sulfide (H_2S): 0-3 vol.%

The properties of biogas are:

1. Change in volume as a function of temperature and pressure.
2. Change in calorific value as function of temperature, pressure and water vapour content.
3. Change in water vapour as a function of temperature and pressure.

12.6.2 Benefits of Biogas Technology

(i) Production of energy (heat, light, electricity) ;

(ii) Transformation of organic waste into high quality fertilizer;

(iii) Improvement of hygienic conditions through reduction of pathogens, worm eggs and flies;

(iv) Environmental advantages through protection of soil, water, air and woody vegetation;

(v) Micro-economical benefits through energy and fertilizer substitution;

(vi) Macro-economical benefits through decentralized energy generation and environmental protection

12.6.3 Biogas Production

Biogas microbes consist of a large group of complex and differently acting microbe species, notable the methane-producing bacteria. The whole biogas-process stages is shown in Figure 12.7.

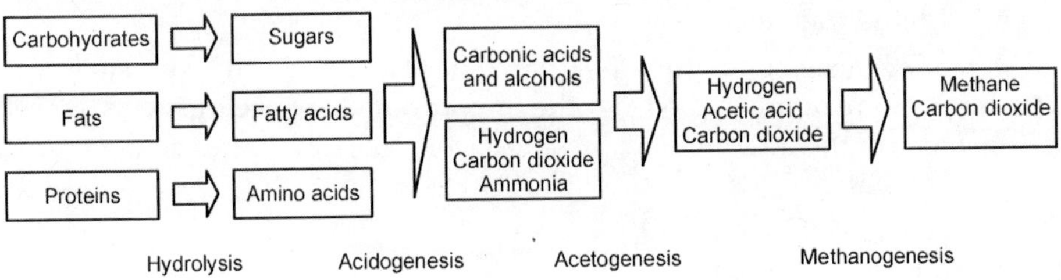

Fig. 12.7 : The key process stages of biogas generation

Stage 1: Hydrolysis

In general, hydrolysis is a chemical reaction in which the breakdown of water occurs to form H+ cations and OH- anions. Hydrolysis is often used to break down larger polymers, often in the presence of an acidic catalyst.

In anaerobic digestion, hydrolysis is the essential first step, as Biomass is normally comprised of very large organic polymers, which are otherwise unusable. Through hydrolysis, these large polymers, namely proteins, fats and carbohydrates, are broken down into smaller molecules such as amino acids, fatty acids, and simple sugars.

While some of the products of hydrolysis, including hydrogen and acetate, may be used by methanogens later in the anaerobic digestion process, the majority of the molecules, which are still relatively large, must be further broken down in the process of acidogenesis so that they may be used to create methane.

Stage 2: Acidification

(i) Acidogenesis

Acidogenesis is the next step of anaerobic digestion in which acidogenic microorganisms further break down the Biomass products after hydrolysis. These fermentative bacteria produce an acidic environment in the digestive tank while creating ammonia, H_2, CO_2, H_2S, shorter volatile fatty acids, carbonic acids, alcohols, as well as trace amounts of other byproducts.

While acidogenic bacteria further breaks down the organic matter, it is still too large and unusable for the ultimate goal of methane production, so the biomass must next undergo the process of acetogenesis.

(ii) Acetogenesis

In general, acetogenesis is the creation of acetate, a derivative of acetic acid, from carbon and energy sources by acetogens. These microorganisms catabolize many of the products created in acidogenesis into acetic acid, CO_2 and H_2. Acetogens break down the Biomass to a point to which Methanogens can utilize much of the remaining material to create Methane as a Biofuel.

Stage 3: Methanogenesis

Methanogenesis constitutes the final stage of anaerobic digestion in which methanogens create methane from the final products of acetogenesis as well as from some of the intermediate products from hydrolysis and acidogenesis. The reactions are:

$$CO_2 + 4\,H_2 \rightarrow CH_4 + 2H_2O$$

$$CH_3COOH \rightarrow CH_4 + CO_2$$

12.6.4 Factors Affecting Biogas Production

There are eight major factors which affect the quality and quantity of biogas.

(a) Solid-to-water ratio

Cattle dung (gobar) contains about 18% solid matter and the remaining 82% is water. Anaerobic fermentation proceeds at a faster rate if the slurry contains about 9% solid matter. Digester feed is prepared by mixing water in the ratio 1 : 1 by weight to reduce the solid content.

(b) Volumetric loading rate

It is expressed as the quantity of organic waste fed into the digester per day per unit volume. It is dependent on the size of the plant. The recommended loading rate is about 0.2 kg/m3 of digester capacity. The under loading and overloading reduces the biogas production.

(c) Temperature

Temperature affects bacterial activity; methane formation is optimum in the temperature range 35°-38°C. Biogas production decreases below 20°C and stops at 8°C. In cold regions a solar canopy is built over the biogas plants to maintain the desired temperature.

(*d*) Seeding

Cattle dung contains both acid forming bacteria and methane forming bacteria. Acid forming bacteria multiply fast, while the methane forming bacteria grow slowly. To start and accelerate fermestation, seeding of methane forming bacteria is required Accordingly, a small quantity of digested slurry rich in methane-forming bacteria is added to freshly charged digester.

(e) pH value

Measure of pH value indicates the concentration of hydrogen ions. Microorganisms are sensitive to pH of the digested slurry. For optimum biogas production, pH can be varied between 6.8 and 7.8. Control on pH should be exercised by adding alkali when it drops below 6.6.

(f) Carbon-to-nitrogen (C/N) ratio

Methanogenic bacteria need carbon and nitrogen for its survival. Carbon is required for energy while nitrogen for building cell protein. The consumption of carbon is 30 to 35 times faster than that of nitrogen. A favourable ratio of C : N can be taken as 30 : 1.

(g) Retention time

The period for which the biomass slurry is retained inside the digester is called 'retention time'. It refers to the volume of digester divided by the volume of slurry added per day, Thus, a 120 litre digester which is fed at 5 litres per day would have a retention time of 24 days.

(*h*) Stirring digester contents

Stirring the contents of the digester is necessary to mix the bacteria rich fluid in the slurry. It provide better contact between micro-organism and the substrate and uniformly distributes the volatile solids in the slurry. Gas production improves by 15% over the full cycle.

12.7 BIOGAS PLANTS

The biogas plant is a device that converts cattle dung and other organic matter into inflammable gas called biogas and into good quality organic manure under anaerobic conditions.

12.7.1 Floating Drum Type Biogas Plant (KVIC Model)

Slurry (mixture of equal quantities of biomass and water) is prepared in the mixing tank. The prepared slurry is fed into the inlet chamber of the digester through the inlet pipe. The plant is left unused for about two months and introduction of more slurry is stopped. During this period, anaerobic fermentation of biomass takes place in the presence of water and produces biogas in the digester. Biogas being lighter rises up and starts collecting in the gas holder. The gas holder now starts moving up. The gas holder cannot rise up beyond a certain level. As more and more gas starts collecting, more pressure begins to be exerted on the slurry.

The spent slurry is now forced into the outlet chamber from the top of the inlet chamber. When the outlet chamber gets filled with the spent slurry, the excess is forced out through the outlet pipe into the overflow tank. This is later used as manure for plants. The gas valve of the gas outlet is opened to get a supply of biogas. Once the production of biogas begins, a continuous supply of gas can be ensured by regular removal of spent slurry and introduction of fresh slurry.

Advantages are the simple, easily understood operation, construction is relatively easy.

Disadvantages of floating gas holder type biogas plant are

(a) Expensive

(b) Steel drum may rust and

(c) Requires maintenance.

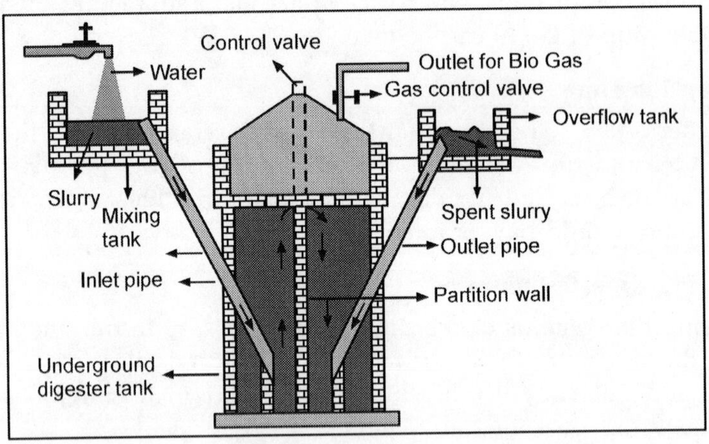

Figure 12.8: Floating gas holder type biogas plant

12.7.2 Fixed Dome Type Biogas Plant (Janata Model)

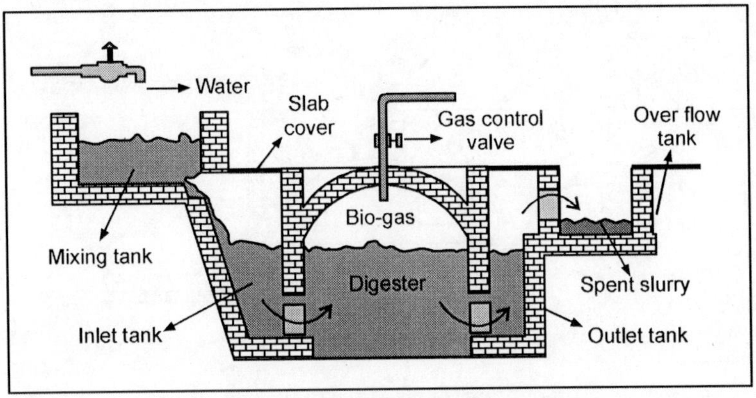

Figure 12.9: Fixed Dome type biogas plant

The various forms of biomass are mixed with an equal quantity of water in the mixing tank. This forms the slurry. The slurry is fed into the digester through the inlet chamber. When the digester is partially filled with the slurry, the introduction of slurry is stopped and the plant is left unused for about two months.

During these two months, an anaerobic bacterium present in the slurry decomposes or ferments the biomass in the presence of water. As a result of anaerobic decomposition, biogas is formed, which starts collecting in the dome of the digester. As more and more biogas starts collecting, the pressure exerted by the biogas forces the spent slurry into the outlet chamber. From the outlet chamber, the spent slurry overflows into the overflow tank. The spent slurry is manually removed from the overflow tank and used as manure for plants. The gas valve connected to a system of pipelines is opened when a supply of biogas is required. To obtain a continuous supply of biogas, a functioning plant can be fed continuously with the prepared slurry.

Advantages of fixed dome type of biogas plant are

- o Requires only locally and easily available materials for construction.
- o Inexpensive.
- o Easy to construct.

Disadvantages are mainly the frequent problems with the gas-tightness of the brickwork gas holder (a small crack in the upper brickwork can cause heavy losses of biogas).

12.7.3 Deenbandhu Biogas Plant

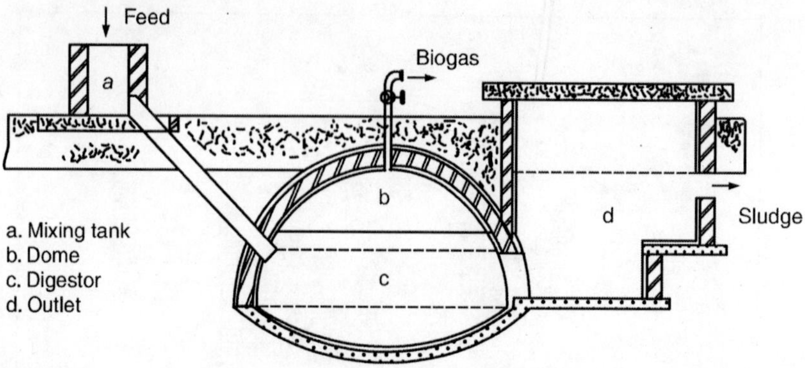

Figure 12.10 Deenbandhu Biogas Plant

The Deenbandhu biogas plant has a hemispherical fixed-dome type of gas holder, unlike the floating dome of the KVIC-design. The dome is made from pre-fabricated ferrocement or reinforced concrete and attached to the digester, which has a curved bottom. The slurry is fed from a mixing tank through an inlet pipe connected to the digester. After fermentation, the biogas collects in the space under the dome. It is taken out for use through a pipe connected to the top of the dome, while the sludge, which is a by-product, comes out through an opening in the side of the digester. About 90 percent of the biogas plants in India are of the Deenbandhu type.

12.7.4 Comparision among Family Size Biogas Plants

Table 12.8

KVIC	Janata	Deenbandhu
1. The digester of this plant is a deep well shaped masonry structure. In plants above 3m^3 there is a partition in the middle of the digester.	Digester of this plant is a shallow well shaped masonry structure. No partition wall is provided.	Digester is made of segments of two spheres one each for the top and bottom.
2. Gas holder is generally made of mild steel. It is inverted into the digester and goes up and down with formation and utilization of gas.	Gas holder is integral part of the masonry structure of the plant, Slurry from the gas storage portion is displaced out of the digester with the formation of gas of and comes back when it is used.	The structure descirbed above includes digester and the gas storage chamber, Gas is stored in the same way as in the case Janata plants.

3. The gasi is available at a constant pressure of about 10 cm of water.	Gas pressure varies from 0 to 90 cm of water.	Gas pressure varies from 0 to 75 cm of water.
4. Inlet and outlet connections are provided through A, C, pipes.	Inlet and outlets tanks are large masonry structures designed to store the slurry displaced out of the digester.	Inlet connection is through AC pipe. Outlet tank is large masonry designed to store displaced slurry.
5. The volume of the gas holder governs gas storage capacity of the plant.	It is the combined volumes of inlet and outlet chambers, (portions of inlet and outlet tanks above the second step.)	It is the volume of outlet displacement chamber.
6. The floating mild steel gas holder need regular maintenance to prevent corrosion. It has short life.	There is no moving part and hence no recurring expenditure. It is also has e long working life.	There is no moving part and hence no recurring expenditure. It also has a long working life.
7. Installation cost is very high A 2m^3 plant costs over Rs. 6900.00	It is cheaper than the KVIC type plants, A 2m^3 plant costs about Rs. 5400.00	It is much cheaper then KVIC and Janate type plants. A 2m^3 plant of this design costs Rs. 4000.00
8. Digester can be constructed locally the gas holder needs sophisticated workshops facilities.	A trained mason using locally available materials can be build entire plant.	Entire plant can be built by a trained mason using locally available materials.

12.8 OTHER TYPES OF BIOGAS PLANTS

12.8.1 Continuous Type Biogas Plant

In a continuous-type digester, feedstock is constantly fed into the digester. The material moves through the digester either mechanically or by the pressure of the newly feed substrate, pushing out the digested material. Unlike batch-type digesters, continuous digesters produce biogas without interruption for loading new feedstock and unloading the digested effluent. Biogas production is constant and predictable.

In continuous type biogas plant, the supply of the gas is continuous and the digester is fed with biomass regularly. Continuous biogas plants may be single stage, double stage or multiple stages. Digestion of waste materials in a single chamber or digester is called single stage process, in two chambers called double stage process while in several digesters is called multi stage process. In double stage process, acidogenic and methanogenic stage are physically separated into two chambers. Thus, the first stage of acid production is carried out in a separate chamber and only diluted acids are fed into the second chamber where biomethanation takes place.

In single stage, acidogenic and methanogenic stage are carried out in the same chamber without barrier. These plants are economic, simple and easy to operate. These plants are generally for small and medium size biogas plants. However, the two stage biogas plants are costlier, difficult in operation and maintenance but they produce more gas. These plants are preferred for larger biogas plant system.

The important features of continuous type biogas plants are:

(i) Gas production is continuous.

(ii) Retention period is less

(iii) Less problems as compared to batch type.

(iv) Small digestion chambers are required

Continuous digesters can be vertical, horizontal or multiple tank systems. Depending on the solution chosen for stirring the substrate, continuous digesters can be completely mixed digesters and plug flow digesters (Table 12.3). Completely mixed digesters are typically vertical digesters while plug-flow digesters are horizontal.

Table 12.3. Digester types

Completely mixed digesters	**Plug flow digesters**
Round, simple tank construction, vertical	Elongated, horizontal tank
Completely mixed	Vertically mixed
Suitable for simple feedstock (liquid manure)	Suitable for difficult feedstock (solid manure)
Fractions of the undigested feedstock can reach the outflow	Normally, no short cut between inflow and outflow; secure sanitation
Process temperature 20°-37°C	Process temperature 35°-55°C
Retention time 30-90 days	Retention time 15-30 days

12.8.2 Batch type Biogas Plant

Batch type biogas plants are appropriate where daily supplies of raw waste materials are difficult to be obtained. A batch loaded digester is filled to capacity sealed and given sufficient retention time in the digester. After completion of the digestion, the residue is emptied and filled again. Gas production is uneven because bacterial digestion starts slowly, peaks and then tapers off with growing consumption of volatile solids.

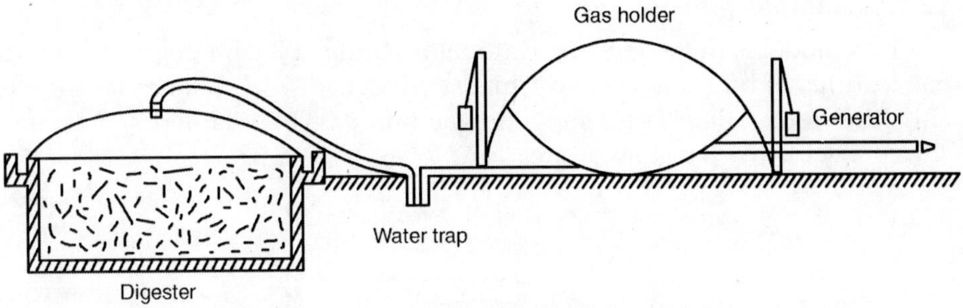

Fig. 12.11 Schematic View of the Batch Digester

The salient features of batch-fed type biogas plants are:

(i) Gas production in batch type is uneven.

(ii) Batch type plants may have several digesters for continuous supply of gas.

(iii) Several digesters occupy more space.

(iv) This type of plants require large volume of digester, therefore, initial cost becomes high.

(v) This plant needs addition of fermented slurry to start the digestion process.

Compared to other systems, batch digestion has the advantage of low operation costs and costs of the mechanical technology behind it and the disadvantage of high process energy consumption and maintenance costs.

12.8.3 Gayatri Model

This model is developed by the Government Implements Factory, Bhubaneshwar. In this model, a prefabricated fiber glass reinforced plastic (FRP) dome is used for collection of gas.

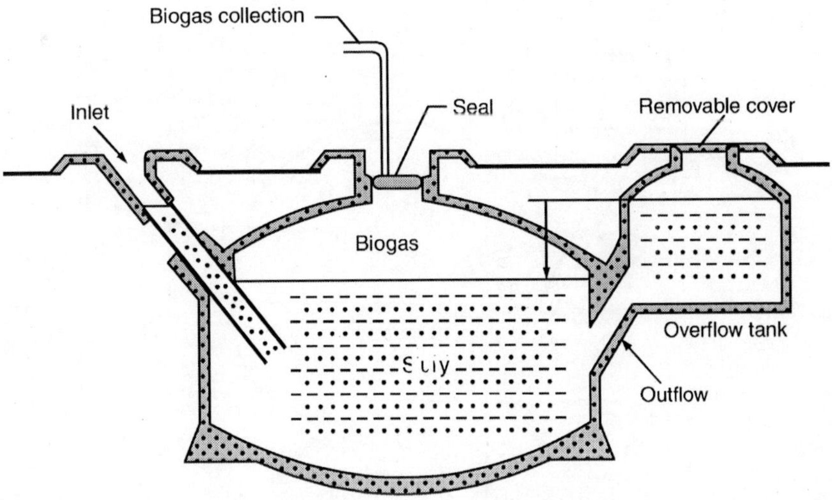

Fig. 12.12 : Gayatri model Biogas Plant

12.8.4 Manipal Model

This model is developed by Manipal Institute of Technology. This model has features of both Indian and Chinese models. It has rectangular digester and RCC roof. There is no separate gas holder. The inclined space above slurry level provides storage area for biogas.

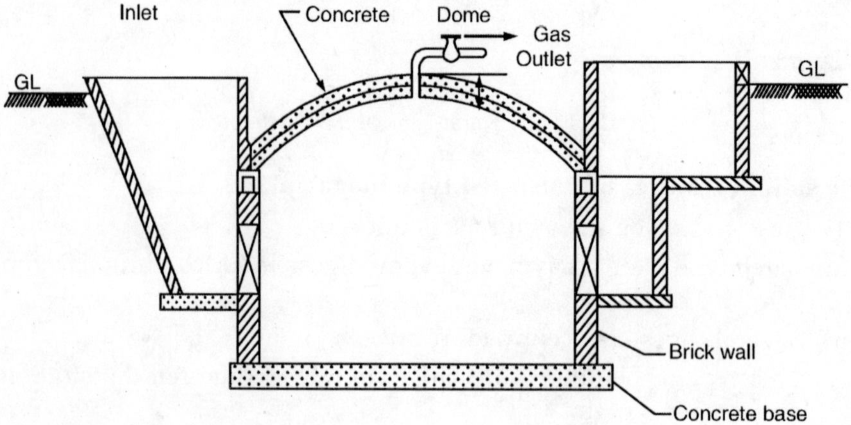

Fig. 12.13 Manipal model Biogas Plant

12.8.5 Spherical Biogas Plant

The spherical biogas plant, a fixed—dome type low-cost model, has been developed by Ae Tata Energy Research Institute (TERI), New Delhi. Besides being a low-cost model it is found to be durable because of its shape which can withstand the pressure of the gas. One of the additional features of this plant is that it uses a nylon net for automatic breaking of the scum formation over the surface of the slurry within fee digester. This plant is designed for a retention period of 50 days with a maximum pressure of 75 cm. Some of the main features of the spherical plant are described below.

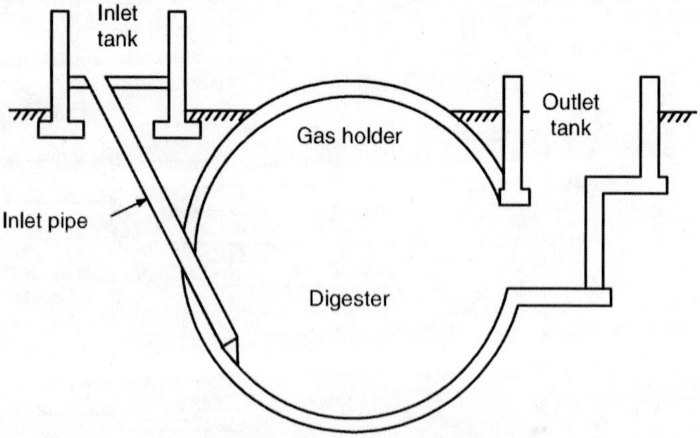

Fig. 12.14 Spherical Biogas Plant

Digester and gasholder together form a complete sphere, in which the top portion serves as the gas-holder, The sphere is made of bricks and the thickness of additional layer of tiles which are laid over the cricks. A GI pipe is provided on top of the dome and a valve is fitted on it to regulate the flow of gas. The mixing tank and outlet lank are on either side of the digester.

The outlet starts towards approximately the middle level of the sphere. A manhole of 60 cm × 60 cms left at this height of the digester wall which facilitates entry and also serves as the opening to the outlet tank. This tank is extended to form a bigger outlet tank. A small passage of 15 cm × 15 cm is provided on top of the wall of the bigger outlet tank. When gas is generated, increased pressure causes the slurry to flow out through this small passage and accumulate in the manure pit.

Scum-breaking Net: The slurry inside the digester may contain lighter particles float on the top surface of the slurry and form a hard layer which obstructs gas production. In order to prevent the formation of his hard layer of scum, a nylon net is spread inside the digester, just above the manhole opening. During the digestion process, is produced and accumulated in the gasholder. The slurry level within the digester goes down due to the pressure of the produced gas and rises up with its consumption. This movement causes the slurry to pass through the nylon net, thereby breaking up the scum.

The reduction in cost of construction of the plant is achieved by it's very shape. The construction of the plant requires minimum number of bricks which in turn reduces the sand, cement and mason days (labour cost) requirements.

12.9 APPLICATION OF BIOGAS

One cubic meter of biogas can do the following operations:

a) It can illuminate a mantle lamp (60 W) for a period of 7 hours.

b) It can be used for cooking three meals for a family of five.

c) It can run 2 hp engines for one hour.

d) It can run 100 lt. capacity refrigerators for 9 hours.

e) It can generate electricity of 1.25 KWH.

12.10 Selection of Site for a Biogas Plant

1. Less distance (about 10m) between the plant and the site of the gas consumption.
2. Minimum gradient
3. The space should be open so that temperature between 15oC to 30oC can be maintained.
4. The plant is normally constructed underground so water table should not be more than 3m.
5. Proper care should be taken from the interference of run-off water during the monsoon season.

6. A distance of minimum 15m should be maintained from the wells.
7. An area of 10 to 12 m2 is needed per m3 of the gas.
8. Plenty of water must be available with solid concentration of 7% to 9%.
9. The distance between the material for biogas generation and the gas plant site should be minimum.

12.11 Energy Farming

Energy farming is defined as the production of fuels or immediate energy as a main or subsidiary product of agriculture, silviculture, aquaculture, and also of industrial or social activities that produce organic waste residues. An example of energy farming is sugarcane industry. The schematic is shown in Figure 12.15. The flow diagram indicates how a single crop (sugarcane) may be processed for both energy supplies and a wide range of products with no other inputs than just the locally grown sugarcane.

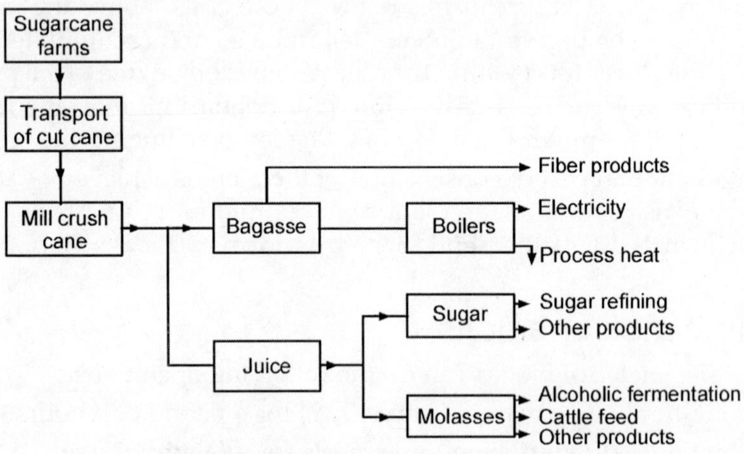

Fig. 12.15 Sugar cane agro-industry : process flow diagram, Bagasse is plant fiber residue; molasses is sugar rich residue.

Advantages of Energy Farming

1. Large potential supply
2. Variety of crops
3. Variety of uses including transport fuel and electricity generation
4. Efficient use of by-products, residues and wastes
5. Environment improvement by utilizing wastes and reduces green house emmisions
6. Encourages rural development

Dangers and Difficulties of Energy Farming

1. May lead to soil infertility and erosion
2. May compete with food production
3. May encourage genetic engineering of uncontrollable organisms
4. Pollutant emissions from poorly controlled processes

Strategies to avoid such disadvantages are

1. Use energy more efficiently
2. Grow plants that can supply both human foods (eg. Grain) and energy from the waste products (e. straw)
3. Do not burn residue biomass in the field
4. Decrease feeding human food crops to animals

SOLVED EXAMPLE

Example 1 : Calculate (1) the volume of a biogas digester suitable for the output of 6000 pigs, (2) the power available from the digester, assuming a retention time of 20 days and a burner efficiency of 0.6.

Solution: Mass of solids in waste is approximately

$$m_0 = (0.3 \text{ kg d}^{-1})(6000) = 1800 \text{ kg d}^{-1}$$

fluids volume is

$$\dot{V}_f = \frac{(1800 \text{ kg d}^{-1})}{(50 \text{ kg m}^{-3})} = 36 \text{ m}^3 \text{ d}^{-1}$$

digester volume is

$$V_d = (36 \text{ m}^3 \text{ d}^{-1})(20 \text{ d}) = 720 \text{ m}^3$$

volume of biogas is

$$V_b = (0.24 \text{ m}^3 \text{ kg}^{-1})(1800 \text{ kg d}^{-1}) = 430 \text{ m}^3 \text{ d}^{-1}$$

So, energy output is

$$\begin{aligned} E &= (0.6)(20 \text{ MJ m}^{-3})(430 \text{ m}^3 \text{ d}^{-1}) \\ &= 5200 \text{ MJ d}^{-1} = 1400 \text{ kWh d}^{-1} \\ &= 60 \text{ kW (continuous, thermal)} \end{aligned}$$

It continuously converted to electricity, this would yield about 15 kW of electricity from a biogas-fired generator set at 25% overall efficiency.

REVIEW QUESTIONS

1. What is a biomass? What are its important characteristics?
2. What are the various types of biomass resources? Explain with examples.
3. What are the various biomass conversion processes? Describe them with examples.
4. What is biomass gasification? Explain the three types of gasifiers with examples.

What are the advantages and disadvantages of various gasifiers?

5. What is Pyrolysis? Explain the Pyrolysis process of biomass.
6. Explain anaerobic digestion process in detail.
7. What is biogas? What is the composition and properties of biogas? Explain the three-stage anaerobic fermentation of biomass.
8. What are the factors which affect biogas production? Explain them.
9. Differentiate between floating drum type and fixed dome type biogas plant with suitable diagrams.
10. Explain the various types of other miscellaneous types of biogas plants. Explain them with suitable diagrams.
11. What are the applications of biogas?
12. What are the various problems and constraints for biogas development?

❑❑❑

13

OCEAN THERMAL ENERGY CONVERSION

13.1 INTRODUCTION

In the tropical and subtropical oceans of the world, a natural temperature difference exists between the surface water and those at depth. According to the fundamental laws of thermo-dynamics, this temperature gradient can be exploited as an energy source. The concept of ocean energy conversion (OTEC) exploits this temperature difference to drive power plants to produce electricity. OTEC can be considered an indirect solar technology because the surface water are warmed by the sun. A reliable OTEC plant would be able to generate electricity continuously because the temperature difference lasts 24 hours a day.

OTEC uses water from the bottom of the sea, which is nutritious, one result of this is that a lot of fish and other seafood will be collected in the outlet flow. This means that OTEC not only produce electricity, it produces water and food too.

The earth's oceans absorb solar radiation, the major part of which they store as thermal energy in the warm surface waters. About one fourth of the 1.7×10^{17} watts of solar energy reaching the earth's atmosphere is absorbed by sea water. In tropical regions, the sun's heat can warm surface water temperatures to as much as 25°C and a temperature of 5°C exist at depth of about 1,000 meters. The power cycles operating with such small temperature differences are low in efficiency and therefore expensive OTEC is only practical where the temperature differences is 20°C.

13.2 History

OTEC technology is not new. In 1881, Jacques Arsene d'Arsonval, a French physicist, proposed tapping the thermal energy of the ocean. But it was d'Arsonval's student, Georges Claude, who in 1930 actually built the first OTEC plant in Cuba. The system produced 22 kilowatts of electricity with a low-pressure turbine. In 1935, Claude constructed another plant aboard a 10,000-ton cargo vessel moored off the coast of Brazil. Weather and waves destroyed both plants before they became net power generators. (Net power is the amount of power generated after subtracting power needed to run the system.)

13.3 WORKING PRINCIPLE

The operation of OTEC plant is based on a well established physical (thermodynamic) principle. If a heat source, is available at a higher temperature and a heat sink at a lower temperature, it is possible in principle, to utilize the temperature difference in a machine or prime mover (e.g. a turbine) that can convert part of the heat taken from the source into mechanical energy and hence into electrical energy. The residual heat is discharged to the sink at the lower temperature. In the OTEC system, the warm ocean surface water is the heat source and the deep colder water provides the sink.

Solar energy absorption by the water takes place according to Lambert's law of absorption, which states that each layer of equal thickness absorbs the same fraction of light that passes through it. Mathematically,

$$-\frac{dI_{(x)}}{dx} = KI$$

Or

$$I_{(x)} = I_o e^{-Kx}$$

Where Io and I(x) are the intensities of radiation at the surface (x = 0) and at a distance x below the surface. K is an absorption coefficient that has unit Length-1. K has values of 0.05 m^{-1} for very clear fresh water, 0.27 m^{-1} for turbid fresh water and 0.50 m^{-1} for very salty water. Thus the intensity decreases exponentially with depth and, depending upon K, almost all of the absorption occurs very close to the surface of deep waters. Because of heat and mass transfer at the surface itself, the maximum temperatures occur just below the surface.

13.4 TYPES OF OTEC SYSTEMS

Ocean thermal energy is used for many applications, including electricity generation. There are three types of electricity conversion systems: closed-cycle, open-cycle, and hybrid.

Closed-cycle systems use the ocean's warm surface water to vaporize a working fluid, which has a low-boiling point, such as ammonia. The vapor expands and turns a turbine. The turbine then activates a generator to produce electricity. Open-cycle systems actually boil and seawater by operating at low pressures. This produces steam that passes through a turbine/generator. Hybrid systems combine both closed-cycle and open-cycle systems.

Open cycle, also known as the Claude cycle, and the other closed cycle system, also known as the Anderson cycle.

13.5 THE CLOSED OR ANDERSON, OTEC CYCLE

The closed cycle schematic is shown in Fig. 13.1. This cycle require a separate working fluid that receives and rejects heat to the source and sink via heat exchangers (evaporator and surface condenser). The working fluid may be ammonia, propane or a Freon. The operating (saturation) pressures of such fluids at the boiler and condenser temperatures are much higher than those of water; being roughly 10kg/cm2 at the boiler, and their specific volumes are much lower, being comparable to those of steam in conventional power plants. Such pressures and specific volumes result in turbines that are much smaller and hence less costly than those that use the low pressure steam of the open cycle.

Closed-cycle systems use fluid with a low boiling point, such as ammonia, to power a turbine to generate electricity. Warm surface seawater is pumped through a heat exchanger to vaporize the fluid. The expanding vapour turns the turbo-generator. Cold water, pumped through a second heat exchanger, condenses the vapor into a liquid, which is then recycled through.

The closed cycle approach was first proposed by Barjot in 1926, but the most recent design was by Anderson and Anderson in the 1960s. The closed cycle is sometimes referred to as the Anderson Cycle. In the cycle propane was chosen as the working fluid. The temperature difference between warm surface and cool surface was 20oC. The cool surface was at about 600m deep. Propane is vaporised in the boiler or evaporator at about 10 bar or more and exhausted in the condenser at about 5 bar.

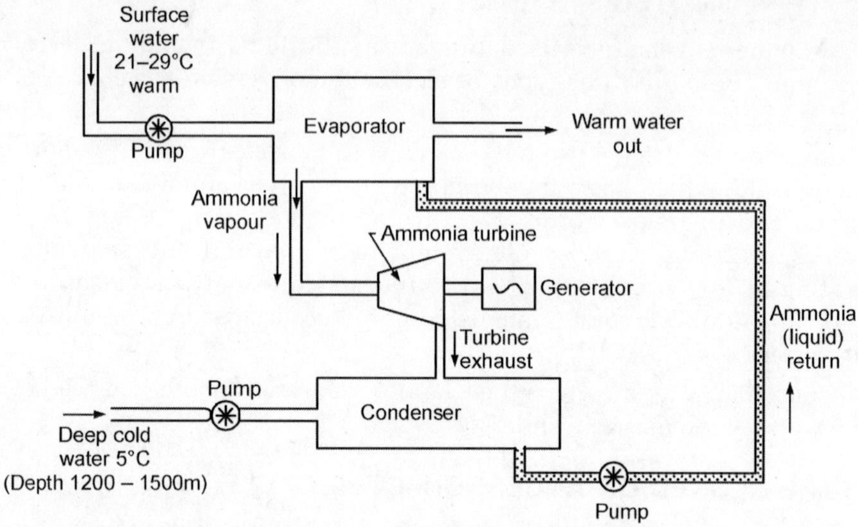

Fig. 13.1 Schematic of a closed OTEC ammonia cycle

13.6 OPEN CYCLE OTEC SYSTEM (CLAUDE CYCLE)

In the open cycle turbine system, sea water is the working fluid. The warm surface water is caused to boil by lowering the pressure, without supplying any additional heat. The low pressure steam is passed through a turbine, which extracts energy from it, and then the spent vapour is cooled in a condenser. This cycle drives the name 'open' from the fact that the condensate need not be returned to the evaporator, as in the case of the 'closed cycle'. Instead the condensate, can be utilised as desalinated water if a surface condenser is used, or if a spray (direct-contact) condenser is used, the condensate is mixed with the cooling water and the mixture is discharged back into the ocean. A schematic diagram of the open cycle system is shown in Fig. 13.2. Its corresponding T - S diagram is also shown in Fig. 13.3.

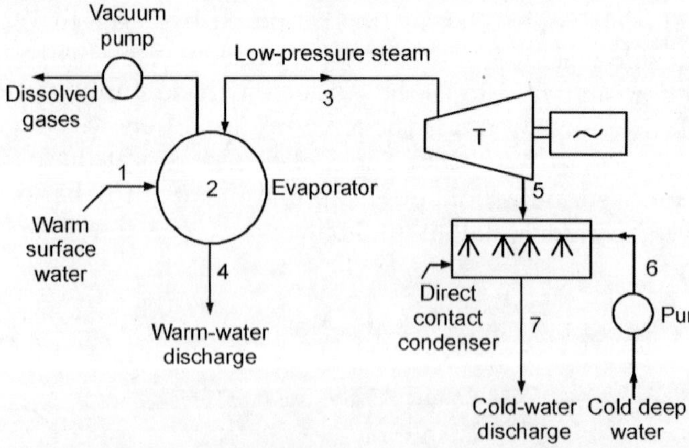

Fig. 13.2 Schematic of the OTEC open cycle

In the cycle shown warm surface water at 27°C is admitted into an evaporator in which the pressure is maintained at a value slightly below the saturation pressure corresponding to that water temperature. At the new pressure, water which is entering the evaporator gets 'superheated'.

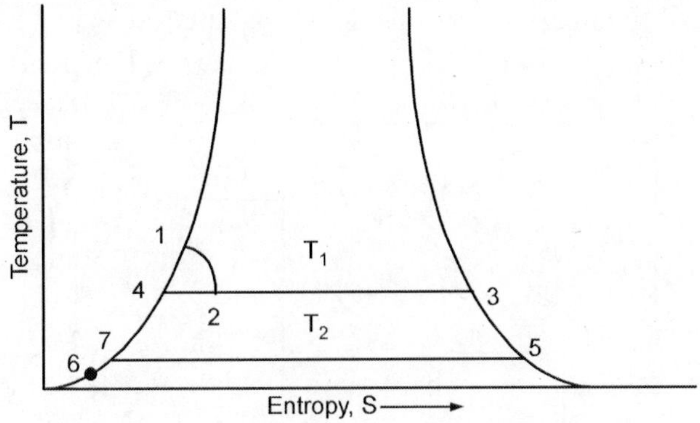

Fig. 13.3 *T – S diagram corresponding to Fig. 13.2*

As shown in Fig. 13.3, the warm water which is at 27oC, has a saturation pressure of 0.0356 bar (point 1). The evaporator pressure is of 0.0317 bar, which corresponds to 25oC saturation temperature. This temporarily superheated water undergoes volume boiling, causing that water to partially flash to steam to equilibrium two-phase conditions at the new pressure and temperature of 0.0317 bar and 25oC (point 2). The low pressure in the evaporator is maintained by a vacuum pump that also removes the dissolved non-condensable gases from the evaporator.

At (point 2), the evaporator contains a mixture of water and steam of very low quality. The steam is separated from the water as saturated vapour at (point 3). The remaining water is saturated at (point 4) and is discharged back to the ocean. The steam at (point 3) has very low pressure and high specific volume. The steam expands in a specially designed turbine that can handle such conditions to (point 5). In the condenser, the exhaust steam is mixed with cold water from the deep cold water pipe at (point 6), which results in near saturated water at (point 7). This water is allowed to discharge to the ocean. The cooling water from deep ocean which is at about temperature of 11°C, on reaching the condenser, rises to about 15oC, due to heat transfer between the progressively warmer outside water and the cooling water inside the pipe, as it ascends towards the top.

Because of the need in the open cycle to harness the energy in low pressure steam, extremely large turbines (compared to wind turbines) must be utilized. Furthermore degasifiers (deaerators) must be used to remove the gases dissolved in the sea water.

13.7 HYBRID CYCLE

A hybrid cycle combines the features of both the closed-cycle and open-cycle systems.In a hybrid OTEC system, warm seawater enters a vacuum chamber where it is flash-evaporated into steam, which is similar to the open-cycle evaporation process. The steam vaporizes the working fluid of a closed-cycle loop on the other side of an ammonia vaporizer. The vaporized fluid then drives a turbine that produces electricity. The steam condenses within the heat exchanger and provides desalinated water.

The line diagram of Hybrid cycle OTEC is (see Fig. 13.4)

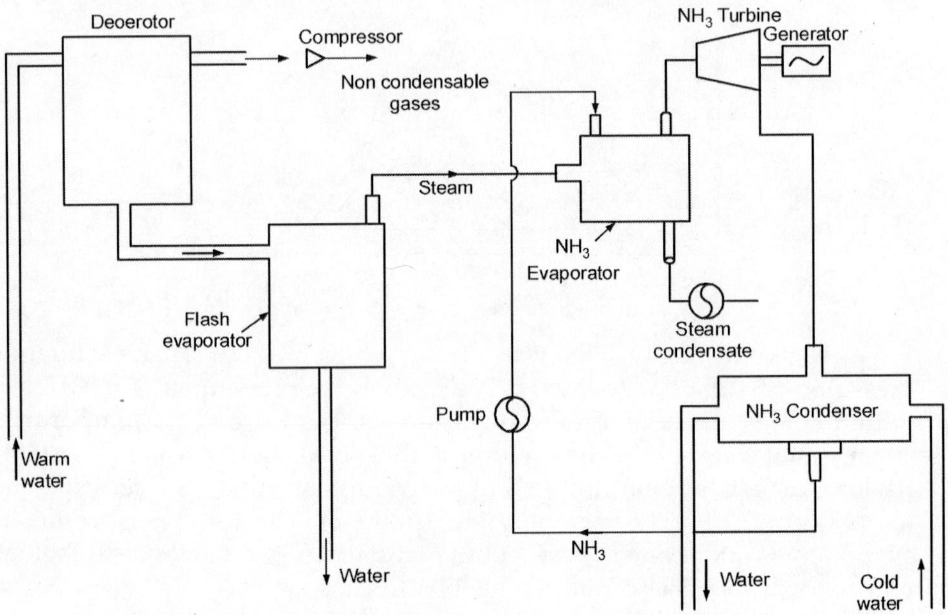

Fig. 13.4 Hybrid Cycle

13.8 EFFICIENCY OF OTEC SYSTEM

The efficiency of OTEC system is given by,

$$\eta = 1 - \frac{T_o}{T}$$

Where To is the deep water temperature in Kelvin and T is the surface water temperature in Kelvin.

The thermal gradient gives OTEC a typical energy conversion of 3 to 4%, whereas conventional oil or coal fired steam plants, often have temperature differentials of 500oF, yielding thermal efficiencies of 30 to 35%.

Remember, the greater the difference between hot and cold temperatures, the greater the efficiency of the energy conversion system. So to compensate for its low thermal efficiency, OTEC has to move a tremendous amount of water. It takes 20 to 40% of the power generated to pump the water through intake pipes in and around an OTEC system. This is why, almost 100 years after the idea was first conceive, OTEC researchers are still striving to develop plants that will consistently produce more energy than is needed to run the pumps, and that will operate in the corrosive marine climate, to justify the development and construction.

13.9 ADVANTAGES AND DISADVANTAGES OF OTEC

13.9.1 Advantages

1. OTEC uses clean, renewable, natural resources. Warm surface seawater and cold water from the ocean depths replace fossil fuels to produce electricity.
2. Suitably designed OTEC plants will produce little or no carbon dioxide or other polluting chemicals.
3. OTEC systems can produce fresh water as well as electricity. This is a significant advantage in island areas where fresh water is limited.
4. There is enough solar energy received and stored in the warm tropical ocean surface layer to provide most, if not all, of present human energy needs.
5. The use of OTEC as a source of electricity will help reduce the state's almost complete dependence on imported fossil fuels.

13.9.2 Disadvantages

1. The power cost is more.
2. The construction and pipe length affects the marine ecosystem.
3. The closed cycle OTEC can cause the pollution, if intermediate chemicals leak into the ocean.
4. Heat exchangers (evaporator and condenser) must be made of highly conductive materials, which increase their capital cost.

13.10 APPLICATIONS OF OTEC PLANT

OTEC has many applications, the most important are the following :

1. Production of electricity
2. Desalination of water
3. Marine culture, due to richness of the deep seawater in nutrients, which can be used to grow a phytoplankton, used to feed marine species.
4. Refrigeration and air-conditioning.
5. Mineral extraction.

13.11 SITE SELECTION

In selecting the site for an OTEC facility, the primary consideration is, a significant temperature difference of atleast 20oC between surface and deep ocean waters that will permit year round operation. The greater the difference, the lower will be the cost of generating electricity.

As a general rule, an OTEC plant would be located offshore in order to provide access to the deep colder water.

REVIEW QUESTIONS

1. Explain the basic principle of ocean thermal energy conversion technology.
2. List the various types of OTEC plants. Explain them in detail.
3. How the efficiency of OTEC plant is calculated? Explain.
4. What are the advantages and disadvantages of OTEC?

❑❑❑

14

TIDAL ENERGY

14.1 INTRODUCTION

Tides are generated by the action of gravitation forces of the sun and the moon on the oceans, by the spinning of the earth around its axis and the relative positions of the earth, moon and the sun.

The *tides* are the periodic vertical rise and fall of ocean water. The period between consecutive high tides is 12.5 hours. The tidal rise and fall of water is accompanied by periodic horizontal to and fro motion of water called **tidal currents**. Tides and tidal currents are intimately related.

Tidal movement differs from wave-movement. Waves have a period of only about 6 s whereas tides have a period of 12.5 h. Waves are caused by surface winds, whereas tides are caused by the gravitation forces of moon and sun on ocean water. The amplitude of tides covers a wide range from 25 cm to 10 cm. The speed of tidal currents is in the range of 1.8 km/h to 18 km/h. The tides and tidal currents possess renewable energy.

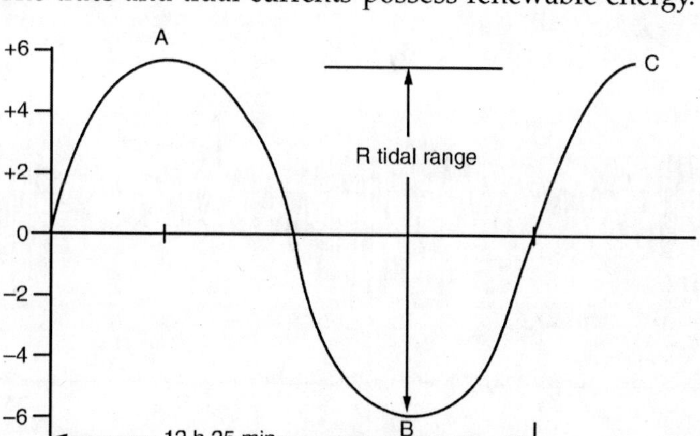

Fig. 14.1 The tides of sea.

The rise and fall of the water level follows a sinusoidal curve, shown with point A indicating the high tide point and point B indicating the low tide point. The average point of time for the water level to fall from A to B and then rise from B to C is each approximately equal to 6 hours 12.5 min (Fig. 14.1).

The difference between high and low water levels is called the range of the tide. The tidal range R is defined as :

R = water elevation at high tide-water elevation at low tide.

Because of the changing positions of the moon and sun relative to the earth, the range varies continuously. There are however, some characteristic features of this variation.

At times during full or new moon, when sun, moon and earth are approximately in a line, the gravitation forces of sun and moon are enhanced. The tidal range is then exceptionally large, the high tides are higher and low tides are lower than the average. These high tides are called **spring tides**. On the other hand, near the first and third quarters of the moon, when the sun and moon are at right angles with respect to the earth, **neap tides** occur. The tidal range is then exceptionally small; the high tides are lower and the low tides higher than the average. Hence the range is not constant. It varies during the 29.5 day lunar month (Fig. 14.2), and is maximum at the time of new and full moons (called the spring tides), and minimum at the time of the first and third quarter moons (called the neap tides). The spring-neap tidal cycle lasts one-half of a lunar month. A typical **mean range** is roughly one third of the spring range. The actual variations in range are somewhat complicated by seasonal variations caused by the ellipticity of the earth's orbit around the sun.

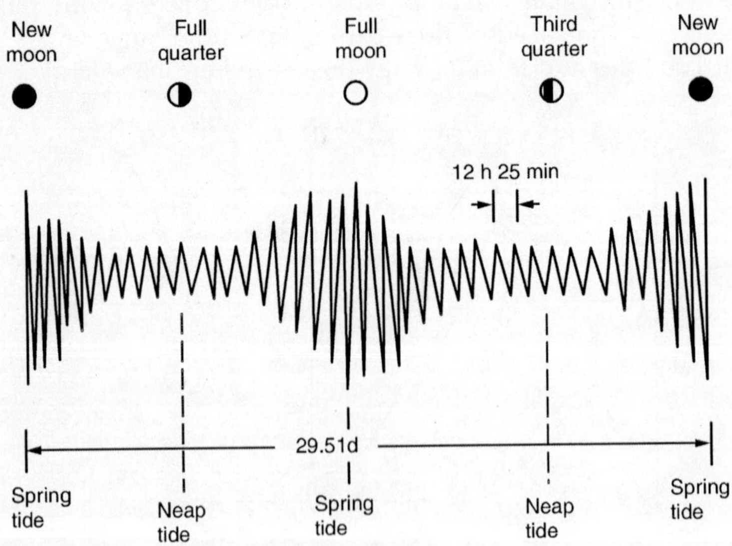

***Fig. 14.2** Relative high and low tides showing variation in range during lunar month.*

The variations in the periodicity and monthly and seasonal ranges must, of course, be taken into account in the design and operation of tidal power plants. The tides, however, are usually predictable, and fairly accurate tide tables are usually available.

Tidal ranges vary from one earth location to another. They are influenced by such conditions as the profile of the local shoreline and water depth. When these are favourable, a resonance like effect causes very large tidal ranges. Ranges have to be very large to justify the huge costs of buildings dams and associated hydroelectric power plants. Such tides occur only in a few locations in the world.

The tides along most coastlines are about a metre high, but in constricted areas where they are amplified by a funneling action, they may rise by 10 metres or more. It is in these constricted areas that the most effective tidal power plants may be located. A dam or sluice gate is placed across an ocean bay or estuary. An incoming tide fills up the enclosed basin while passing through a row of hydraulic turbines. After the basin is filled with water, the gates are closed and the turbines are shut down. Then the turbine blades are reversed and the gates opened again to let the water surge out. Thus turbines would be rotated either way generating electric power.

Following points have to be specially noted in connection with the tidal phenomenon:

1. The tides are a periodical phenomenon but no two tides in any cycle are alike. Since the relative positions of sun and moon and their distances from earth are continuously changing, the tides are also influenced accordingly. Of the two tides in a single day, one tide is higher than the other. In any month, the tides on the full moon and no moon days are particularly higher than the rest, as on these days sun's and moon's attraction acts in a directly additive manner. These are termed as the spring tides. In any year, the tides that occur at the time of versnal and autumnal equinoxes will be even higher due to the relative location of the sun and earth. Thus the tidal range, R shown in the Figure 14.1 varies from time to time. Generally, a long time mean value of R is designated as mean tidal range at any particular place.
2. The mean tidal range varies from place to place. The shape of the tidal cycle depends upon the interaction of the sea with the coast-line. Where the coast-line offers a resonating influence, the tidal range gets accentuated, at the other places; the land may produce a dampening effect on the tidal phenomenon. For instance, in land locked seas, the tidal phenomenon is always much subdued. Because of this interacting effect, the tidal range varies from place to place. For example, the mean tidal range on the west coast of India is high as 7 to 8 meters near the Gulf of Kutch, whereas it is only one meter or so near Kerala, down south. Bay of Fundy (Canada) has one of the greatest tidal

ranges in the world i.e. of 20m, whereas the Adiatic Sea at the Zara has virtually static water with the range being only of a few cm. Thus the tidal phenomenon is a unique feature of every coast-line.

3. In spite of their complexity, the tides are amenable to mathematical analysis. As a result the exact time and the water level for a high tide and a low tide can be forecast with great accuracy.

14.2 COMPONENTS OF TIDAL POWER PLANTS

The following are the components of a tidal power plant:

1. The dam or dyke or barrage (low wall) to form the pool or basin.
2. Sluice-ways from the basins to the sea and vice versa.
3. The power house.

Dam or Barrage: The function of dam or dyke is to form a barrier between the sea and the basin or between one basin and the other in case of multiple basins.

Sluice-ways: These are used to fill the basin during the high tide or empty the basin during the low tide, as per operational requirement. These are gate controlled devices.

Power house: A power house comprises turbines, electric generators and other auxiliary equipment. As far as possible the power house as well as sluice-ways should be in alignment with the dam or dyke.

The design cycle may also provide for pumping between the basin and the sea in either direction. If reversible pump turbines are provided, the pumping operation can be taken over at any time by the same machine. The modern tubular turbines are so versatile that they can be used either as turbines or as pumps in either direction of flow. In addition, the tubular passages can also be used as sluice-ways by locking the machine to a stand still. As compared to conventional plants, this, however, imposes a great number of operations in tidal power plants. For instance, the periodic opening and closing of the sluice-ways of a tidal plant are about 730 times in a year.

Fig. 14.3 Sluice gate

14.3 CLASSIFICATION OF TIDAL POWER PLANTS

The power generation from tides involves flow between an artificially developed basin and the sea. However in order to have a more or less continuous generation, this basic scheme can be elaborated by having two or more basins. Accordingly we can distinguish the following types of arrangements:

1. Single basin arrangement
2. Double basin arrangement

Single-basin schemes can generate power only intermittently, but a double basin scheme can provide power continuously, or on demand, which is a tremendous advantage. The drawback is that the civil works become more extensive. In the simplest double-basin scheme there must be a dam between each basin and the sea, and also a dam between the basins, containing the power house. One basin is maintained always at a lower level than the other. The lower reservoir empties at low tide, and the upper reservoir is replenished at high tide. If the generating capacity is to be large; the reservoirs must be large, which usually means that the dams will be long.

14.3.1 Single Basin Arrangement

In a single basin arrangement there is only one basin interacting with the sea. The two are separated by a dam (or barrage) and the flow between them is through sluice ways located conveniently along the dam. Potential head is provided by rise and fall of tidal water levels, this is usually accomplished by blocking the barrage embodies a number of sluice gates and low head turbine sets. The generation of power can be achieved in a single basin arrangement either as a

(*a*) Single ebb-cycle system, or

(*b*) Single tide-cycle system, or

(*c*) Double cycle system.

(*a*) Single Ebb-Cycle System

When the flood tide (high tide) comes in, the sluice gates are opened to permit sea-water to enter the basin or reservoir, while the turbine sets are shut. The reservoir thus starts filling while its level rises, till the maximum tide level is reached. At the beginning of the ebb tide the sluice gates are closed. Then the generation of power takes place when the sea is ebbing (flowing back of tide) and the water from the basin flows over the turbines into the lower level sea water. After two or three hours when there is sufficient difference between the full reservoir level and the falling tide level, to run the turbines, they are started and keep working until the rising level of the next flood tide and the falling reservoir level together reduce the effective head on the turbines to the extent where it can no longer work safely and efficiently. The turbines are then closed and the sluice gates opened again; to repeat the cycle of operations. Since in an estuary, the ebb tide has a long duration than the flood tide, the ebb operation provides an increased period of actual work.

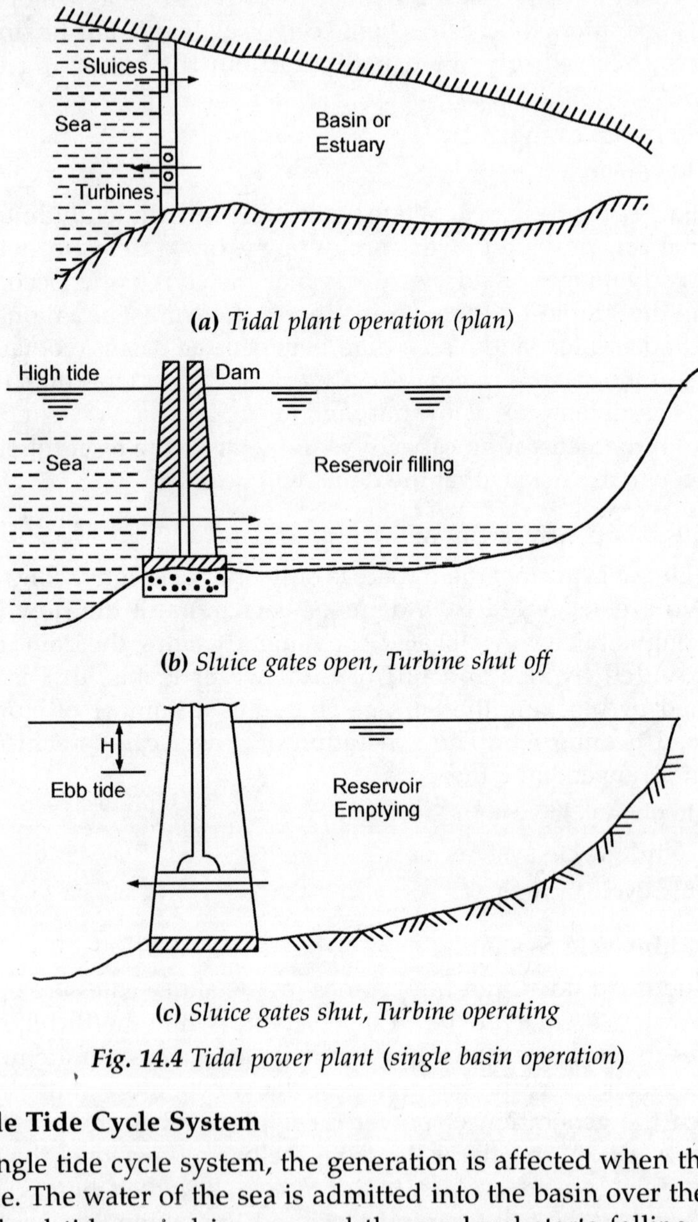

***Fig. 14.4** Tidal power plant (single basin operation)*

(*b*) Single Tide Cycle System

In single tide cycle system, the generation is affected when the sea is at flood tide. The water of the sea is admitted into the basin over the turbines. As the flood tide period is over and the sea level starts falling again, the generation is stopped. The basin is drained into the sea through the sluice ways.

Flood operation scheme needs larger size plant, operating, for shorter period and hence less efficient as compared to ebb tide operation. The ebb operation plant will be of smaller size, but will operate over a large period. The aim and effort should be to obtain as long a period of operation as possible at the beginning and finishing the work at the minimum operating head. Adjustable blade bulb turbines area specially suited for such operations under low and variable heads. All these turbines may be reversible which can work as pumps after the high tide, to increase the amount of water in the storage lake, until the generation can start. This way the turbine operation period may be prolonged to ten or more hours, out of the twelve hours-twenty five minutes of the tidal cycle.

The tide-cycle requires a deeper reservoir so as to locate the sills of the sluice gates deeper and, thus, requires greater construction costs. It has been estimated that the energy produced by an ebb cycle system can be as much as 1.5 times that by a tide cycle system.

The main disadvantage in both the ebb-cycle as well as the tide cycle systems is the intermittent nature of their operation. However, since the intermissions occur at regular intervals, there is possibility of connecting another supplementary system, so as to balance the discontinuity. Such possibilities can regulate the output. The system can be so geared as to generate power, both during the ebb and flood tides with the help of single basin only. This system is known as the double-cycle system.

(*c*) Double Cycle System

As stated above in double cycle system, the power generation is affected during the ebb as well as in flood tides. The direction of flow through the turbines during the ebb and flood tides alternates, but the machine acts as a turbine for either direction of flow. In this method, the generation of power is accomplished both during emptying end filling cycles. Both filling and emptying processes take place during short periods of time, the filling when the ocean is at high tide while the water in the basin is at low tide level, the emptying when the ocean is at low tide and the basin at high-tide level.

The flow of water in both directions is used to drive a number of reversible water turbines, each driving an electrical generator. Electric power would thus be generated during two short periods during each tidal period of 12h, 25 min. or once every 6h, 12.5 min.

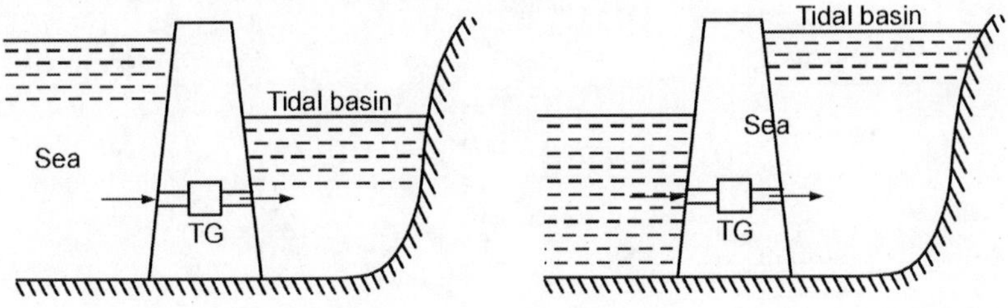

(a) High tide (b) Low tide

Fig. 14.5 *Double Cycle System*

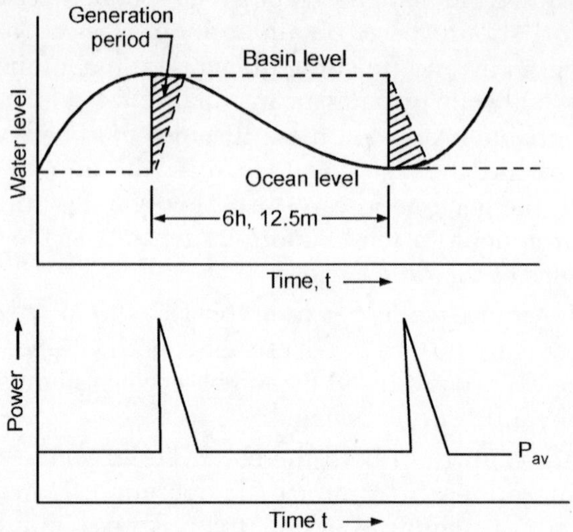

Fig. 14.6 Ocean and pool levels and power generated in a single-basin tidal system

Though the double cycle system has only short duration interruptions in the turbine operation, yet a continuous generation of power is still not possible. Furthermore the periods of power generation coincide only occasionally with periods of peak demand. These problems are solved to some extent in the two-basin scheme described below. However, a fundamental drawback to all methods for generating tidal power is the variability in output caused by the variations in the tidal range.

14.3.2 Double Basin Arrangement

It requires two separate but adjacent basins. In one basin called upper basin (or high pool), the water level is maintained above that in the other, the low basin (or low pool). Because there is always a head between upper and lower basins, electricity can be generated continuously, although at a variable rate.

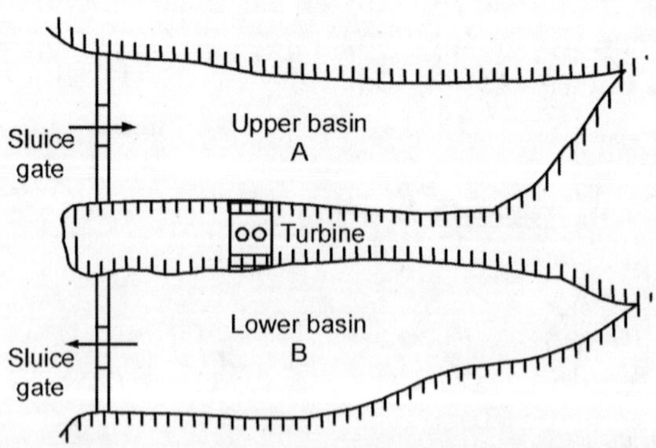

Fig. 14.7 Tidal power plant (Double basin operation)

In this system the turbines are located in between the two adjacent basins, while the sluice gates are as usual embodied in the dam across the mouths of the two estuaries. At the beginning of the flood tide, the turbines are shut down, the gates of upper basin A are opened and those of the lower basin B are closed. The basin A is thus filled up while the basin B remains empty. As soon as the rising water level in A provides sufficient difference of head between the two basins, the turbines are started. The water flows from A to B through the turbines, generating power. The power generation thus continues simultaneously with the filling up the basin A. At the end of the flood tide when A is full and the water level in it is the maximum, its sluice gates are closed. When the ebb tide level gets lower than the water level in B, its sluice gates are opened whereby the water level in B, which was arising and reducing the operating head, starts falling with the ebb. This continues until the head and water level in A is sufficient to run the turbines. With the next flood tide the cycle repeats itself. With this twin basin system, a longer and more continuous period of generation per day is possible. The small gaps in the operation of such stations can be filled up by thermal power.

The operation of the two basin scheme can be controlled so that there is a continuous water flow from upper to lower basin. However since the water head between the basins varies during each tidal cycle, as well as from day to day, so also does the power generated. As in the case with single basin scheme, the peak power generation does not often correspond in time with the peak demand. One way of improving the situation is to use off-peak power, from the tidal power generators or from an alternative system, to pump water from the low basin to the high basin. An increased head would then be available for tidal power generation at times of peak demand. This is very similar to pumped storage system in hydro-electric power stations.

14.4 ESTIMATION OF ENERGY AND POWER IN SIMPLE SINGLE BASIN TIDAL SYSTEM

The expression of maximum energy that can be generated during one generation period can be derived with the help of Fig. 14.8 which shows the case of the basin beginning at high-tide level, emptying through the turbine to the ocean, which is at low tide. (The identical energy will be generated in reverse process).

During the emptying process, the differential work done by the water is equal to its potential energy at the time. Considering a tidal range R, and intermediate head, at a given tune, the amount of work is calculated, considering a small head dh, for a intermediate head h, as shown in Figure 14.8.

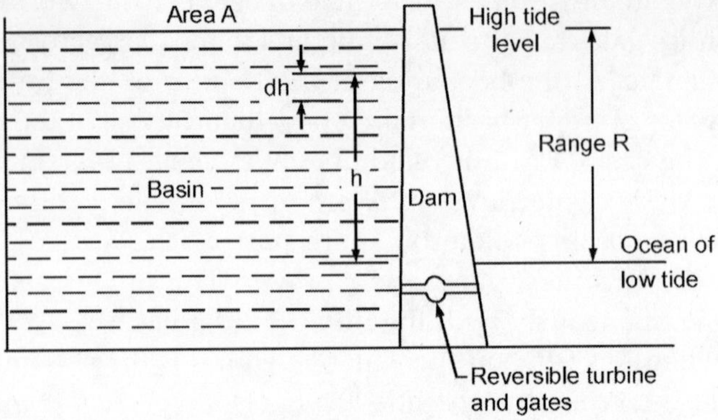

Fig.14.8 Single Basin Tidal System

We can write,

$$dw = dm.\ g.\ h \qquad ...(14.1)$$

but $$dm = -\rho.\ A.\ dh \qquad ...(14.2)$$

so that $$dw = -\rho.\ A.\ dh.\ g.\ h \qquad ...(14.3)$$

where W = workdone by water, kcal/kg or Joule

g = gravitational constant

m = mass flowing through turbine, kg

h = head, m

= water density, kg/m^3

A = basin surface area, considered constant, m^2

The total theoretical work during a full emptying (or filling) period is obtained by integrating the expression (14.3) i.e.

$$W = \int_R^0 dW = -g\rho A \int_R^0 h\,dh$$

$$= \frac{1}{2} g\rho A R^2 \qquad ...(14.4)$$

The work is proportional to square of the tidal range.

The power is the rate of doing work.

The power is generated during emptying (or filling) and no power is generated during rest of the time. The average theoretical power delivered by the water is W divided by the total time it takes each period to repeat itself. Duration is 6 h, 12.5 minutes (22,350 seconds).

Thus average theoretical power in watts,

$$P_{average} = \frac{W}{time} = \frac{\rho g A R^2}{2 \times 22350}$$

$$= \frac{1}{44700} g\rho A R^2 \qquad ...(14.5)$$

Assuming an average sea water density = 1025 kg/m3, the average power per unit basin area is given by,

$$\frac{P_{average}}{A} = \frac{1}{44700} \times 9.80 \times 1025\, R^2$$

$$= 0.225\, R^2 \text{ watts/m}^2 \text{ (MW/km}^2\text{)} \qquad ....(14.6)$$

The actual power generated by a real tidal system would be less than the average theoretical power obtained by the above expressions due to frictional losses and conversion efficiencies of turbine and electric generators. The actual power generated may be about 25 to 30 per cent of the theoretic power.

14.5 SITE REQUIREMENTS

The utilization of tidal energy requires construction of a barrier (or barriers) across a narrow inlet to an estuary or bay, thus forming an enclosure (or basin) in which ocean water can be impounded. Electricity can be generated by allowing water to flow through a turbine from the basin filled at high tide to the open ocean during falling tides and also as the basin is being filled from the ocean during rising tides.

In each case, the maximum amount of electrical energy that can be generated depends on the product of the tidal range (R) and the mass (or volume) of water flowing through the turbine. The volume is equal to the range multiplied by the area of the impounded water. Hence, the electrical energy is proportional to the square of the range and the area of the enclosed basin. A favourable site for a tidal power plant should then have a large tidal range, and the geographic features should permit enclosure of large areas with reasonably short dams or other barrages. Sluice gates in the dams permit water to pass to or from the enclosed basin (or basins).

14.6 ADVANTAGES AND DISADVANTAGES OF TIDAL POWER GENERATION

ADVANTAGES:

(*i*) Tidal power is free from pollution as it does not use any fuel and also does not produce any unhealthy waste like gases, ash, and atomic refuse.

(*ii*) The biggest advantage of the tidal power is besides being inexhaustible; it is completely independent of the precipitation (rain) and its uncertainty. Even a continuous dry spell of any number of years can have no affect whatsoever on the tidal power generation.

(*iii*) The land cost of the tidal plant is less because such plants are located at seashore (or bays).

(*iv*) The plant does not require large space.

LIMITATIONS

(*i*) The power output of the plant will fluctuate continuously, because it depends on tidal range.

(*ii*) The construction of a tidal plant in a sea or in estuaries is found difficult.

(*iii*) The transmission cost of tidal power is costlier because such plants are located far away from the load centre.

(*iv*) The initial cost of the plant is high.

(*v*) Plant equipment will be subjected to corrosion due to seawater as it is corrosive in nature.

(*vi*) The efficiency of plant will be affected due to the variable tidal range due to which turbines have to work on a wide range of head variation.

(*vii*) The tidal power plant would hamper the other natural uses of estuaries such as fishing, or navigation.

14.7 STORAGE

Storage is necessary when alternative electricity production schemes are not, or cannot be, connected with the electrical grid. Tidal power plants are not an exception to this rule; there is a strong case for associating them with storage to provide for the varying needs of the consumer, also taking into account the eventual presence close-by of other plants.

For tidal power being produced in 'mechanical form' only *batteries, compressed air,* and *hydraulic storage* can be considered. Flywhere could be used, but its technology is not yet ready.

Flywheel Storage : By connecting a flywheel to a motor/generator, it is spinned up to high speed and absorbs energy. This energy can be returned to the motor-generator by decreasing the flywheel's speed. However only small quantities can be stored and they are limited to short periods of time.

Batteries Storage : Perhaps most flexible and practical are electro-chemical batteries. These batteries are the most common, but researches being conducted with less expensive and lighter types. Also presently available are aqueous solution nickel and nickel cadmium types, but they are much more costly. Again, this type of storage is suited to small plants, particularly self contained ones.

Hydraulic Storage: Hydraulic (or pumped-water) storage is most frequently mentioned in connection with tidal power plants. Two reservoirs, at different elevations, are linked by pumps and turbines and their motors and generators. They constitute the accumulator (a reversible pump-turbine, connected to motor-generator achieves the same result). Off-peak energy, which could be used, is put to work to pump water from the lower into the upper reservoir, which can be run through the turbine and generator and provide energy when needed at a later time.

Power can be provided immediately on demand; storage stabilizes an otherwise intermittent source and constitutes an efficiency improvement, Reservoirs must be found or built, of course, and a certain amount of energy is lost, to activate and work the pump.

Compressed Air Storage : Air is compressed during off-peak periods and thus stored underground. It can then be called upon to work gas turbines and provide electricity. Tidal energy can be used directly to drive air turbo compressors.

14.8 PROSPECTS OF TIDAL ENERGY IN INDIA

The possible sites for tidal power generation in India are obviously those where high tidal ranges occur for e.g. Gulf of Cambay (Bhavnagar Sonrai), Gulf of Kutch (Kandla, Navalakhi) and of Houghly River. The maximum tidal range in the Gulf of Cambay (10.8 m) and is attractive for a tidal plant.

There are two possible sites on the western bank namely, Sonrai creek and Bhavnagar creek which have the essential requirements for locating probable plants. However, the silt change of the Gulf of Cambay is about 5000 ppm which is thought to be high and needs a closer study for future development. Gulf of Kutch has a maximum spring tide range of 7.5 m. The silt change here (near Navalakhi in the Gulf of Kutch) is much lower (nearly 1000 ppm). The tidal ranges and power potential of these sites are indicated in the Table 14.1 below.

Table 14.1 Tidal Power Potential in India

Sites	Spring Tidal range in metres	Assumed area in Sq. kms.	Total maximum potential energy, 10^6 kWh/yr	Single Basin cycle, 10^6 kW/yr		Two basins			
						Alternatively operating, 10^6kWh/yr		Cooperating, 10^6 kWh/yr	
Gulf of Kutch Navalakhi	7.5	10	1110	43	376	48	419	16.4	143
Gulf of Cambay	10.8	10	2300	89.4	784	100	880	34.2	300
Sagar	4.85	10	464	18	157	20.1	176	6.9	60
Diamond Harbour	3.9	10	686	26.6	233	29.7	262	10.15	89

There is at present no indication regarding the cost of generation from tidal power. Preliminary studies already carried out by the CPWD and for tidal station in the Gulf of Cambay indicated higher cost of generation from conventional sources. However, the cost of coal and other allied materials is increasing which may open up the possibility of exploitation of this source of power. Adequate data will have to be collected for any realistic assessment of tidal power potential and possible impact on the environment, current patterns, tidal reflections, sedimentation, erosion etc. Detailed feasibility reports based on full technology assessment are called for before venturing into this field.

SOLVED EXAMPLE

Example 1 : A tidal project has installed capacity of 2176 MW in 64 units each of 34 MW rated output. The head at rated output is 5.52 m. The embankment is 4 miles long = 6.4 km. Again assume 93% efficiency for both turbine and generator. The generation is 5 hours twice a day. Calculate

(*a*) The quantity of water flowing through each turbine and the total flow out of the tidal basin.

(*b*) The surface area of reservoir behind the embankment, and the wash.

(*c*) Energy produced in TW-h per year.

Solution:

(*a*) $$P = 2176 \times 10^6/0.93 \times 0.93 = 9.81 \times 1025 \times 5.52 \times Q$$

Therefore $$Q = 45.33 \times 10^3 \text{ m}^3/\text{sec in 64 units}$$

and $$q = 708 \text{ m}^3/\text{s through each turbine.}$$

(*b*) $$\text{Surface area of reservoir} = 45.33 \times 10^2 \times 5 \times 3600/5.52 = 14.78 \times 10^7 \text{ m}^2 = 147.8 \text{ km}^2$$

Therefore wash behind the embankment = 147.8/6.4 = 23.1 km

(*c*) Energy produced per day = 0.5 × 2176 × 10 = 10,880 MW-h

$$\text{Therefore energy generated per year} = 10{,}880 \times 365 \text{ MW-h} = 10.88 \times 0.365 \text{ TW-h} = 3.97 \text{ TW-h.}$$

This example corresponds to one of the possible power development sites studied for Bay of Fundy in Canada.

Example 2 : A tidal power station has 24 generators each of 10 MW operating at a maximum head of 13.5 m. It generators for two 6-hour periods per day.

Calculate the basin capacity in m^3, and annual energy production. Again assume 93% efficiencies.

Solution:

$$Q = 240 \times 10^6/(9.81 \times 13.5 \times 1025 \times 0.93 \times 0.93) = 2044 \text{ m}^3/\text{s}$$

For 6 hour, total quantity involved is

$$2044 \times 6 \times 3600 = 44.15 \times 10^6 \text{ m}^3$$

Annual energy production

$$= 0.5 \times 240 \times 12 \times 365 \times 10^{-6} \text{ TW-h/yr} = 0.5256 \text{ Tw-h} = 525.6 \text{ GW-h}$$

Example 3: A tidal power plant of the simple single basin type has a basin area of 30 X 106 m2. The tide has a range of 12m. The turbine, however, stops operating when the head on it falls below 3m. Calculate the energy generated in one filling (or emptying) process, in kilowatt hours if the turbine generator efficiency is 0.73.

Solution: The total theoretical work,

$$W = \int_R^r dw$$

R is the range = 12m

r is the head below turbine stops operating = 3m

$$W = \int_R^r -g\rho Ah\, dh = -g\rho A \int_R^r h\, dh = \frac{1}{2} g\rho A(R^2 - r^2)$$

Thus the average power,

$$P_{average} = \frac{W}{time} = \frac{pgA(R^2 - r^2)}{44700}$$

The average power generated

$$= \frac{1}{44700} \times 9.80 \times 1025 \times 30 \times 10^6 \,(12^2 - 3^2) = 911.25\ MW$$

$$= \frac{911.25}{1000} \times 3600 \times 10^6\ kWh = 3280.5 \times 10^6\ kWh$$

Considering turbine generator efficiency, the energy generated,

$$= 3280.5 \times 10^6 \times 0.73 = 2395 \times 10^6\ kWh$$

REVIEW QUESTIONS

1. What are tides? Explain the different types of tides.
2. How tides are caused? How this energy is used as a renewable resource. Explain.
3. What are the components of tidal power plant? Explain them.
4. Discuss the classification and operation of tidal power plants in detail.
5. What are the advantages and disadvantages of tidal power?
6. What are the various applications of tidal energy?
7. The basin area of a tidal power plant is 20×10^6 m^2. The tidal range is 8m, calculate the energy generated in kWh. [Ans. 10.368 X 10^8 kWh]

❑❑❑

15

Wave Energy

15.1 INTRODUCTION

Wave energy is an irregular and oscillating low frequency energy source that can be converted to a 50 Hertz frequency and can then be added to the electric utility grid. Waves get their energy from the wind, which comes from solar energy.

Ocean waves are generated by wind passing over stretches of water. The precise mechanisms involved in the interaction between the wind and the surface of the sea are complex and not yet completely understood. Three man processes appear to be involved.

1. Initially, air flowing over the sea exerts a tangential stress on the water surface, resulting in the formation and growth of waves.
2. Turbulent air flow close to the water surface creates rapidly varying shear stresses and pressure fluctuations. Where these oscillations are in phase with exisiting waves, further wave development occurs.
3. Finally, when waves have reached a certain size, the wind can exert a stronger force on the upwind face to the wave, causing additional wave growth.

Because the wind is originally derived from solar energy we may consider the energy in ocean waves to be stored, moderately high-density, from of solar energy. Solar power levels, which are typically of the order of 100 Wm^{-2} (mean), can be eventually transformed into waves with power levels of over 100 kW per metre of crest length.

Waves are characterised by their wave length, L, wave height, H, and wave period, T. The size of the waves generated by any wind field depends upon three factors: the wind speed; its duration; and the 'fetch' or distance over which wind energy is transferred into the ocean to form waves.

Waves located within or close to the areas where they are generated are called 'storm waves'. They from a complex, irregular sea. However, waves can travel out of these areas with minimal loss of energy to produce 'swell' waves, at great distances from their point of origin.

World sites that may be suitable for harvesting of energy from waves include the Molakai and Alenuihaha channels in the Hawalian islands, where 2 to 3 m high (crest to trough) waves are typical during normal trade wind periods, the Pacific coast of North America, the Arabian sea of India and Pakistan, the North Atlantic coast of Scotland, the coast of New England etc.

15.2 ADVANTAGES OF WAVE ENERGY

(*i*) It is renewable in nature. There will always be waves crashing upon the shores of nations, near the populated coastal regions. The waves flow back from the shore, but they always return.

(*ii*) It is environment friendly as creating power from waves creates no harmful byproducts such as gas, waste, and pollution. The energy from waves can be taken directly into electricity-producing machinery and used to power generators and power plants nearby. It is a clean source of energy.

(*iii*) It is abundant and widely available.

(iv) There are a variety of ways to gather wave energy. Current gathering methods range from installed power plant with hydro turbines to seafaring vessels equipped with massive structures that are laid into the sea to gather the wave energy.

(v) The biggest advantages of wave power as against most of the other alternative energy sources is that it is easily predictable and can be used to calculate the amount that it can produce. The wave energy is consistent and proves much better than other sources which are dependent on wind or sun exposure.

(vi) Dependence on foreign companies for fossil fuels can be reduced if energy from wave power can be extracted up to its maximum. Not only it will help to curb air pollution but can also provide green jobs to millions of people.

(vii) Unlike fossil fuels which cause massive damage to land as they can leave large holes while extracting energy from them, wave power does not cause any damage to earth. It is safe, clean and one of the preferred method to extract energy from ocean.

15.3 DISADVANTAGES OF WAVE ENERGY

1. **Suitable to Certain Locations:** The biggest disadvantage to getting your energy from the waves is location. Only power plants and towns near the ocean will benefit directly from it. Because of its source, wave energy is not a viable power source for everyone.
2. **Effect on marine Ecosystem:** As clean as wave energy is, it still creates hazards for some of the creatures near it. Large machines have to be put near and in the water to gather energy from the waves. These machines disturb the seafloor, change the habitat of near-shore creatures (like crabs and starfish) and create noise that disturbs the

sea life around them. There is also a danger of toxic chemicals that are used on wave energy platforms spilling and polluting the water near them.

3. **Source of Disturbance for Private and Commercial Vessels:** Another downside is that it disturbs commercial and private vessels. Power plants that gather wave energy have to be placed by the coastline to do their job, and they have to be near cities and other populated areas to be of much use to anybody. But these are places that are major thoroughfares for cargo ships, cruise ships, recreational vehicles and beach goers. All of these people and vessels will be disrupted by the installation of a wave energy gathering source. This means that government officials and private companies that want to invest in wave energy sources have to take into account and consider the needs of those they may be disturbing.
4. **Wavelength:** Wind power is highly dependent on wavelength i.e. wave speed, wave length and water density. They require a consistent flow of powerful waves to generate significant amount of wave power. Some areas experience unreliable wave behavior and it becomes unpredictable to forecast accurate wave power and therefore cannot be trusted as reliable energy source.
5. **Weak Performance in Rough Weather:** The performance of wave power drops significantly during rough weather. They must withstand rough weather.
6. **Noise and Visual pollution:** Wave energy generators may be unpleasant for some who live close to coastal regions. They look like large machines working in the middle of the ocean and destroy the beauty of the ocean. They also generate noise pollution but the noise is often covered by the noise of waves which is much more than that of wave generators.

15.4 ENERGY AND POWER FROM THE WAVES

In deep water where the water depth is larger than half the wavelength, the wave energy flux is

$$P = \frac{\rho g^2}{64\pi} H_{m0}^2 T_e \approx (0.5 \frac{kW}{m^3.s}) H_{m0}^2 T_e$$

with P the wave energy flux per unit of wave-crest length, H_{m0} is the significant wave height, T_e is the wave energy period, ρ is the water density and g is the acceleration by gravity.

The above formula states that wave power is proportional to the wave energy period and to the square of the wave height. When the significant wave height is given in metres, and the wave period in seconds, the result is the wave power in kilowatts (kW) per metre of wavefront length.

In a sea state, the average (mean) energy density per unit area of gravity waves on the water surface is proportional to the wave height squared, according to linear wave theory:

$$E = \frac{1}{16}\rho g H_{m0}^2$$

where E is the mean wave energy density per unit horizontal area (J/m^2), the sum of kinetic and potential energy density per unit horizontal area. The potential energy density is equal to the kinetic energy, both contributing half to the wave energy density E, as can be expected from the equipartition theorem. In ocean waves, surface tension effects are negligible for wavelengths above a few decimetres.

As the waves propagate, their energy is transported. The energy transport velocity is the group velocity. As a result, the wave energy flux, through a vertical plane of unit width perpendicular to the wave propagation direction, is equal to:

$$P = Ec_g$$

with c_g the group velocity (m/s). Due to the dispersion relation for water waves under the action of gravity, the group velocity depends on the wavelength λ, or equivalently, on the wave period T. Further, the dispersion relation is a function of the water depth h. As a result, the group velocity behaves differently in the limits of deep and shallow water, and at intermediate depths.

15.5 WAVE ENERGY CONVERSION METHODS

Wave energy technologies rely on the up-and-down motion of waves to generate electricity. There are three basic methods for converting wave energy to electricity.

(i) **Float or buoy systems** that use the rise and fall of ocean swells to drive hydraulic pumps. The object can be **mounted** to a floating raft or to a device fixed on the ocean bed. A series of anchored buoys rise and fall with the wave. The movement is used to run an electrical generator to produce electricity which is then transmitted ashore by underwater power cables.

(ii) **Oscillating water column devices** in which the in-and-out motion of waves at the shore enters a column and force air to turn a turbine. The column fills with water as the wave rises and empties as it descends. In the process, air inside the column is compressed and heats up, creating energy. This energy is harnessed and sent to shore by electrical cable.

(iii) **Tapered channel** rely on a shore mounted structure to channel and concentrate the waves driving them into an elevated reservoir. Water flow out of this reservoir is used to generate electricity using standard hydropower technologies.

15.6 WAVE ENERGY COLLECTING DEVICES

The wave energy collecting devices are characterized in two broad categories in terms of placement or location:

15.6.1 Shoreline Devices

These devices are fixed to or embedded in the shoreline itself, which has the advantage of easier maintenance and/or installation. In addition these would not require deep-water moorings or long lengths of underwater electrical cable. However, they would experience a much less powerful wave regime. This could be partially compensated by natural energy concentration. The deployment of such schemes could be limited by requirements for shoreline geology, tidal range, preservation of coastal scenery, etc.

There are three types of shoreline devices:

(*a*) Oscillating Water Column (OWC) Devices

One major class of shoreline device is the oscillating water column partly submerged concrete or steel structure, which has an opening to the sea below the water line, thereby enclosing a column of air above a column of water. As waves impinge on the device, they cause the water column to rise and fall, which alternately compresses and depressurizes the air column. This air is allowed to flow to and from the atmosphere through a turbine, which drives an electric generator. Both conventional (i.e. unidirectional) and self-rectifying air turbines have been proposed.

The axial-flow Wells turbine, invented in the 1970s, is the best-known turbine for this kind of application and has the advantage of not requiring rectifying air valves.

A number of OWC devices have been installed world wide, with several of them being built into a breakwater to lower overall construction costs.

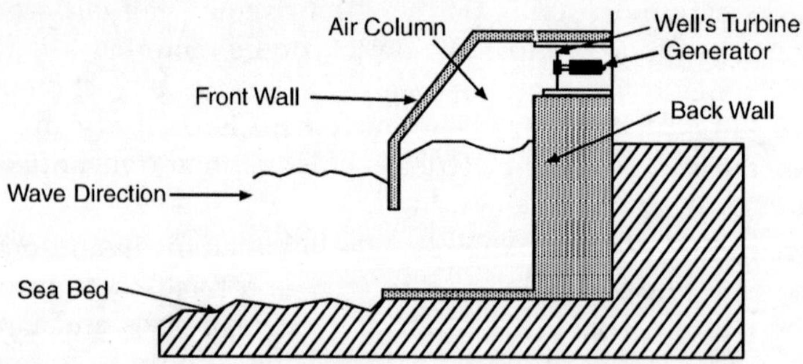

Fig. 15.1 Oscillating Water Column Device

(*b*) Tapered Channel Devices (TAPCHAN)

The TAPCHAN comprises a gradually narrowing channel with wall heights typically 3 to 5 m above mean water level. Waves enter the wide end of the channel and, as they propagate down the narrowing channel, the wave height is amplified until the wave crests spill over the walls to the reservoir, which is raised above sea level. The water in the reservoir returns to the sea via a convention allow head turbine, which generates a stable output due to the storage effects of the reservoir.

A demonstration device with rated output of 350 kW began operating in 1985 at Toftesfallen, in Norway. The device functioned successfully until the early 1990s, when work on modifying the device destroyed the tapered channel. The potential market for such a device is limited within Europe, because the design requires a small tidal range.

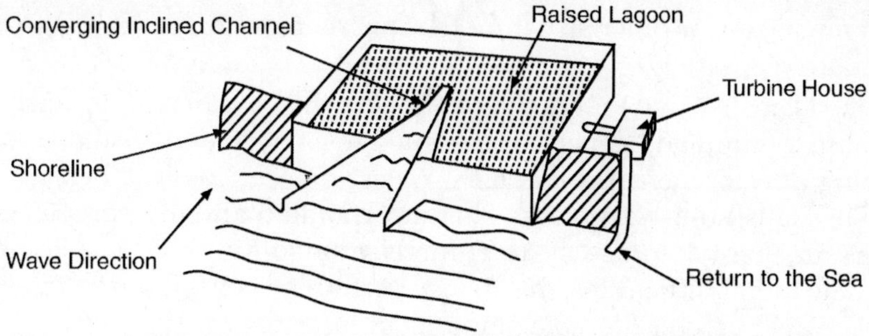

Fig. 15.2 Tapered Channel Device (TAPCHAN)

(*c*) The Pendulor Device

A 5 kW Pendulor test device has been operating in Hokkaido since 1983. It consists of a rectangular box, which is open to the sea at one end. A pendulum flap is hinged over this opening, so that the actions of the waves cause it to swing back and forth. This motion is then used to power a hydraulic pump and generator.

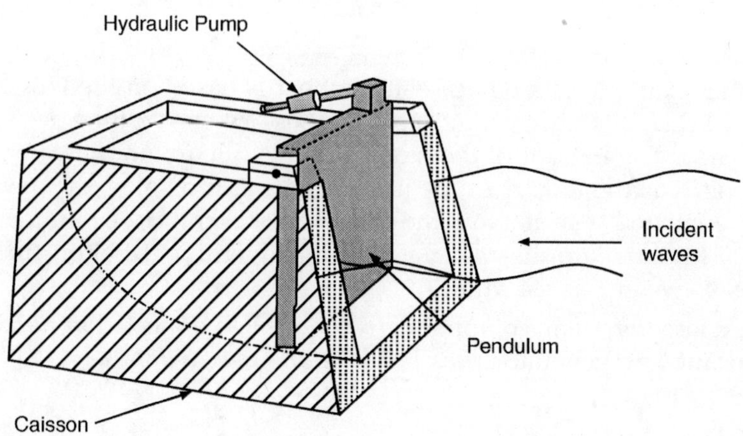

Fig. 15.3 Pendulor Device

15.6.2 Offshore Devices

This class of device exploits the more powerful wave regimes available in deep water (> 40 m depth) before energy dissipation mechanisms have had a significant effect. In order to extract energy from the waves, the devices need to be at or near the surface (i.e. floating) and so they require flexible moorings and electrical transmission cables.

There are many different types of offshore device, some of which are:

(*a*) Float-Based Devices

The simplest concepts extract energy from the vertical motion of a float as it rises and falls with each wave. If the motion of the float is reacted against an anchor or other structure that resists motion, then energy can be extracted.

In the Danish Wave Power (DWP) device, this is achieved by anchoring the float to a pump and generator mounted in a concrete box on the seabed. Following developmental work, a 1 kW test device was installed near the harbor of Hanstholm, Denmark. This incorporated an air reservoir, which acted as an energy storage system, thereby smoothing the device output. After some initial difficulties, this device performed continuously for several months providing considerable amounts of information.

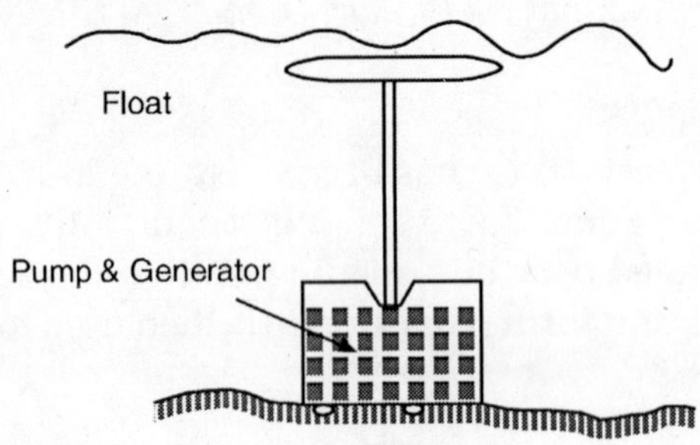

Fig. 15.4 DWP Float

Another example of a device using a float is based on the Hose pump, which is a specially reinforced elastomeric hose whose volume decreases as it is stretched. The interior of the Hose pump is filled with seawater, which is pressurized as the float rises. By using a non-return valve, the device can supply pressurized seawater to a line connecting several Hose pump modules together. This line supplies seawater to a conventional Pelton turbine at pressures between 1 and 4 MPa).

Later a larger system, comprising five modules connected in parallel to a single turbine and generator, was installed in Lake Lygnern.

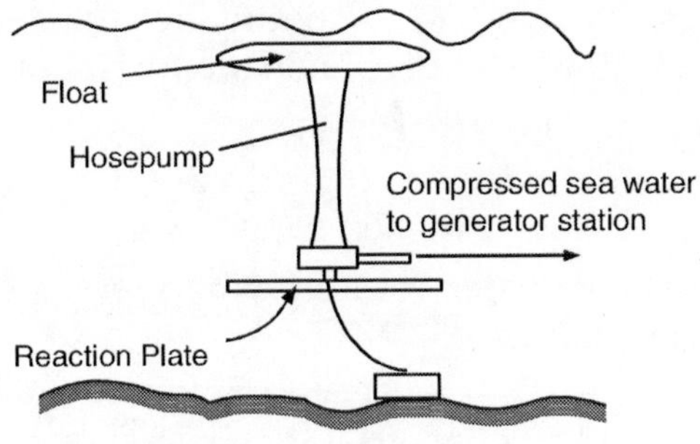

Fig. 15.5 Hosepump

(*b*) Pelamis

The Pelamis device is a semi-submerged, articulated structure composed of cylindrical sections linked by hinged joints. The wave-induced motion of these joints is resisted by hydraulic rams, which pump high-pressure oil through hydraulic motors via smoothing accumulators. The hydraulic motors drive electrical generators to produce electricity. A novel joint configuration is used to induce a tuneable, cross-coupled resonant response, which greatly increases power capture in small seas and control of the restraint applied to the joints allows tuning to the particular sea state.

(*c*) The Archimedes Wave Swing

This consists of a cylindrical, air filled chamber (the "Floater"), which can move vertically with respect to the cylindrical "Basement", which is fixed to the seabed. The air within the 10m –20m diameter Floater ensures buoyancy. However, a wave passing over the top of the device alternatively pressurizes and depressurizes the air within the Floater, changing this buoyancy. This causes the Floater to move up and down with respect to the Basement and it is this relative motion that is used to produce energy.

The design for a 2 MW Pilot scheme is currently being finalized.

(d) The McCabe Wave Pump

This device consists of three narrow (4 m wide) rectangular steel pontoons, which are hinged together across their beam. These pontoons are aligned so that their longitudinal direction heads into the incoming waves and they can move relative to each other in the waves.

The essential aspect of the scheme is the damper plate attached to the central pontoon this increases the inertia of the central pontoon (by effectively adding mass), ensuring that it stays relative still. Therefore, the fore and aft pontoons move in relation to the central pontoon by pitching about the hinges. Energy is extracted from the rotation about the hinge points by linear hydraulic rams mounted between the central and two outer pontoons near the hinges.

Control of the characteristics of the hydraulic system allows the device to be tuned to the prevailing sea state and so optimize energy capture.

This energy can be used in two ways:

(*i*) To provide electricity by driving a hydraulic motor attached to a generator, with a rating of ~ 400 kW.

(*ii*) To produce potable water by supplying pressurized seawater to a reverse osmosis plant.

A 40 m long prototype of this device was deployed off the coast of Kilbaha, County Clare, Ireland and a commercial demonstration scheme is currently being built.

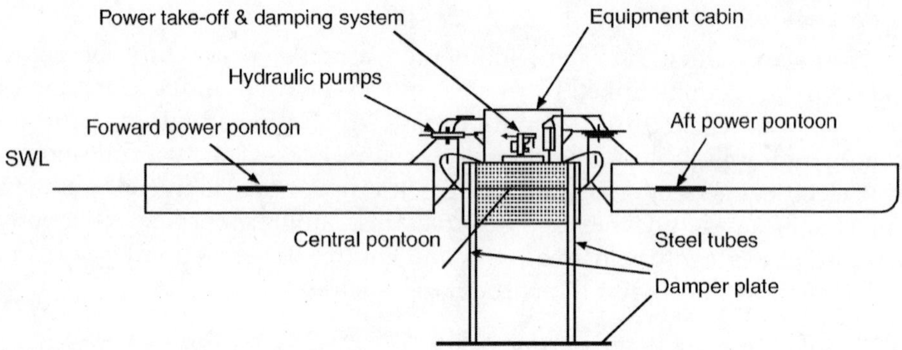

Fig. 15.6 Outline of the McCabe Wave Pump

15.7 WAVE ENERGY POTENTIAL IN INDIA

India is estimated to have a potential of 40-60 GW of Wave Energy around it cost with the current state of technology. The wave energy potential is estimated to be 5-15 MW per metre of coastline. There are no big wave energy plants in India except the pilot plant at Vizinjham Fisheries Harbor near Trivandrum in Kerala.

Maharashtra government has built project would generate 15 to 20 kilowatt of electricity located at Borya and Budhal villages in coastal Ratnagiri district. Similar pilot projects exploiting the tidal waves are being undertaken in 15 coastal villages.

Sagar Shakthi is a 1 MW OTEC plant built off the Tuticorn coast which utilizes the temperature different wave energy device.

REVIEW QUESTIONS

1. Write a short note on wave energy.
2. Briefly discuss advantages and disadvantages of wave energy.
3. Discuss an expression for energy and power from the waves.
4. Briefly discuss various wave energy conversion methods.
5. Briefly discuss various wave energy collecting devices.

❑❑❑

16

ENERGY CONSERVATION

16.1 INTRODUCTION

Energy plays a key role in achieving the desired economic growth. Energy is a pivotal prerequisite of developed economy and social structures.

Energy conservation means reduction in energy consumption but without making any sacrifice of quantity and quality of production.

Energy conservation refers to reducing energy consumption through using less of an energy service. Energy conservation differs from efficient energy use, which refers to using less energy for a constant service. For example, driving less is an example of energy conservation. Driving the same amount with a higher mileage vehicle is an example of energy efficiency. Energy conservation and efficiency are both energy reduction techniques. Energy conservation is sometimes known as sufficiency.

Even though energy conservation reduces energy services, it can result in increased environmental quality, national security, personal financial security and higher savings. It is at the top of the sustainable energy hierarchy. It also lowers energy costs by preventing future resource depletion.

16.2 SALIENT FEATURES OF "ENERGY CONSERVATION ACT, 2001"

Energy Conservation Act is introduced to provide the efficient use of energy and its conservation and for matters connected therewith. Some of the salient features of this act are:

- Specify standards, specify appliances and equipment to be subjected to labeling regime
- Prohibit manufacture, sale, import or deal in appliances and equipment not meeting S&L requirements/standards
- Inspect and enforce compliance
- Order mandatory energy audits in specified industries and for "designated consumers"
- Designate consumers, with powers to exempt

- Prescribe energy consumption norms
- Direct any consumer to furnish energy related information
- Directions for appointment of energy manager
- Direct any designated consumers to prepare and implement energy efficiency measures (if not meeting norms, and if economical)
- Prescribe energy conservation building codes
- Enforce compliance to: building codes, mandatory norms, mandatory energy audit regime, energy efficiency measure implementation
- Levy penalties (Company as well as individuals in Company)
- Certification of energy auditors and energy managers
- Adjudication and appellate procedures
- Training in techniques for efficient use of energy and its conservation
- Awareness and dissemination, pilot project demonstration and innovative financing

16.3 VARIOUS ASPECTS OF ENERGY CONSERVATION

There are three important aspects of energy conservation:

1. **Economic Aspect**

   (a) Reduction in Cost of product: Energy conservation leads to economic benefit as cost of production is reduced. The cost of energy forms a significant part of cost of product. Energy cost as a percent of total cost of product in India varies from 0.36% to 65%. Economy can be improved by using energy efficient technologies. This reduces manufacturing cost and leads to cheaper and better quality products.

   (b) New Job Opportunities: Energy conservation requires new investments in efficient equipments, monitoring of energy consumption, training of manpower etc. Thus, new job opportunities are created.

2. **Environmental Aspect**

   As we know that energy utilization affects environment. During every energy conversion stage, a part of energy escapes to the surroundings and appear in the form of heat. Adoption of energy conversion minimizes damage to environment.

3. Conservation of Non Renewable Energy Assets

   We know that most of the energy comes from fossil fuels which are non-renewable. Within finite time the prices of these fuels are bound to go up. Thus we must save non renewable resources for future.

16.4 PRINCIPLES OF ENERGY CONSERVATION

There are two principles of energy conservation policies:

1. **Maximum efficiency:** A device, system or process is working at maximum efficiency when maximum work is done for a given magnitude of energy input. But only a part of the input energy is converted into useful work. The remainder is lost in energy conversion transfer process and energy discharge. It is defined in the following form:

   Maximum Work = Energy Input – Energy loss in transfer process and energy discharge.

2. **Maximum cost effectiveness in energy use:** Implementation of energy conservation entails additional investment. This investment increases as more and more energy conservation measures are adopted. Because of implementation of these measures the fuel costs decrease as extent of conservation is increased. The total cost per unit output is the sum of annual charges on investment per unit output and fuel costs per unit output. Evidently maximum cost effectiveness in energy use is obtained when total costs are the least.

16.5 ENERGY CONSERVATION PLANNING

Energy conservation planning can be divided into four steps:

1. **Specifying targets and preparing detailed plans:** It is the first step in energy conservation planning. The targets and plans can be divided into three categories viz. programmes which do not require any additional investment, programmes which require small additional investment and need a year or so for implementation and programmes which require major changes and large investment.

2. **Identifying energy inefficient facilities and equipment:** In this step the facilities and equipment which are energy inefficient are identified. The indices used for this purpose are energy efficient index, EEI and energy quality index, EQI.

   EEI = energy used / energy input

   EQI = availability of energy output / availability of energy input

3. **Implementation of energy conservation measures:** The energy conservation measures includes method of installation (i.e., recycling, retrofitting) , method of energy use (e.g. installation of equipment for waste heat recovery and utilisation) and size of investments.

4. **Evaluation of benefits:** In this step overall costs and benefits of programmes are studied and calculated. A behaviour model and a cost function are used to evaluate costs and benefits.

16.6 BENEFITS OF ENERGY CONSERVATION

1. **Industrial Benefits**
   - Reduced energy bills
   - Increased competitiveness
   - Increased productivity
   - Improved quality
   - Increased profits
2. **National Benefits**
   - Reduced energy imports
   - Avoided costs can be used for poverty reduction
   - Conservation of limited resources
   - Improved energy security
3. **Global Benefits**
   - Reduced GHG and other emissions
   - Maintains a sustainable environment

16.7 GENERAL ELECTRICAL ECO'S (ENERGY CONSERVATION OPPORTUNITIES)

1. **Energy Conservation in Lighting system**
   (i) Optimum use of natural light
   (ii) Replacing incandescent lamps by Compact Fluorescent Lamps (CFL's)
   (iii) Replacement of Mercury/Sodium Vapor Lamp by Halides Lamp
   (iv) Replacing HPMV Lamps by High pressure sodium Vapour Lamp (HPSV)
   (v) Replacing filament lamps on panels by LED
   (vi) Replacement of conventional ballast by Electronic ballast
   (vii) Installation of separate transformer for lighting
   (viii) Installation of servo stabilizer for lighting feeder
   (ix) Control over energy consumption pattern
   (x) Periodic survey and adequate maintenance program
2. **Energy Conservation in Transformers**
   (i) Optimization of loading of transformer
   (ii) By Improvisation in Design and Material of Transformer
   (iii) Replacing By Energy Efficient Transformers
3. Energy Conservation in Transmission Line
   (i) To reduce line resistance, solid conductors are replaced by stranded conductors (ACSR or AAC) and by bundled conductors in HT line.

(ii) High Voltage Direct Current (HVDC) is used to transmit large amount of power over long distances or for interconnections between asynchronous grids

(iii) By transmitting energy at high voltage level reduces the fraction of energy lost due to Joule heating.

iv) As load on system increases terminal voltage decreases.

v) Voltage level can be controlled by using voltage controllers and by using voltage stabilizer

vi) To control receiving end voltage, reactive power controllers or reactive power compensating equipments such as Static VAR controllers are used.

4. Energy Conservation in Distribution Line

(i) Optimization of distribution system

(ii) Balancing of phase load

(iii) Distribution Static Compensator and Harmonic filters can reduce harmonics.

(iv) Energy Conservation by using power factor controller

(v) Energy Conservation By Demand side management control

5. Energy Conservation in Motors

(i) Improving power supply quality

(ii) Optimum loading

(iii) Improving transmission efficiency

(iv) Stopping idle or redundant running of motors or lights will save 100% power

(v) By use of Soft Starter

(vi) By improving power factor

(vii) Use of high efficiency or Energy efficient motors

16.8 CO-GENERATION

Cogeneration or combined heat and power (CHP) is the use of the heat engine or power station to generate electricity and useful heat at the same time.

Cogeneration offers energy savings ranging between 15-40% when compared against the supply of electricity and heat from conventional power stations and boilers.

Types of Cogeneration

On the basis of energy use, cogeneration systems are classified as

(i) Topping Cycle

In a topping cycle, the fuel supplied is used to first produce power and then thermal energy, which is the by-product of the cycle and is used to satisfy process heat or other thermal requirements.

The four types of topping cycle cogeneration systems are:

- A gas turbine or diesel engine producing electrical or mechanical power followed by a heat recovery boiler to create steam to drive a secondary steam turbine. This is called a *combined-cycle topping system.*
- The second type of system burns fuel (any type) to produce high-pressure steam that then passes through a steam turbine to produce power with the exhaust provides low-pressure process steam. This is a *steam-turbine topping system.*
- A third type employs heat recovery from an engine exhaust and/or jacket cooling system flowing to a heat recovery boiler, where it is converted to process steam / hot water for further use.
- The fourth type is a *gas-turbine topping system.* A natural gas turbine drives a generator. The exhaust gas goes to a heat recovery boiler that makes process steam and process heat

(ii) Bottoming Cycle

In a bottoming cycle, the primary fuel produces high temperature thermal energy and the heat rejected from the process is used to generate power through a recovery boiler and a turbine generator. Bottoming cycles are suitable for manufacturing processes that require heat at high temperature in furnaces and kilns, and reject heat at significantly high temperatures. Typical areas of application include cement, steel, ceramic, gas and petrochemical industries.

Benefits of Cogeneration

(i) Increased efficiency of energy conversion and use.

(ii) Lower GHG emissions to the environment.

(iii) Large cost savings and provides affordable heat for domestic users.

(iv) An opportunity to move towards more decentralised forms of electricity generation, where plants are designed to meet the needs of local consumers, providing high efficiency, avoiding transmission losses and increasing flexibility of system use. This will particularly be the case if natural gas is the energy carrier.

(v) Improved local and general security of supply. In addition, the reduced need for fuel resulting from cogeneration reduces import dependency.

(vi) Increased employment

REVIEW QUESTIONS

1. Explain the salient features of "Energy Conservation Act, 2001".
2. Explain the various aspects of Energy Conservation.
3. Explain the principles of energy conservation.
4. Write a short note on General Electrical ECO's (Energy Conservation Opportunities).
5. Explain benefits of Energy Conservation.
6. Explain energy conservation planning.
7. Write a short note on 'cogeneration'.

❑

17

Other Applications of Solar Energy

17.1 INTRODUCTION

Solar energy is abundant in nature and can be stored for millions of years. It can be utilized for many purposes. Few other applications of solar energy are discussed in the following sections.

17.2 SOLAR WATER HEATER

Solar water heating (SWH) is the conversion of sunlight into renewable energy for water heating using a solar thermal collector.

A solar water heater is a combination of solar collector array, an energy transfer system and a storage tank. The main part of the solar water heater is the solar collector array, which absorbs solar radiation and converts it into heat. This heat is then absorbed by a heat transfer fluid (water, non-freezing liquid or air) that passes through the collector. This heat can then be stored or used directly.

Two types of solar water heating systems are:

1. *Direct or open loop systems* in which portable water is heated directly in the collector.
2. *Indirect or closed loop systems* in which portable water is heated indirectly by a heat transfer fluid that is heated in the collector and passes through a heat exchanger to transfer its heat to the domestic or service water.

Systems differ also with respect to the way the heat transfer fluid is transported:

1. Natural (or passive) systems
2. Forced circulation (or active) systems

Natural circulation occurs by natural convection (thermosiphoning), whereas *forced circulation* systems use pumps or fans to circulate the heat transfer fluid through the collector.

17.2.1 Passive Solar Water Heating Systems

There are two types of passive solar water heating systems:

(a) THERMOSIPHON SYSTEM

As the sun shines on the collector, the water inside the collector flow-tubes is heated. As it heats, this water expands slightly and becomes lighter than the cold water in the solar storage tank mounted above the collector. Gravity then pulls heavier, cold water down from the tank and into the collector inlet. The cold water pushes the heated water through the collector outlet and into the top of the tank, thus heating the water in the tank. Connecting tubes are insulated to prevent heat loss and sloped to prevent formation of air pockets, which would stop circulation.

This system features a thermally operated valve that protects the collector from freezing. It also includes isolation valves, which allow the solar system to be manually drained in case of freezing conditions, or to be bypassed completely.

The advantages of thermosiphon systems are that they do not rely on pumps and controllers, are more reliable and have a longer life than forced circulation systems.

The main disadvantage is that because the storage tank should be above the collector they are comparatively tall units, which makes them not very attractive aesthetically. Another disadvantage is that as the system is open, extremely hard or acidic water can cause scale deposits that clog or corrode the absorber fluid passages.

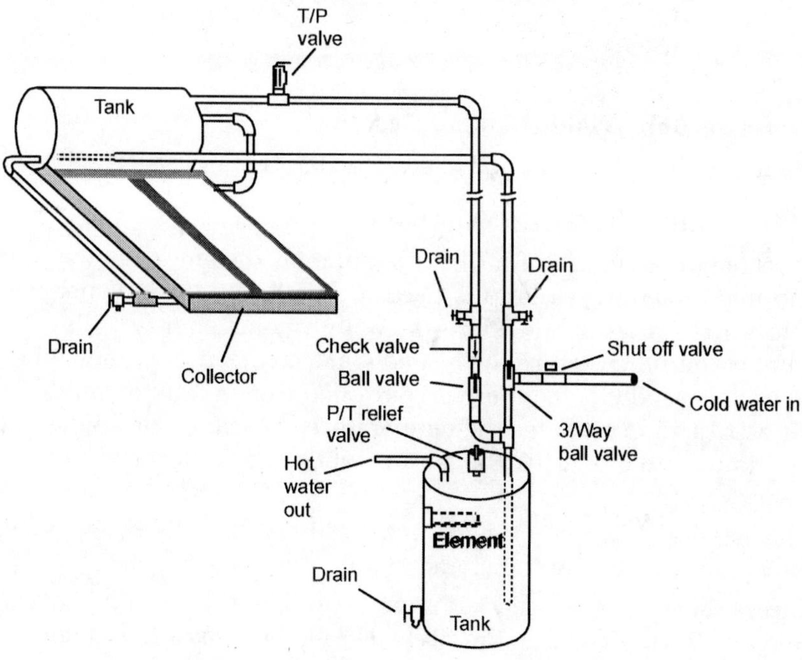

Figure 17.1: Schematic diagram of thermosiphon solar water heater

(b) INTEGRATED COLLECTOR STORAGE

ICS systems are simple units in which the hot water storage is part of the collector i.e. the surface of the storage tank is also the absorber.

The storage tank is usually a horizontal cylinder and to improve stratification, hot water is drawn from the top of the tank whereas cold make-up water enters to the bottom of the tank on the opposite side.

The main problem of the ICS systems is the high thermal losses from the storage tank to the surroundings, which occurs because most of the surface area of the storage tank cannot be thermally insulated since it is intentionally exposed for the absorption of solar radiation.

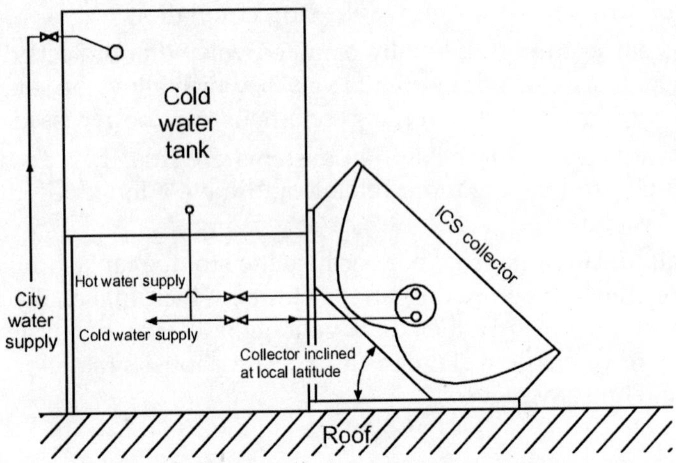

Figure 17.2: Schematic diagram of ICS system

17.2.2 Active Solar Water Heating Systems

There are three types of active solar water heating systems:

(a) DIRECT CIRCULATION SYSTEMS

A schematic diagram of a direct circulation system is shown is Figure 17.3. In this system, the pump is used to circulate potable water from the collectors to storage when there is enough solar energy to increase its temperature and then return the heated water to the storage tank where it is stored until is needed. The pump is controlled from a differential thermostat that measures and compares the temperature at the collector outlet and the storage tank and operates the pump whenever a certain temperature difference exists.

Because the pump is used to circulate the water, the collectors can be mounted above or below the storage tank.

These systems can be used with water supplied from a cold water storage tank or connected directly to the city water mains. Pressure-reducing valves and pressure relief valves are required, when the city water pressure is greater than the working pressure of the collectors.

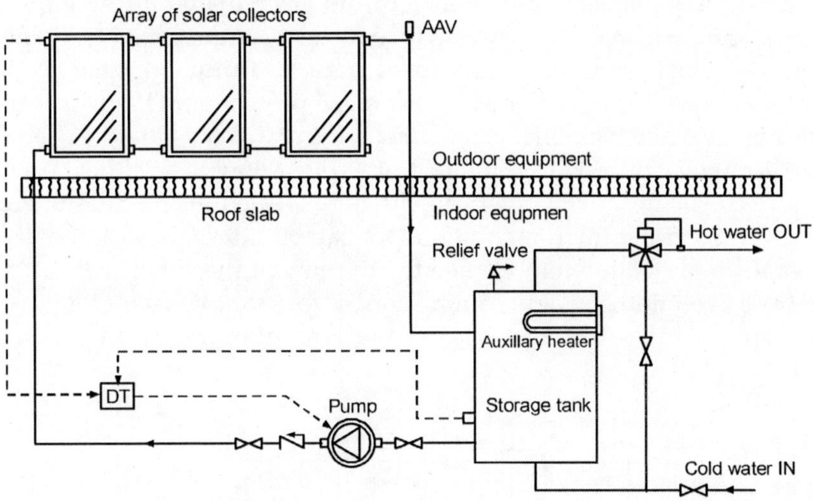

Figure 17.3: Schematic diagram of direct circulation system

For freeze protection, a variation of the direct circulation system, called the drain-down system, is used. The schematic diagram is shown in Figure 17.4. In this case, potable water is also pumped from storage to the collector array, where it is heated. When a freezing condition or a power failure occurs, the system drains automatically by isolating the collector array and exterior piping from the make-up water supply with the normally closed (NC) valve and draining it using the two normally open (NO) valves.

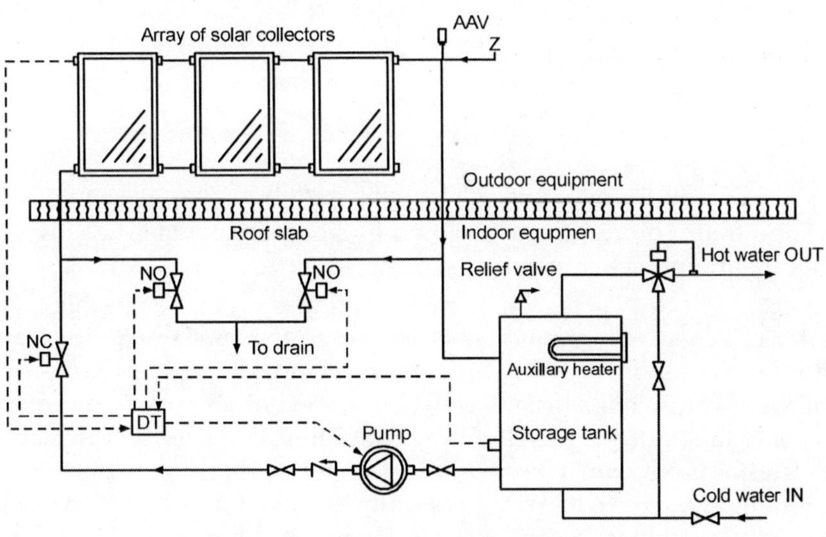

Figure 17.4: Drain down system

(b) INDIRECT WATER HEATING SYSTEMS

A schematic diagram of an indirect water heating system is shown in Fig. 17.5. In this system, a heat transfer fluid is circulated through the closed collector loop to a heat exchanger, where its heat is transferred to the portable water. The most commonly used heat transfer fluids are water/ethylene glycol solutions, which offer also antifreeze protection. Other heat transfer fluids however, such as silicone oils and refrigerants may also be used. When the heat transfer fluid is non-potable or toxic, a double-wall heat eachanger is required. The heat exchanger can either be located inside the storage tank, around the storage tank (tank mantle), or can be external. Additionally over-temperature protection may be needed to prevent the collector heat transfer fluid from decomposing or becoming corrosive. As the collector loop is closed, an expansion tank and a pressure relief valve are required as shown in Fig. 17.5.

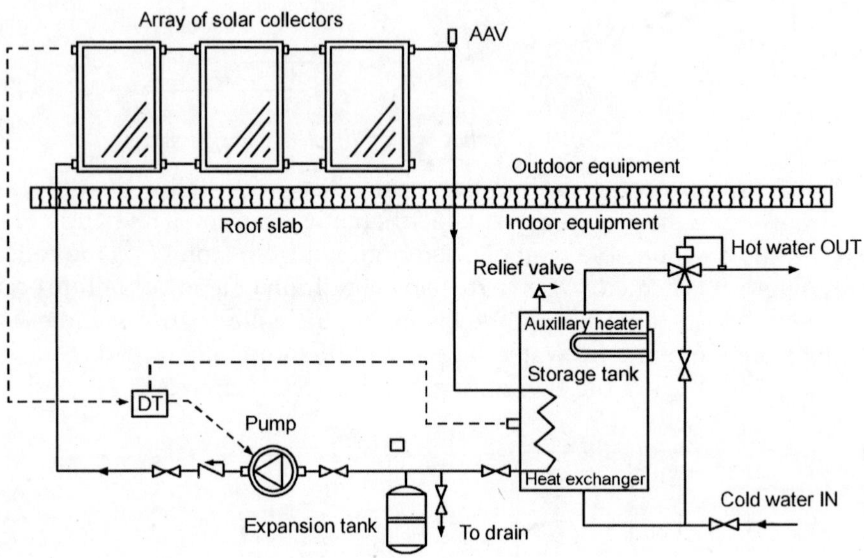

Figure 17.5: Indirect water heating systems

For a freeze protection, a variation of the indirect water heating system, called the drain-back system is used.

In drain-back systems, circulation continues as long as usable energy is available. When the circulation pump stops the collector fluid drains by gravity to a drain-back tank. This system provides a high level of protection as no valves are needed to actuate draining and it does not rely on controllers that could fail under adverse freezing conditions however, the collector array and exterior piping must be adequately sloped to dain completely. As can be seen in Fig. 17.6, the solar circuit is un-pressurized and the drain-back tank is open and vented to the atmosphere. Finally, as the collector loop is isolated from the potable water, scaling is not a problem.

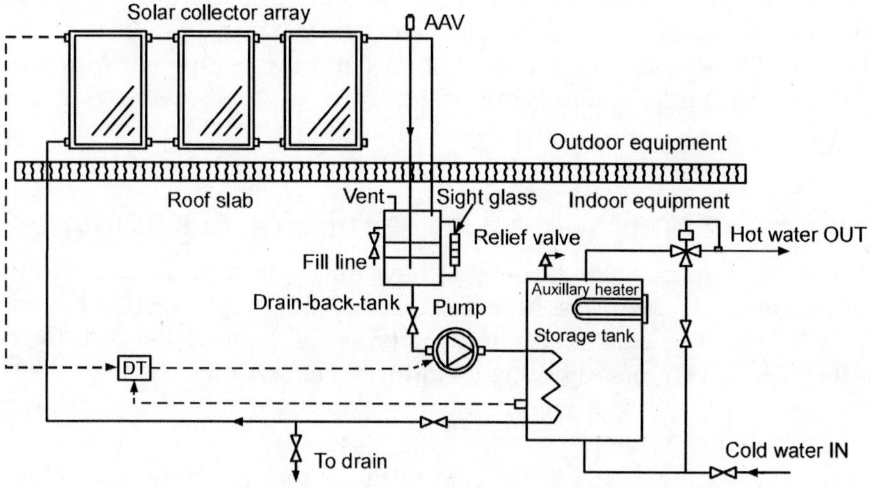

Figure 17.6: Drain-back system

(c) AIR WATER HEATING SYSTEMS

Air systems are indirect water heating systems that circulate air through the collectors to an air-to-water heat eachanger, thus the heat is transferred to the potable water, which flows through the heat exchanger and return to storage tank. Fig. 17.7 shows a schematic of a double sotrage tanks ystem. This type of system is usually preferred as air systems are generally used for preheating domestic hot water and in this way auxiliary is used only in on oe of the tanks as shown.

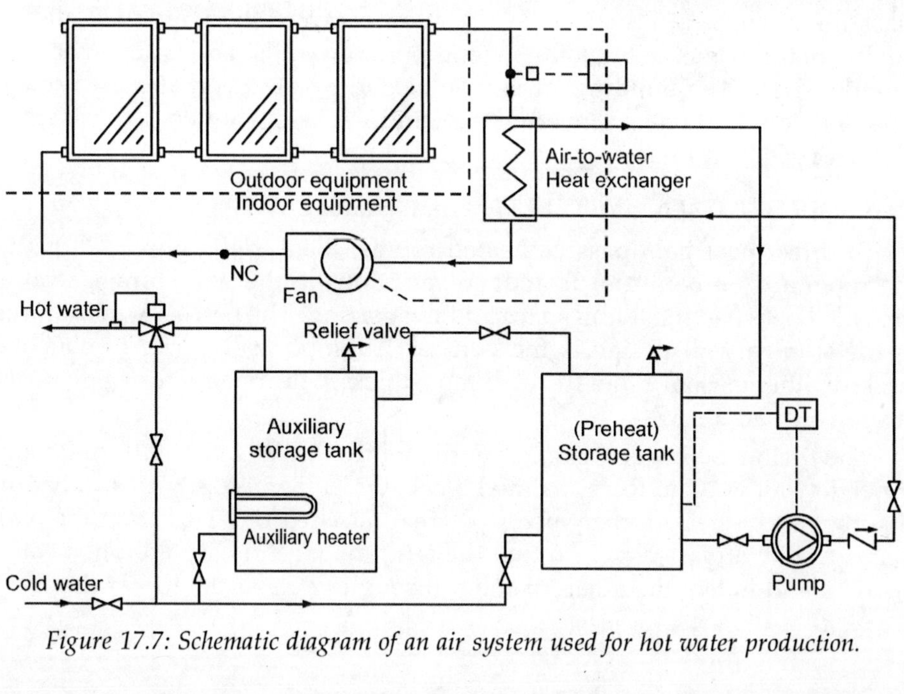

Figure 17.7: Schematic diagram of an air system used for hot water production.

There are numerous advantages of air systems. The most important ones are that air needs no protection from freezing or boiling, is non-corrosive, and is free. The disadvantages are that air-handling equipment (ducts and fans) are more bulky than piping and pumps, air leaks cannot be easily detected and parasitic power consumption is higher than that of liquid systems.

17.3 SPACE- HEATING (OR SOLAR HEATING OF BUILDINGS)

There are two primary categories into which virtually all solar heating systems may be divided. The first is *passive systems*, in which solar radiation is collected by some element of the structure itself, or admitted directly into building through large, south facing windows. The second is the *active systems* which generally consist of (a) separated solar collectors, (b) storage devices, and (c) a back up system.

Passive heating systems operate without pumps, blowers, or other mechanical devices; the air is circulated past a solar heated surface and through the building by convection (i.e. less dense, cooler air tends to rise while denser, cooler air moves downward). In active heating systems, fans and pumps are used to circulate the air and often a separate heat absorbing fluid is used.

17.3.1 Passive Solar Space Heating Systems

(a) DIRECT GAIN SYSTEM

This technique is generally used in cold climates. In this system, the building has a south wall with a large number of windows; two layers of glass minimize heat losses. Solar radiation entering the windows falls on thick concrete, slate, or brick floors (and possibly walls) and is absorbed and stored as heat. The building air is then heated by radiation and convection from the floor and walls. Covering the windows with shutters or curtains at night reduce heat losses.

(b) INDIRECT GAIN SYSTEM (Thermal Storage Wall)

In direct heat gain passive heated rooms, there are large variations in the room air temperature. To reduce variations, a thermal storage wall is provided between the living space and the glazing. The best known example of the storage wall design is the vertical Troumbe wall, made of concrete crick, or other masonry some 0.3m or more thick. A Troumbe wall arrangement is shown in Figure 17.8.

The distance between glazing and concrete wall is about 10 to 20 cm. concrete wall is 20cm thick, painted black, which serves as both a radiation absorber and a heat storage medium. Heat radiated outward from the wall is trapped by a glass cover, so that the air in between is heated. The heated air rises and enters the adjacent room through vents at the top of the wall;

the air circulates by natural convection and is returned by way of ducts at the bottom of the storage wall. Electric strip heaters are provided for standby purposes during excessively cold weather and during days with little sunshine.

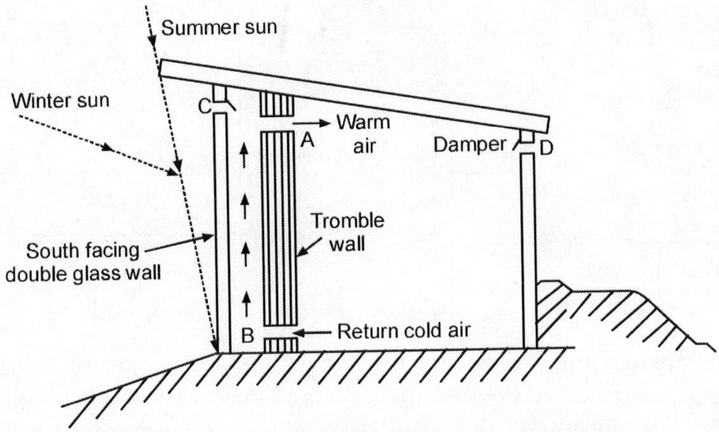

Fig. 17.8 : Trombe Wall passive solar heating system

During summer the vent A at the top of the south-facing wall is kept closed while the vents B, C and D are opened. The hot air between the glazing and the wall then flows out through the vent C and the air from the room flows into fill this space. Simultaneously, the air is pulled ino the room through the vent D which is located in a shaded cool area. The construction of the building is done in such a way that the overhanging roof prevents direct sun rays to heat glazing during summer.

17.3.2 Active Solar Space Heating Systems

(a) BASIC HOT WATER SYSTEM

The schematic of a basic hot water active system is shown in Figure 17.9. The sloping flat plate collector is located on the roof of the building. Heat is transferred to the water in the storage tank, commonly located in the basement of the building. The solar heated water from the tank passes through an auxiliary heater, which comes on automatically when the water temperature falls below a prescribed level. For space heating, the water may be pumped through radiators or it may be used to heat air in a water to air heat exchanger.

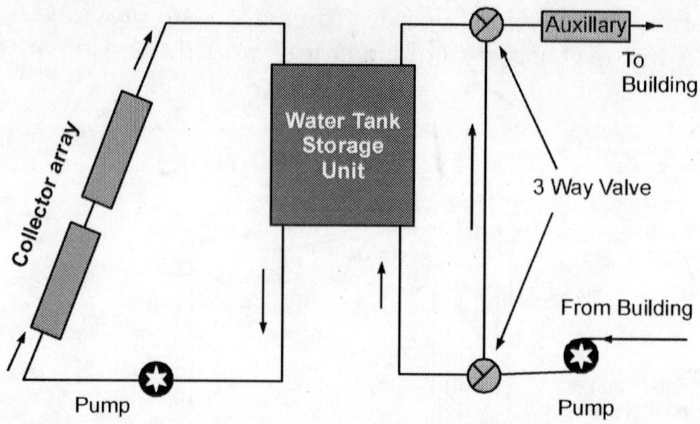

Fig. 17.9 Scheme of a Basic Hot Water Active System

During normal operation, the three way valves are set to permit solar heated water to flow from the storage tank and auxiliary heater to the distribution system and back to the tank. If after several cloudy days, the heat in storage is depleted. The valves will adjust automatically to bypass the storage tank.

If the temperature in the heater at the top of the collector should fall below that at the bottom of the tank, the pump would be switched off automatically.

If in this system, the heat transport medium is an anti-freeze solution, then there is a closed circuit of it, with the heat exchanger coil in the storage tank. This type of solar space heating systems with hot water system is shown in Figure 17.10.

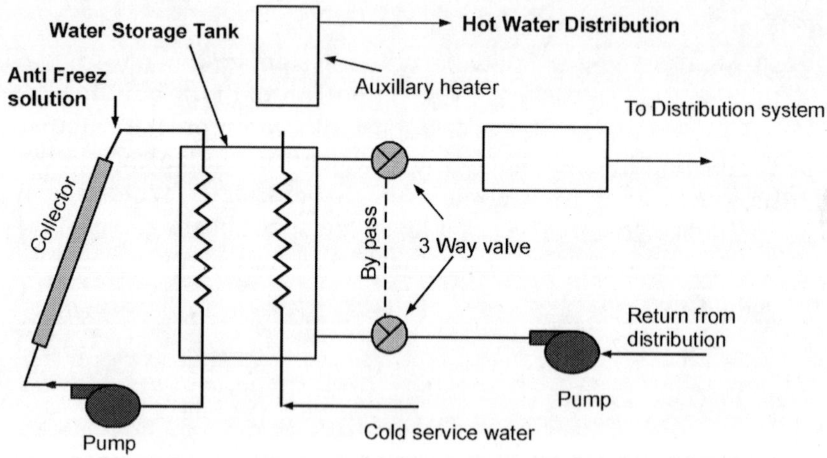

Fig. 17.10 Solar Space Heating and Hot Water System

ADVANTAGES OF BASIC HOT WATER SYSTEM

1. A common heat transfer and storage medium, water is used, this avoids temperature drop during transfer of energy into and out of the storage.
2. It requires relatively smaller storage volume.
3. It can be easily adopted to supply of energy to absorption air conditioners.
4. Relatively low energy requirements for pumping of the heat transfer fluid.

DISADVANTAGES OF BASIC HOT WATER SYSTEM

1. Freezing problems are there.
2. Leakage problems are there.
3. Corrosion problems are there thus water chemistry needs monitoring.
4. Heat exchanger is required for collector-storage and storage-building loops.
5. Boiling and fluid expansions provisions are required.

(b) BASIC HOT AIR SYSTEM

A schematic of a basic solar heating system using air as the heat transfer fluid, with people bed storage unit and auxiliary heating source is shown in Fig. 17.11. The various modes of operations are achieved by appropriate positioning of the dampers. In most air systems it is not practical to combine the modes of adding energy to and removing energy from storage at the same time. Auxiliary energy can be combined with energy supplied from collector or storage to top-up the air temperature in order to cover the building load. As shown in Fig.17.11 it is possible to bypass the collector and stoage unit when auxiliary done is being used to provide heat.

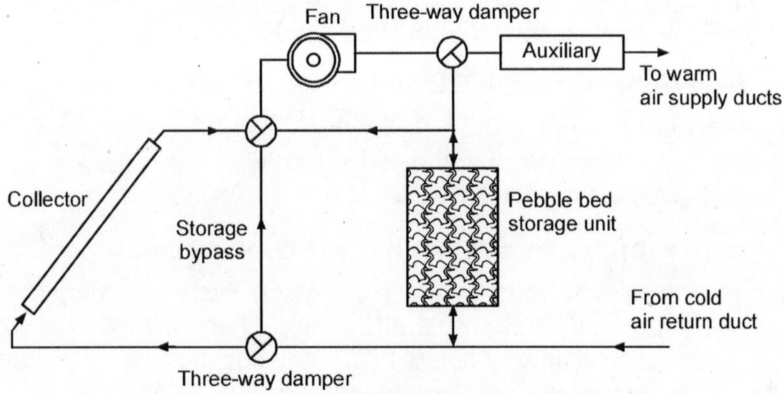

Fig. 17.11 Schematic of Basic Hot Air System

Fans are placed so that the pressure in the collector is not above ambient pressure, which might be advantageous in controlling leakage.

ADVANTAGES OF BASIC HOT AIR SYSTEM

1. There is no freezing problem in the collectors.
2. Corrosion problems are minimized.
3. Conventional control equipment for air heating is already available.
4. Problems of designing for over heating during periods of no energy removal are minimized.

DISADVANTAGES OF BASIC HOT AIR SYSTEM

1. Relatively higher power costs for pumping air through the storage medium.
2. Relatively large volumes of storage units.
3. Difficulty of adding absorption air conditioners to the system.

17.4 SOLAR SPACE COOLING AND REFRIGERATION

The two most common refrigeration techniques are vapour compression and absorption. Both can be adopted for use with solar energy, although the temperatures required are higher than those adequate for space heating.

In the vapour compression technique, solar heated water could vapourise propane or ammonia at a moderate pressure. The vapour could then drive a turbine which would in turn, operate a vapour-compression cooling unit. This technique has a very low efficiency.

Absorption cooling with solar energy is regarded as more practical.

In humid climates, removal of moisture from the air represents a major portion of air conditioning. In such climates, desiccant systems can be used for dehumidification, in which solar energy can provide most of the energy requirements.

Also, other than the above active cooling methods, several passive cooling techniques such as natural cooling etc. are there.

17.4.1 Absorption Air Conditioning

The two types of absorption air conditioners are

a) Lithium-bromide water ($LiBr-H_2O$) system
b) Ammonia-water (NH_3-H_2O) system

(a) LITHIUM-BROMIDE WATER ($LiBr-H_2O$) SYSTEM

In the Lithium-bromide water ($LiBr-H_2O$) system, water vapour is a refrigerant. The absorption air conditioning system is shown schematically in Fig. 17.12. The system consists of four major parts, i.e., a generator, a condenser, an evaporator and an absorber.

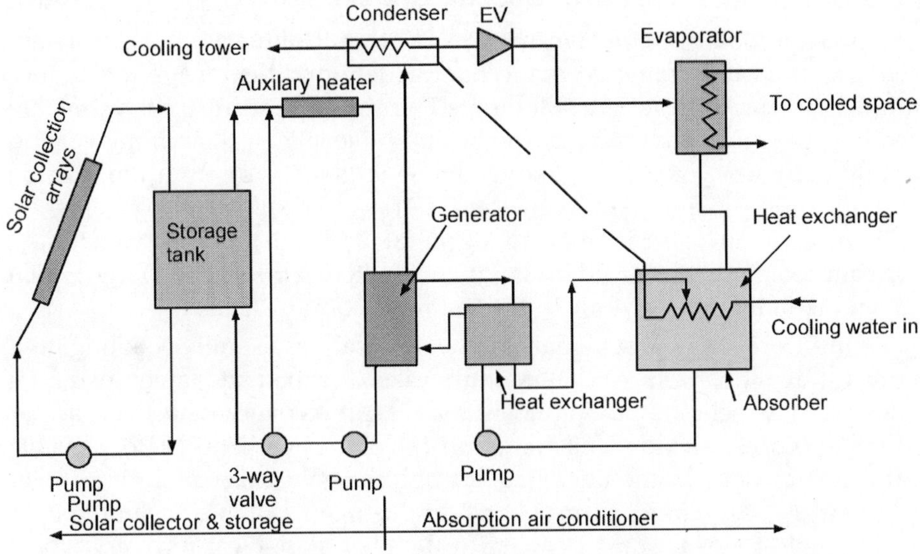

Figure 17.12: Schematic of Solar Operated Absorption Air Conditioner

Initially, the collector receives energy from sunlight and heat is accumulated in the storage tank. Subsequently, the energy is transferred through the high temperature energy storage tank to the refrigeration system. The solar collector heat is used to separate the water vapour from the lithium bromide solution in the generator at high temperature and pressure resulting in higher lithium bromide solution concentration. Then, the water vapour passes to the condenser where heat is removed and the vapour cools down to form a liquid. The liquid water at high pressure is passed through the expansion valve, to the evaporator, where it gets evaporated at low pressure, thereby providing cooling to the space to be cooled. Subsequently, the water vapour goes from the evaporator to the absorber. Meanwhile, the strong lithium bromide solution leaving the generator for the absorber passes through a heat exchanger in order to preheat the weak solution entering the generator, and then expanded to the absorber. In the absorber, the strong lithium bromide solution absorbs the water vapor leaving the evaporator to form a weak solution. The weak solution is then pumped into the generator and the process is repeated.

Generally, the heat is removed from the system by a cooling tower. The cooling water passes through the absorber first then the condenser.

In the case that the sun is not shining, an auxiliary heat source is used by electricity or conventional boiler to heat the water to the required generator temperature.

17.4.2 Desiccant Evaporative Cooling System

Desiccant cooling is effective in warm and humid climates. In the desiccant cooling method, desiccant salts or mechanical dehumidifiers are used to reduce humidity in the atmosphere. Materials having high affinity for water are used for dehumidification. They can be solid like silica gel, alumina gel and activated alumina, or liquids like tri-ethylene glycol. Air from the outside enters the unit containing desiccants and is dried adiabatically before entering the living space. The desiccants are regenerated by solar energy. Sometimes, desiccant cooling is employed in conjunction with evaporative cooling, which adjusts the temperature of air to the required comfort level.

Figure 17.13 shows a schematic of the desiccant evaporative cooling unit. In process air side, room air that including sensible load and latent load goes to desiccant wheel to removing latent load. Heat recovery wheel acts as per cooling in process air side. The main purpose of the heat wheel is for sensible heat recovery only. In the next step, air become cold by evaporative cooler and then air goes to room as supply air. In the regeneration side, ambient air becomes cold by evaporative cooler. In the next step, Heat recovery wheel acts as pre heater in regeneration air side. Then heat from heat exchanger and heater transfers to air. So, in the last step of regeneration side, hot air takes humidity of desiccant wheel and releases to ambient as exhaust air.

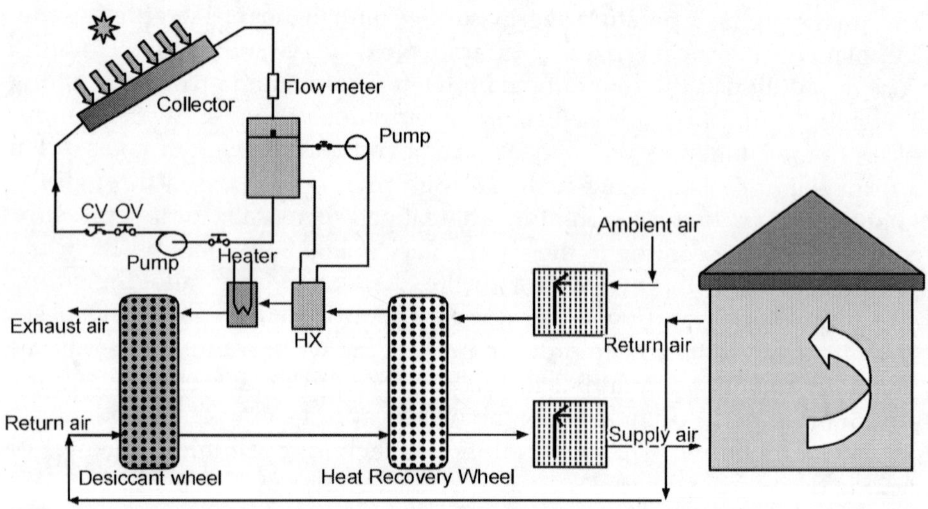

Fig. 17.13 Desiccant Evaporative Cooling System Schematic

17.4.3 Passive Solar Space Cooling

A 'passive' solar design involves the use of natural processes for heating or cooling to achieve balanced interior conditions. The flow of energy in passive design is by natural means: radiation, conduction, or convection without using any electrical device. Maintaining a comfortable environment within a building in a hot climate relies on reducing the rate of heat gains into the building and encouraging the removal of excess heat from the building.

Some of the passive cooling techniques are:

1. **Solar Shading**
   - *Shading by overhangs, louvers and awnings etc.*
   - Shading of Roof by providing roof cover of concrete or plants or canvas or earthen pots etc.
   - *Shading by trees and vegetation*
2. Insulation in the exterior of the building reduces heat gain and heat loss
3. Induced ventilation techniques such as solar chimney, air vents, wind tower.
4. Radiative cooling
5. Evaporative cooling
6. Earth coupling
7. Desiccant cooling

17.5 SOLAR FURNACES

A solar furnace is a structure that captures sunlight to produce very high temperatures, used for industrial purposes. This is done with a curved mirror (or an array of mirrors) that acts as a parabolic reflector (device used to collect or project energy such as light, sound, or radio waves), concentrating light onto a focal point. The temperature at the focal point may reach 3,500 °C (6,330 °F), and this heat can be used to generate electricity, melt steel, and make hydrogen fuel or nano materials.

WORKING PRINCIPLE OF SOLAR FURNACE

The operation principle of a solar furnace is quite simple entailing the use of two mirrors, plane mirror and parabolic mirror. The plane mirror is known as Heliostat and is angled such that it directs parallel beam of light to the parabolic mirror. The parabolic mirror then brings the light beam to focus at the focal point.

When the number of mirrors is increased to ten, then it is possible to achieve energy and heat levels where one can actually boil water and cook food. The amount of energy and efficiency of the solar furnace rely completely on how accurate the mirrors are focused on one point. The shutter is opened and closed partially to different degrees to control the amount of radiation that is allowed to enter the system.

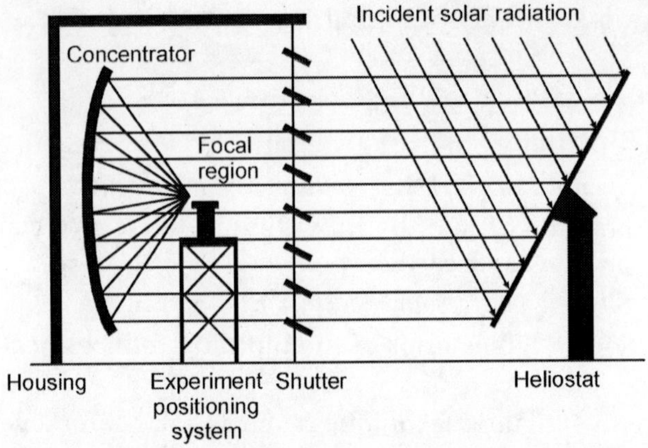

Figure 17.14: Principle of Solar Furnace

ADVANTAGES OF SOLAR FURNACE

1. Heat produced is very clean.
2. It provides extremely high temperatures.
3. Reduces the need to burn fossil fuels
4. Reduces the need to cut down forests for firewood

LIMITATIONS OF SOLAR FURNACE

1. This technology has existed for many years but has never fully explored or used on a widespread commercial basis.
2. Large solar concentrators are expensive.
3. They occupy large amount of space.

APPLICATIONS OF SOLAR FURNACE

1) It is used in melting of steel
2) It is used for solar water pasteurization
3) It is used in space to provide energy for manufacturing process.
4) It is used in solar powered barbecues.

17.6 SOLAR GREEN HOUSE

Solar greenhouses are designed not only to collect solar energy during sunny days but also to store heat for use at night or during periods when it is cloudy.

A greenhouse is a structure covered with transparent material that utilises solar radiant energy to grow plants and may have heating, cooling and ventilating equipments for temperature control.

ADVANTAGES OF GREENHOUSE

1. Manipulation of growing season
2. Round the year production of most desired crop
3. Higher production per unit area is obtained
4. Higher value and higher quality crops can be grown
5. Drastic reduction in wastage of fertilisers and pesticides
6. Efficient use of irrigation water

TYPES OF GREEN HOUSES

Mainly there are two types of greenhouse:

1. FREE STANDING GREENHOUSE

They can be situated on any convenient patch or piece of waste ground. They are not directly attached to any other building for green house and are separate structures sitting all by themselves. They have insulated walls on the north east and west sides. The walls are suitably designed to permit maximum reflection of the incoming radiation onto the plant canopy. Enough storage facilities are provided to meet the requirements.

Freestanding solar greenhouses are large enough for the commercial production of ornamentals, vegetables, or herbs.

2. ATTACHED TYPE GREENHOUSE

A greenhouse which does not have a separate structure and is a part of a house is known as attached type. Thus, it is quite cheaper to build a greenhouse as an addition to the existing house. It has an advantage that it can draw heat from an already structure when required and can return excess heat when conditions are sunny. Thus with a right location, is can be a very good heat source for the house.

There are various designs of attached type greenhouses, but one elongated along the east-west axis is the most efficient shape for the solar energy collection.

These structures provide space for transplants, herbs, or limited quantities of food plants.

DESIGN PRINCIPLES OF SOLAR GREENHOUSE

1. **Orientation**

   Since the sun's energy is strongest on the southern side of a building, glazing for solar greenhouses should ideally face true south. However, if trees, mountains, or other buildings block the path of the sun when the greenhouse is in a true south orientation, an orientation within 15° to 20° of true south will provide about 90% of the solar capture of a true south orientation.

In addition to north-south orientation, greenhouse glazing should be properly sloped to absorb the greatest amount of the sun's heat. A good rule of thumb is to add 10° or 15° to the site latitude to get the proper angle.

2. **End walls**

The south-east or south-west end walls should almost always be glazed. Glazed east-west end walls can allow light from the south glazing to pass straight through and thus there is an argument for insulating these walls.

3. **Site**

Proper site selection is important. It is necessary to understand how the sun travels through the sky at that place. Thus, heat gain can be calculated. This will also help in deciding requirements for heat storage, insulation and shading facilities.

4. **Glazing**

Two or more layers of glazing are required in cold climate. If however movable insulation is used at night, one layer of glazing is used. Glass has been the most widely used material, though fibre glass, polyethylene, acrylics or polycarbonates are also used.

5. **Ventilation**

Adequate ventilation is required as inside air changes per hour. Also more air may be required under some conditions to keep plants dry enough to prevent from moulds and fungus infection.

Outside air can be introduced into the interior through air tunnels at a depth of 2.5 to 3m below the surface of the ground so that the growing area will be warmed in winter and cooled in summer. Exhaust vent to the outside can be used in warmer weather.

6. **Increased solar gain**

The solar gain can be increased by providing exterior insulating shutter, by coating the frame of the south wall with a highly reflecting white paint and by making the backside surface of greenhouse silvered with reflective surface.

7. **Heat storage**

For solar greenhouses to remain warm during cool nights or on cloudy days, solar heat that enters on sunny days must be stored within the greenhouse for later use. The most common method for storing solar energy is to place rocks, concrete, or water in direct line with the sunlight to absorb its heat.

Brick or concrete-filled cinder block walls at the back (north side) of the greenhouse can also provide heat storage. However, only the outer four inches of thickness of this storage material effectively absorbs heat. Medium to dark-colored ceramic tile flooring can also provide some heat storage. Walls not used for heat absorption should be light colored or reflective to direct heat and light back into the greenhouse and to provide a more even distribution of light for the plants.

17.7 SOLAR DRYER

Solar dryers are devices that use solar energy to dry substances, especially food. Drying helps in reducing the moisture content of a product to a level below which deterioration does not takes place and the product can be stored for a definite period.

Thebasicprinciplesemployedinasolardryerare:

- Converting light to heat
- Trapping the heat
- Moving the heat to the food

TYPES OF SOLAR DRYER

Solar dryers are basically of three types:

1. DIRECT TYPE OR NATURAL CONVECTION TYPE DRYERS

They consists some kind of enclosure and a transparent cover. The food products get heated due to direct absorption of heat or due to high temperature in the enclosure and therefore, moisture from the product evaporates and goes out by the natural circulation of air.

The problems with these dryers are: slow drying, not much control on temperature and humidity, small quantities can be dried, and some products change colour and flavor due to direct exposure to sun.

A simple direct solar cabinet dryer is shown in Fig. 17.15

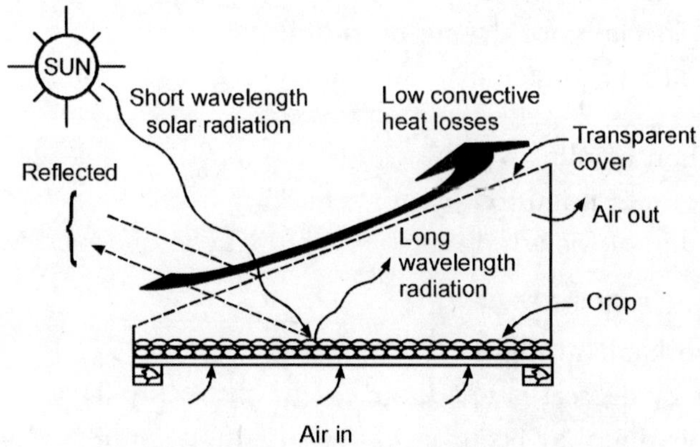

Fig. 17.15 Solar Cabinet Dryer (Direct Type Dryer)

2. INDIRECT TYPE DRYERS

In this type of drying, the products are not directly exposed to the sun but, the solar radiation is used to heat the air which then flows through the product to be dried. Thus, moisture from the product may be lost by convection and diffusion. The indirect type solar dryers are classified into natural convection (passive) type and forced convection (active) type depending upon the method used to pass the air over the products.

In natural convection indirect type solar dryers, the products are stored in the cabin or hot box units. Solar collector is used to absorb the incident solar radiation and heat the air which passes over the stored products. As the air is heated, its density gets reduced and it flows into the drying section naturally. Since, in this case, the flow of air is by density difference only, these are called natural convection solar dryers.

In forced convection solar dryers, the heated air is forced into the drying cabinet by means of an external device, (eg. blower, fan, etc.). Thus they offer better control over drying, but, require more power.

3. MIXED MODE TYPE DRYERS

Many types of drying systems utilize both direct and indirect solar radiation. In these types of systems, radiant energy from the sun falls directly onto the product being dried; however, in addition, a preheater also is used to raise the air temperature, which in turn, accelerates the drying rate. Acceleration of drying rate can occur in two ways: hot air can transfer some of its heat to the product being dried, thus raising its vapour pressure causing a faster moisture loss; or as temperature of air mass increases, the water-holding capacity also increases

ADVANTAGES OF SOLAR DRYER

(*i*) Much less time is required for drying as compared to direct drying because of black body.

(*ii*) Protection of the drying products from insects but also from birds, dogs, especially for drying meat and fish.

(*iii*) The product is higienic because micro-organisms, insects and flies are killed.

(*iv*) Protection of rain.

(*v*) Protection of pollution by dust etc.

(*vi*) Protection of the wind which can blow away the food.

LIMITATIONS OF SOLAR DRYER

(*i*) Not workable at night.

(*ii*) Efficiency decreases to a large extent on cloudy days.

(*iii*) Over heating may occur if regular attention is not paid.

(*iv*) Due to over heating it can decreae the quality of food.

(*v*) Change in taste and flavor of food may occur if regular monitoring is not done.

(*vi*) We cannot get the accurate amout of sun rays and heat.

17.8 SOLAR DISTILLATION

Solar distillation also known as solar still is a simple way of distilling water. It uses solar energy to distill water. It removes impurities such as salt and other microbiological organisms.

WORKING OF SOLAR STILL

1. The impure water (brine) is added to the center trough. The center trough usually will have a black bottom, which helps to attract sunlight.
2. The heat from the sun evaporates the salt water that is sitting in the center trough. The process of evaporation only lifts pure molecule of H_2O into the air of the container, leaving the dirty parts of the water sitting in the center trough.
3. Next, the process of condensation occurs. When the water vapour molecules hit the glass or plastic ceiling of the solar still, they turn into water droplets.
4. After condensation, the water droplets are forced by gravity and slide down the glass or plastic ceiling into a second clean trough along the inside edge of the solar still. They cling to the edge of the glass or plastic and follow it all the way down into an outer rim that flows into the 'clean water' area. Because the water is clinging to the angled glass or plastic, it does not get mixed back in dirty water.
5. After a certain amount of time enough water is collected and the water is ready to drink. This is usually done with a hose that is connected from the clean trough to the outside of the contraption.

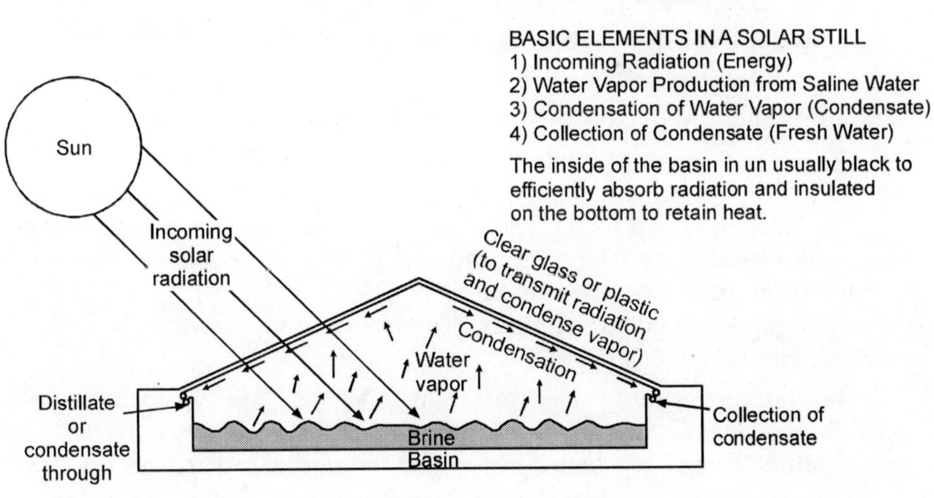

Fig. 17.16 Solar Water Still

The solar still efficiency is defined as

$$\eta = \frac{w\Delta h}{H}$$

Where 'w' is weight of distillate per square meter per day, '?h' is enthalpy change from cold water to vapour and 'H' is solar radiation intensity per square meter per day.

REQUIREMENTS FOR MAKING GOOD SOLAR STILL

(*i*) The cover can be either glasss or plastic.

(*ii*) Glass is preferable to plastic because most plastic degrades in the long term due to ultra violet light from sunlight.

(*ii*) The use of the mirror reflector will increase the temperature of the solar still basin.

(*iv*) Sufficient Insulations of wool, thermocol, sealants etc. must be provided inside the basin in order to prevent loss of heat.

ADVANTAGES OF SOLAR DISTILLATION

(*i*) Free of charge sun energy (during sunlight it eliminates 500 Watt electric consumption per one hour of sunlight).

(*ii*) There are no moving parts; it is therefore reliable and almost maintenance free (cleaning is required though).

(*iii*) Water taste is claimed to be better since the device act as a Solar Water Vaporizer and it doesn't boil the water (resembling rain water).

(*iv*) Neutral pH is claimed (like rain water), not like the not neutral pH of steamed distilled water.

LIMITATIONS OF SOLAR DISTILLATION

(*i*) Low distillate output per unit area.

(*ii*) Leakage of vapour through joints.

(*iii*) High maintenance.

(*iv*) Productivity decreases with time for a variety of reasons.

17.9 SOLAR BATTERIES

A solar battery is a rechargeable battery that integrates a solar cell with battery power storage. They are used especially in stand-alone systems for storage of energy produced by solar panels. A solar cell produce the dc current required for battery charging. The stored energy can then be delivered as electricity upon discharge.

The most commonly used for solar batteries battery type was in the past, the lead-acid battery. Lithium-ion batteries are also used recently as a solar battery as they are better in terms of charging and release cycles.

Also, the dc current from the solar cell can be used to decompose the water (by electrolysis) into hydrogen and oxygen gases. These gases can be stored in a suitable form and utilized as needed to generate electricity in a fuel cell.

17.10 SOLAR POWERED WATER PUMPING SYSTEM

Solar cells are used to run water pumps. From crop irrigation to stock watering to domestic uses, photovoltaic-powered pumping systems meet a broad range of water needs.

COMPONENTS

1. Solar Panel: Solar panels, or modules, generate direct current (DC) electricity.
2. Controller / Solar Inverter: The pump controller protects the pump from high or low voltage conditions and maximizes the amount of water pumped in less than ideal light conditions. An AC pump requires an inverter, an electronic equipement that converts DC to AC electricity to operate the pump.
3. Pump: A pump is a device that moves fluids (liquids or gases), or sometimes slurries, by mechanical action. DC pumps are classified as either displacement or centrifugal, and can be either submersible or surface types.
4. Other equipment: A float switch turns on pump on and off when filling the storage tank. Low water cut-off electrodes protect the pump from low water conditions in the well.

TYPES OF SOLAR POWERED PUMP SYSTEM

1. Battery Coupled Water Pumping System

Battery-coupled water pumping systems consist of photovoltaic (PV) panels, charge control regulator, batteries, pump controller, pressure switch and tank and DC water pump (Figure 17.17). The electric current produced by PV panels during daylight hours charges the batteries and the batteries in turn supply power to the pump anytime water is needed. During the night and low light periods, the system can deliver a constant source of water for livestock.

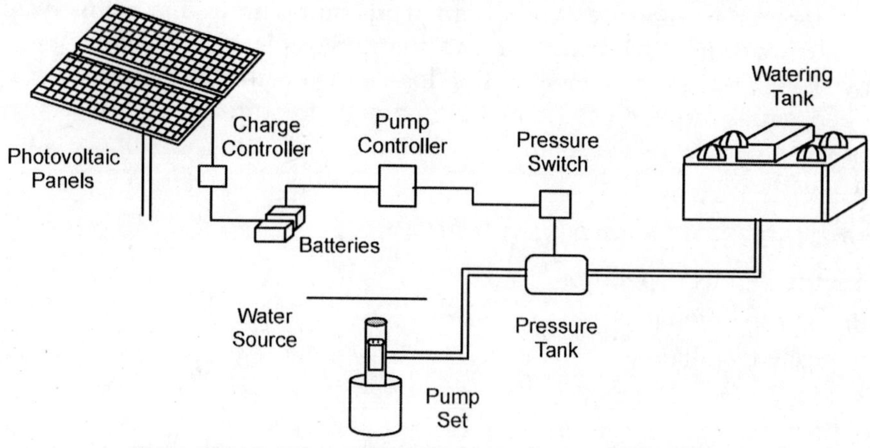

Figure 17.17: Battery-coupled solar water pumping system

The use of batteries reduces the efficiency of the overall system because the operating voltage is calculated by the batteries and not the PV panels. This can be improved by using appropriate pump controller that boosts the battery voltage supplied to the pump.

2. Direct Coupled Water Pumping System

In direct-coupled pumping systems, electricity from the PV modules is sent directly to the pump, which in turn pumps water through a pipe to where it is needed (Figure 17.18). This system is designed to pump water only during the day.

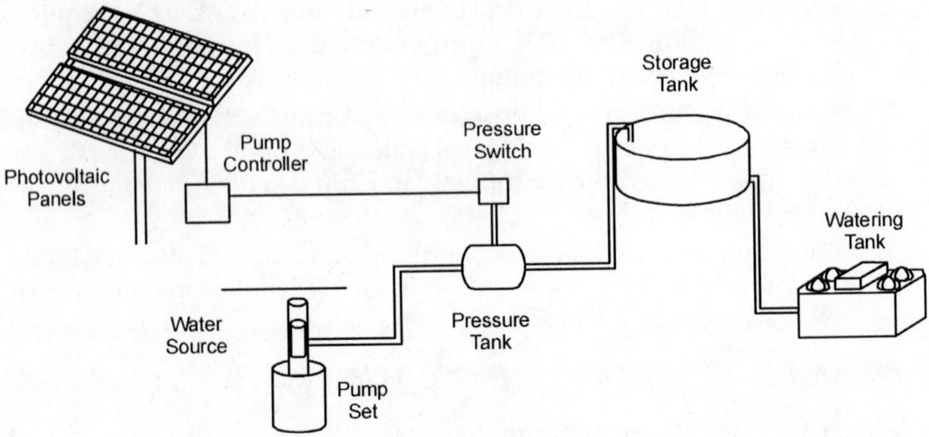

Figure 17.18: Direct coupled solar pumping system

The amount of water pumped is totally dependent on the amount of sunlight hitting the PV panels and the type of pump. Because the intensity of the sun and the angle at which it strikes the PV panel changes throughout the day, the amount of water pumped by this system also changes throughout the day.

Water-storage capacity is important in this pumping system as this system does not work in cloudy days and in night. Storing water in tanks has its drawbacks. Considerable evaporation losses can occur if the water is stored in open tanks, while closed tanks big enough to store several days water supply can be expensive. Also, water in the storage tank may freeze during cold weather.

ADVANTAGES OF SOLAR WATER PUMPING

1. unattended operation
2. low maintenance
3. easy installation
4. long life

DISADVANTAGES OF SOLAR WATER PUMPING

1. high capital costs
2. water storage is required for cloudy periods
3. repairs often require skilled technicians

17.11 SOLAR LIGHTING

Solar-powered lighting consists of a solar panel or photovoltaic cell that collects the sun's energy during the day and stores it in a rechargeable gel cell battery. Solar power is used with LEDs for the creation of stand alone (off grid) lighting devices.

WORKING

According to principle of photovoltaic effect, the solar panels receive solar radiation during the day time and then convert it into electrical energy through the charge and discharge controller, which is finally stored in the battery. When the light intensity is reduced during night and open circuit voltage of the solar panels reaches at a certain value, the controller acts the Battery. The battery offer the energy to the LED light to drive the LED and emits visible light at a certain direction. Battery discharges after certain time passes, the charge and discharge controller will act again to end the discharging of the battery in order to prepare next charging or discharging again.

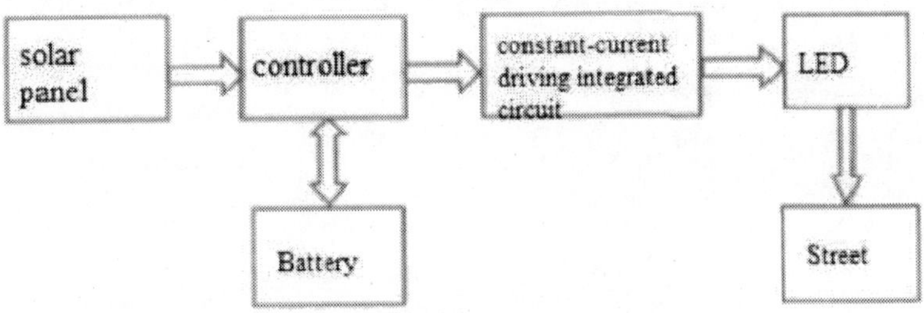

Fig. 17.19 Solar Lighting System Workflow

ADVANTAGES OF SOLAR LIGHTING

1. high efficiency
2. energy-saving
3. long-life
4. high color rendering index
5. environmental protection

17.12 SOLAR ENERGY IN INDIA

Solar Power a clean renewable resource with zero emission has got tremendous potential of energy which can be harnessed using a variety of devices. With recent developments, solar energy systems are easily available for industrial and domestic use with the added advantage of minimum maintenance.

Solar power has so far played an almost non-existent role in the Indian energy mix. The grid-connected capacity (all PV) in India now stands at 481.48 MW as of 31st January 2012. However, the market is set to grow significantly in the next ten years, driven mainly by rising power demand and prices for fossil fuels. With the cost of solar photovoltaic cells falling, the prices are dropped by 50% last year.

India has a great potential to generate electricity from solar energy and the Country is on course to emerge as a solar energy hub. The techno-commercial potential of photovoltaics in India is enormous. With GDP growing in excess of 8%, the energy 'gap' between supply and demand will only widen. Solar PV is a renewable energy resource capable of bridging this 'gap'.

Most parts of India have 300 – 330 sunny days in a year, which is equivalent to over 5000 trillion kWh per year – more than India's total energy consumption per year. Average solar incidence stands at a robust 4 – 7 kWh/sq.meter/day. About 66 MW of aggregate capacity is installed for various applications comprising one million industrial PV systems – 80% of which is solar lanterns, home/street lighting systems and solar water pumps, etc. The potential of the solar thermal sector in India also remains untapped. In terms of all renewable energy, currently India is ranked fifth in the world.

❑❑❑

MODEL TEST PAPER

MODEL TEST PAPER 1

1. (a) What are the prospects of various renewable energy resources in India?
   (b) Describe the general principles of Energy management with suitable examples.
2. (a) What are different types of solar energy collectors? Explain any two in detail.
   (b) List advantages and limitations of photovoltaic solar energy conversion.
3. (a) Enumerate the advantages and disadvantages of wind power.
   (b) Write short notes on potential wind power in India.
   (c) List few companies manufacturing WEC devices.
4. (a) Explain the operation of a closed cycle OTEC system.
   (b) Discuss its advantages and disadvantages compared to open cycle OTEC plant.
5. Discuss the methods of harnessing wave energy.
6. (a) Describe the difference between spring tides, neap tides, high tide, and low tide.
   (b) Discuss the possible reasons why energy output in double-effect generation is usually lower than for single-effect generation.
7. (a) Explain Hot Dry rocks (petrothermal) resources of geothermal energy and how they can be exploited as a source of energy.
   (b) Explain vapour dominated hydrothermal power plant with neat sketch and its representation on T-S diagram.
   (c) Describe various disadvantages and operational problems associated with geothermal energy.
8. (a) What is meant by anaerobic digestion? What are the factors, which affect biodigestion? Explain briefly.
   (b) What is a community biogas plant? What are the main problems encountered in its operation?

MODEL TEST PAPER 2

1. (a) Briefly explain the following
    i. Energy Planning.
    ii. Energy Efficiency.

   (b) Explain what energy efficient electric motors are. How do they differ from conventional motors?

2. What is pyrheliometer? With neat sketch, explain about the method of measuring solar radiation using Angstrom compensation pyrheliometer.

3. (a) Enumerate the advantages and disadvantages of wind power.

   (b) Write short notes on potential wind power in India.

   (c) List few companies manufacturing WEC devices.

4. (a) Draw the schematic diagram and explain the Open cycle OTEC system. What are the operational difficulties encountered in OTEC plants?

   (b) Find the quantity of water to be pumped to OTEC plant working with surface water at 270C and with cold water at 80C at a depth of 600 m from the surface to obtain 1.0MW of energy. Assume the density of ocean water as 1010 kg/m^3 and the specific heat of water as 4200 J/kg K.

5. Explain in brief the energy potential of ocean waves and methods of harnessing the wave energy.

6. (a) Show by sketches the method of harnessing the energy potential associated with ocean tides.

   (b) A tidal power station has 24 generators each of 10 MW operating at a maximum head of 13.5m. It generates for two 6 hour periods per day. Calculate the basin capacity in m3, and annual energy production. Assume 93% efficiencies.

7. (a) What are the sub classifications of hydrothermal convective system?

   (b) Describe a liquid dominated system or wet steam field.

   (c) A hot water geothermal plant of the total flow type, receives water at 2500C. The pressure at turbine inlet is 10bar. The plant uses a direct contact type condenser that operates at 0.3bar. The turbine has a polytropic efficiency of 70%. For a cycle, net output of 10MW. Calculate:
    i. The hot water flow rate,
    ii. The condenser cooling water flow rate,
    iii. Cycle efficiency and
    iv. Plant heat rate.

8. (a) How are biogas plants classified? Explain the batch type and floating drum type of biodigesters with sketch.

   (b) What are the advantages and disadvantages of floating drum plant?

   (c) Enumerate the advantages and disadvantages of fixed dome type plant.

MODEL TEST PAPER 3

1. (a) Discuss the need for development of renewable energy resources.
   (b) What do you understand by energy management and what is its role in industry.
2. What is the difference between a pyrheliometer and a pyranometer? Describe the principle of operation of Eppley pyranometer.
3. (a) Describe the working of a vertical axis Savonius Rotor with a neat sketch.
   (b) What are the advantages and disadvantages of Savonius rotor?
4. (a) What is the basic principle of OTEC? Discuss the advantages of the closed cycle system over open cycle system.
   (b) The efficiency of power plant working on OTEC system is very less. However, the secondary advantages make it commercially attractive. Discuss.
5. Discuss the advantages and limitations of wave energy conversion.
6. (a) Explain with neat sketches the energy extraction techniques from tidal waves
   (b) A tidal power development has total installed generation of 7500 MW operating at a maximum head of 8 m. The minimum head at the end of cycle of generation is 2.5 m after 5 hours. Assume two cycles of generation in 24 hr. The generated power decreases linearly from 7500 MW to zero. The turbine and generator have efficiencies of 93% and 97%, respectively. The length of embankment is 20 km. Calculate:
      i. Quantity of water flowing through the turbines a maximum output in m^3/s.
      ii. Surface area of reservoir in km^2.
      iii. Wash behind the embankment at maximum reservoir capacity.
      iv. Energy delivered per year at a load factor of 0.8.
7. (a) Describe a Binary cycle system for liquid dominated system.
   (b) What are the limitations of a flashed steam system?
   (c) What are the advantages of double flash system?
8. (a) What is the difference between biomass and Biogas?
   (b) What are the techniques suggested for maintaining the biogas production?
   (c) What is community biogas plant? What are the main problems encountered in its operation?

MODEL TEST PAPER 4

1. (a) List out Various non -Conventional Sources of energy.
   (b) Briefly explain the advantages of renewable sources of energy.
   (c) Explain briefly the causes of low power factor and how it can be corrected?
2. (a) Write short notes on the following:
      i. Solar constant
      ii. Local solar time
      iii. Surface azimuth angle.

(b) Determine the local solar time and declination at a location latitude 23015′N, longitude 77030′E at 12.30 IST on June 19. Equation of time correction is given from standard table to be = – (1′ 01″).

3. (a) Explain the concept of Darrieus rotor principle.
   (b) Describe the working of vertical axis Darrieus type vertical axis machine with a neat sketch.
4. (a) What is the basic principle of OTEC? Discuss the advantages of the closed cycle system over open cycle system.
   (b) The efficiency of power plant working on OTEC system is very less. However, the secondary advantages make it commercially attractive. Discuss.
5. Discuss the advantages and limitations of wave energy conversion.
6. Describe the following schemes for tidal generation, with suitable figures:
   (a) Ebb generation;
   (b) Flood generation;
   (c) Two-way generation;
   (d) Single-basin scheme;
   (e) Two-basin scheme.
7. (a) Describe a vapour dominated or dry steam field.

   (b) A vapour dominated system of 100MW capacity uses saturated steam with a shut off pressure of 30 bar and enters turbine at 5.0 bar and condenses at 0.15 bar. Polytropic efficiency of turbine is 80%, generator - turbine combined mechanical and electrical efficiency is 90% water output temperature from cooling tower is 200C. and reinjection occurs prior to cooling tower. Calculate:
   i. Steam required.
   ii. Heat rate.
   iii. Plant efficiency and
   iv. Cooling water rate.
8. (a) What are the different inputs which produce Biogas? List out the factors affecting bio-digestion
   (b) Give a neat sketch of Biogas production plant for domestic use for a family of 5-6 persons.
   (c) Explain "Energy Plantation" and state its advantages and disadvantages.

❑

INDEX

N

O

P

R

S

❑❑❑